The Undocumented Everyday

Contents

Acronyms

CAFTA-DR	Central America–Dominican Republic Free Trade Agreement
COMO	Centro de Orientación de la Mujer Obrera
DACA	Deferred Action for Childhood Arrivals
DAPA	Deferred Action for Parents of Americans and Lawful Permanent Residents
DHS	Department of Homeland Security
DOJ	Department of Justice
DOL	Department of Labor
DREAM Act	Development, Relief, and Education for Alien Minors Act
FAIR	Federation for American Immigration Reform
HRHCare	Hudson River HealthCare
ICE	Immigration and Customs Enforcement
IIRIRA	Illegal Immigration Reform and Immigrant Responsibility Act
INS	Immigration and Naturalization Service
IRCA	Immigration Reform and Control Act
IYJL	Immigrant Youth Justice League

MALDEF	Mexican American Legal Defense and Education Fund
NAFTA	North American Free Trade Agreement
NDLON	National Day Labor Organizing Network
NFOP	National Fugitive Operations Program
NIYA	National Immigrant Youth Alliance
1199SEIU	Local 1199 Service Employees International Union
PEP	Priority Enforcement Program
PRWORA	Personal Responsibility and Work Opportunity Reconciliation Act
SB 1070	Arizona Senate Bill 1070 (Support Our Law Enforcement and Safe Neighborhoods Act)
S-COMM	Secure Communities Program
USA PATRIOT Act	Uniting and Strengthening America by Providing Appropriate Tools Required to Intercept and Obstruct Terrorism Act
USCCR	U.S. Commission on Civil Rights

Preface

I began work on this project in 2003, as labor–community coalitions were starting to organize the Immigrant Workers Freedom Ride (IWFR) to protest the U.S. federal government's inaction on comprehensive immigration reform. As part of the IWFR, close to one thousand migrant workers and their allies rode buses originating from nine U.S. cities, meeting up in Washington, D.C., and then traveling to join one of the largest immigrant rights rallies in history held in New York City on October 2, 2003.[1] This event was organized following the passing of laws after 9/11, including the USA PATRIOT Act, which criminalized undocumented migrants.[2] It was in this context that the Freedom Ride participants "manifested their political message and defiantly asserted their subjectivity," by what Nicholas De Genova contends was "their physical and bodily *presence*."[3] De Genova argues that the "migrant Freedom Riders not only moved 'the question of the speaking subject front and centre,' but also provoked a kind of dialogue that was above all about the question of the *moving* subject—migrant subjectivities manifested through the insubordinate mobility of their bodies."[4] In his analysis of the IWFR, De Genova emphasizes migrant *subjectivity*, *presence*, and *mobility*, which relate to the organizers' interest in involving migrant activists in documentary projects of self-representation, including "Unseen America."

In early 2003, the staff of Bread and Roses Cultural Project, then the cultural arm of Local 1199 of the Service Employees International Union

(1199SEIU), suggested that the organizers of the Freedom Ride could help host cities coordinate "Unseen America" photography workshops on the buses to Washington, D.C. The Bread and Roses staff provided the photography teachers and cameras for a fee, enabling the activists to document their experiences on the buses, in Washington, D.C., and at the closing ceremony in Flushing, New York. While this type of strategy was not new, it was especially meaningful in view of the historic conjuncture of the post-9/11 moment. In other words, the strategy of self-representation in documentary photography took on specific meanings for undocumented migrants during this time due to intensifying regimes of state-mandated documentation.[5]

Although the organizers of the Freedom Ride were interested in Unseen America—with its focus on self-representation and its capacity to generate images and leadership opportunities for the participants—only a small number of the host cities were able to fund the project. In Minneapolis, photographer Quito Ziegler led the Unseen America photo workshop for the nine-day bus ride, handing out 35mm point-and-shoot film cameras and documentary photography books to ninety riders on two buses. When the bus returned to Minneapolis after the Freedom Ride, Ziegler set up a curatorial committee of individuals who took the photographs and who selected some for an exhibition. Also, in preparation for a planned demonstration in Minneapolis in late 2003, these activists taped their photographs inside the windows of a school bus, producing a mobile photography exhibit.[6] In creating and exhibiting these images, these activists centered their *subjectivity*, while also visualizing their *presence* and *mobility* within the United States.

This book is informed by the context of 9/11, the effects of U.S. immigration policy on Mexican and Central American migrants in the United States, and increased immigration enforcement in the U.S.–Mexico borderlands. Specifically, it examines the particular salience of self-representation as a common trope in documentary projects that primarily involve undocumented Mexican and Central American migrants during the post-9/11 period through 2012.[7] Although Presidents Vincente Fox and George W. Bush were in negotiations about a binational agreement on the status of undocumented Mexicans in the United States in the summer of 2001, following 9/11, agencies of the U.S. state viewed these migrants in particular as representative of the threat that immigration presented. In this context, the U.S. government created laws and policies that criminalized undocumented migrants without allowing them the space or place to contest them. *The Undocumented Everyday* examines how these individuals have used documentary forms to respond to a political context in which they have been both racialized and criminalized. One way that they have contested their circumstances has been through the production and circulation of documentary media, including photography, film, video, and audio projects. These projects have taken place in locations across the United States and in the U.S.–Mexico borderlands during the 2000s and 2010s.

Despite the high-profile and contentious debates over immigration during the early twenty-first century, the terms of visibility and the prevalence of self-representation as a form of visibility have yet to be adequately addressed and analyzed. Although some of these projects are based on the premise that visibility will provide recognition and inclusion of Latina/o migrants by the U.S. state, visibility can also produce heightened conditions of vulnerability and exposure, especially within the context of the intensification of the U.S. state's regimes of surveillance, detention, and deportation following 9/11. While this book examines the ways in which some documentary projects of self-representation emphasized migrants making themselves "visible," I argue that they represent themselves in ways that are directed toward other goals and political projects, too.

In this book, I focus on representation as a practice, not only as an image or idea.[8] I bring a critical approach to the study of documentary forms, and I am also interested in how Mexican and Central American migrants have used documentary media to challenge how they are represented in the mainstream media in the United States and Mexico. Some create images that contrast with these representations, while others use documentary media to engage other migrants. Although the projects that I write about are quite distinct from one another—in their use of specific forms of media, in how they are mediated or curated, and to what purposes they are put—all of them involve some form of self-representation in documentary form.

In addressing an audience largely (although not entirely) outside of those who created these artworks, I challenge liberal humanist approaches to documentary as well as what Wendy Hesford refers to as the "seeing-is-believing" paradigm. She contends that this "model presumes the power of the image to persuade . . . instead of emphasizing the rhetorical and material power and the confluence of the discourses and apparatuses . . . that deploy the image and that guarantee or hinder its circulation."[9] Hesford argues for a "seeing-is-power" model, which understands the visual as a "structuring agent for a specific set of historical, social, and economic interests."[10] The mediation, curation, exhibition, and distribution of documentary work involving self-representation shape its production, as well as how it is viewed. These aspects address issues of who has the power to represent whom and what events are made visible or invisible. I focus on how these documentary projects are shaped by exhibitionary practices, as well as by audience engagement.

Similar to some of the organizers of these projects, I am not a member of the communities that produced these works. This book is mediated by my own perspective, and thus the arguments that I make about these projects are not a matter of "giving voice" or speaking on behalf of those whom I am writing about. One of the ways that I have attempted to be accountable to those whose work is represented in the book is by the decisions that I have made about which projects to write about. The documentary works that I have included were made public through exhibitions, books, film screenings, and websites, as well as livestreams on the Internet.

It is my intention that this book speak to the significance of these documentary photography, film, and video projects and their relation to migrant organizing in the early twenty-first century. My stake in bringing together these projects in this book is related to my understanding of the role of culture in the terrain of struggle. Stuart Hall argued that "culture is always being negotiated and inflected, to resonate with new situations," and is "often contested, and sometimes bitterly fought over."[11] He also contended that "counter-strategies in the 'politics of representation'" relate to "the way meaning can be struggled over," as well as "whether a particular regime of representation can be challenged, contested, and transformed."[12] In this book I examine the context of undocumented Mexican and Central American migrants' exclusion from citizenship in the United States in relation to their use of aesthetic and political strategies.

As such, I understand the aesthetic strategies deployed by Mexican and Central American migrants in their documentary projects not as secondary to politics but as primary—as their decisions relate to the address of the work as well as to the purposes that they want it to serve. Sonia E. Alvarez, Evelina Dagnino, and Arturo Escobar argue that "cultural contestations are not mere 'by-products' of political struggles but are instead constitutive of the efforts of social movements to redefine the meaning and the limits of the political system itself. . . . When movements deploy alternative concepts of woman, nature, race, economy, democracy, or citizenship that unsettle dominant cultural meanings, they enact cultural politics."[13] While many of these projects were not produced within the context of organized social movements, I argue that between 2000 and 2012 Mexican and Central American migrants employed documentary media to visualize "ways of belonging" in the United States and U.S.–Mexico borderlands that did not rely on notions of citizenship.[14] Further, in centering their *subjectivity*, *presence*, and *mobility* they created alternative representations of themselves that challenged the framing of some of these projects as attempts to "humanize" them for a broader audience or as part of efforts to gain the "gift" of citizenship or some other form of immigration status.[15] These projects convey the significance of migrant organizing in the early twenty-first century, but they also engage with the documentary form itself.

I started researching this project in 2003, and I completed it during the final months of President Barack Obama's second term and the first months of the Trump administration. The aftershocks of Donald J. Trump's November 2016 victory rippled across many communities throughout the United States, raising concerns about how his administration would approach immigration policies, especially those affecting undocumented Mexican and Central American migrants. These reactions were in response to hostile statements made during Trump's campaign that were specifically directed toward Mexicans and Trump's near-constant refrain about the need to build a wall between the United States and Mexico. Trump also threatened to end Deferred Action for Childhood Arrivals (DACA), deport two to three million undocumented "criminals," and defund "sanctuary cities."

Trump's win unleashed preemptive organizing against his proposed policies through efforts to establish "sanctuary campuses" and to reaffirm the commitments of sanctuary cities and counties. The strategies developed by undocumented youth and migrant activists during President Obama's two terms have proven to be useful in the Trump era, evident in campaigns such as Alto Trump.[16] In recent years, this organizing has taken place on the local and grassroots levels—such as in Arizona, where undocumented migrant activists filed lawsuits against Sheriff Joseph Arpaio, and in campaigns they coordinated, such as ¡Bazta Arpaio!, which worked to vote Arpaio out of office. On the national level, groups like the National Day Labor Organizing Network initiated antideportation campaigns, including #Not1More.

On January 14, 2017, days before President Obama left office, "We Are Here to Stay," a nationwide immigrant rights rally, was held in Washington, D.C., and in fifty other cities throughout the United States. Organizing for the rally included a diverse group of undocumented migrants, most of whom were people of color; recent migrants from Haiti; and LGBTQ activists from Make the Road New York (MRNY).[17] The rally was held when Obama was still in office, since some organizers hoped that he would take executive action to allow these Haitian migrants into the United States. Similar to the IWFR, migrant activists from across the country participated in this national rally to protect migrants and refugees.

Migrant rights activists associated with Somos un Pueblo Unido in Santa Fe—an organization that has been successfully organizing against anti-immigrant laws on the local level—sent community leaders representing counties in New Mexico to Washington, D.C., to attend the rally. Before leaving New Mexico, Sergio, who represented Familias Unidas por Justicia, an affiliate of Somos un Pueblo Unido in Farmington, stated, "We are already living what the incoming Trump administration is threatening to do," and furthermore, "that is why I am going to Washington,

D.C., to share how we are fighting back locally and despite all the uncertainty and everything going against our community, we will continue to fight and win."[18] While the activists were in D.C., they met with New Mexico's congressional delegation to discuss how sanctuary policies have helped their communities. They also participated in the national rally at an African Methodist Episcopal (AME) Church.

After Trump took office on January 20, 2017, his administration acted quickly on his campaign promises, mostly through executive orders. On January 25, 2017, Trump announced two executive orders: "Border Security and Immigration Enforcement Improvements" and "Enhancing Public Safety in the Interior of the United States." As part of his order on Border Security, Trump directed the secretary of the Department of Homeland Security to construct a wall along the U.S. border with Mexico (section 4), as well as to "allocate resources to . . . detain aliens at or near the land border with Mexico."[19] This executive order emphasized border security, while also reaffirming that federal immigration authorities would enter into 287(g) agreements with local and state authorities to detain and deport undocumented migrants.[20]

The executive order on "Enhancing Public Safety in the Interior of the United States" included enforcement priorities, such as deporting undocumented migrants who had committed criminal offenses. However, this executive order expanded who could be categorized as a criminal and identified acts such as presenting a false social security number to a government agency as crimes.[21] While this executive order ended Immigration and Customs Enforcement's Priority Enforcement Program (PEP), it reactivated Secure Communities (S-COMM), a program that led to mass deportations during the Obama administration.[22] The executive order also specified that sanctuary jurisdictions "are not eligible to receive Federal grants, except as deemed necessary for law enforcement purposes."[23]

In response, numerous migrant rights organizations held rallies and press conferences at which speakers challenged these executive orders. At El Centro de Igualdad y Derechos in Albuquerque, executive director Rachel LaZar stated, "We will organize locally to pass and strengthen local immigrant-friendly policies," asserting that "we'll use strategic litigation to fight back and we will ramp up some of our organizing efforts to fight back against Trump's deportation machine and agenda of hate."[24] At the press conference, some activists held signs that read "We're Not Going Anywhere" and "Mayor Berry Reject Trump's Immigration Machine #heretostay." Less than two weeks later, speaking at an Immigrant Day of Action rally organized by Somos un Pueblo Unido and held at the New Mexico State Capitol in Santa Fe, state representative Javier Martínez declared, "Estamos aquí para quedarnos. We are here to stay." Further, he proclaimed, "We're going to fight for our rights. We're going to fight against that wall. We're going to fight against that ban and we're going to tell President Trump this is our country too."[25] At the end of the rally, members of Somos un Pueblo Unido started a round of chants shouting, "Aquí estamos y no nos vamos" (Here we are and we're not going), their voices echoing in the rotunda of the state capitol. Activists have chanted these words during many immigrant rights rallies and marches over the last decade, and yet as one activist noted in recent months, they have "never been so much of a declaration of defiance."[26]

This book explores a set of strategies regarding visibility and documentation that Mexican and Central American migrants have used in response to the political context of the early twenty-first century. It is dedicated to undocumented migrants who engage in "impossible activism" on behalf of all migrants in the United States.[27]

Migrant Lives and the Promise of Documentation

This photograph (Figure 1) was taken by Jonathan Alvira during a "Shut Down ICE" protest, organized by the National Day Labor Organizing Network (NDLON), the Puente Movement of Arizona, and other groups in Phoenix, Arizona, on October 14, 2013, as part of the

Figure 1. A "Shut Down ICE" protest in Phoenix, Arizona, on October 14, 2013. Photograph by Jonathan Alvira.

#Not1More campaign.[1] During this day of protests activists chained themselves together on a road leading to the Eloy Detention Center in Eloy, Arizona—run by the Corrections Corporation of America—in order to disrupt its daily operations of deporting undocumented migrants. This photograph was taken at a concurrent protest held that day outside an Immigration and Customs Enforcement (ICE) building in Phoenix, Arizona.[2] As described by an activist involved in the #Not1More campaign, "The protest transformed the building with *papel picado* and decorations" and "became a dance party in the driveway of ICE with no buses or vans moving in or out."[3] The fence around the ICE building is featured prominently in this photograph, along with signs, posters, and images that are displayed on it, some of which were screen-printed ("Alto a la Migra," "Not One More Deportation," "Deferred Action for All Now," and "Vamos a Quebrar el ICE"), while others were handwritten ("Leave my dad here we need him").[4] There are also paper flowers on the fence, as well as a photograph of a man flanked by two boys, all of whom are posing for the photograph.

If you are unfamiliar with contemporary migrant activism, you may wonder why a photograph, presumably of a father with his two sons, was enlarged to the size of a poster and hung on a fence along with political signs and posters. As indicated by the handwritten text below the photograph, this poster-sized image was probably held up during the protest by members of this man's family, who were fighting his deportation. Family and personal photographs have been used in recent years as part of antideportation campaigns.[5] These images circulate within a range of different locations, including political actions and as part of online petitions on activist websites. Although some scholars and activists have noted the limitations to emphasizing the family ties of undocumented migrants (within either mixed-status families or not), Amalia Pallares contends that within the context of antideportation activism, highlighting the family "challenge[s] the divisions and categorizations of the state" and specifically the way in which the state views undocumented adults as less "deserving" of citizenship or some other official "legal" status than undocumented children and young adults.[6] The strategic use of this photograph among signs and posters is indicative of this book's primary concern with struggles over the idea of documentation, documentary forms, and self-representation by Mexican and Central American migrants in the early twenty-first century.

My interest in starting off the book with an analysis of this image from the "Shut Down ICE" protest is related to the significance of "subjective" aesthetic forms within projects that primarily involve the self-representation of undocumented Mexican and Central American migrants.[7] In the early 2000s, these projects began to proliferate in the United States and U.S.–Mexico borderlands, resembling those developed by nonprofits, social service organizations, filmmakers, and photographers in the 1960s and 1970s, which attempted to put the "mode of production" into the hands of members of "marginalized" groups. Still, I wondered why there was a resurgence of this approach in the post-9/11 era in projects that specifically included Mexican and Central American migrants. This book aims to respond to this question. I contend that although nonprofits, social service organizations, filmmakers, and artists initiated projects for these migrants to "document" elements of their lives through photography, film, and video, those who participated did not only *use* the documentary form, but also *revised* the aesthetics of documentary. They did this by combining documentary with "subjective" aesthetic forms, including family and personal photography and performative elements within film and video.

The Undocumented Everyday specifically focuses on projects created in the United States and U.S.–Mexico borderlands between 2000 and 2012 during the administration of George W. Bush and the first term of Barack Obama's administration. Starting in the early 2000s and continuing after 9/11, labor unions, nonprofit social service organizations, advocacy groups, filmmakers, artists, and activists developed documentary projects that included Mexican and Central American migrants, which were presented to a range of different audiences. As compared with conventional approaches to documentary media, the organizers of these projects envisioned self-representation as a way for members of these groups to portray themselves on their own terms, and thus differently from how they were presented in the mainstream media or by documentary photographers and filmmakers. This approach can also be distinguished from other autobiographical forms within nonfiction media, as these projects involved groups of people, rather than individuals.[8]

The Undocumented Everyday also examines the choice of documentary modes and corresponding realist aesthetics in the self-representation of Mexican and Central American migrants. I analyze what is assumed in the imperative for "documentation" in this context, and I consider the presumptions and formal conventions that valorize self-representation as a visual and political strategy. This book explores the conventions and constraints of documentation, understood both as an aesthetic practice and as an administrative procedure for policing boundaries of inclusion within the nation-state. I use the phrase "documentary realist forms" to emphasize the ways in which documentary is an aesthetic based on the visual conventions of social realism, with genealogical connections to state (juridical-administrative) record keeping and scientific modes of visual documentation.[9] The use of visual technologies as part of state documentation can be traced back to the late nineteenth century, when, as Anna Pegler-Gordon argues, "the United States's differential politics regarding immigration and photo documentation were part of state-based practices of racial formation."[10] The majority of the documentary projects that I write about were produced following 9/11, a time when the U.S. state gathered biometric data, including photographs, ostensibly as a form of defense against terrorism. The government also utilizes "biometric imaging technologies that digitally recognize racial 'types'" at entry points to the country, including the U.S.–Mexico boundary.[11] Consequently, I understand "documentary" as a form of knowledge and a technique of power, and I explore the possibilities and limitations of the production and circulation of works of self-representation in documentary form in the context of U.S. neoliberal governance.

In this book, I argue that in their use of documentary media, Mexican and Central American migrants have created alternatives to liberal tropes of "visibility." Within a liberal model, "giving" visibility is individualized, focusing on the ways individuals are depicted, rather than highlighting the predicament of undocumented migrants as a result of state policies and legislation and their collective circumstances more generally. However, as Dimitris Papadopulos and Vassilis Tsianos suggest, "Visibility, in the context of illegal migration, belongs to the inventory of the technologies for policing migrational flows."[12] In contemporary U.S. society, visibility is associated with empowerment and invisibility with powerlessness, including an absence from political and cultural life.

While some scholars see visibility as a means for marginalized groups to claim rights, Lisa Marie Cacho suggests that "because the state renders criminalized populations of color [including undocumented migrants] ineligible for personhood, and consequently, ineligible for the right to ask for rights, they cannot be incorporated in rights-based politics."[13] It is "the exclusionary aspects of citizenship that shape the experiences of undocumented residents as the 'present absents' in the U.S. polity," as Amalia Pallares argues.[14] However, Pallares also notes that scholars must study the subjectivity of undocumented migrants and "focus on the specific agency of the undocumented—that is, on the relationship between the exclusion from citizenship and the forms of political representation, strategies, and identities that undocumented people can potentially deploy."[15] *The Undocumented Everyday* examines how Mexican and Central American migrants use documentary media as part of their "counter-representational practices" and "to generate uncertainty about 'commonsense' understandings of belonging."[16]

Rather than presuming the value of visibility, I analyze how Mexican and Central American migrants deploy strategies of visibility and invisibility within specifically situated contexts that expose the relations of power at work in the terms of visibility itself. Although the general liberal claim about "visibility" is frequently touted as necessary in order for certain marginalized groups to have a "voice" and be fully included in U.S. society, what is significant about these migrants' approach to visibility in the examples that follow is their attention to the specific context of their enunciation. As such, I contend that in these projects migrants do not make general claims about the importance of being "visible" as an abstract form of empowerment, identitarian affirmation, and inclusion, but instead employ documentary forms to draw attention to as well as challenge the effects of neoliberal policies and U.S. immigration laws on undocumented migrants.

Mexican and Central American migrants have used and revised the aesthetics of documentary realism to represent themselves in ways that push back against liberal concepts of "political incorporation into national belonging."[17] This approach relates to arguments scholars have made that in the late twentieth and early twenty-first centuries undocumented Mexican and Central American migrants have asserted their political presence in the United States in opposition to liberal citizenship rights.[18] I argue that in some of these documentary projects migrants narrate forms of social belonging that do not involve state forms of recognition, while in others they refuse recognition from the state.[19] This study contributes to scholarship on contemporary U.S. im/migration through its examination of how Mexican and Central American migrants use documentary media to provide alternative representations of themselves, which center their subjectivity and visualize their presence within the United States and in the U.S.–Mexico borderlands.

These documentary works created by Mexican and Central American migrants are a response to U.S. immigration policies and neoliberal economic policies in the U.S.–Mexico border region. In the case of Mexican migrants, Alicia Schmidt Camacho contends that as they "narrate a condition of alterity to, or exclusion from, the nation, they also enunciate a collective desire for a different order of space and belonging across the boundary."[20] Drawing on Charles Taylor's work on social imaginaries, Schmidt Camacho suggests that we should understand these migrants' cultural forms not as "a reflection of the social, or merely a detached 'set of ideas,' but rather the means by which subjects work through their connections to a larger totality and communicate a sense of relatedness to a particular time, place, and condition."[21] In analyzing these projects of self-representation, I situate them within the historical moment in which they were developed in the post-9/11 era, as well as their locations, their modes of address, and their contexts of production.

The Undocumented Everyday begins during a period marked by a shift from a collaboration between the U.S. and Mexican governments on a 2001 binational agreement regarding the status of undocumented Mexicans in the United States to the immediate post-9/11 era, wherein these migrants were viewed as part of the threat that immigration presented to the country.[22] As I outline in the next section, laws established after 9/11 limited the ability of Mexican and Central American migrants to leave and then return to the United States. Consequently, there were major changes in migration patterns, increasing the number of undocumented people living for extended periods in the United States. Almost all of the projects that I analyze were produced after 9/11, when the federal government subjected undocumented migrants to more punitive and carceral practices, leading to dramatic increases in the numbers of those arrested, detained, and deported. This period was also characterized by neoliberal austerity programs in Mexico, escalating violence in Central America, heightened security in the U.S.–Mexico borderlands, and the installation of surveillance technologies in public spaces—including worksites— throughout the United States. *The Undocumented Everyday* concludes at the end of Obama's first term in office, by which time close to two million undocumented migrants, primarily from Mexico and Central America, had been deported.[23]

The development of localized strategies of immigration enforcement distinguishes the post-9/11 era from earlier periods.[24] While these strategies were partly the result of federal immigration policies, state governments also implemented stricter immigration enforcement, such as Arizona Senate Bill 1070: "Support Our Law Enforcement and Safe Neighborhoods Act" (SB 1070). Jonathan X. Inda and Julie A. Dowling note that policies like SB 1070, which are based on "attrition through enforcement," focus on "depriving [undocumented migrants] of the ability to participate meaningfully in quotidian life" and are thus "designed to isolate this population from society and render them ultimately powerless."[25] Further, federal agencies like Immigration and Customs Enforcement (ICE) developed programs, such as Secure Communities (S-COMM), that had local law enforcement policing and reporting on migrants' immigration status, leading to huge increases in the detentions and deportations of undocumented migrants.[26]

In the post-9/11 era, federal immigration policies and state laws like SB 1070 have increased the racial profiling and surveillance of Latina/o migrants.[27] The documentary projects of self-representation that I examine developed within a political context in which, as Wendy Hesford notes, these "specular and panoptic logics are mobilized by governments to harden ideological support for the curtailment of rights."[28] Jodie M. Lawston and Ruben R. Murillo have related the spectacle of enforcement by state agents—including Sheriff Joe Arpaio of Arizona—and the escalation of ICE raids—leading to the detention and deportation of undocumented migrants—to the actions performed by civilian anti-immigrant organizations, such as the Minuteman Project in the U.S.–Mexico borderlands.[29]

This book is informed by theoretical insights from visual culture studies, as it seeks to place questions of visuality at the center of U.S. immigration politics. The theoretical perspectives that I draw upon emphasize how the visual is invested in relations of power. As Susan Jeffords has argued, "It is how citizens *see* themselves and how they *see* those against whom they define themselves that determines national self-perception. . . . The very idea of a nation is itself dependent on the visual realm."[30] Various scholars have written about how state and nonstate actors use visual surveillance technologies to produce spectacles of enforcement, drawing on the work of Guy Debord, who described the spectacle not as "a collection of images," but as "a social relationship between people that is mediated by images."[31] According to Diana Taylor, the spectacle "ties individuals into an economy of looks and looking."[32] Further, Nicholas Mirzoeff has argued that laws such as SB 1070 are intended to "intensify the racialized divide between the citizen and undocumented migrant worker, creating a normative border that can be instantiated whenever a 'citizen' looks at a person suspected of being a migrant."[33]

The projects that I discuss emerged out of distinct sites, political contexts, and historical moments. Some involved photography workshops arranged by labor groups or social service organizations in places where migrants were either temporary residents or where they were part of a well-established community. Other projects involved migrants taking photographs as they traveled through the U.S.–Mexico borderlands. Still others had filmmakers and artists collaborating with migrant activists on film and video projects that became part of their political organizing. The migrants who contributed to these documentary works include male day laborers from Central America and Mexico living in Long Island, New York; a multigenerational group of men, women, and teenagers who were primarily from Oaxaca living in Poughkeepsie, New York; Mexican and Central American migrants journeying through the

U.S.–Mexico borderlands; *promotoras* (community activists) in Tijuana, most of whom migrated there to work in the *maquiladoras*;[34] Latina/o migrants who were part of mixed-status families in the Bay Area in California; and "undocumented 1.5 generation activists," some of whom are Latina/o, but not Mexican or Central American, or are undocumented, but not Latina/o, who collaborated with migrant activists on campaigns against anti-immigrant laws.[35] I further investigate their different circumstances, as well as the distinct discourses that informed perceptions of these groups, in the next section of the introduction.

In these locations, the dynamics of conflict took a variety of forms. In some places, local residents developed policies in efforts to drive out undocumented migrants, whereas in others residents and policies were less hostile and more inclusionary. In Hempstead, Long Island, anti-immigrant groups such as Sachem Quality of Life (SQL) actively attempted to push out Mexican and Central American migrants. Anti-immigrant organizations—such as the Federation for American Immigration Reform (FAIR)—worked with politicians and residents to create anti-immigrant ordinances, such as the Neighborhood Preservation Act, which limited day laborers' ability to wait for work on street corners in parts of Long Island.[36] FAIR also generated anti-immigrant legislation on the state level through its legal arm, the Immigration Reform Law Institute, which employed politicians such as Kris Kobach, coauthor of Arizona Senate Bill 1070.[37] Migrant activists in Arizona and elsewhere challenged both SB 1070 and copycat laws in Alabama and Georgia. Other projects were organized in the U.S.–Mexico borderlands, where vigilante groups such as the Minuteman Project (MMP) had set up "observation sites" to "guard" the U.S.–Mexico boundary, reporting migrants trying to cross "illegally," or where cross-border organizing related to labor and environmental issues was taking place.

Other projects were produced in towns and cities that were more inclusionary of Latina/o migrants, including Poughkeepsie and San Francisco, the latter of which has a "sanctuary" ordinance for undocumented residents. Sanctuary ordinances offer what Jennifer Ridgley calls "an alternative vision of security and political membership" for undocumented migrants because these laws position migrants as residents of a locality, rather than as criminals within the United States.[38] However, the disjuncture between local sanctuary ordinances and federal immigration law and policies can create conditions of vulnerability for undocumented migrants.

The production of Mexican and Central American migrants' documentary media has also been shaped by dominant ideological discourses, including neoliberalism. Neoliberal discourse on immigration began dominating the political landscape in the mid-1990s. The discussions about immigration resembled prevailing approaches to so-called welfare reform, which insisted that poor people—in this case noncitizens—were making illegitimate claims on the state. One major tenet of the Personal Responsibility and Work Opportunity Reconciliation Act (PRWORA)— which emphasized "personal responsibility" over "public dependency" (shifting liability from the state to the individual)—was that migrants, whether "legal" or "illegal," could not receive welfare benefits.[39] According to Nicholas De Genova, the PRWORA and 1996 Illegal Immigration Reform and Immigrant Responsibility Act (IIRIRA) "together represented the two-pronged material and practical culmination of a more generalized ideological onslaught against 'immigration' and 'welfare' that had raged in the United States during the early and mid-1990s."[40] In this context Jonathan X. Inda argues that "illegal" migrants have been "typically imagined as criminals, job takers, welfare dependents" and "have essentially been constructed as imprudent, unethical subjects incapable of exercising responsible self-government and thus as threats to the overall well-being of the social body."[41] Neoliberalism not only "represents a change in the way political subjects are perceived," as Rebecca Hester suggests, but it also shifts "the way they perceive themselves."[42] Further, as Lisa Duggan argues, neoliberalism is a cultural project, and its political and economic objectives can be conveyed in forms of cultural production.[43] Some of the documentary projects produced by Mexican and Central American migrants were responses to neoliberal policies and discourses that positioned them as "illegal" and as "takers" in relation to the welfare system.

Within the context of their exclusion from citizenship, Latina/o migrants deployed specific strategies and forms of cultural and political representation. The documentary projects that I analyze in this book were shaped by a political context whereby migrants' marginalization from national belonging is, as Amalia Pallares argues, "sustained ideologically through the use of repeated images and representations that help to create and reinforce exclusion."[44] Undocumented migrants have been constrained in their attempts to portray themselves in both legal and political contexts. Due in part to the limitations of immigration law and the predominance of neoliberal ideology, immigration advocates and lawyers have sometimes pressured migrants to represent themselves as exceptional, particularly in the ways "that appeal to dominant populations' sympathies and sense of morality," as part of antideportation cases.[45] This strategy—to highlight the "worthiness" of their migrant clients—has been used by lawyers to defend undocumented migrants in deportation proceedings. Muneer Ahmad argues that there are many problems with this tactic, noting that while it "may expand the contours of the rights-bearing community," it "do[es] so at the risk of reinforcing the subordinating regime that produces the substantive inequality in the first place."[46] It has also been used as part of antideportation cases involving undocumented youth, who have been encouraged to represent themselves in ways that emphasize their "worthiness" by focusing on their "productivity and competitiveness," "their individuation," and "their potential for self-care and self-responsibility."[47] This approach has been challenged in recent years by undocumented youth and migrant activists, whose strategies are aimed at disrupting the ways in which some migrants are represented as "exceptional" and thus "deserving," and others are positioned as "undeserving" and thus deportable.[48]

Some of these migrants' approaches to self-representation in documentary media developed out of their political strategies and activism. In these projects, migrants use documentary media to represent visual forms of "migrant counter-conducts," which Jonathan X. Inda and Julie Dowling define as "acts or forms of comportment that contest the criminalization and exclusion of the undocumented."[49] Migrant counter-conducts can occur as part of organized political actions or everyday forms of resistance, what Inda and Dowling refer to as "everyday counter-conducts."[50] The different forms of migrant counter-conducts also relate to how scholars have defined "migrant struggles." For example, Nicholas De Genova and his coauthors provide one meaning that "indicates more or less organized *struggles* in which migrants openly challenge, defeat, escape or trouble the dominant politics of mobility (including border control, detention, and deportation) or the regime of labor, or the space of citizenship."[51] Some of the organized struggles that inform the migrants' projects include the nationwide immigrant rights marches in the spring of 2006. They also include the activism of migrant-led organizations, such as NDLON, the National Immigrant Youth Alliance (NIYA), and the Puente Movement of Arizona.[52] These activists have engaged in what I refer to as "unauthorized acts," in which they disrupt or interrupt the business of the state in order to contest immigration laws and policies. The second meaning of "migrant struggles," as defined by De Genova and his coauthors, "refers to the daily strategies, refusals, and resistances through which migrants enact their (contested) presence—even if they are not expressed or manifested as 'political' battles, demanding something in particular."[53] The documentary projects that developed out of these contexts narrate how Mexican and Central American migrants respond to being racialized and criminalized in the United States.

In their documentary projects, these migrants emphasize their points of view and everyday lives as forms of counter-knowledge and counter-representation. By centering their lives and their political projects, they also revise documentary realism by mixing documentary aesthetics with those of amateur photography (such as personal, family, or snapshot photography) and performative elements in the film, video, and audio projects. This mixed-genre aesthetic relates to Imogen Tyler's contention that, in contemporary immigration politics, "the intellectual and the political challenge is precisely about the necessity of working at the borders of older and different genres and forms of practice as a means of reinventing," what Lauren Berlant refers to as "new idioms of the political, and of belonging itself."[54] Although this book charts the various ways that undocumented migrants have organized, from working within the constraints of U.S. immigration policy to critiquing state power, I focus on how they have used documentary media as part of their political strategies. These documentary projects emphasize not only the migrants' respective subjectivities, but also their collective presence and mobility.

At the same time, this photographic, film, and video work needs to be contextualized in relation to the "aesthetic and cultural conditions of post-9/11 carceral governmentality."[55] Inherent in some of these projects is what Yates McKee describes as the challenges of making "disappearance appear as such, which is to say, as an intolerable governmental practice premised on the dismembering of particular subjects from the realm of both legal protection and public memory."[56] Some of these works involving Latina/o migrants take up an aesthetics of disappearance, such as those in which they refuse to be represented visually in order to protect themselves from harassment or identification leading to arrest, detention, and deportation. In not visually representing migrants, these artworks focus attention on state practices of surveillance. The representation of migrant disappearance takes numerous forms in these works. Some migrants choose not to represent their bodies photographically as engaged in certain activities, while others photographed crosses marking places where migrants had perished in the U.S.–Mexico borderlands, which had the effect of "re-membering" those who lost their lives. In other images, such as those taken by the migrants' family members who live across national boundaries, they portray themselves and their lives, but in doing so they make the *absence* of migrants *present*, at least in the eyes of their community members.

This book also considers issues of address as well as audiences for these projects, including how these works are mediated, curated, and distributed. Although documentary projects of self-representation frequently involve the circulation of images, Martha Rosler argues that what is "underestimate[d] [is] the shaping effect of institutions and the context of reception, which are likely to reimpose the unequal power relationship banished from the photographic transaction."[57] Thus, *The Undocumented Everyday* critically examines the exhibition and distribution of migrant self-representation. The earlier chapters focus on photography projects that are shown within more traditional forums, including exhibitions, slideshows, and coffee-table books. The later chapters consider film, video, and audio projects—which involve migrant organizing and coalition-building—that are distributed through binational film tours, as projections onto public buildings, on the Internet, and in galleries. These works are exhibited and distributed in local, translocal, transborder, and national contexts.[58]

Sometimes the organizations and individuals who coordinated these projects had goals that differed from those who created the documentary work, which entailed presenting the photographs, films, and videos in specific ways for broader audiences. For example, some of the photography exhibitions were curated by staff members at nonprofit organizations or by members of advocacy groups who saw these images as tools for creating awareness and reflexivity among viewers from outside the community. These projects were framed by the liberal humanist belief that the images will elicit an emotional response from the audience, and this affect will compel reform.[59] Other projects—such as videos of activists' political actions—feature performative elements and are recorded and viewed through digital and social media by other undocumented migrants as a means of political mobilization. The emphasis on performance and "the movement of bodies" in these works provides what Ramón Rivera-Servera and Harvey Young argue is "an opportunity to envision a more articulate theory of political mobilization; one that accounts for the ways in which participation is actually encouraged and attained."[60] Further, Diana Taylor's notion of the repertoire as an embodied practice—"a form of knowing as well as a system of storing and transmitting knowledge"—is also relevant to the context of contemporary political activism whereby videos of actions circulate through forms of digital and social media.[61]

Counter-Documentation

The first part of this book begins with two labor union–affiliated documentary projects from the early 2000s, featuring migrants' photographs of their everyday lives. These images were produced as part of Unseen America, a nationwide project organized by the Bread and Roses Cultural Project, the cultural arm of 1199SEIU (Local 1199 of the Service Employees International Union). In these photography projects—including one involving day laborers affiliated with the Workplace Project (Centro de Derechos Laborales) in Long Island—Mexican and Central American migrants portray their ordinary existence, their indispensability to everyday economies, and their everyday "counter-conducts." In these images, migrants represented their everyday lives—what I refer to as the *undocumented everyday*—which also involved mixing documentary with other photographic genres. Their approach to self-representation was meant to challenge anti-immigrant discourses and policies that associated undocumented migrants with criminality and illegality within locations in which they were limited from participating in aspects of everyday life.[62] While the Unseen America participants used documentary in ways that associated their photographs with certain truth claims, they also revised elements of documentary realism through their creation of a mixed-genre aesthetic, which drew on personal, family, and snapshot photography. This aesthetic relates to the emphasis of Unseen America on documentary photography, as well as the migrants' address to individuals within their local or translocal communities. In their images, migrants construct alternative representations of themselves and local and translocal "ways of belonging."[63]

In addition to their portrayal of the undocumented everyday, some of the Unseen America participants also developed a *translocal aesthetic*, which relates the mixed-genre approach to the translocal address of the photographers. Their translocal aesthetic envisions migrants' simultaneous belonging to multiple locations. For example, Mexican migrants who were part of Hudson River HealthCare (HRHCare)'s Communities without Borders project created photographs that represent elements of their everyday lives, which they addressed to family members, from whom they were separated by national borders. However, the photographs produced by these migrants' families in Oaxaca—who also participated in the project—made visible the *absence* of the family members who had migrated. The absence of migrants in the photographs, which could only be seen by members of the translocal community, narrates a critique of neoliberal globalization that pressures Mexicans to migrate, while also referencing the fact that once in the United States, post-9/11 immigration laws and policies prevent them from returning home.

The second part of *The Undocumented Everyday* examines collaborative projects that focus on U.S.–Mexico border enforcement and the effects of neoliberal economic policies on border communities. In my analysis of the documentary photography and film projects produced in the U.S.–Mexico borderlands, I distinguish between different approaches to "collaboration" and the address of the work to nonmigrants or as related to coalition building and self-representation. For example, as part of the Border Film Project—which also included members of the nativist, anti-immigrant Minuteman Project—migrants took photographs while traveling surreptitiously through the U.S.–Mexico borderlands. Their photographs combine documentary aesthetics with those of personal and snapshot photography, and they represent themselves engaging in "migrant counter-conducts," which challenge their exclusion from the United States. Their images—such as those of crosses marking migrant deaths—also narrate alternative "ways of seeing" how U.S.–Mexico boundary policing and militarization affect undocumented migrants. In addressing a U.S. audience, the Border Film Project organizers obscured the migrants' perspectives by emphasizing a U.S. nationalist point of view in the exhibitions and the book, which also featured photographs by members of the Minuteman Project. In contrast, the collaboration between the filmmakers and promotoras (community activists) who created *Maquilápolis: City of Factories* (2006) prioritized the promotoras as political subjects, and the film was addressed to other *maquila* workers.

In addition to photography, some of these projects involve collaborations between filmmakers, artists, and activists in the creation of film, video, and audio projects that emphasize migrant organizing and employ both performance and documentary aesthetics. This combining of genres relates to the attention given to what Thomas Keenan refers to as "aesthetic categories," which Yates McKee contends "[imply] both a general acknowledgment that evidence itself is not self-evident—the difficulty of effectively 'making an issue' out of the practice of a governing agency, rather than simply revealing it to the presumably morally sensitive 'eyes of the world'—and a vigilant attention to the specific conditions, mediations, and tactics of such issue making."[64] By combining documentary with performance, migrant activists used and revised forms of documentary media to center their point of view. In *Maquilápolis*, the filmmakers and promotoras juxtapose documentary elements with performance sequences that emphasize the promotoras' subjectivity and also reframe and recontextualize the aesthetic logic of documentary.[65] In this film and other projects, media makers also employ varying aesthetic strategies to address the complexities of representing the effects of neoliberal globalization on workers in Mexico and restrictive U.S. immigration policies on undocumented migrants, specifically in contexts where visibility can bring vulnerability.

The third part of the book analyzes video, multimedia, and social media projects that focus on U.S. immigration laws and policies. These projects also feature affective and performative elements that make visible the effects of state practices on undocumented migrants and provide a critique of state forms of policing and surveillance. The art installation *Sanctuary City/Ciudad Santuario, 1989–2009*, which was exhibited in San Francisco, included migrants' oral testimonies along with state forms of documentation. Their testimonies are examples of "migrant counterconducts," in which they contest the criminalization of undocumented migrants. The artists' inclusion of Latina/o migrants' oral testimonies on the effects of ICE raids in the Bay Area without a visual counterpart was a response to the migrants' request that their faces not be shown. In doing so the artists made these individuals present within the space, while also countering the expectation for their voices to correspond to visual representation, thus disrupting the desire of the audience for the realization of the promise of documentation. In addition, the artwork relates to what McKee describes as the "paradoxical aesthetics of disappearance articulated by [a] cluster of practices that resonates with Judith Butler's call for a 'critical image,'" which, according to Butler, "must not only fail to capture its referent, but *show* this failing."[66] The absence of visual representations of those testifying was also a means to focus attention on state practices, including the surveillance of Latina/o migrants.

Both the artists who created *Sanctuary City/Ciudad Santuario* and the undocumented migrant and youth activists whose media work I discuss

in the final chapter use specific aesthetic and political strategies—
including counter-surveillance—in addition to affective and performative
elements as part of documentary projects that visually depict migrants'
"counter-conducts." Undocumented youth and migrant activists deployed
counter-surveillance and performance as part of their efforts to document state agents' processes of arresting and detaining undocumented
migrants. In their use of documentary media to record their performances of "unauthorized acts," undocumented migrant activists took
up strategies of *counter-visibility* in which they publicized their political
actions in order to shield themselves from detention and deportation.
They also created what I term *counter-documents*, which combine documentary aesthetics with performance elements that are part of their
actions in which they demand social justice for undocumented migrants.[67]
Their counter-documentation is a form of image practice that references
the truth claims of traditional social documentary film and video as a
means to provide evidence that challenges official forms of documentation and the state's ability to determine the parameters of political inclusion. Further, they circulated these counter-documents through digital
and social media in efforts to mobilize other undocumented migrants.
This emphasis on mobility and mobilization counters what some scholars have referred to as the "dominant politics of mobility."[68]

In the remainder of the Introduction I provide an overview of the
broader political context surrounding the migration of Mexicans and
Central Americans to the United States and the U.S.–Mexico borderlands in the 1990s and 2000s, which was largely prompted by neoliberal economic policies. I analyze how undocumented migrants respond
to restrictive immigration policies both before and after they have entered
the country, focusing on the direction of migrant activism since 2010.
In the section on "Documentary and Self-Representation," I contextualize the projects developed by nonprofit and advocacy organizations,
photographers, artists, and filmmakers by tracing a longer history of this
approach, dating back to collaborations between "marginalized" groups
and photographers, filmmakers, and video makers in the 1960s, 1970s,
and 1980s. The final section of the Introduction outlines the chapters and
the Conclusion.

Mexican and Central American Migration, U.S. Immigration Policy, and Migrant Activism

The photography, film, video, and audio projects by Mexican and Central American migrants that I examine in this book emerged out of the political context of the United States following 9/11. In part because laws established after 9/11 limited the ability of Mexican and Central American migrants to leave and then return to the United States, this period saw major shifts in migration patterns, leading to an increase in the number of undocumented Mexican and Central American migrants in the United States.[69] According to a Pew Research Center Report, Mexicans generally make up the largest percentage of undocumented residents, which was six million in 2012 (52 percent), a decline from 6.9 million (57 percent) in 2007.[70] Between 2008 and 2012, more migrants to the United States came from Central America than from Mexico.[71] The 2008 recession was a factor in this, since it affected construction and other industries that employed undocumented workers, which led some to return home. But it was also an outcome of violence in parts of Central America—including Honduras, El Salvador, and Guatemala—which was partially a consequence of U.S. covert military policies and counter-insurgency in addition to neoliberal economic policies, such as the 2006 Central America–Dominican Republic Free Trade Agreement (CAFTA-DR), which led to significant job loss in various industries in participating countries.[72]

The majority of Mexican and Central American migrants involved in the projects described in this book are undocumented. These individuals relocated from countries in Central America and Mexico to the United States and the U.S.–Mexico borderlands. Central Americans from El Salvador, Nicaragua, and Guatemala started leaving their countries in large numbers during wars that began in the late 1970s and early 1980s.[73] At the time the U.S. government failed to acknowledge the role that its foreign policy played in creating Central American refugees; however, María Cristina García explains that while the United States granted a limited number of Central Americans political asylum in the 1980s and 1990s, very few who came to the United States during the mid-1990s through the early 2000s were granted refugee status.[74] This was due to the 1996 IIRIRA, which changed immigration law, especially for undocumented migrants. The act made it more difficult for these migrants to stay in the United States, and it also significantly limited the ability of Central Americans to receive political asylum in order to become U.S. residents.[75]

Much of the migration of Mexicans and Central Americans to the United States in the early twenty-first century was the result of the North American Free Trade Agreement (NAFTA), CAFTA-DR, and neoliberal globalization that has restructured production. These changes also affected both the demand for and the regulation of a low-wage labor force, which was composed in part of undocumented migrants in the United States.[76] In Mexico, neoliberal economic policies, including NAFTA—which established a free-trade zone among the United States, Mexico, and Canada—displaced millions of people in Mexico, including many indigenous agricultural workers, increasing both unemployment and migration within and beyond Mexico.[77] During the mid-1990s, Mexicans who had difficulty making a living migrated to northern border cities to work in export processing factories—known as maquiladoras—while others attempted to cross the U.S.–Mexico boundary into the United States.[78]

The locations of the documentary projects featured in this book correspond to the post-1990 migration patterns of Mexicans and Central Americans into northern Mexico and the United States.[79] Some projects were created by those who moved to northern border cities such as Tijuana to look for work in the maquiladoras. Their circumstances were quite different from those who entered the United States. In the 2000s, Mexican and Central American migrants in the United States increasingly found jobs in places far away from established migrant border communities. According to Monica Varsanyi, Mexicans and Central Americans have in recent years journeyed to the U.S. South, the Midwest, and the Northeast to look for work.[80] In addition to agriculture, migrants from Mexico and Central America have found jobs in the service industry, meat-packing and processing, and as day laborers, employed in construction, janitorial work, or landscaping. Some women are also employed as domestic workers, cleaning homes or caring for children.

Migrants who cross the boundary from Mexico into the United States experience the effects of militarized border policing, U.S. immigration policy, and limited rights as workers. As Alicia Schmidt Camacho argues, "However ineffective border policing appears as immigration *law enforcement*, official sanctions against unauthorized entry function effectively as instruments of *labor regulation*."[81] She asserts that undocumented migrants see "U.S. immigration policy as a check on their labor power and their capacity to defend their rights as workers."[82] Once in the United States, immigration laws such as IIRIRA racialized and criminalized undocumented Mexicans and Central American migrants.[83] The IIRIRA included 287(g) agreements, which "allow a state and local law enforcement entity to enter into a partnership with ICE, under a joint Memorandum of Agreement (MOA)." Thus, "the state or local entity receives delegated authority for immigration enforcement within their jurisdictions."[84] However, as Varsanyi notes, it was not until after 9/11 that state and local enforcement agencies signed 287(g) agreements.[85]

The political context of the early twenty-first century—specifically the ways that migrant "illegality" has been reconfigured since 9/11—is essential to the analyses of migrants' documentary media in this book. Nicholas De Genova argues that "the dominant metaphysics of antiterrorism ultimately has had labor subordination as one of its decisive conditions of possibility."[86] Scholars have stated that the topic of "immigration reform" was "unspeakable" following 9/11, and since that time politicians have failed to pass any significant immigration reform bills.[87] In the early 2000s, U.S. immigration policy has been shaped by a tension between federal immigration laws and laws passed by state and municipal governments.[88] Contemporary U.S. immigration policy can be characterized by what Varsanyi and others have described as the devolution of federal immigration powers to states, counties, and municipalities.[89] Federal immigration laws determine how undocumented migrants become eligible for legal residence, apply for citizenship, or are deported from the United States. Still, state and municipal policies have significant effects on many other aspects of migrants' lives. Since 2005, immigration-related legislation has grown on the state and local level.[90] Some of these laws are inclusionary—for example, recognizing undocumented migrants as residents in a community—including sanctuary ordinances, the granting of drivers' licenses, or the offering of municipal ID cards. Other local laws are exclusionary, such as those that criminalize the solicitation of work by unauthorized migrants or deny them access to residential leases.[91]

In addition to the punitive quality of some local and state laws, federal programs and policies that were enacted following 9/11—such as the USA PATRIOT Act—criminalized undocumented migrants.[92] In 2002 the Homeland Security Act was passed, leading to the creation of the U.S. Department of Homeland Security (DHS), which established ICE in 2003.[93] ICE describes its role as protecting "national security and public safety." One outcome of its programs has been the criminalization of undocumented migrants within the United States, leading to detentions and deportations.[94] For example, ICE framed the National Fugitive Operations Program (NFOP) as part of a plan to "protect" U.S. citizens from the "dangers" associated with "aliens," who were sometimes referred to as criminals. After 2006, when ICE developed an arrest quota system, raids, detentions, and deportations targeted nonfugitives (those who had never been charged in an immigration court but were instead arrested based on ICE's suspicion that they were in the country unlawfully).[95] In order to justify defining undocumented workers as "criminals" during the administration of President George W. Bush, government officials represented their operations—including workplace raids—as targeting document fraud and identity theft. These violations brought criminal charges, rather than mere administrative immigration violations.[96]

In lieu of comprehensive immigration reform, during the administration of President George W. Bush the federal government established policies that increased the numbers of undocumented migrants arrested, detained, and deported. Although politicians developed Comprehensive Immigration Reform bills in 2005 and 2006, they failed to get the legislation through both houses of Congress. The House passed HR 4437, the Border Protection, Antiterrorism, and Illegal Immigration Act (Sensenbrenner-King Act) in 2005; if it had been approved by the Senate, it would have made residing in the United States without immigration documents a felony, along with criminalizing anyone who aided undocumented migrants.[97] The Senate passed the Comprehensive Immigration Reform Act of 2006, which provided undocumented migrants who had been in the United States for at least five years a path to citizenship. Still, the bill did not obtain a majority vote in the House.[98] Meanwhile, the laws that *were* approved in the 2000s—including the REAL ID Act (2005)—made the lives of undocumented migrants more difficult by trying to limit states' ability to issue them drivers' licenses. Further, the Secure Fence Act (2006), which included constructing seven hundred miles of fence along sections of the U.S. border with Mexico, attempted to keep Mexican and Central American migrants out of the country entirely.[99] According to Wendy Brown, these acts "situate the U.S. walling project as a response to a 'state of emergency,' bidding to protect the vulnerable nation under siege."[100]

From President George W. Bush's second term to President Barack Obama's first, federal agencies like ICE developed new programs to detain and deport undocumented migrants, including S-COMM. In 2008, George W. Bush's last full year in office, ICE established S-COMM, which involved local law enforcement agencies in policing and reporting migrants' immigration status.[101] The coauthors of *Policing Immigrants: Local Law Enforcement on the Front Lines* argue that these policies are part of a larger trend of "crimmigration."[102] The number of undocumented migrants placed in detention or removal (deportation) proceedings increased significantly after President Obama took office. During Obama's first term, S-COMM became one of his administration's key initiatives for immigration enforcement. However, the Obama administration's "silent raids" through E-Verify—which involved auditing employee files, searching for undocumented workers—can be contrasted with the spectacle of ICE's Bush-era workplace raids.[103] The Obama administration focused on detaining and deporting "criminal aliens" through ICE's S-COMM, Operation Community Shield, and NFOP.[104] As Anna Sampaio argues, "most of those apprehended with criminal records were actually noncitizens guilty of minor offenses, such as traffic violations, disorderly conduct, or simply unlawful entry."[105] As such, she contends that ICE, in emphasizing the detention and deportation of "criminal aliens," was also "utilizing broad definitions of criminality" that "unjustly affected Latina/o communities across the country."[106] Although the Bush and Obama administrations differed on some aspects of immigration policy, one similarity is that only a small percentage of undocumented migrants who were arrested, detained, and deported through S-COMM had criminal records.[107]

When President Obama was unable to get comprehensive immigration reform bills through Congress in the early 2010s, his administration instead turned to providing administrative relief to certain groups of undocumented migrants, including students. On June 17, 2011, John Morton, then director of the DHS, wrote a memo in which he stated that ICE agents should exercise "prosecutorial discretion" so as to eliminate "low priority" cases and instead focus on detaining and deporting undocumented migrants convicted of crimes.[108] While Morton explained that prosecutorial discretion was "the authority of an agency charged with enforcing the law to decide to what degree to enforce the law against a particular individual," the "Morton Memo" was ignored by numerous federal immigration officials who continued to arrest, detain, and deport undocumented migrants who had committed only civil violations.[109] Two months later—on August 18, 2011—the Obama administration made an official announcement that undocumented migrants who fit certain eligibility criteria should *not* be placed in deportation proceedings.[110] Young, undocumented migrants, many of whom came to the United States as children, were among those to benefit. The following year, on June 15, 2012, Obama signed an executive order that created Deferred Action for Childhood Arrivals (DACA). DACA allows undocumented youth to apply for "deferred action," which enables them to remain in the United States for two years and to apply for work permits.[111] As I note in chapter 6, President Obama's executive order regarding DACA was enacted as a response to the organizing work of undocumented youth activists.

The documentary works of self-representation referenced in this book are intimately connected to how Mexican and Central American migrants had been organizing in response to restrictive immigration laws. Much of this organizing has occurred on the local level, although some has taken place on a national level. Nationwide events include the 2003 Immigrant Workers Freedom Ride and the May 1, 2006, "A Day without an Immigrant" strike and boycott, which was a response to HR 4437, the Border Protection, Antiterrorism, and Illegal Immigration Act (Sensenbrenner-King Act).[112] Nicholas De Genova has argued that in the context of the "A Day without an Immigrant" strike and boycott,

> undocumented labour, which the legislative debate had sought to render its *object*, audaciously stepped forward again, now on a genuinely massive scale, to effectively reaffirm that migrant workers were truly *subjects* in the struggle. Indeed, they were the subjects in a double and inextricably contradictory sense. They were subjects as labour *for* capital and thus, the veritable source of value, upon which capital is constitutively dependent. They were also subjects as labour *against* capital, engaged in a mass act of insubordination and an expression of the irreconcilable antagonism that conjoins labour and capital in a mutually constitutive social relation.[113]

The increase in ICE raids in the two years following "A Day without an Immigrant," however, tempered the involvement of some undocumented migrants in public political struggles.

Around 2010, some undocumented youth activists shifted their focus from legalization to decriminalization, and they developed new political strategies, including civil disobedience actions and collaborations with migrant-led organizations.[114] Some of these undocumented youth activists had worked to get the DREAM (Development, Relief, and Education for Alien Minors) Act passed, and some had campaigned in support of comprehensive immigration reform.[115] These activists increasingly distanced themselves from mainstream immigrant rights organizations and became more involved in antideportation activism. Amalia Pallares and Gabriela Marquez-Benitez argue that "the creation of a movement within a movement evidences a politics of motion," as activists "challenge their criminalization in more explicit and confrontational ways."[116] These activists formed organizations such as NIYA, the Immigrant Youth Justice League (IYJL), and DreamActivist.org.[117] They also began to organize with migrant-led groups, such as NDLON, and the Puente Movement, a grassroots organization based in Arizona, among others.

Working together, undocumented youth and migrant activists coordinated actions to protest the exponential increase in ICE arrests, detainments, and deportations, through S-COMM and other policies.

Undocumented youth and migrant activism is dynamic, with activists initiating new strategies and approaches all the time. Starting in 2010, some of these activists became more publicly disruptive in challenging local, state, and federal laws and policies. The strategies of undocumented youth have changed significantly since the DREAM Act was proposed in the early 2000s, when mainstream immigrant rights organizations advised youth to represent themselves as "ideal protocitizens" and in ways that appealed to politicians.[118] Undocumented youth sometimes portrayed themselves as "exceptional" in campaigning for the DREAM Act, but by 2010, some activists began to engage in other political strategies, which Pallares argues involved "challenging the use of exceptionalism in the exclusion and potential deportability of all the undocumented."[119] While activist Tania Unzueta Carrasco and Hinda Seif contend that "normative articulations and performances continue to be a key strategy among advocates," they also suggest that "there are segments of undocumented immigrants who have found ways to disrupt and challenge these definitions."[120] In organizations such as the IYJL and DreamActivist.org, undocuqueer (undocumented and queer) activists have played important roles, especially within positions of leadership, and have contested the hierarchy of "deserving" versus "undeserving" migrants, an idea perpetuated by the U.S. state and some mainstream immigrant rights organizations.[121] In recent years, groups such as Mijente have brought an intersectional approach to their organizing in support of LGBTQIA+ Latinx migrants, among many other groups.[122]

As such, undocumented youth and migrant activists have organized actions critiquing the false dichotomy between politicians' representations of undocumented migrants as either "deserving" (young people/DREAMers) or "undeserving" (adults/undocumented workers).[123] Unzueta Carrasco and Seif argue that "undocumented organizers are moving away from justifying access to rights by measuring worthiness according to the nation-state's norms and towards articulating rights based on the needs of the undocumented immigrant, their ties to the community and family, and their mental health."[124] This emphasis was evident when NDLON established the No Papers, No Fear Ride for Justice with NIYA, the Puente Movement, and other organizations in the summer of 2012. These actions mobilized undocumented migrants in states with anti-immigrant laws and in counties with 287(g) agreements.[125] In 2013 NDLON and other groups organized the #Not1More campaign to end the detention and deportation of *all* undocumented migrants.[126]

Undocumented youth have collaborated with migrant activists in what Pallares and other scholars call "impossible activism," referring to the way that undocumented migrants' "political rights are not recognized as legitimate."[127] As part of their "impossible activism," they organize against restrictive and punitive immigration laws and policies— including SB 1070 (and copycat laws), 287(g), and S-COMM. In their actions they also critique neoliberal globalization, which has contributed to the rise of undocumented migrants in the United States.[128] The emphasis on challenging laws that affect undocumented migrants relates to what Carlos, executive director of Arizona's Puente Movement, describes as "centering the movement around the people affected . . . who live it every day." Further, this focus allows undocumented people to, in Carlos's words, "speak for ourselves."[129]

There are differences between the documentary projects I analyze that were coordinated by social service organizations and advocacy groups and those developed by migrant-led organizations, in which undocumented migrants were in positions of authority. Some of the documentary projects developed by social service organizations and advocacy groups were focused on reinforcing liberal beliefs about migrants' humanity in efforts to gain support from individuals outside these communities. In so doing, these projects were framed by liberal notions of empathy, which Marjorie Garber has described as that which "denotes the power of projecting one's personality into the object of contemplation."[130] A similar approach was taken up by mainstream immigrant rights organizations, which emphasized undocumented migrants representing themselves in specific ways as part of attempts to gain rights and citizenship. The work of migrant-led organizations can be distinguished from mainstream immigrant rights organizations that, as Gabriela Marquez-Benitez and Amalia Pallares argue, "marginalized, silenced and treated [undocumented migrants] as subjects of policy."[131] Instead, documentary projects initiated by migrant-led organizations center migrants' subjectivity. Consequently, I also examine the relation of migrant-led organizing work and self-representation within documentary.

Documentary and Self-Representation

The development of projects involving the self-representation of Mexican and Central American migrants in documentary form—that is, in which the people who are taking the photographs or recording the film/video identify as members of the groups they are depicting—has become a familiar strategy used by nonprofit organizations, advocacy groups, artists, filmmakers, and activists. Although documentary photography, film, and video are often associated with objectivity and the portrayal of "others," self-representation in documentary form highlights the image makers' subjective viewpoints. Further, as Keith Beattie contends, "the assertion of subjective and personal points of view and representation of one's self, family, and culture, forces a significant revision of an objective, externalizing, documentary practice."[132] I write about projects that draw on documentary and its association with "objective truth," as well as serving as examples of "subjective experience," in which individuals portray elements of their lives. This emphasis on subjectivity is reinforced by the aesthetics associated with "amateur" photography, film, and video.

The interest of nonprofit organizations, advocacy groups, filmmakers, artists, and migrant activists in these projects is related to the predicaments of Mexican and Central American migrants in the context of neoliberalism and post-9/11 immigration policy, but it is also a response to and a critique of power relations within documentary media. Some scholars, artists, and film and video makers have viewed self-representation as challenging aspects of documentary because it is produced by amateurs rather than professionals, yet others have noted the way in which these forms are limited by similar truth claims. Although self-representation within documentary media can be seen as distinct from conventional social documentary forms, it is also continuous with this genre. While one convention or promise of documentary is that it will motivate viewers to support and pursue reform of the injustice depicted, it can also reinscribe normative frameworks that limit responses to these forms of injustice. This can occur when projects individualize and personalize issues to evoke sympathy and compassion in viewers outside the represented group.

The approach to documentary realist aesthetics in these projects partly depends on the context as well as the form of media employed. This book includes analyses of various media—including photography, film, video, and audio—as well as projects that circulate on the Internet. In these documentary projects, migrants create a mixed-genre aesthetic, drawing on personal, family, and snapshot photography, as well as performative elements in film and video. In combining documentary with family, personal, and snapshot photography, Mexican and Central American migrants create images that are meaningful to them, which relate to a broader political project or which connect family members separated by national borders. The photographic work in the first half of the book differs from the film, video, and audio projects in the second half. The migrants' self-conscious use of performance adds another dimension in these latter works. These projects—which were developed in collaboration with filmmakers, artists, and activists—extend and disrupt documentary conventions through their performative and experimental elements.

The projects involving Mexican and Central American migrants are informed by a longer history in which community arts organizations, photographers, and filmmakers instructed members of disenfranchised groups in how to use cameras so that they could visually represent themselves or, in the case of film and video, "speak on their own behalf."[133] This "hands-on" form of media education was facilitated by technological inventions in the late 1960s, such as the Porta Pak, a portable video recorder. Patricia Aufderheide suggests that contemporary projects have "roots in several traditions" and that "disenfranchised social groups and their supporters have long used documentary to communicate directly their point-of-view to a broader audience—often with a pointed political objective."[134] Some of the first U.S. projects involving documentary film-makers working with community groups developed in New York City in the 1960s. One such organization was Young Filmmakers' Foundation (later Film/Video Arts). The idea behind Young Filmmakers' Founda-tion was to put the "mode of production" into the hands of young people who did not have access to these technologies in order for them to por-tray aspects of their lives, as well as those of their family members, friends, and members of their communities.[135]

There was a similar development within photography in the 1970s, which continued into the 1980s and 1990s. U.S.-based photographers, such as Ann Marie Rousseau, Wendy Ewald, and Jim Hubbard, taught groups of homeless women and children, Native American youth, and economically disadvantaged children in Appalachia and Mexico how to use cameras.[136] Self-representation in photography was also being taken up by advocacy groups who viewed this form as empowering to disenfranchised sectors of the population.[137] Some scholars of photogra-phy have written that this approach provides an active—rather than a passive—relationship to image production. For example, Don Slater has argued that "the camera as an *active* mass tool of representation is a vehicle for documenting one's conditions . . . for creating alternative representations of oneself and one's sex, class, age-group, race," as well as "of gaining power . . . over one's image; of presenting arguments and demands; of stimulating action; of experiencing visual pleasure as a producer, not consumer of images; of relating to, by objectifying, one's personal and political environment."[138] Since self-representation extracts its value from the connection between the photographer and the sub-jects as members of the same community, pictures taken by amateur photographers have also been viewed as less mediated—and thus more "truthful"—than the work of documentary photographers.

Starting in the 1970s, as these early projects of self-representation developed within documentary film, video, and photography, scholars, writers, and artists began to question the documentary genre's historical practices and claims to represent the "truth." Some artists challenged the concept of photograph as "document," while scholars contended that it was not in fact an "impartial witness."[139] Susan Sontag in *On Photography*

(1977) and Martha Rosler in "In, Around, and Afterthoughts (on Documentary Photography)" (1981) also wrote critically about the power relations involved in documentary photography.[140] Allen Sekula and John Tagg analyzed documentary's genealogical connections to state record-keeping and scientific modes of visual documentation in the work of Alphonse Bertillion and Francis Galton.[141] Tagg called into question the ability of the documentary form to represent "reality," which he argued "is already implicated in the historically developed techniques of observation-domination."[142] Abigail Solomon-Godeau wrote about the U.S. state's use of documentary photography during the 1930s and 1940s, noting how that the Farm Security Administration's (FSA) staff encouraged photographers to portray groups who it viewed as "worthy" subjects, namely those envisioned as the "deserving" poor.[143] This scholarship attempted to address what Solomon-Godeau referred to as the "structural limitations of conventional documentary imagery to disrupt the textual, epistemological, and ideological systems that inscribe and contain it."[144] In the 1990s and 2000s scholars of photography also analyzed the ways in which documentary photography has been used as a means to differentiate between "races" dating back to nineteenth-century ideas that racial hierarchies had a basis in science.[145] For example, Coco Fusco has written about the specific relationship between "race" and representation, arguing that "photography *produced* race as a visualizable fact" starting in the nineteenth century.[146]

In recent years, scholars have also written about how activists of color have used documentary forms, including photography, to represent themselves and publicize their political actions. In her book *Imprisoned in a Luminous Glare*, Leigh Raiford analyzes how activists involved in the antilynching, civil rights, and the Black Power movements "intervene[d] in the complicity of racial ideology and visual technology" by deploying photography as a means to publicize their political goals and mobilize supporters.[147] As part of this study, Raiford examined the ways in which African Americans have used photography "as a liberatory tool of black self-representation." At the same time, she contends that black photographic self-representation "must be understood [then] as a constant dialectic between private and public, personal and political, fiction and biography."[148] This point resonates with the work of scholars in film and cultural studies—such as Stuart Hall and others at the Centre for Contemporary Cultural Studies—who "challenged the notion of media texts as 'transparent' bearers of meaning."[149]

Along with critical scholarship on documentary photography, film, and video, in the 1990s documentary film and video makers in the United States were developing more collaborative media-making practices with their subjects. Jay Ruby described these practices as "offer[ing] the possibility of perceiving the world from the viewpoint of the people who led lives that are different from those traditionally in control of the means for imagining the world."[150] The availability of camcorders led to an exponential growth in amateur video making, and first-person storytelling became a popular genre in the 1990s. Patricia Aufderheide described these projects as "collaborative efforts between artists and otherwise disenfranchised voices" who use "the strategy of social activism through documentary."[151] Some of these projects include documentary filmmakers teaching people to use video cameras to create diaries of their lives, such as filmmaker Ilan Ziv's work with Palestinians in the making of *Palestinian Diaries* (1991).[152] Yet other documentary filmmakers who have used this approach, such as John Caldwell, have also been critical of the ways in which giving cameras to members of disadvantaged groups emphasizes self-representation while making absent the role of the filmmaker within the film.[153]

Another important component of this book concerns the collaboration among nonprofit organizations, advocacy groups, filmmakers, and artists working with Mexican and Central American migrants on these projects. In the first half of the book, I examine projects coordinated by advocacy groups, social service organizations, and individuals that relate migrant self-representation and "visibility" within documentary photography to political agency and empowerment. In these contexts, self-representation acquires value from the connection between the photographer and the subjects, who are members of the same community. Nonprofit organizations and advocacy groups draw from a long history of these types of projects. These works are rooted in liberal humanism, but they are also informed by neoliberalism. I distinguish between the photography projects developed by individuals and organizations working with Mexican and Central American migrants in the first three chapters and those coordinated by filmmakers, artists, and activists in migrant-led organizations in the second half of the book. These latter projects display a more critical approach to the notion of "visibility" for undocumented Latina/o migrants, some of which are engaged in struggles over what constitutes the terms of visibility, explicitly recognizing that the visual is always positioned within larger structures of power and control. Although these works are always mediated through the specific context of presentation, it is only the latter projects that call attention to these dynamics.[154]

The deployment of different media in these projects speaks to changing documentary practices and the politics of self-representation. In the last twenty years, documentary film and video have transformed as a consequence of the availability of inexpensive digital video cameras, better editing software, and the dispersion of these forms through digital and social media, such as on YouTube.[155] The type of technology and documentary form utilized for a project affects not only how the work is produced, but also how it can be viewed. Works circulate on the Internet, even via cell phones, where documentary forms are brought into personal space. Thus, Mexican and Central American migrants' images are distributed not only in exhibitions and at screenings, but also on personal mobile devices, which addresses the fluctuations in the circulation of documentary forms as well as in the audiences who are seeing them. These different platforms for viewing documentary photographs, films, and videos are significant, and as Yates McKee and Meg McLagan point out, these are not "neutral spaces." They explain, "Images circulate within institutional and discursive networks, anchored by the specificity of their formal mediation and attentive to the aesthetic and generic commands of their particular platforms." As such, they argue that "politics do not lie within an image," but instead, "modes of circulation and making public are forms of political action in and of themselves."[156]

In interrogating the proliferation of documentary projects involving the self-representation of Mexican and Central American migrants in the early twenty-first century, this book has primarily drawn from scholarship in the fields of American studies, visual culture studies, media studies, Latina/o studies, U.S.–Mexico border studies, and im/migration studies. Over the past two decades, groundbreaking scholarship has studied the effects of transnational and transborder contexts on Mexican, Mexican American, and Mexican migrants' cultural production and representation, including Claire F. Fox's *The Fence and the River: Culture and Politics at the U.S.–Mexico Border* (1999) and Alicia Schmidt Camacho's *Migrant Imaginaries: Latino Cultural Politics in the U.S.-Mexico Borderlands* (2008). While *The Undocumented Everyday* is informed by this and other scholarship that examines the intersection of Mexican and Central American migration and forms of cultural production, including documentary film, video, and photography, it is also distinct from this work because it addresses the links between documentary forms, U.S. immigration politics, and neoliberal economics during the post-9/11 period and focuses on self-representation as a common trope throughout this moment.[157]

Overview of Chapters

The Undocumented Everyday: Migrant Lives and the Politics of Visibility is organized in loose chronological order from 2000 to 2012. It is comprised of six chapters and divided into three parts. Each part of the book contains two chapters, and each chapter focuses on a case study of the self-representation of Mexican and Central American migrants in documentary form. I understand each case study as a struggle over meaning—from projects produced within highly mediated contexts to those that intervene into dominant discourses and challenge the spectacle of migrant apprehension. I analyze how the political context shaped these projects as well as the goals of advocacy groups, nonprofit organizations, artists, and activists in producing these works. I further explore their circulation within exhibitions, books, screenings, and activist campaigns on the Internet.

Part I, "Ordinary Identifications and Unseen America," studies projects developed in the early 2000s as part of Unseen America, coordinated by the Bread and Roses Cultural Project, the cultural division of 1199SEIU. One of the main goals of Unseen America was to make low-wage laborers "visible" in U.S. society. Chapter 1, "'We See What We Know': Migrant Labor and the Place of Pictures," considers the predicaments of photographic self-representation through an analysis of images produced by Mexican and Central American day laborers who were members of the Workplace Project (Centro de Derechos Laborales) as part of Unseen America. The Workplace Project is an organization of Central American and Mexican day laborers and domestic workers based in Hempstead, Long Island, New York. In their photographs the day laborers represented their everyday lives to counter the images of undocumented Latina/o migrants circulating in the mainstream media and to challenge the discourses of local politicians and anti-immigrant activists. They employed a mixed-genre aesthetic, comprised of documentary, personal, and snapshot photography, to link their images with certain truth claims and to convey intimacy within a hostile environment. I analyze the political uses to which these images were put in the context of local and national exhibitions, as well as the distinct registers that were used to frame the images, including liberal notions of empathy as well as the ideology of "compassionate conservatism." These registers speak to the limits of documentary as a genre in an era of neoliberalism and the compassionate conservatism of the George W. Bush administration.

While the involvement of Workplace Project members in Unseen America was motivated by their broader political commitments, the photographs produced by Mexican migrants in Poughkeepsie, New York, described in chapter 2, "The Border's Frame: Between Poughkeepsie and La Ciénega," narrated their translocal affiliations. This chapter focuses on another Unseen America project, Communities without Borders: A Bridge for Health, organized in 2003 by HRHCare and Bread and Roses. The participants in this project were migrants from Mexico, many of whom were originally from La Ciénega, Oaxaca, who worked and lived in Poughkeepsie. The Communities without Borders project involved two photography workshops in the summer of 2003—one for Mexican migrants in Poughkeepsie and another for their family members in La Ciénega. I argue that participants in HRHCare's project in Poughkeepsie developed a *translocal aesthetic* that narrates the migrants' simultaneous belonging to multiple locations.

Part II, "Documentary, Self-Representation, and 'Collaborations' in the U.S.–Mexico Borderlands," examines "collaborative" photography and film projects that present alternative ways of envisioning the effects of U.S. border policy and neoliberal policies within the United States and Mexico in spaces where migrant workers are regarded as disposable. These chapters also focus on the mediation and curation of migrants' documentary photography and film projects, including the Border Film Project and *Maquilápolis: City of Factories* (2006). Chapter 3, "Visible Frictions: The Border Film Project and the 'Spectacle of Surveillance,'" focuses on a "collaborative art" project developed to address conflicts over U.S.–Mexico border policy. The organizers of this project distributed disposable cameras to Mexican and Central American migrants headed to the United States and also to members of the Minuteman Project, who were positioned at self-made "observation sites" along the U.S. side of the U.S.–Mexico boundary. The organizers saw these groups as representing "both sides" of the debate over U.S. border policy. The migrants' photographs made visible the effects of U.S. border policy and policing on undocumented migrants and represent visual forms of "migrant counter-conducts" that challenges their exclusion from the United States.

Chapter 4, "Refusing Disposability: Representational Strategies in *Maquilápolis: City of Factories*," investigates two distinct approaches to collaborating with women maquiladora workers in Tijuana and how they impact forms of self-representation. The chapter focuses on *Maquilápolis: City of Factories* (2006), produced by filmmaker Vicki Funari and artist Sergio De La Torre in collaboration with women who were being trained as promotoras at Casa de La Mujer/Grupo Factor X, an organization that campaigned for the health and labor rights of women maquila workers. This film was produced after the promotoras in Grupo Factor X were involved in *Tijuana Projection* with the artist Krzysztof Wodiczko, which was performed at inSite 2000–2001, a binational art event between Tijuana and San Diego. Although Wodiczko saw *Tijuana Projection* as representing the perspectives of the women workers, his preconceptions of their lives largely overdetermined the project. In contrast, the collaborative process taken up by Funari, De La Torre, and the promotoras in *Maquilápolis* emphasizes their subjectivity as well as their role as agents in their political organizing against the effects of neoliberal policies within Mexico. However, while *Maquilápolis* focuses on the grassroots campaigns of the promotoras, it is not just a "document" of their struggles. Rather, the film combines multiple conventions, including documentary and staged sequences that are not "reenactments," but rather performances. In addition, the film critiques both the positioning of these workers as "objects of labor" and documentary's claim to "unmediated" representation.

Part III, "Counter-Optics: Disruptions in the Field of the Visible," examines work by artists and activists that focuses on U.S. immigration laws and policies and emphasizes migrant absence, presence, disruption, and mobility. These projects include *Sanctuary City/Ciudad Santuario, 1989–2009*, an exhibition that involved projections in public space produced by artists in San Francisco, and videos created by migrant activists and artists in NIYA, NDLON, and the Puente Movement in 2011 and 2012. The works featured in these chapters call attention to the use of disruption to make visible state practices that were not seen in public spaces. These projects also emphasized mobility—as an aesthetic and in the context of political mobilization—as a means to reclaim space.

Chapter 5, "Disappearance and Counter-Spectacle in *Sanctuary City/ Ciudad Santuario, 1989–2009*," examines an exhibition by Sergio De La Torre and a group of art students, which focused on issues of safety and security for Latina/o migrants in San Francisco. *Sanctuary City/Ciudad Santuario* included a gallery exhibition, as well as projections of text drawn from the testimonies of undocumented Latina/o migrants and their family members onto buildings in the Mission District in San Francisco in 2010. In *Sanctuary City/Ciudad Santuario*, the artists employed an aesthetics of disappearance in an installation in the "sound room" that conveyed the absence of migrants—due to fear of or actual detention and deportation—while also representing their presence through testimonies taped during hearings to denounce ICE raids. In taking this project beyond the gallery, the artists both claimed space and contested law enforcement officials' surveillance of Latinas/os. The projections occupied spaces in the Mission District as a form of "counter-spectacle," making the state's practices of migrant apprehension visible. The projections also illuminated the disjuncture between the effects of the ICE raids and racial profiling on Latina/o migrants and the statements made by local politicians about the city's sanctuary ordinance.

Using documentary media to make the state's violence visible was also a strategy employed by undocumented youth and migrant activists after 2010. Chapter 6, "Reconfiguring Documentation: Mobility, Counter-Visibility, and (Un)Documented Activism," focuses on undocumented youth and migrant activists' use of media tactics, examining how they utilized documentary aesthetics and performance to test the terms of "prosecutorial discretion," as well as to organize against anti-immigrant state and federal laws, policies, and programs. In these contexts, migrant activists employed documentary media as part of their strategies of counter-surveillance and *counter-visibility*. The tactics of undocumented youth activists include counter-surveillance to document state agents' process of arresting and detaining migrants. Further, they create *counter-documents*, including videos of their actions, which are deliberately oppositional.

In the Conclusion, I explore what attending to these projects of self-representation in documentary form—including changes in genre—does for understanding the politics of this particular conjuncture. One of this book's main arguments is that by centering their own *subjectivity* and *presence* in their use of documentary media, Mexican and Central American migrants have envisioned alternatives to liberal tropes of "visibility." Further, in creating alternative representations of themselves they revised forms of documentary media and intervened in the cultural politics of U.S. immigration and neoliberal globalization. Their photographs, films and videos, and art projects emphasize their political presence in the United States and U.S.–Mexico borderlands and gesture toward the ways in which they are disrupting the presumed association between citizenship and belonging.

PART ONE

Ordinary Identifications and Unseen America

CHAPTER ONE

"We See What We Know"

Migrant Labor and the Place of Pictures

The photograph titled *Waiting for Work* (Figure 2), taken by a day laborer affiliated with the Workplace Project (Centro de Derechos Laborales) on Long Island in 2000, portrays five men standing outside in the wintertime looking cold and somewhat bored. Four of the men stand in a line facing toward the camera, while one man is turned away from the camera. Of the group facing the camera, only one of the men engages the photographer's gaze, as the other three men are looking down at their feet. The way that the photograph is cropped highlights the trees behind them and the snow on the ground, but obscures the street by which they are positioned. In this sense, the photograph brackets out the place where they are standing as overtly a site of contention. However, in examining this image more closely, one sees that a section on the photograph's left-hand edge directs viewers toward the outside world of the street. It is here that viewers can see the broader context of the photograph—namely that these men are not in the woods, but rather they are standing by a street in a residential area.[1] Although local viewers of this image would be able to situate the men within this broader context, nonlocal viewers would not know that this street is a gathering spot for day laborers.

Further, the photograph itself would probably appear fairly innocuous to someone for whom its specific context may not be evident. What is clear from the title is that these are men waiting for work—however, what is not conveyed to an audience unfamiliar with the day laborers'

Figure 2. *Waiting for Work* depicts day laborers on a street corner in Long Island. It was taken by a member of the Workplace Project as part of Unseen America, a project of Bread and Roses, 1199SEIU.

experiences is that these individuals often wait fruitlessly on street corners such as this one for jobs that never appear. Nor would it be known to a nonlocal audience that while the day laborers are waiting they are also subjected (especially on Saturdays when this photograph was taken) to the angry tirades of anti-immigrant groups who picket the site or drive by with cameras to "document" those who they believe to be "illegal" while threatening to report these individuals to what was at that time the Immigration and Naturalization Service (INS).[2] Nor would the ever-present threat and actuality of violence against the day laborers be apparent. *Waiting for Work* is a photograph that references some of the difficult conditions that the day laborers experience, but it does not explicitly represent what it references. This relates to a statement made by one of the day laborers, who during his involvement in a photography workshop coordinated by the Workplace Project wrote that "We see what we know. What's hard to see is the unknown, and then to understand what we're looking at, to make sense of what we see."[3]

This chapter considers the predicaments of photographic self-representation through an analysis of images produced primarily by Central American migrants who were members of the Workplace Project, as part of Unseen America in 2000–2001. Unseen America was the first nationwide project to provide photography workshops for groups of workers and to present these images in exhibition form to audiences both within and outside their communities. Bread and Roses Cultural Project—the cultural division of 1199SEIU (Service Employees International Union), United Healthcare Workers East—developed the program. As the project's name indicates, Unseen America was intended to make visible what Bread and Roses considered to be the invisibility of low-wage workers within American society, and emphasized the role of culture in bringing power and attention to the low-wage workforce.[4] With this mandate in mind, Bread and Roses collaborated on Unseen America with numerous social service and advocacy organizations between 2000 and 2008. One of the first Unseen America projects was coordinated by Bread and Roses and the Workplace Project, comprised of Central American and Mexican migrant workers who have organized for better working conditions in the Hempstead, Long Island, area in the 1990s and 2000s. Photography exhibitions produced by Workplace Project participants were shown on Long Island in 2001, and some images were included in a larger show at the Department of Labor (DOL) in 2003.

Workplace Project participants used photographic self-representation to reframe perceptions of themselves within Long Island, where they lived and worked. The workers' interest in participating in Unseen America was as a means to contest how they had been portrayed by immigration restrictionists as an "illegal," illegitimate, or disposable workforce. To challenge these discourses, the participants in the Unseen America Project visually presented themselves both as being diligent workers and as having personal lives. As Israel, one of the participants, stated, "I want to show the work we do and how we live, our homes, our livelihood. I would like them to see we are the human beings we are."[5] The day laborers had a politicized understanding of how images would affect their local Long Island audience and chose to represent themselves in ways that they felt would depict them as part of that community. The strategies taken up by the Workplace Project members are a result of how undocumented migrants have been positioned as exterior to liberal selfhood. This onto-logical exclusion provides the basic conditions in which the project's participants sought to mobilize the conventions of self-representation.

The Workplace Project participants who were involved in the Unseen America workshop created photographs of what I refer to as the *undocu-mented everyday*, in which they portrayed their ordinary lives and their importance to everyday economies in Long Island. In their photographs of the *undocumented everyday*, the Workplace Project participants revised documentary forms in order to construct alternative representations of themselves. The pictures the day laborers took challenged Long Island residents' understandings of them only in terms of the labor they per-formed or their perceived "criminality" due to their undocumented sta-tus. In representing their everyday lives, Unseen America participants also contested how anti-immigrant activists attempted to limit their abil-ity to make a living—and even to reside—in Long Island. The Workplace Project participants developed a mixed-genre aesthetic, combining forms of documentary, personal, and snapshot photography. Participants used black-and-white film and aesthetic elements associated with documen-tary photography to align their images with certain truth claims. In addi-tion, drawing on personal and snapshot photography enabled them to portray themselves in more intimate ways. The intimate relationship between photographer and subject is transposed to that between viewer and photograph.

In addition to examining the Workplace Project participants' photo-graphs from the Unseen American workshop, I also analyze the framing of these photographs in exhibitions at SUNY–Stony Brook in the fall of 2001 and at the Department of Labor in the spring of 2003. Members of the Workplace Project chose to display images that represented all facets of their lives in Long Island—at work, at home, and involved in political organizing. In their images, participants represented their engagement in organized struggles, as well as their daily resistances in which they "enact their (contested) presence" by their visibility within public spaces like street corners.[6] Later, in curating the exhibition at the DOL in 2003, the staff members at Bread and Roses emphasized images of the personal and, to some extent, work lives of Workplace Project members, but they did not include images of their political activism. Bread and Roses staff also included captions with each image in an attempt to further elicit empathy. At the Department of Labor exhibition, the emphasis on encouraging viewers to identify with those depicted in the photographs served to make empathy an end in itself, a point to which I will return.

Although Bread and Roses' exhibition choices stressed empathy, the DOL staff approached these images with the ideology of "compassionate conservatism," which was embraced by the administration of George W. Bush. In my analysis of the exhibition at the DOL, I focus on what happens when a photography project based on the self-representation of Mexican and Central American migrants appears before a broader audience. This national exhibition of Unseen America images at the DOL in 2003 helped to consolidate the discourse of "compassionate conservatism" by positioning the bureau as sympathetic toward low-wage workers. In defining compassionate conservatism, Kathleen Woodward argues that "if the liberal focus is on the uncertain connection between feeling and action, the calculated response of conservatives has been to sever incisively the link between feelings of compassion for people and action, eliminating the feeling of compassion altogether."[7] Staff members at the DOL initiated the exhibition of Unseen America in their lobby, and they used the rhetoric of compassionate conservatism to describe images in the show. In so doing, they ignored the broader contexts shaping these images, including the many challenges faced by low-wage (including undocumented) migrant workers in the United States. The exhibition gave the DOL a chance to convey its "compassionate conservatism" toward the subjects in the photographs, while ignoring its legislative assaults on low-wage workers and unions.[8] Although the strategies and tactics of the three groups (Workplace Project, Bread and Roses, and the DOL) overlap, they also can be distinguished from one another.

Their distinct registers speak to the limits of documentary—including self-representation—in an era characterized by neoliberalism and compassionate conservatism.

In this chapter, I start by situating Unseen America's photography initiative within the context of the merger between 1199 and the SEIU. I also examine how Unseen America's projects take their cue from similar projects of self-representation involving marginalized groups in the 1960s and 1970s, as well as from traditions of social documentary photography. In the section that follows I explore the history of the Workplace Project in order to explicate the interest of members in participating in Unseen America. In the final two sections, I analyze two exhibitions produced by members of the Workplace Project—one at SUNY–Stony Brook in 2001 and one at the Department of Labor in Washington, D.C., in 2003.

The Labors of Looking

Unseen America began in 2000 as a national project, developed within the context of the merger between Local 1199 and the SEIU.[9] Bread and Roses was established in 1979 at the initiative of Moe Foner, one of Local 1199's staff members, who envisioned the organization as a cultural resource for union members in New York City.[10] According to historians Leon Fink and Brian Greenberg, Bread and Roses profoundly influenced the way that Local 1199 was viewed outside the union. Fink and Greenberg specifically note that the contributions of Bread and Roses gave 1199 significant public recognition, which helped the union politically.[11] Bread and Roses's contributions to Local 1199 assumed nationwide significance when 1199 joined the SEIU in 1998. After the merger, Bread and Roses was given a new mandate to develop national—rather than regional—projects that would be exhibited throughout the United States.[12]

Unseen America was instigated by a volunteer from Bread and Roses who found a camera store willing to give one hundred 35mm point-and-shoot film cameras to the organization. Executive director Esther Cohen announced the creation of a free photography class in *1199 News*. Since Bread and Roses had more cameras than it had interested students, staff members contacted ten other nonprofit organizations in New York State to see who would like to participate.[13] One of the first initiatives to develop was the collaboration between Bread and Roses and the Workplace Project.

When Bread and Roses launched Unseen America in 2000, the organization had three primary goals for the project. The first was to empower workers by giving them the means of self-representation. The second was to create images that would showcase the labor of working-class people and their contributions to U.S. society. The third goal was to enact legislation to improve the lives of low-wage laborers in the United States.[14] Although Unseen America started in New York State, between 2000 and 2008, over eight hundred groups throughout the country participated in Unseen America.

As a project of photographic self-representation, Unseen America can be differentiated from, and yet was also influenced by, the ways in which documentary photography has functioned in relation to issues of labor, surveillance, and reform since the late nineteenth century. Although photographic self-representation has been viewed as distinct from traditional social documentary photography, it is in fact a subgenre of this broader category. One similarity between Unseen America and the work of social documentary photographers is their shared desire to shape perceptions of the working and living conditions of low-wage laborers. As Karin Becker Ohrn has argued, "Primarily, documentary was thought of as having a goal beyond the production of a fine print. The photographer's goal was to bring the attention of an audience to the subject of his or her work and, in many cases, to pave the way for social change."[15] Although distinct in their own right, photographers Jacob Riis, Lewis Hine, Dorothea Lange, and others share the conceit that "representing" poor and working-class people will provoke awareness, and this awareness will inspire social change, usually in the form of legislation.[16] In the social documentary photographic tradition, reformist projects—such as Hine's involvement with the National Child Labor Commission or Lange's work for the Farm Security Administration (FSA) in the 1930s—highlighted the heroism of workers in the face of overwhelming hardship.[17] One important element that distinguishes Unseen America from the work of these photographers is that the "subjects" themselves are taking the pictures.

The particular historical moment also serves to differentiate among these ideologies and images. During the mid-1930s, the Historical Section of the FSA was established to photograph the effects of the Depression on the agricultural workforce. By then, the economic crisis was widespread, and documentary photography was aligned with the initiatives of the reformist state. FSA photographers portrayed Americans who demonstrated "quality of character," and the director of the program, Roy Stryker, along with the photographers saw their subjects as representing "American values."[18] In the current context, the state no longer has the same regulatory function, in part the result of a backlash against the New Deal. Since the 1980s, the state has transferred wealth from the public to the private sphere and consolidated elite fractions of capital in the name of "free enterprise." The New Deal's emphasis on social insurance—in which the state attempted to safeguard the conditions of social well-being—has transformed into a neoliberal mode of rule, in which individuals take responsibility for their own social well-being.

In the 1960s and 1970s community arts organizations and photographers developed projects that involved putting cameras into the hands of individuals who did not previously have access to the medium. This strategy of self-representation has recently become prevalent among advocacy groups working with undocumented Latina/o migrants, who view this form as less mediated than social documentary photography. Unseen America was founded on the belief that viewing low-wage workers' photographs will produce an emotional reaction in the audience, which is considered to be one outside working-class communities, and that this emotive resonance will compel reform. The goals of Bread and Roses for Unseen America reiterate the liberal reformist notion that making the problems of poor people visible through photography will result in these problems being dealt with through the rational workings of social institutions. This approach assumes a causal relationship between image and action and is dominated by the belief that making social inequities "visible" would allow them to be rectified.

The presumed transparent correspondence between images and their meanings espoused by a group like Bread and Roses is reminiscent of the way that documentary photography was understood during the

1930s—that the camera was an unmediated form of communication.[19] These ideas extended into the 1950s, when photographers like Edward Steichen and others "believed that the photographic medium ha[d] an intrinsic emotional immediacy, or humanism, understood by all."[20] This approach sees an image's meaning as being inherent and immediate for the viewer, rather than being actively produced within multiple contexts, including the particular social and institutional conditions of reception and the interpretive dispositions of different viewers.[21] Like all visual artifacts, photographs can be read many ways—depending not just on individual viewers, but also on the various contexts of exhibition.[22]

Part of the support for the Unseen America project outside the community of the photography workshops, from the mass media and agencies of the federal government such as the DOL, is related both to the framing of these exhibitions as well as to the selective vision of these audiences. Although one of the goals of Unseen America was that the photographs displayed influence the way that those who have power in our society perceive low-wage laborers, viewers of the exhibitions interpret the photographs in their own ways. This is how Unseen America workshops from New York State could be shown at the DOL with positive commentary from Secretary of Labor Elaine Chao. In this institutional context, the photographs could just as easily serve to "humanize" the DOL's public image as to contest its policies. Although the staff at Bread and Roses had broad goals for Unseen America that related to low-wage workers' empowerment and visibility, members of the Workplace Project had more specific ideas regarding their participation, to which I will now turn.

Self-Determination, Self-Representation, and the Workplace Project

The Workplace Project's involvement in Unseen America and the participants' approach to image production were both part of the political strategizing to shape how members of the organization were perceived in the Long Island community. Specifically, Workplace Project staff saw their members' involvement in Unseen America as an intervention into the public discourse dominated by a vocal minority of anti-immigrant activists. When they exhibited their images locally, day laborers represented themselves through images of their home and work lives, as well as their political organizing and activism. However, the inclusion of relatively few images representing their participation in political activism lessened the specificity of the challenges faced by the photographers— such as not receiving fair wages, not being paid, and not being protected from verbal and physical harassment while they waited outside for work—as well as the ways in which they organized in response.[23]

The Workplace Project's approach to Unseen America was similar to their political organizing, which emphasized workers' self-determination, as well as politically expedient strategies, which involved reframing issues to appeal to politicians and business owners. In 1992 Jennifer Gordon, a young law school graduate, founded the Workplace Project. The organization was originally located in the offices of the Central American Refugee Center (CARECEN), a community organization serving Central Americans on Long Island. By the early 1990s, a large number of Central Americans—many of whom were from El Salvador—were living on Long Island. Approximately ninety thousand Salvadorans resided on Long Island at this time, most of whom had relocated to the United States after the civil war in El Salvador.[24] Other than CARECEN, there were very few advocacy organizations that helped migrants from Central America and Mexico living on Long Island in the early 1990s. To fill this void, the Workplace Project decided to focus solely on organizing Latina/o workers from various industries.[25]

In addition to educating undocumented migrants about workers' rights, the organization also worked to uphold these rights through organizing. The battles chosen corresponded to the issues that migrant workers presented to the Workplace Project staff, which were primarily related to difficulties in the workplace, often due to lack of enforcement of certain labor laws, such as being paid minimum wage.[26] By 1994, the Workplace Project developed into an organization based on the model of a workers' center, which was run by members and focused on organizing. At this time, towns like Farmingville, Long Island, saw an increase in Mexican migrants—partly because of the North American Free Trade Agreement (NAFTA)—which led to the growth in membership of the

Workplace Project. During these early years, the Workplace Project improved working conditions for their members by defending day laborers' right to use public space to wait for work, by developing the "Workplace Project's Domestic Worker Bill of Rights," and by starting an employment agency and a cleaning cooperative. One of the Workplace Project's biggest successes was their 1996–1997 campaign for an Unpaid Wages Prohibition Act in New York State.[27]

Two aspects of the Workplace Project are essential to understanding its members' involvement in Unseen America: the organization's emphasis on "self-determination" and its concomitant focus on workers' rights. The emphasis on self-determination followed from the Workplace Project's commitment to being run by its members. In its transformation from a legal clinic to a workers' center, the Workplace Project stressed the "internal power" of migrant workers to organize themselves.[28] This "path to participation" started with a requirement that members take the Worker's Course, and continued through the "organizing culture" of the Workplace Project, which gave even new members the ability to influence the organization's direction.[29] Early organizing included the creation of committees that worked to set minimum wages for day laborers. The organization also focused on the rights of workers, which, as Gordon argues, "is a way of both demanding and demonstrating inclusion within the broader community."[30] Learning their rights through the Worker's Course helped members in their organizing, and they began to understand their struggle as a collective one.

However, Workplace Project campaigns—such as the one for the Unpaid Wages Prohibition Act—demonstrate how the organization's focus on self-determination could also be framed in ways that appealed to neoliberal policies emphasizing "personal responsibility." The Unpaid Wages Prohibition Act was part of the Workplace Project's strategy to focus on the enforcement of "minimum rights," rather than expanding or developing new rights claims. Through this campaign, members addressed the problem of migrant workers who were underpaid—or not paid anything—for their work. For years, the Workplace Project had dealt with these problems on a case-by-case basis, but eventually, the membership decided it would be more effective to create legislation to enforce minimum-wage laws.[31] This campaign signified the transition of the Workplace Project from a legal clinic to an Alianza para la Justicia (Alliance for Justice), which—as Janice Fine has argued—more broadly situates the issues raised by workers.[32] The Workplace Project decided to focus on this legislation in New York State for numerous reasons, including the fact that the federal DOL does not cover all workers, and this agency shared information with the Immigration and Naturalization Service (INS), which members feared might lead to workplace raids.[33]

The Workplace Project's strategies need to be situated within the political context of the mid-1990s. In 1996, as members of the Workplace Project were attempting to get their bill passed in New York State, two other bills were being debated in Congress: the Personal Responsibility and Work Opportunity Reconciliation Act (PRWORA) and the Illegal Immigration Reform and Immigrant Responsibility Act (IIRIRA). Although PRWORA restricted welfare benefits, completely cutting them for undocumented migrants, IIRIRA had even broader consequences for migrants living in the United States. According to the House Subcommittee on Immigration's chief counsel, one of the aims of the IIRIRA was "making it more difficult for illegal aliens to have jobs in this country."[34] Numerous scholars have found correlations between these two pieces of legislation. Jonathan X. Inda has examined how neoliberal governments function through mechanisms of exclusion, which "have produced a highly naturalized—and often racialized—division between those who can and do secure their own well-being through judicious self-promotion and those who are deemed incapable of managing their own risks: the criminal, the underclass, the homeless, the vagrants, the truly disadvantaged."[35] Positioning migrants as "illegal" and as a drain on the welfare system characterized the ideological framework that the Workplace Project had to confront during their campaign.

During the mid-1990s, neoliberal discourse around immigration resembled that of welfare reform. Confronted with this political context, Workplace Project members used neoliberal discourse in their representation of the Unpaid Wages Prohibition Act to appeal to Republican state senators and businesspeople in New York State.[36] Workplace Project members tactically represented the bill as facilitating the elimination of migrants as "fiscal burdens" to the state. Specifically, they argued that by "putting money in the hands of immigrants," the bill would enable workers not "to rely on public benefits."[37] Furthermore, members emphasized that the employers' penalties for not paying employees would go directly to the coffers of New York State. Members also stressed that the act would benefit "good" businesses. Thus, as Jennifer Gordon argues, for the New York State Restaurant Association "saying 'no' to the bill would translate into admitting their members were 'bad' employers."[38]

The Workplace Project's success hinged on its members' ability to represent their bill within the discourse of neoliberalism; at the same time, they "challenge[d] conventional ideas about citizenship and political participation" by becoming participants in the political system.[39] Members of the Workplace Project prepared for meetings with Republican senators by choosing one individual out of a ten-worker team to make a presentation, and each team member researched the answers to at least one of the questions they expected to field from the senators.[40] Workplace Project members were involved every step of the way—from developing strategies to address a senator's political interests to learning to run meetings themselves.[41] Gordon argues that Workplace Project members "developed a vision of themselves as legitimate and capable actors in the political system."[42] Further, she suggests that in the campaign for the Unpaid Wages Prohibition Act, these members came to act "in ways not envisioned by the law, in ways beyond the boundaries of the law's definition of who is entitled to do the work of citizenship."[43] Alicia Schmidt Camacho has described how undocumented migrants attempt to inhabit the status of citizen within the United States, noting that this is unrecognized by "proponents of anti-immigration measures," who "commonly represent the undocumented as people with no respect for the rule of law."[44] Their ability to participate in the political system enabled these individuals to be successful in the political arena, even without making financial contributions or having the ability to vote.

In order to win over the state senators, however, members of the Workplace Project could not challenge senators' beliefs that migrant workers' presence negatively affected those who were born in the United States. The Workplace Project framed the bill as benefiting *workers in general,* not just *migrants.* In fact, during their lobbying meetings, members deemphasized the bill's effects on migrants, and they were prepared to answer questions about the bill's possible effects on "illegal" immigration, the business community, and state finances.[45] Although the Workplace Project members took up the role of political participants in their meetings with senators, they deemphasized the benefits of the Unpaid Wages Prohibition Act for migrants, instead highlighting how this bill would affect U.S. citizens who supposedly competed with migrants for jobs.

The Workplace Project's strategy in promoting the Unpaid Wages Prohibition Act demonstrates the political constrictions within which undocumented migrants had to work in the late twentieth century. Although members of the Workplace Project organized their own campaign for the Unpaid Wages Prohibition Act, their strategy used the terms of neoliberalism to win the support of Republican legislators in New York State. There were clearly limitations to the approach used by the Workplace Project—to represent themselves as "workers" not "takers," and thus as "good" migrants, who help build the United States, as opposed to "bad" migrants, who "take from" rather than "give to" the country. The Workplace Project's approach created fictitious lines between workers and people on benefits and between authorized and unauthorized migrants. As Gordon describes, the Workplace Project members did not believe in these lines themselves, but this is how the bill was framed and "read" by senators.[46]

The limitations of political representation for noncitizens in an era of neoliberalism also shaped the Workplace Project's involvement in Unseen America. The Workplace Project's emphasis on workers' self-determination relates well with Unseen America's focus on self-representation. Workplace Project members used self-representation as a strategy to reframe perceptions of themselves within the broader Long Island community. However, just as Workplace Project members took up the terms of neoliberalism to win support for the Unpaid Wages Prohibition Act, their involvement in the Unseen America project reinforced certain liberal beliefs that representing the migrants' "humanity" would be an effective weapon against the dehumanizing representations portrayed by immigration restrictionists. This approach—to emphasize the "humanity" of the migrants—trades on liberal constructions of empathy and recognition, which constrained their political efficacy, even as they appear to counter these limited representations of undocumented migrants.

Seeing Long Island

The Workplace Project's emphasis on legal self-representation in its campaign for the Unpaid Wages Prohibition Act corresponded to Unseen America's focus on photographic self-representation. In the late 1990s and early 2000s in Farmingville, Long Island, where many day laborers lived and worked, a visible group of residents were outwardly hostile toward the recent migrants to their towns. They went so far as to form anti-immigrant organizations, such as the Farmingville Citizens for Immigrant Reform, later renamed the Sachem Quality of Life (SQL).[47] The SQL and its supporters picketed near where the day laborers gathered to wait for work, holding signs labeling the day laborers as criminals. They also drove around, photographing or videotaping the day laborers to report to the INS.[48] Since most day laborers were undocumented and could potentially be deported, they did not take these activities lightly. The staff at the Workplace Project and Bread and Roses thought the day laborers could use cameras to fight back by representing themselves and by taking pictures of those who harassed them on a daily basis.

The Unseen America workshop occurred in 2000, following a few intense years of anti-immigrant organizing by SQL and other Long Island groups.[49] In the mid-1990s, migration from Mexico and Central America to the United States increased significantly, and migrants in Long Island found jobs primarily as day laborers working in seasonal construction and landscaping. However, by the late 1990s, a backlash against migrants was gaining momentum in Farmingville and other Long Island towns. SQL members viewed the migrants as "illegal," believing that they did not share the same values as other Long Island residents and thus were negatively affecting their "quality of life."[50] These perspectives were evident in the interviews that Elizabeth Druback-Celaya conducted in 2001 and 2002, after which she contended that Farmingville residents believed that migrants had "put a strain on the maintenance of space, not so much through numbers as through the altering of the concept of community" (e.g., by living in "overcrowded slum housing"). She argued further that "many residents feel as though they have been invaded because the Mexican [and Central American] community has taken over some of their most basic definers of place: home, work, streets. Beyond this, however, is the feeling that Farmingville residents lack a sense of control over these changes."[51]

In the late 1990s, the main source of tension between Mexican and Central American migrants and the broader Farmingville community was the latter's views of the migrants' use of space—both public and private.[52] To begin with, long-term residents and migrants viewed public space very differently. According to Ken Greenberg, a suburban community such as Farmingville "vastly increased 'open space,' but its primary purpose was different, i.e., to separate functions, open up distance between buildings, allow for the penetration of sunlight and greenery, not to provide places for extensive social contact."[53] Longtime residents of Farmingville viewed street corners as open spaces that were not supposed to be utilized. However, migrants appropriated these spaces, using the street corners as gathering spots for individuals waiting to be hired for jobs.

Open space was contested because longtime residents and migrants had such distinct ideas about what Don Mitchell has described as "what constitutes public space, and furthermore who constitutes 'the public.'"[54] Farmingville residents reacted to the migrants' spatial "appropriation" by trying to control open spaces to "keep order" in their community. From the perspective of the long-term Farmingville residents, the migrants' use of this space to obtain work contributed to disorder in their community. Through intimidation—and a host of other means—these residents tried to force out migrants from these visible spaces. Farmingville residents were clearly influenced by neoliberal "law and order" policies employed by New York mayor Rudolph Giuliani's administration. These policies included the "'war on crime,' and 'war on drugs,' 'zero tolerance' policy and quality-of-life crackdowns as crimes against public order," as Lisa Duggan has described.[55] During Mayor Giuliani's terms in office, city agencies tried to remove the homeless and other street users from public spaces, claiming that their presence constituted an infringement on the "quality-of-life" of those whom the city viewed as legitimate members of the community.[56]

Longtime residents were also critical of undocumented Latina/o migrants' use of private space.[57] Most day laborers in Farmingville were single men who worked seasonally and rented housing.[58] The migrants' use of private space threatened their neighbors, most of whom were white and working- or middle-class families.[59] It provided further evidence that they had different values than long-term residents, who viewed migrants as nonnormative subjects.[60] Residents targeted what they believed to be "overcrowding" in the homes of migrants. SQL addressed this issue by proposing a Neighborhood Preservation Act, which would limit the number of people living in rental properties.[61]

The Unseen America workshop occurred in the fall of 2000, as SQL continued to disseminate information accusing undocumented male Latino migrants of being predisposed to rape, robbery, and other violent crimes.[62] This propaganda was effective. Residents of towns like Farmingville benefited from the labor of Mexican and Central American migrants working in landscaping, construction, and domestic service, but the battles around migrants' use of private and public spaces indicated that many long-term residents did not want day laborers as part of their communities. In the words of *New York Times* reporter Michael Cooper, migrants "find themselves valued as workers but not as neighbors."[63]

In addition to working on the Neighborhood Preservation Act, SQL members and their supporters attempted to develop legislation to deny health-care and welfare benefits to noncitizens. SQL also enlisted support from national anti-immigrant groups, including the Federation for American Immigration Reform (FAIR).[64] SQL members initially harassed the day laborers just on street corners, but over time, their actions took a more violent turn. They threw rocks and bottles, shot BB guns, and accosted Latinas/os on the street. There was also an increase in vandalism, including broken windows at Latina/o migrants' houses and apartments.[65] In September 2000, two day laborers, Israel and Magdaleno,

were picked up for what they believed was a job, but instead, they were
dropped off in an isolated spot, brutally attacked, and left for dead by two
white men from the local community.[66] (Israel later became involved
in the Unseen America workshop.) In response, the Workplace Project
tried to create a day laborer center in Farmingville, in which day laborers
could wait for work in a more protected location. However, members of
SQL defeated the campaign to establish a day laborer center.[67]

Workplace Project members' involvement in Unseen America was
not just about countering the harassment by anti-immigrant groups.
Unseen America also offered ways for the day laborers to interject their
own representations of their lives into the public sphere. Staff member
Carlos Canales—who had previously organized agricultural workers in
El Salvador—thought that Unseen America would enable the day laborers to create a "graphic history of their lives," a document of their everyday experiences that had not previously existed.[68] Canales felt that the
project would allow day laborers to record elements of their personal
and civic lives, which they could circulate to their families in Central
America and to communities on Long Island.

The Workplace Project's staff reasoned that Unseen America would
benefit their members, but due to the volatile circumstances on Long
Island, both Bread and Roses and the Workplace Project thought that
some issues needed to be discussed before starting the collaboration.[69]
One of the main concerns of the Bread and Roses' staff was that the day
laborers might put themselves in danger by carrying cameras and taking
pictures in their workplaces.[70] Some day laborers were also worried
about the implications of becoming involved in Unseen America. A few
even wondered if they would lose their jobs for participating. Some were
concerned that taking pictures either on the job or off might even en-
danger their lives.[71]

The day laborers also had questions about the effectiveness of the
project. In a report on Unseen America, Nathalis Wamba and Carolyn
Curran wrote, "The day laborers from Long Island who first met with
Esther [Cohen, the executive director of Bread and Roses] questioned
whether photographs would change the attitudes of people in Suffolk
County. They wondered if taking photography classes was worth their

time and investment."[72] These day laborers, many of whom were from Central America, had a complex relation to being visible in U.S. society due in part to their past experiences, issues regarding their immigration status, as well as their hypervisibility on street corners in Long Island, which exposed them to harassment.[73] In their discussions with the staff at Bread and Roses, the day laborers brainstormed how they could depict themselves on their own terms.[74] Although there were many potential drawbacks for day laborers participating in Unseen America, a photography workshop did ensue.

The Workplace Project participants' decision to work in black and white—rather than color 35mm film—conveys specific aesthetic associations. The choice of black-and-white film was a strategy, a way for workshop participants to relate their images to the social documentary tradition of photography and a validation of their own perspectives through an aesthetic form associated with truth claims and humanitarian dispositions. Although Bread and Roses provided 35mm cameras, other decisions regarding the content of the workshops were left up to individual photography teachers. At this point, there was no established guide for teachers, so photography instructors developed their own curricula.[75] Two photography teachers led the workshops: Jim Cassidy, a member of the SUNY–Stony Brook faculty, and Matthew Septimus, a professional photographer from New York City. The photography teachers drew on the aesthetics of documentary photography, and they encouraged the day laborers to portray their everyday lives. Septimus started the class with a slideshow on the history of photography from the 1930s to the present in which he included the documentary work of Dorothea Lange and other FSA photographers, photojournalist Henri Cartier-Bresson, and contemporary art photographers like Duane Michals. The instructors introduced workshop participants to the aesthetic aspects of photography, such as lighting and composition, and they also addressed the technical elements of 35mm cameras and the processes of working in a darkroom. They assigned the students weekly themes to address when taking pictures. During the workshops, the instructors focused on hands-on work in the darkroom. In class, participants talked about their photographs and their inspirations.[76]

This Unseen America workshop—the first one organized by Bread and Roses—demonstrated the interest of an established labor organization (1199) in issues concerning migrant labor. However, attending the workshop was challenging for the day laborers for a number of reasons, and many did not see how the primary goal of Unseen America—to make low-wage laborers more visible in U.S. society—would help them directly. The workshop initially included fifteen Workplace Project members, but over time, many participants dropped out, in part due to their migratory lives and also due to questions about the effectiveness of the project. Bread and Roses initially scheduled the workshops to last between twelve weeks and sixteen weeks, but the classes for the Workplace Project's constituency were held over one year, because many day laborers went back to Central America in the winter. When they returned in the spring, the class resumed.

Considering the circumstances of the day laborers, Carlos Canales (the coordinator of Unseen America at the Workplace Project), Jim Cassidy, and Matthew Septimus felt that they needed to focus on the potential benefits of the workshop to keep up attendance. Septimus and Cassidy explained that by presenting a fuller representation of their experiences at home and at work, participants could influence the larger Long Island community to rethink the ways that day laborers were viewed.[77] However, according to Wamba and Curran in their report on Unseen America, "The cynicism was so deep among these participants that out of 15 people who signed [up] to take the classes, a core group of only five attended regularly. And even after successful completion of the workshop and much acclaim for its participants . . . one of the organizers [Carlos Canales] still has reservations." Canales told the authors, "We understand the philosophical part of it. Trying to become more visible to society. But I had a really hard time recruiting people to be in the workshop. They kept asking, how does this help our lives? And I couldn't come up with enough concrete reasons." Canales did suggest that the photographs could inform both Long Island community members and state legislators about the issues concerning migrant workers in New York State.[78]

The day laborers who remained in the Unseen America workshop photographed multiple facets of their life experiences—on the job, at home, as well as their involvement in political activism—as a means to counter the limited ways they were viewed by some Long Island residents, politicians, and anti-immigrant groups. They created these images using assigned themes: to represent their everyday lives at work or their involvement in extracurricular or leisure activities on Long Island. The photographers envisioned themselves and their fellow day laborers not only as workers but also as having personal lives. Portraying themselves at work was challenging, however, and only some were able to take photographs in the workplace, such as Figure 3, which was later titled *What I Planted* by the Bread and Roses staff.[79] Images of their home lives include Figure 4 (*The Barbeque*) by Israel, which featured four men around a grill cooking dinner and laughing; Figure 5 (*Who We Are*) by Luis, which depicts the photographer's former housemate, Pedro, dancing with Ouri, the woman who cooked for them, inside their house; and Figure 6 (*We Have Lives*) by Antonio, which portrays a young man cooking dinner on a stove.[80] The aesthetic style of these images undercuts conventions of documentary photography, as they emphasize shared moments between photographers and subjects. These photographs are not self-consciously artful, but instead they address our relation to the people pictured. These images portray casual moments that are more characteristic of personal photographs or snapshots than documentary conventions. The connection between photographer and subject contributes to the intimacy between viewer and image.

The participants from the Workplace Project developed a mixed-genre aesthetic form in representing their everyday lives that drew from a number of different genres including documentary, personal, and snapshot photography. In creating these images of their everyday lives that represent what I refer to as the *undocumented everyday*, workshop participants combined the aesthetics of documentary photography that they were introduced to in their photography workshop with personal and snapshot photography. Their use of the aesthetics of social documentary photography buttressed the association of their work with certain truth claims, which are linked to the form, while elements of personal and snapshot photography gave the images a sense of intimacy. Their use of the aesthetics of personal and snapshot photography developed out of the close relation between photographer and subject. Art historian Liz Wells suggests that "personal photographs are made specifically to portray the individual or the group to which they belong *as they would wish to be seen* and as they have chosen to show themselves to one another."[81] Like Wells, Catherine Zuromskis notes that snapshots "allow us to record ourselves and our histories as we would have them remembered." She also argues that snapshots are "often viewed as a useful tool for members of subaltern or marginalized groups to construct alternative visual cultures to those perpetuated by mainstream society."[82]

These photographs can also be distinguished from the use of close-ups of migrants' faces by humanitarian organizations as part of their campaigns.[83] For example, while photographs like Figure 3 (*What I Planted*) draw on social documentary traditions, such as the "heroic" images of workers created by FSA photographers in the 1930s, the photographer also employs the aesthetics of personal photography that convey intimacy between photographer and subject. This photograph portrays a day laborer working outside. Although the aesthetics of the photograph relate to the documentary genre, the image is also an example of a personal photograph, suggested by the exchange of looks between the subject of the picture and the photographer. The photograph's intimacy is related to other aesthetic choices, such as composition. A day laborer stands in front of a wall of dirt, where he and the photographer are physically separated (and thus protected) from the world outside the closely cropped frame. This approach is common in outdoor photographs taken by Workplace Project participants, as they frequently portray day laborers as separated from the outside world by walls, fences, trees, or dirt. In indoor photographs, the subjects are sheltered and often pictured in close-up or medium-range shots. These aesthetic choices relate to Wells's point about the contract between photographer and subject in personal photographs. By creating these images, the day laborers were protective of both where and how they represented one another.

Other photographs taken by Workplace Project participants also emphasized elements of personal and snapshot photography. Zuromskis suggests that snapshot photography is itself a hybrid form, "perceived as

Figure 3. *What I Planted* is an intimate portrait of a day laborer working outside. This photograph was taken by a member of the Workplace Project as part of Unseen America, a project of Bread and Roses, 1199SEIU.

documentary and the aspirational fiction it often records."[84] One example includes *The Barbeque* by Israel (Figure 4) that seemingly captures a
jovial exchange between the photographer and his subjects. Four men
are pictured outside in what appears to be a backyard, positioned in a
circle around a grill. Although this image has documentary qualities,
there are aesthetic elements in this photograph that relate to personal
and snapshot photography. For example, two of the men are facing the
camera, with one man centered within the frame. The photographer is
situated behind one of the men, and, so, he becomes part of this circle
of men laughing while they cook dinner.

Through the use of a mixed-genre aesthetic—which combined documentary, personal, and snapshot photography—the Workplace Project
participants pictured their lives in ways that were quite distinct from
how anti-immigrant groups represented the day laborers. Some of these

Figure 4. *The Barbeque* portrays a group of men laughing while cooking
dinner outside on a grill. It was taken by Israel, a member of the Workplace
Project as part of Unseen America, a project of Bread and Roses, 1199SEIU.

images, such as Figure 5 by Luis (*Who We Are*), challenged how anti-immigrant groups portrayed the largely male day laborer community as "threatening." The image conveys a joyous moment—a day laborer dancing with a woman who cooks for his (all-male) household—and emphasizes heteronormativity. However, Workplace Project participants also produced photographs that did not attempt to fit within certain normative representations of men and women occupying traditional gender roles. For example, in Figure 6 by Antonio (*We Have Lives*), a young man prepares his own meal on the stove, without the help of a woman.

These images, which contain elements of documentary, personal, and snapshot photography, are less accessible to outside audiences than traditional social documentary photographs. Although many of the actual conditions that undocumented Latina/o migrants encountered were not

Figure 5. *Who We Are* pictures a day laborer dancing with a woman who cooks for his household. This photograph was taken by Luis, a member of the Workplace Project as part of Unseen America, a project of Bread and Roses, 1199SEIU.

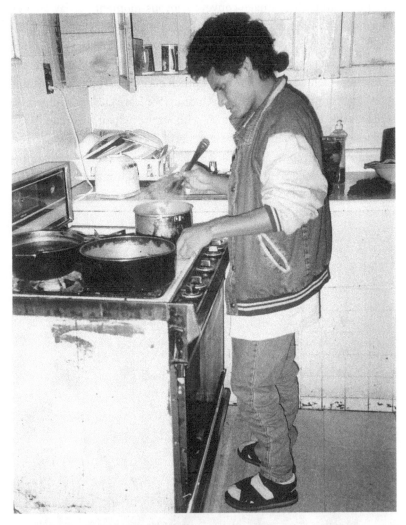

Figure 6. *We Have Lives*, a photograph of a young man cooking dinner on a stove, was taken by Antonio, a member of the Workplace Project as part of Unseen America, a project of Bread and Roses, 1199SEIU.

made explicit in *Waiting for Work*, in portraying other day laborers waiting for work, the individual who took Figure 2 appropriated the strategy of photographing day laborers on the street corners from those who harassed them, but with a very different sense of purpose. The image is a visual form of migrant counter-conduct. This individual's decision to take this photograph was a political act, as he represented day laborers as inhabiting (and taking an informal ownership over) the contested space of the street corner.[85] Although many Long Island residents had protested against day laborers' use of open spaces as hiring halls in their towns, here the day laborers position themselves as legitimately occupying that space. This image challenges Long Island residents' conception of open spaces—including street corners—as forms of private property. In addition to this photograph, which was included in multiple exhibitions, there were others taken by day laborers when they used their cameras against the anti-immigrant groups who videotaped them on the street corner. One image in particular demonstrates how the day laborers countered the harassment directed toward them by these groups and their supporters. In this photograph one of the day laborers portrayed an individual who is videotaping the photographer (and presumably other day laborers) as he drives by the street corner where the day laborers wait for work.[86] Here, the Workplace Project participant uses the camera as part of a strategy to challenge members of anti-immigrant groups who videotaped day laborers and threatened to show the footage to the INS in an attempt to get them deported.

Just as some of the day laborers were unsure about joining the workshop, Matthew Septimus mentioned that they were equally cautious about where the images would be shown and who would see them.[87] Because of their fear of possible repercussions from displaying their photographs, the day laborers wanted to be identified only collectively in the exhibition. This collective identification was a practical and protective mechanism, since some photographs depicted protests or referenced their political organizing. Curating the exhibition was also a collective process, including both instructors and participants. The photography teachers chose four or five images by each student, and the students edited their collections down to two or three images each. The images in the exhibition addressed a range of subjects, covering aspects of the day laborers' lives at home, at work, as well as involved in political activism. Many decisions regarding which images would appear in the exhibition were related to the day laborers' concerns about how their photographs would be perceived by the broader Long Island community.[88] After the images were chosen, a writing teacher helped the participants to compose brief captions in Spanish, some of which were displayed with the pictures at the exhibition.[89]

Although members of the Workplace Project, such as Carlos Canales, viewed the photographs of day laborers waiting for work as political, the workshop participants felt limited in the images they could include in the exhibition.[90] For example, even though they had photographed their political activity, some of the pictures they chose to exhibit represented their political involvement, but did not include their physical bodies.[91] The day laborers had concerns about displaying images of their involvement in political organizing or their protests due to fears of possible repercussions for their engagement in these activities. In an image that was later titled *Child Writing* by Nelson, a toddler stands in front of a whiteboard that displays a list in Spanish.[92] At the top of the list is the statement "Salario que refleje el costo de la vida en Long Island" (Salary that reflects the cost of living on Long Island), which references one of the main goals of the Workplace Project, which was to secure better wages for day laborers.[93] The notes on the board were probably drawn up at a meeting held at the Workplace Project, but there are no adult bodies in the photograph. Another untitled image at the exhibition was photographed at one of many demonstrations against the policies of Farmingville's mayor, Joseph M. Trudden. The photograph focuses on a sign proclaiming, "Mayor Trudden, let us work," which hangs on a bicycle. The sign responds to Trudden's plan to shut down the site where laborers were hired for jobs. There are no bodies in the photograph, but local residents would recognize this bicycle as belonging to a day laborer, since many used bicycles as their primary mode of transportation. In this photograph, there is a direct reference to the day laborers' political activity, but since there are no bodies in the picture, no one can be singled out for retribution.

The goal of eliciting support from local audiences guided the participants' curatorial decisions for the local exhibitions in Long Island during fall 2001. After the completion of the workshop, two galleries on the campus of SUNY–Stony Brook exhibited Unseen America's photographs. In the fall of 2001, the day laborers displayed their work as part of a show titled *Unseen America on Long Island: A First Look* at the Latin American Caribbean Center and the Stony Brook Union Art Gallery at SUNY–Stony Brook.[94] Although the shows took place on the campus of SUNY–Stony Brook because of the workshop's location, the university setting was also a site that gave symbolic clout to the project.[95] An exhibition was also held at the Sachem North High School library in Lake Ronkonkoma, New York, during "sensitivity week." The teacher who organized the exhibition invited Workplace Project staff and participants in Unseen America to talk with students about the photographs and the lives of day laborers. This dialogue with students enabled the day laborers to make broader appeals to the Long Island community.[96]

Although the Workplace Project participants decided to be credited collectively for the photographs, some day laborers allowed their names to be included with their captions. The captions for the photographs—which were presented in Spanish and English—were part of their attempt to address viewers outside of their community by creating a counternarrative to the discourses that anti-immigrant groups employed to characterize day laborers. In one caption, Luis wrote: "Pienso que este es un cuadro que ayudaría a cada uno a saber que venimos a este país no a hacer cosas malas como la gente dice. Venimos aquí para trabajar y divertirnos" (I think that this is a picture that would help everyone else know that we come to this country not to do bad things like people say. But we come here to work and have fun). In a second caption, Luis noted: "Todos nos conocen solamente como trabajadores. Ellos solamente saben lo que la gente dice sobre nosotros, y ellos no son capaces de pensar más allá" (Everyone knows us only as workers. They know only what other people tell them about us, and they're not able to go any further).[97] Some day laborers might have felt more comfortable including their names with the captions, because the captions did not challenge the audience in the same way as the images.[98] These captions—written by a small number of participants who remained at the end of the workshop—suggest that those who stayed involved believed that the Unseen America project would be an effective way to elicit support.

In the following section, I analyze the effects of moving the exhibit to a national context at the DOL in 2003. The Workplace Project had little to do with this arrangement, since unlike 1199, at this time the organization had purposely decided not to focus its organizing on a national level.[99] At the time of the exhibition, President George W. Bush's DOL was outwardly hostile toward the low-wage labor force. Under Secretary of Labor Chao, the DOL consistently ignored complaints by low-wage and minimum-wage workers about their employers' failure to pay minimum wage or overtime. These were the same issues that led the Workplace Project to campaign for the Unpaid Wages Prohibition Act years earlier in New York State.[100] Considering that the DOL's "unofficial" policy toward low-wage laborers was to ignore their complaints, it is surprising that the agency was interested in hosting an exhibit of Unseen America. In many ways, however, the exhibition was a public relations coup for the agency under Chao, whose "vision," to "promote the economic well-being of workers and their families," did not correspond to its actions.[101]

Eliciting Empathy, Exhibiting Compassion

In fall 2002, Secretary of Labor Chao invited the Bread and Roses Cultural Project to display a selection of photographs from Unseen America at the DOL. After Executive Director Cohen accepted Chao's offer, she and fellow staff members traveled to Washington, D.C., to view the gallery space, which they discovered was located within the massive lobby of the building. This created a dilemma. Despite the lobby's monumentality, it was nonetheless an entryway, a transient space designed for people passing through the room. The Bread and Roses staff had to think about how to construct the exhibition so that the images actually had an impact, to encourage those passing through the space to engage with the images. They did this by having the photographs printed much larger than they had been when displayed in local exhibitions. According to Cohen, "The idea was to be strong and visible in that environment [the lobby of the DOL], official and big."[102]

The staff's experience designing the exhibition for the DOL can be seen as a metaphor for their attempts to deal with the labor policies of the George W. Bush administration, which worked to contain and appropriate counter-discourses for its own ends. Just as the Bread and Roses staff had to think of ways for the Unseen America photographs to be noticed in the DOL lobby, the organization also struggled to have a presence within the purview of the DOL. The impact of the exhibition could be diminished by both the transient space of the lobby and the DOL's pro-business labor politics.

The "shaping effect" of the DOL on the Unseen America show relates to Martha Rosler's argument about the problems with exhibiting works of photographic self-representation. She comments, "As the sole form of representation, this work seems vulnerable to those with no desire to change political realities. In the words of a municipal bureaucrat, it represents a tool for 'managing diversity': thus, it has come to be seen as therapeutic or cathartic."[103] Bread and Roses staff's curatorial decisions for the DOL exhibition emphasized personal images to elicit the empathy of viewers toward the subjects of the photographs. The DOL's strategy, however, was to approach the Unseen America photographs with the ideology of compassionate conservatism, as the agency sought to contain and appropriate the exhibition for its own ends.

In curating the exhibition held at the DOL in May 2003, Bread and Roses' staff drew from the organization's (by then extensive) archive, which included photographs from workshops during the first two years of Unseen America.[104] During the early years of Unseen America, the emphasis on migrant workers was part of a broader strategy to "revitalize" 1199SEIU through the workshops, which served as a "tool for recruitment" for the union.[105] The staff chose images from the Workplace Project and five other workshops in New York State for the first national exhibition of Unseen America, which was sponsored by the DOL, 1199SEIU, and Bread and Roses.[106] In an interview, Cohen explained that their decision to send these images to the DOL was intentional, as the staff members of Bread and Roses felt that the pictures would increase awareness of issues that concerned these workers.[107] The focus on migrant workers also related to the goals of 1199SEIU, which had recruited a substantial number of these workers between 2000 and 2002, significantly increasing their membership base.[108]

This growing membership base led 1199SEIU in new directions, including building coalitions among workers who had previously been viewed as having little in common. These connections could be seen at the DOL exhibit, which contained images created by union members, non-unionized workers, U.S. citizens, and migrants. Positioning photographs by Chinese garment workers—who were affiliated with the Union of Needletrades, Industrial and Textile Employees (UNITE) Local 23–25— next to those of day laborers from Mexico and Central America emphasizes this collectivity among the working classes and, more specifically, within unions.[109] At the DOL show of Unseen America, Bread and Roses included forty photographs, which were printed seven feet high and more than three feet wide. The photographs were mounted onto self-standing boards and placed side by side along the DOL's lobby walls.

An important shift took place between the local exhibition produced by the Workplace Project participants and the national exhibition at the DOL. This included both decreasing the number of images by the Workplace Project participants and Bread and Roses' curatorial decisions that emphasized personal images of the day laborers' lives while editing out images of their political activity. Although the personal images had also been a significant part of the SUNY–Stony Brook exhibition, they were even more pronounced at the DOL show. Of the seven images chosen for exhibition, almost half portray the day laborers at home in Long Island (for example, *The Barbeque, Who We Are,* and *We Have Lives*). Of the remaining images, one portrays a day laborer on the job (*What I Planted*), one shows day laborers waiting for work (*Waiting for Work*), one makes reference to the day laborers' involvement in the Workplace Project (*Child Writing*), and one features a woman handing a cup (presumably of coffee) to the photographer (*Have Some* by Aron). The shift from the local Long Island venue to the lobby of the DOL meant that only images of day laborers in their homes, on the job, or waiting for work were included, rather than a wider range of images including those portraying their political activism.

Although the choice to include photographs of many aspects of their daily lives was a strategy for the day laborers in the local context of exhibition, using a more limited number of these images before a national audience that had little understanding of their experiences had different repercussions. At the DOL, these "personal" images were considerably less alienating to middle-class viewers than those of day laborers organizing, of anti-immigrant groups picketing the day laborers, or of demonstrations against government officials or employers. What disappears when the experiences of marginalized people are understood to be "just like (middle-class) us" are the specific conditions that these individuals experienced as low-wage workers and (in this case) as undocumented migrants within communities that were hostile toward them.

While narrowing down the images from local to national exhibition sites limited the range of photographs presented to viewers, the images that *are* included also lose their specificity when they are relocated from a local to a national context. Thus, when the photographs were displayed for a national audience, the reduced selection criteria were amplified by the loss of context. These decisions were made partly because of the need to narrow down the numbers of images for the DOL. Still, the photographs exhibited in their local context provided for a more layered understanding of these images. Although the staff at Bread and Roses created titles and attached captions written by the Workplace Project participants for all the photographs displayed, the particularities of these images remained obscured. They lacked critical information that implicitly relied on local knowledge to evoke the multidimensionality of what was pictured. The change of institutional framing set the terms for a decidedly different manner of interpretation.

Cohen, the executive director of Bread and Roses, had hoped that the Unseen America exhibition would influence viewers to "raise a cry for equal rights for all American workers."[110] However, the show did not have this effect on the person who had the most influence on U.S. labor policies, Secretary of Labor Chao. After seeing the exhibition, Chao commented, "Unseen America invites us to personally experience [the workers'] world. It reminds us that all work is meaningful and that all workers have dignity. It calls upon us to stop for a moment, reflect, and appreciate the often invisible labor that makes America work every day."[111] The rhetoric that Chao uses is characteristic of "compassionate conservatism." She focuses on the "dignity" that comes from work, disengaging the images from the lived experience of the day laborers and disavowing the economies, inequalities, and geopolitics that shape their experiences.[112]

Bread and Roses' emphasis on eliciting support for low-wage workers did not account for the DOL's strategy of framing these images through the ideology of "compassionate conservatism." Kathleen Woodward argues that "compassionate conservatism trades on the rhetoric of feeling even as it is curiously empty of it."[113] Chao's words, which are characteristic of "compassionate conservatism," indicate the degree to which the images can be removed from the lived experiences they depict. Chao's response withheld "compassionate attachment," as described by Lauren Berlant, in which Chao does not "connect, sympathize, or recognize an obligation" by the state to the people portrayed in the images.[114] Chao, a "compassionate conservative," was utterly indifferent to rectifying the problems experienced by low-wage workers through the mechanisms of the state—by regulating wage and hour laws or workplace safety.[115] This inaction is characteristic of what Berlant refers to the "compassionately conservative state," which "wants to limit these mechanisms [laws and programs of the expanding liberal state] severely and in particular to shift its economic obligations from redressing poverty to protecting income by taking less from and giving less back to workers and citizens."[116]

The Unseen America exhibition at the DOL was a negotiation between Bread and Roses' attempt to elicit support for low-wage workers and the DOL's approach to images, which was dominated by the ideology of "compassionate conservatism." Aspects of Bread and Roses' political project for Unseen America lost in translation when the images move from a local to a national context.[117] For these photographs to have a political impact, they needed to be framed by the local circumstances in which they were produced. In the case of the Workplace Project exhibitions it is the *local* context that is always already overdetermined by geopolitical economies, where the day laborers are harassed, treated as criminals, and occasionally physically brutalized, which provides the everyday details and familiar history of events that frame and infuse the images with broader significance. However, if that context is *not* made explicit, the photographs lose their ability to convey what is politically important about them—namely their localized circumstances or the locally specific ways in which larger conditions of possibility and limit are engaged. The emotive form of the photographs cannot bear the weight of their intended effect. The context of reception is also indicative of the constraints faced by Bread and Roses in curating a national exhibition of photographs at the DOL during an administration that was outwardly hostile toward unions and the low-wage labor force. The DOL's "vision" during George W. Bush's administration was ostensibly to help workers and their families "share in the American dream through rising wages, pensions, health benefits and expanded economic opportunities," yet the staff managed to achieve the opposite effect.[118]

Conclusion

In representing what I refer to as the *undocumented everyday*, the participants in Unseen America created a mixed-genre aesthetic, comprised of elements of social documentary, personal photography, and snapshot photography. This aesthetic—while drawing on documentary to associate this work with certain truth claims—also includes the aesthetics of personal and snapshot photography, which creates a sense of intimacy between viewer and image. Workplace Project participants understood that these photographs had political objectives, and they viewed these images in relation to their own political goals. As the day laborers learned to use cameras, process film, and print photographs, they also thought about what images might influence individuals in their local communities to rethink their perceptions of undocumented migrants and to gain support and safety for themselves. Thus, their photographs of the undocumented everyday employed a mixed-genre aesthetic form for particular purposes.

The undocumented Mexican and Central American migrants who participated in the Unseen America project used photographic self-representation to counter the everyday racism that they encountered

working in Long Island, New York. Similar to what Ann Cvetkovich contends about the public cultures that she writes about in *An Archive of
Feelings*, the trauma experienced by undocumented migrants "doesn't
always lend itself to media spectacle since it frequently operates in
the less dramatic terrain of everyday experience and involves groups of
people who make no claim to being representative citizens."[119] However, these migrants' experiences as day laborers on Long Island are
only alluded to in their photographs and, thus, the meanings of these
images only obliquely reference individuals' experiences as the targets
of racist acts.

The Workplace Project participants viewed these images in relation to
a broader political project, yet Bread and Roses' staff conceived of these
photographs as serving political ends by being intimate and personal,
rather than explicitly political. Bread and Roses associated the intensely
personal point of view in the Unseen America photographs with the
fact that the images were taken by amateur—rather than professional—
photographers. Bread and Roses' emphasis on the "authenticity" of the
images relates to the idea that viewers will identify with the inner lives
of low-wage laborers through these images, which they perceive to be
"genuine." As Bread and Roses' executive director Cohen noted in a
report on Unseen America, "Something about the authenticity of the
emotional engagement in explaining what it means to be unseen, perhaps taps into some universal feelings most of us have about the need to
be seen (accepted) as we really are."[120] Bread and Roses overwrites the
particular with the universal and, therefore, the images are framed as
encompassing the viewer's own emotional self-reflection. The photographs are positioned as ends in themselves, rather than as catalysts for
social change.

Although both the Workplace Project and Bread and Roses traded on
the circulation of personal photographs, the Workplace Project participants chose strategies of representation that were situated and specific.
They believed these images would enable them to appeal to individuals
in their local community. In exhibiting their work in Long Island, the
photographers saw the images they chose to include as part of their overall strategy to influence the way that they were perceived in the broader

community. These images could be more easily framed within their local conditions, as opposed to the inclusion of these photographs at an exhibition at the DOL.

Bread and Roses had a different investment in the project and, thus, they emphasized different aspects of it. This organization's strategy was based on the idea that political change will follow from the identification of the viewer with the universal human qualities portrayed in the photographs, and this identification would translate into a specific repertoire of social justice action. This maneuver, to emphasize the humanity of the migrants as a means through which viewers are assumed to identify with the migrants, and to have consequences that are political, is intended to put the depoliticization of the images in the service of a particular political project that aims to align and activate the sentiments of the viewer in relation to the conditions and plight of the migrants depicted.

Despite the fact that these photographs were a political project for Bread and Roses and the Workplace Project participants, the reaction of Chao to the exhibition at the DOL demonstrates how the readings and institutional framings of these images can limit—rather than prompt—particular forms of engagement and action. The exhibition did not change how the DOL viewed the state's obligations toward the low-wage workforce. Instead, the images were cynically appropriated for the state's neoliberal disavowal of the conditions both labor groups aimed to address. The DOL exhibition contained the counter-representation of these workers and incorporated their resistance within a framework of government benevolence and sentimentalization. I have argued that the meanings attached to these photographs were largely influenced by the ways in which they were framed, as well as their specific conditions of reception. I also contend that these modes of reception need to be recognized as situated practices and understood analytically for how their significance is linked to particular places and times.

In the next chapter, I analyze another Unseen America photography project that was developed by Hudson River HealthCare in Poughkeepsie, New York, in 2003. This project had very different purposes than the one developed by the Workplace Project participants, as it focused on bringing together a translocal community comprised of Oaxacan migrants in Poughkeepsie and their family members in La Ciénega, Oaxaca. At that time family members were not able to see one another, due to post-9/11 laws in the United States that affected the mobility of undocumented migrants. Similar to the Workplace Project, participants in Poughkeepsie also employed a mixed-genre aesthetic form in their photographs. They did this to portray aspects of their everyday lives in Poughkeepsie for members of their translocal community in La Ciénega.

CHAPTER TWO

The Border's Frame

Between Poughkeepsie and La Ciénega

In the summer of 2003, staff at Hudson River HealthCare (HRHCare), a network of ten community and migrant health centers based in the Hudson River Valley, traveled to La Ciénega, Oaxaca, to lead a photography workshop. The workshop was for the families of the Oaxacan migrants who had participated in an Unseen America project in Poughkeepsie. As part of an initiative called Communities without Borders: A Bridge for Health, HRHCare staff presented a PowerPoint of photographs taken by the Poughkeepsie workshop participants to their families and other residents of La Ciénega. The presentation provided audience members with an opportunity to view photographs of their family members in Poughkeepsie, including some grandparents who saw images of grandchildren that they had never met in person.[1] In an interview about the Communities without Borders project, HRHCare CEO Anne Nolon commented on the challenges faced by the workshop participants, noting that "people can't travel, but photographs do."[2]

At the same time that HRHCare staff framed the Communities without Borders project as providing a "photographic bridge" between Poughkeepsie and La Ciénega, the photographs themselves were symptomatic of the obstacles faced by members of this translocal community.[3] The Communities without Borders project highlighted the separations among members of these communities, as well as the difficulties faced by those who remained behind in Oaxaca. This photography project emphasized the connections among these communities at a time when U.S. immigration laws limited the movement of undocumented Mexican and Central American migrants across the U.S.–Mexico boundary. The HRHCare staff's goal for Communities without Borders was to link members of a translocal community, but there were limits to this objective, not the least of which is the militarized border between them.

HRHCare viewed Communities without Borders as a way to reach out to Oaxacan migrants living in Poughkeepsie and to encourage them to serve as *promotores* and *promotoras de salud* (health advocates) for the organization.[4] Further, staff members added the photography workshop in La Ciénega to help to connect the two sectors of this translocal community. The HRHCare staff members believed that if family members in La Ciénega knew about their organization's services, they would encourage their migrant relatives in Poughkeepsie to use them. These extensive outreach efforts to Oaxacan migrants took place in the post-9/11 political context, during which laws such as the USA PATRIOT Act (2001) and the Homeland Security Act (2002) were enacted. In this political environment, undocumented migrants avoided health and social service organizations, fearing that their immigration status would be discovered and that they would be arrested, detained, or deported. In these difficult circumstances, HRHCare staff believed that promotores and promotoras de salud could help the organization reach out to, build trust with, and familiarize migrants with their services.

Similar to the Unseen America photographs that I analyze in chapter 1, the images produced by Oaxacan migrants in Poughkeepsie can also be characterized by what I call the *undocumented everyday*. These images, which feature a mixed-genre aesthetic comprised of documentary, family, and snapshot photography, resulted from the collaboration between the documentary-style project of Unseen America and the goals of HRHCare to provide a "photographic bridge" between members of this translocal community. In Poughkeepsie, Oaxacan migrants photographed elements of their everyday lives specifically for their family members in La Ciénega. Their photographs portray community members engaged in daily activities—at home, at work, and at play. The participants took photographs in public and private settings, attesting to the integration of Oaxacan migrants in Poughkeepsie.

Although there are some similarities between the images produced in the Unseen America workshop in Long Island and the one in Poughkeepsie, the participants in the latter workshop had goals that were distinct from those in the former. Consequently, they used a mixed-genre aesthetic for different purposes. While documentary approaches span all the Unseen America workshops, what differentiates the Communities without Borders photographs from those by the Workplace Project participants is the former group's address to family members in La Ciénega. In directing their work to relatives in La Ciénega, participants in Poughkeepsie drew upon the genres of family and snapshot photography and the documentary aesthetics they learned in Unseen America. The mixed-genre aesthetic that the Poughkeepsie participants employed related to their translocality as a mode of address. I contend that these images can be characterized by a *translocal aesthetic*, which relates the mixed-genre aesthetic form to the translocal address of the photographs. This translocal aesthetic distinguishes this project from Bread and Roses' framing the photographs produced in the Unseen America workshops as forms of national culture.[5] This, according to HRHCare social worker Barbara Hill, transformed "Unseen America into Unseen *Americas*."[6]

Through their translocal aesthetic, participants in Poughkeepsie's Communities without Borders project visualized what Lynn Stephen describes as "simultaneous belonging in multiple localities" or what Denise A. Segura and Patricia Zavella refer to as "subjective transnationalism," which they argue "reflects the experience of feeling 'at home' in more than one geographic location."[7] In addition to promoting HRHCare's goals, Communities without Borders narrates the workshop participants' local and translocal "ways of belonging," as well as highlighting the separations among members of this community.[8] The joint exhibitions of images by Oaxacan migrants in Poughkeepsie and their family members in La Ciénega—which took place in Poughkeepsie, La Ciénega, and Oaxaca City in the fall of 2003—imagine community networks across national borders. By placing images of migrants in Poughkeepsie next to photographs taken by family members in La Ciénega, these exhibitions envisioned an alternative reality in which daily life in these disparate locations existed side by side. However, the spaces between the photographs also represent the separation of the people within them. At that time neither the Oaxacan migrants in Poughkeepsie nor their family members in La Ciénega could see each other—except in photographs.

The Communities without Borders project did provide a means of connecting members of this translocal community whose mobility was constrained by strict U.S. immigration laws limiting undocumented migrants' movements across the U.S.–Mexico boundary. However, there were other outcomes to the project. In the words of one participant, the Communities without Borders project and exhibitions "broke the boundary between public and private" for those who were involved.[9] Communities without Borders also strengthened the bonds with Oaxacan as well as with other Mexican migrants in Poughkeepsie and encouraged their engagement with HRHCare as promotores and promotoras de salud. The project prompted some Communities without Borders participants to organize around broader issues concerning undocumented Latina/o migrants in the United States by helping to plan political events, including the 2006 "A Day without an Immigrant" boycott, march, and rally in Poughkeepsie.[10]

Within the translocal frame of Communities without Borders, however, there were limits to addressing the effects of transnational capitalism and neoliberal trade policies that cause migration. In La Ciénega, participants in the Communities without Borders project created photographs that represented aspects of their daily lives that they hoped would encourage their family members to come home or that would inform outsiders about the conditions that forced their family members to migrate.[11] Participants in La Ciénega thus directed their work not only to their family members in Poughkeepsie, but also to a much broader audience. Although participants in La Ciénega portrayed the everyday lives of those left behind, only their families and friends would notice the *absence* of those who migrated in the photographs. So, although participants in La Ciénega were addressing a translocal audience comprised of community members in Poughkeepsie and La Ciénega, and a broader audience outside of those communities, only the former group would be able to "see" the effects of migration in these photographs.

I begin this chapter by contextualizing the history of Oaxacan migration to Poughkeepsie from the 1980s to the post-9/11 era in order to historically situate my analysis of the Unseen America project held at HRHCare in the summer of 2003. Due to the increased settlement of Oaxacan migrants in Poughkeepsie, HRHCare's role shifted from providing mobile medical services for migrant farmworkers to offering a broader range of services to all undocumented migrants residing in the Hudson River Valley. In addition to HRHCare, more social service organizations responded to the needs of the growing population of Oaxacan migrants residing in Poughkeepsie, fostering a very different environment than in Long Island, where the Workplace Project's Unseen America project took place. I relate the development of the translocal Communities without Borders project to HRHCare's efforts to reach out to undocumented Latina/o immigrants in Poughkeepsie and to fulfill the organization's mandate to cultivate leadership among clients of their community healthcare centers. The second half of the chapter focuses on the workshops in Poughkeepsie and La Ciénega and analyzes some of the photographs produced within them. In the final section, I examine the photographic exhibitions in Poughkeepsie and La Ciénega, as well as the impact of the exhibition in Poughkeepsie on participants.

The Formation of a Community of Oaxacan Migrants in Poughkeepsie

HRHCare's Communities without Borders project was rooted in the community of Oaxacan migrants in Poughkeepsie, which had been growing from the 1980s through the post-9/11 era. In the 1980s, Oaxacan migrants came to the Hudson River Valley as seasonal workers. Over time, some settled in Poughkeepsie and the surrounding area, creating a community base for later migrants. In transitioning between accommodating seasonal migrants to supporting longer-term residents, Hudson River HealthCare expanded from delivering medical services by mobile van in the fields to reaching out to new residents to familiarize them with the services provided by their community and migrant

health-care centers. Beyond HRHCare, other Poughkeepsie social service organizations worked to address the needs of Oaxacan migrants
living in town. In contrast to the experiences of migrants in Farmingville
and Hempstead, Long Island, as described in chapter 1, many Poughkeepsie residents viewed the settlement of Oaxacan migrants as contributing to the economic revitalization of this small city.[12] The context in
Poughkeepsie was quite distinct from Long Island, and these differences
affected the photographs that the participants in each of the Unseen
America workshops produced.

This different context influenced the work of social service organizations—including HRHCare—in serving the needs of migrant farmworkers in the Hudson River Valley. HRHCare has a long history of
providing health-care services to low-income residents of the Hudson
River Valley, as well as to seasonal farmworkers, recent migrants, and
day laborers. The organization has been involved with migrant health
care since the 1970s, when the Peekskill Area Ambulatory Health Center began treating migrant farmworkers from the United States and
Mexico in the Hudson River Valley.[13] Starting in the late 1970s, this
precursor to Hudson River HealthCare delivered health-care services
in a mobile van that went to the fields where migrant farmworkers
worked. The workers were mainly African American; Mexican American;
individuals who migrated from southern U.S. states, including Texas;
and a smaller number of farm laborers from Mexico. All were seasonal
migrants, arriving to work the harvest in the fall, going home for the
holidays, and returning in the spring for the growing season.

During the early 1990s, an increasing number of migrants from
Oaxaca and elsewhere in Mexico arrived in towns and small cities in the
Hudson River Valley.[14] Starting in the early 1990s, outmigration from
Oaxaca to the United States for work in agriculture, among other occu-
pations, grew, spurred by the privatization of public lands in Mexico
and neoliberal foreign policies such as the North American Free Trade
Agreement (NAFTA).[15] In the early 1990s, the Mixteca-Sur region of
Mexico was significantly affected by President Carlos Salinas's efforts
to reform Article 27 of the Mexican Constitution (1917), which allowed
peasants land rights for farming.[16] Wayne Cornelius and David Myhre

have related the changes to Article 27 to structural transformations within the Mexican economy. These changes promoted privatization and deregulation and were part of a wider set of neoliberal policy adjustments instituted prior to NAFTA.[17] The policies of NAFTA further exacerbated the financial crisis in Mexico.[18] NAFTA effectively lowered the price of corn in Mexico by increasing the importation of U.S. corn to Mexico, which put small farmers in Mexico out of business. Many agricultural workers lost their livelihood.[19]

By the early 1990s there were thousands of Mexican migrants living in Poughkeepsie, most of whom were from Oaxaca.[20] Poughkeepsie was one of many smaller cities and towns located far from the U.S.– Mexico border that saw a significant rise in Mexican migrants before the turn of the century.[21] According to Allison Mountz and Richard Wright, higher wages for labor in New York State attracted Mexican migrants.[22] Although most of the jobs Oaxacans found in Poughkeepsie paid only minimum wage, this amount was still a substantial increase over the 1990s wages in Oaxaca, where 80 percent of rural households brought home less than ten U.S. dollars a day.[23] Oaxacans who found work in Poughkeepsie relayed this information to residents in their hometowns, some of whom moved to join them.[24] As Lawrence Brown, Tamara Mott, and Edward Malecki argue, it is not push factors or jobs that dictate why Mexicans migrate to a specific U.S. location; rather, migrants choose places based on information they receive from family and friends. This sharing of information can lead to a "migration chain," whereby migrants follow those who have come before them.[25] In Poughkeepsie, Oaxacan migrants such as Honorio "Pie" Rodríguez, who opened El Bracero restaurant in 1991, played a significant role in the social networks on which La Ciénega residents depended.[26]

The long-term settlement of Oaxacan migrants in Poughkeepsie grew substantially between the 1980s and 2000s. In the 1980s and 1990s, most Oaxacan migrants working in the United States did not plan to stay there.[27] During this period, the majority of Oaxacans who migrated to New York State were male and traveled there to earn money, after which they planned to return to Oaxaca.[28] Oaxacan migrants in the 1980s and 1990s remained in the United States less than nine years on average, with most migrants taking only two trips to the country. As a result, as Cohen and Rodríguez argue, migrants at this time were primarily connected to their sending households and communities.[29] From the early to late 1990s—a period in which there was more movement across the U.S.–Mexico boundary—Oaxacan migrants in Poughkeepsie could be characterized as a transnational community, composed of migrants whose "daily lives, work, and social relationships extend across national borders."[30] By the 1990s, a quarter of the adult men from La Ciénega, Oaxaca (population three thousand), were working in Poughkeepsie.[31] According to the 2000 census, 85 percent of Mexicans living in Poughkeepsie had moved there between 1990 and 2000, with most arriving between 1995 and 2000, the years following NAFTA.[32] By 2000, 46 percent of Oaxaca's Central Valley households included one migrant.[33] Of this group, 76 percent were men.

As I mention in the introduction, the decade following the mid-1990s exemplified a major shift in migration patterns for Mexicans in the United States. Alicia Schmidt Camacho and other scholars have argued that this contributed to an increase in undocumented migrants, partly because of harsher security on both sides of the U.S.–Mexico boundary.[34] The rise in border enforcement discouraged some Mexicans from migrating to the United States, and it dissuaded others who had arrived in the United States from returning to Mexico if they later wanted to reenter the United States.[35] Due to the challenges of crossing the U.S.–Mexico boundary without immigration documents, many migrants from Oaxaca started to put down roots in Poughkeepsie. In their research on Mexican migrant communities in New York State, Pilar Parra and Max Pfeffer noted a decline in the number of short-term migrants in the area after the year 2000, which they argue mirrors the general increase in Mexican settlement in the United States.[36] Parra and Pfeffer contend that this increased settlement has also led to the need for services in health care, transportation, and housing, and with assistance obtaining work permits and visas, which HRHCare, among other local organizations, has helped provide.[37]

Comité Latino, a group that was established in the early 1990s, was one of the most direct ways that HRHCare drew in this relatively new population of Latina/os and informed them of the organization's services.[38] In forming Comité Latino, HRHCare located potential community leaders to advise newer migrants about the health-care services that they offered and to get to know people's individual needs and problems. This model helped forge a bond between HRHCare and the community, so that newer migrants felt that they could trust the organization to help them.[39] Comité Latino provided an institutional context in which Latina/o community members could gather and talk about their concerns. Over time, the organization grew and interacted more with local politicians to update them about the community's needs. Comité Latino also organized events in Peekskill, New York, which made certain aspects of Latina/o lives—such as the celebration of holidays—public.[40]

The growth in Oaxacan settlement in Poughkeepsie partially resulted from the intensification of immigration enforcement along the U.S.–Mexico boundary, but other factors contributed to the influx of migrants. For example, more women, children, and other relatives of the male migrants started arriving in the mid-1990s, as many Oaxacans found steady employment in Poughkeepsie and sent for their family members.[41] By the early 2000s, some migrants in Poughkeepsie had purchased homes, and parents had enrolled children in school. In addition, some undocumented migrants began trying to change their immigration status so they could remain in the country.[42] As a result of these factors and others, many migrants living in Poughkeepsie had not returned to Oaxaca for years. Most did not want to risk a trip to Mexico, since they could be deported if they were caught crossing the U.S.–Mexico boundary without immigration documents and lose what they had worked so hard to attain in Poughkeepsie.

The settlement of Oaxacans had a significant impact on Poughkeepsie, especially on the growth of businesses on Main Street. The revitalization of the city that started in the 2000s is partially related to the influx of Mexican migrants.[43] Poughkeepsie had experienced economic challenges since the mid-1970s—especially between the late 1980s and the late 1990s—which was evident in the downtown area, much of which was filled with vacant buildings.[44] The rise of Oaxacan entrepreneurs began in the early 1990s, starting with Honorio "Pie" Rodríguez, who established El Bracero restaurant. After El Bracero opened in 1991, at least twenty-five other Spanish-language businesses were launched before 2004.[45] These businesses included nine restaurants, eight variety stores, three groceries, two bakeries, two delis, and one hair salon, all primarily serving the Mexican population. Brian Godfrey characterizes Poughkeepsie's Main Street as an "incipient urban landscape of ethnic arrival" developed by "an aspiring Latino entrepreneurial class," which included Rodríguez and Francisco del Moral—the owner of Casa Latino grocery store and president of the Asociación Hispana de Benito Juárez (Benito Juárez Hispanic Association)—among others.[46]

The contribution of Mexican (and specifically Oaxacan) migrants to the revitalization of Poughkeepsie has been significant, and along with a number of other aspects of the city's population has led to the integration of this community within Poughkeepsie.[47] Mexican migrants have been part of what Jo Margaret Mano and Linda Greenow have described as the "bottom-up" growth in small Hispanic and Mexican businesses. Along with the "top-down" investment in government and private projects, "bottom-up" growth has brought commercial life back to the city.[48] Elizabeth Druback-Celaya has argued that because of this, the Mexican migrant population has not been viewed as "invading and thwarting Poughkeepsie's overall goals for itself, but rather presenting another way in which the city needs to expand and rejuvenate."[49] The inclusion of Mexican migrants in the community was aided by other social service organizations, such as those housed in the Family Partnership Center; governmental agencies; and other groups who supported migrants, including the Latino Roundtable and the Association for Hispanics to Obtain Resources and Assistance (AHORA).[50]

Unlike in Farmingville, Long Island, where some longtime residents viewed Mexican and Central American migrants' use of public space in their community as negatively affecting their "quality of life," Poughkeepsie residents overwhelmingly viewed Mexican migrants as improving this small city as they became the owners, workers, and consumers of new businesses that were sprouting up on Main Street.[51] The integration of Oaxacan migrants into the broader Poughkeepsie community significantly increased during the 2000s. The city established support services for the Mexican community, and when the number of migrants increased, these service organizations grew to meet their needs.[52] These service organizations reached out to Mexican migrants to inform them about their rights and the services that existed for them.[53] Still, as Druback-Celaya contends, the integration of Mexican migrants "goes beyond simple structural integration, such as inclusion in systems of health care," to an "effort to foster linguistic and cultural understanding among all members of the community."[54] This context has made Poughkeepsie more welcoming to migrants than other towns in the Hudson River Valley, and migrants from Puebla and Veracruz, Mexico—and a smaller number of migrants from Central America—followed those from Oaxaca to Poughkeepsie.[55]

This context in Poughkeepsie created a different environment for Unseen America than that of Long Island, and this distinction affected the photographs that participants produced. Unlike the photographs created by participants in the Workplace Project's workshop, the images produced by Oaxacan migrants in Poughkeepsie were not intended primarily for an outside audience. This was also an outcome of the Communities without Borders frame, which emphasized the building of a "photographic bridge" between Poughkeepsie and La Ciénega. As I will explain further in the coming sections, HRHCare focused on strengthening the connections between migrants in Poughkeepsie and their families in La Ciénega. However, I also contend that as a result of their involvement in the Communities without Borders project, participants worked beyond HRHCare's goals to address broader issues that concerned them, including the effects of restrictive and punitive U.S. immigration laws on members of their communities.

"The Photographic Bridge": Hudson River HealthCare and Unseen America

HRHCare's interest in Unseen America was related to the organization's desire to share information about the organization's services with the Latina/o community in Poughkeepsie. HRHCare staff's focus on recruiting promotores and promotoras de salud was partly a response to the health disparities experienced by undocumented Latina/o migrants in the United States. Federal funding to cover health-care costs for seasonal migrants and farmworkers has existed since 1962, and in 1975, Congress allowed for the development of "community and migrant health centers."[56] In recent decades, neoliberal economic policies contributed to the increased privatization of health care, which limited the funding allocated for undocumented migrants. For example, the 1996 Personal Responsibility and Work Opportunity Reconciliation Act (PRWORA) restricted migrants' eligibility for Medicaid, which had both direct and indirect effects on migrants' health care.[57] Gilbert Gee and Chandra Ford note that "legislation can harm immigrants, not only directly via eligibility standards but also indirectly via a climate of fear."[58] They also assert that, due to the political climate around immigration in recent years, undocumented Latina/o migrants have avoided accessing health and social services due to fear of arrest, detention, or deportation. In this context, community health-care organizations have viewed promotores and promotoras de salud as a means to reach migrant communities that have been marginalized within the U.S. health-care system, as well as U.S. society as a whole.[59]

Unseen America's focus on having working-class communities photograph their lives corresponded well with HRHCare's promotion of their clients' participation in the running of the organization. As a Federally Qualified Health Center (FQHC), HRHCare is mostly overseen by its clients. In fact, 51 percent of the boards of Federally Qualified Health Centers are required to be comprised of their clients. This mandate is based on the model developed by Dr. Jack Geiger and Dr. Count Gibson, leaders in the 1960s community health-care movement. In the first grant they submitted to the Office of Economic Opportunity (OEO), Geiger and Gibson indicated that community participation would be required in the health-care centers, primarily through board membership. When the OEO started promoting community health centers in 1970, it developed guidelines based on Geiger's proposal.[60] Thus, the "clients" of community health-care centers are not just patients, but also participants in the organization.[61]

Staff members at HRHCare were interested in Unseen America because of several emphases within the organization. First, HRHCare had a history of using art as a means to connect with communities. Specifically, HRHCare staff member Wilfredo Morel, who worked on the Communities without Borders project, stated that the organization "uses art as a way to break barriers" with the members whom it serves.[62] Second, the staff at HRHCare believed that the photography workshop would help them to identify potential promotores and promotoras de salud who would tell Oaxacan migrants about the services offered at a two-year-old HRHCare site at the Family Partnership Center in Poughkeepsie.[63] Although there are many distinctive aspects of the community health-care model, one of the most important for a discussion of Communities without Borders is the central role that community members played in these health-care centers. In writing about the importance of "community" in community health, Jenna Loyd suggests that "the valence of community health hinges on specific articulations of geographically-based and group-based understandings of community." Further, she notes that "community-oriented primary care (COPC) practitioners argue that community health is not only the sum of individuals in a geographic space but also the capacity of a group to create community." Thus, the "role of the clinic should be to help mobilize people to *create* a place-based community through the collaborative identification of needs."[64] Creating community was central to the development of Communities without Borders.

The HRHCare staff's aim of recruiting Oaxacan migrants to use the community health-care center challenges the division between institutions that support *either* seasonal farmworkers *or* (to a limited extent) the health care of U.S. citizens but do not provide services for undocumented migrants.[65] Further, HRHCare's goals should be situated within the political context of the early 2000s, a period characterized by neoliberal economic policies as well as the privatization of health care in the United States. What is interesting is that politicians' support for community health centers—including those that provide services for migrants, such as HRHCare—has not been taken up in "politically predictable cycles," as Loyd notes, citing the example of President George W. Bush, who "championed community health centers as a mark of his 'compassionate conservatism.'"[66] Notwithstanding Bush's support for community health centers, Loyd draws on the work of Michel Foucault to argue that community health can be a "political object . . . taken at face value and turned back against the system that was bent on controlling it."[67] Further, she contends, "Although practices under the banner of community health can entrench biopower, they can also serve to subvert state biopolitical practices."[68]

The decision of HRHCare to provide health care to undocumented migrants suggests a more expansive understanding of who deserves health-care services in the United States. This inclusive approach reflects what Loyd calls "the radical potential of community health," which also involves "exposing the contradictory reality of biopower and organizing in such a way that collective well-being is possible."[69] HRHCare's Communities without Borders project demonstrates how, as Loyd notes, "the state's inability to meet current needs is part and parcel of the biopolitical—that is, racialized—organization of scarcity that extends beyond the state to the structure of the economy."[70] Seen in this context, HRHCare's recruiting of undocumented migrants as clients challenges the limits of the U.S. health-care system to accommodate all U.S. residents, regardless of their citizenship status.

HRHCare staff's focus on developing the Communities without Borders project to reach out to the growing population of Oaxacans living in Poughkeepsie was a practical means of providing access to health-care services. Their emphasis on "building the bridge" to connect the translocal communities of Poughkeepsie and La Ciénega—so those in La Ciénega could encourage their family members in Poughkeepsie to use the community health-care center—was built on ties the organization had been cultivating with Mexican health-care agencies. Starting in the early 2000s, HRHCare began relationships with both the Secretaría de Salud (Ministry of Health) in Mexico and local and state departments of health—specifically in Oaxaca and Puebla—to support health care for Mexican migrants in the Hudson River Valley.[71] These connections were especially important after 2000, when Mexican migrants were joining their families in the Hudson River Valley in large numbers.[72]

The Communities without Borders project benefited from one of the lessons learned by the participants in Workplace Project's Unseen

America, which was to have clear goals from the beginning. In January 2003, Bread and Roses contacted HRHCare about becoming involved with Unseen America. After an initial meeting with representatives from Bread and Roses and the Workplace Project, HRHCare staff decided that the project would commence in mid-June.[73] The HRHCare staff then sought out migrants from La Ciénega for the photography workshop. This decision was based on HRHCare's contact with a state department of health employee in Oaxaca, who informed the staff that a significant number of residents from La Ciénega had migrated to Poughkeepsie. After HRHCare hired Juan Garcia-Nuñez, a bilingual artist who taught photography and videography at Dutchess County Community College, the organization started to promote the workshop to Mexican migrants in Poughkeepsie. Staff and volunteers at the health-care center in Pough-keepsie—including Hortensia from La Ciénega—recruited participants by circulating flyers in churches, laundromats, and other locations where the organization had previously advertised ESL classes. Volunteers gave presentations about the workshop around Poughkeepsie, and they also spread the word through the Family Partnership Center.[74] The organi-zation's choice to focus on recruiting individuals from La Ciénega was one of the project's biggest draws.[75] Although HRHCare had originally intended to hold only one photography workshop in Poughkeepsie, the project staff had always planned to display the photographs in both Poughkeepsie and La Ciénega.[76]

According to Nathalis Guy Wamba and Carolyn Curran—authors of *Shadow Catchers: A Look at Unseen America,* a report on the Unseen America workshops held between 2000 and 2003—Workplace Project members suggested that Bread and Roses hold discussions at the begin-ning of each workshop to determine the most important political issues facing the group and how photography could further the group's politi-cal goals.[77] In 2003, the year of the HRHCare workshop, the majority of participants could not travel to Mexico for a visit and then return to the United States because of their undocumented status. They did not get to see their family members regularly, unlike the Workplace Project participants who visited family members in Central America during the winter of 2000–2001.[78] When the HRHCare staff conferred with the participants about their objectives for the photography project, they agreed that their primary political aim was to use photography to connect with their family members in La Ciénega.

The vast majority of participants were recent migrants from La Ciénega, although at least one participant was from elsewhere in Mexico. The group of twenty-three individuals ranged from teenagers to senior citizens, with a mix of men and women. Some participants had come to the United States as early as the mid-1990s, but most had arrived more recently, including some younger workshop members who had moved with their parents in the months before 9/11. A few of the younger members planned to return to Mexico within a year or so, while others, including some of the older members of the workshop, had chosen to settle in the United States, since their family members lived in Poughkeepsie. Some of these participants were students, but most were adults who primarily worked in the service industry, including restaurants, hotels, landscaping, childcare, and housekeeping. A few participants had previously been employed as seasonal farmworkers.[79] Others included volunteers from the health-care center in Poughkeepsie, including Hortensia, and three members of the HRHCare staff from Peekskill, New York: Vilma Velez, Wilfredo Morel, and Nick Cannell. These staff members commuted from Peekskill to Poughkeepsie for the two-hour workshops, which were held for two nights a week for twelve weeks.[80]

From the very beginning, HRHCare staff members emphasized the goals of the workshop, which sustained participation levels.[81] According to participant Elizabeth Druback-Celaya, the staff frequently discussed the primary goal of the project: to support the connection between the communities of Poughkeepsie and La Ciénega. The organizers informed the workshop participants that their family members would see their images in La Ciénega. This would enable Poughkeepsie residents to share photographs representing their daily lives with their family and community members. As the HRHCare staff described, this project highlighted the "connection/migration pattern and dependence of two communities for economic and social reasons."[82] Because the participants had limited contact with their family members, the concept of "building the bridge" was attractive to them.[83] In this sense, the organization's framing of the project as a "photographic bridge" appealed to the participants from La Ciénega and motivated them to attend the workshop regularly.[84]

Although photography teacher Juan Garcia-Nuñez did not follow the *Unseen America Teacher's Guide* (2003) particularly closely during the Family Partnership Center workshop, he did emphasize some project options suggested in the book. The choices included documenting one's own life or the life of another. In the early classes, Garcia-Nuñez taught participants how to use a camera, while also covering composition, framing, and lighting. Garcia-Nuñez focused on a documentary approach, familiarizing the attendees with the work of photographers Eugene Smith, Sebastião Salgado, and Josef Koudelka. As the participants started using the cameras, he encouraged them to use "the eye of the documentarian" and to see photographs as a means to interpret the world around them. In contrast to documentary photographers who portrayed the lives of individuals in different communities, Garcia-Nuñez followed Unseen America's emphasis on self-representation and encouraged the participants to use the camera to depict their own lives, concerns, interests, and experiences. Photographers were directed to "portray aspects of life that are integral, rather than distinct from daily life" and to avoid posed pictures or snapshots.[85] Most workshop participants took photographs of friends and family members at home, during special events, and working or waiting for work, and landscape shots of backyards and streetscapes.[86]

HRHCare's framing of the project as a link between migrants in Poughkeepsie and their families in La Ciénega, combined with Unseen America's emphasis on individuals representing their daily lives in documentary form, influenced the photographs that the participants produced in the workshop. In the HRHCare workshop in Poughkeepsie, most participants created personal photographs that were significant to themselves and their translocal communities in Poughkeepsie and La Ciénega. Their photographs also represented the social integration of Oaxacan migrants, by picturing their settlement in Poughkeepsie. In addition, much like the photographs produced by Workplace Project participants in Unseen America, those involved in HRHCare's workshop also created images that mixed documentary aesthetics with family and snapshot photography, although they did so for different reasons. In the HRHCare workshop, the mixed-genre aesthetic form narrated the participants' translocal mode of address as well as the primary goal of Communities without Borders, to connect two communities divided by national borders.

Similar to Workplace Project participants in Unseen America, those in HRHCare's workshop produced photographs of their family and community members that represent what I referred to as the *undocumented everyday*. The majority of their photographs focus on the "nonevents of daily life," and they depict adults in the private sphere—watching over children, eating, cooking dinner, or otherwise engaged in activities at home. In addition, there are photographs commemorating special events, as well as numerous images of young children that share some aspects of family and snapshot photography. Although using elements of these photographic genres enabled participants to create images that were meaningful to their families, these pictures also narrated the social integration of Oaxacan migrants in Poughkeepsie. Thus, while these photographs represent personal (and private) histories, they also relate to public narratives of community and the translocal identities of the participants. The mixed-genre aesthetic in the photographs by the workshop participants narrated their translocality as a mode of address.

As mentioned above, most of the images produced by workshop participants bear a resemblance to family and snapshot photographs, as they focus on symbolic points in family life, including celebrations, such as baptisms, as in *My Son, Grandson, and Angela* by Esther (Figure 7). They also portray children in everyday scenarios, including *Pichus Bathing* by Edith (Figure 8), and *Las Niñas* (The Girls) by Roberto (Figure 9). The aesthetic qualities of these photographs—such as *My Son, Grandson, and Angela*—also look like family snapshots, since there is "no attempt to conceal the process of picture taking," and as such, "participants present themselves directly to the camera."[87] As Tina Campt explains, "Family photography is . . . far more than a documentary reproduction of its subjects; it is instead a performative practice that enacts complicated and particular sets of social and cultural relationships."[88] Still, some elements of this photograph are more indicative of a documentary style, as

Figure 7. *My Son, Grandson, and Angela* by Esther was exhibited as part of Hudson River HealthCare's Communities without Borders project, in collaboration with Unseen America. Courtesy Hudson River HealthCare.

Figure 8. *Pichus Bathing* by Edith was exhibited as part of Hudson River HealthCare's Communities without Borders project, in collaboration with Unseen America. Courtesy Hudson River HealthCare.

Figure 9. *Las Niñas* (The Girls) by Roberto was exhibited as part of Hudson River HealthCare's Communities without Borders project, in collaboration with Unseen America. Courtesy Hudson River HealthCare.

the photographer did not crop the photograph and, thus, the image includes figures who appear marginal within the frame. *Pichus Bathing* portrays a baby in a bathtub, an iconic subject in the genres of family and snapshot photography. However, what differentiates this image from these genres is the angle from which it was taken. As opposed to the usual snapshot showing the baby's face, this photograph is taken from above, looking down at the back of the baby's head as he sits in the bathtub. *Las Niñas* portrays two young girls who appear to be posing for (but not looking at) the camera, resembling family or snapshot photography. However, this image also draws upon documentary or art photography, as the photographer Roberto composed the image using the rule of thirds, which is a basic rule of composition that Garcia-Nuñez taught in the workshop. In this photograph, Roberto positions the girls on one side, rather than centering them in the frame.[89]

By combining family and snapshot photography with documentary aesthetics, some participants produced images that countered the norms associated with these genres. Scholars of photography have written about the ways in which family and snapshot photography can have both private and more public meanings. Catherine Zuromskis argues that snapshot photographs can be "a means of linking private symbols of domestic harmony to explicitly public ideas of social conformity and American nationalism."[90] Sonja Vivenne and Jean Burgess also note that "everyday practices of such forms of personal photography insistently invited us to construct and expect a normative family gaze."[91] Through their use of a mixed-genre aesthetic, some of the workshop participants in Poughkeepsie challenged normative conventions of these genres. For example, in Gloria's *The Children Enjoying the Lake* (Figure 10) a group of adults and children sit around on a picnic blanket, as the adults play cards. Most of the subjects appear to be enjoying themselves, yet the photographer focuses on a boy who is visibly upset, centering him in the frame. Although the genre of the family snapshot is "closely guided by rigorous cultural norms" that "preserves an ideal (and often idealized) facet of experience," as Zuromskis suggests, this photograph diverges from normative ideals by centering on the boy who appears upset in what is otherwise a cheerful depiction of a family picnic.[92] In the context of family and snapshot photography, this image might be discarded, yet the photographer decided both to print and to exhibit it, which speaks to its significance for the photographer as well as (possibly) for those to whom it was addressed. This image deviates from the "ideal" family photograph, and yet the image has other meanings as it effectively narrates the social integration of Oaxacan migrants in Poughkeepsie.

Many images are of personal subjects, yet some photographs from the Communities without Borders workshop in Poughkeepsie also depict Oaxacan migrants' connections to public life in that city, especially in the workplace. These photographs portray Oaxacan migrants working in restaurants, stores, garages, and in domestic settings, as well as traveling to and from work. Similar to the photographs mentioned above, these images resemble family and snapshot photographs. For example, Edith's *Restaurant Workers* (Figure 11) portrays two smiling coworkers (one Anglo and one Mexican) positioned side by side. The Anglo woman has her arm over the shoulder of the man as they pose for the photograph. Another

Figure 10. *The Children Enjoying the Lake* by Gloria was exhibited as part of Hudson River HealthCare's Communities without Borders project, in collaboration with Unseen America. Courtesy Hudson River HealthCare.

image, Roberto's *Ms. Rafa and Her Store* (Figure 12) features Ms. Rafa from La Ciénega in her Mexican products store in Poughkeepsie. A young boy in the center of the image smiles at the camera. He is dressed in what look like Spiderman pajamas and is sitting on top of a display case with a pillow. The other subjects of the photograph are portrayed in a more candid fashion, including Ms. Rafa, who is preoccupied with work, and a customer who is examining a catalog. The boy appears to be getting ready to take a nap, and his centrality to the photograph highlights the blending of the private life of the home with the public life of the store. Although the images of individuals at work represent the integration of Oaxacan migrants in Poughkeepsie—particularly as store owners and workers—they also resemble private photographs.

Some images provide counterexamples to the majority of photographs that link a translocal address with a mixed-genre aesthetic. As mentioned earlier, most of the workshop participants were from La Ciénega, and they established specific goals and employed a mixed-genre aesthetic within

Figure 11. *Restaurant Workers* by Edith was exhibited as part of Hudson River HealthCare's Communities without Borders project, in collaboration with Unseen America. Courtesy Hudson River HealthCare.

Figure 12. *Ms. Rafa and Her Store* by Roberto was exhibited as part of Hudson River HealthCare's Communities without Borders project, in collaboration with Unseen America. Courtesy Hudson River HealthCare.

their photographs. However, at least one participant—Roberto, who is from Mexico, but not La Ciénega—took photographs that primarily employed a documentary style. In part because his images were not addressed to a translocal audience, Roberto prioritized Garcia-Nuñez's suggestion to take up "the eye of the documentarian." He composed numerous photographs referencing the predicaments of Mexican migrants in the United States, including *The Man on the Wall Waiting to Complete His American Dream* (Figure 13). This photograph portrays a man, presumably a Mexican migrant, who is waiting—perhaps for work, for another person, or for a ride. This image is composed using the rule of thirds. The left side of the photograph portrays the subject—a man leaning against a building near the corner, his face directed toward the right. The building, which is shot at an angle, dominates the center and right side of the image, as does the sidewalk. The diagonal lines of the building and sidewalk direct our eyes to the end of the block, suggesting a possible path for this man. What is conveyed by the image is the waiting involved for migrants—for work, for immigration papers, and thus a "dream" delayed.

Figure 13. *The Man on the Wall Waiting to Complete His American Dream* by Roberto was exhibited as part of Hudson River HealthCare's Communities without Borders project, in collaboration with Unseen America. Courtesy Hudson River HealthCare.

Although many of these images represent the integration of Oaxaca migrants in Poughkeepsie, some photographers took a more critical stance toward the treatment of Latina/o—and specifically Mexican—migrants in the United States. These sentiments were largely conveyed in the captions of the images. In *The Man on the Wall Waiting to Complete His American Dream*, Roberto references the challenges that migrants face in the United States in his caption: "The quiet and silent wall supports us while we await a better future. Thousands of immigrants await an uncertain future. Similarly, this immigrant waits to realize his dreams." Roberto's photograph thus narrates how the lives of Mexican migrants are constrained due to restrictive U.S. immigration policies. Other participants explained that they took photographs to represent the difficulties faced by Mexican migrants, specifically as low-wage workers, in the United States. For example, Francisca took a photograph of a dishwasher because in her words, "it is representative of how many Mexican migrants to this area find work in the restaurant industry and often in unskilled positions such as dishwashers, which barely pays minimum wage."[93]

HRHCare staff members' experiences working with the participants in Poughkeepsie prompted their extension of the photography workshop to Oaxaca. Before the end of the Poughkeepsie workshop, Anne Nolon, the CEO of HRHCare, decided that the organization would put together a one-week photography workshop in La Ciénega with its own funding. During the planning process, HRHCare staff contacted the state department of health in Oaxaca, explaining that they wanted to hold a workshop to increase awareness of HRHCare services in the community. HRHCare staff members felt that the project would enable them to inform relatives about the health-care services available to them in Poughkeepsie, building trust between the organization and the family members of their client base.[94] The Poughkeepsie participants greeted the plans for the workshop in La Ciénega with great enthusiasm.[95] HRHCare's goal was to locate potential participants in La Ciénega with family members in Poughkeepsie. Before they traveled to Oaxaca, they contacted Carmelo Ortiz Castellanos, the local municipal president of La Ciénega, to ask for his assistance. The office of the municipal president responded by distributing information about the workshop throughout the small town. Many residents were interested in the workshop, since almost everyone had at least one family member in the United States, the majority of whom lived in Poughkeepsie. On the day that HRHCare staff members Anne Nolon, Vilma Velez, Wilfredo Morel, and Nick Cannell arrived in La Ciénega, three hundred people showed up in the *zócolo* (central plaza) to take the workshop. Because of the limited number of cameras, not everyone could be involved, so the local municipal president selected a smaller number of people to participate.[96]

Rather than creating an Unseen America project in Oaxaca, HRHCare chose to familiarize those in La Ciénega with the organization, so it would become trusted in the community. The one-week photography workshop in La Ciénega was a way to introduce family and community members to HRHCare and the Communities without Borders project and to instruct participants on how to use cameras. In their presentation to participants in Oaxaca, HRHCare staff members spoke about their organization and informed participants about the health-care services that they provided in Poughkeepsie. They also gave a PowerPoint presentation that explained the Communities without Borders project and included photographs taken by and of participants in the Poughkeepsie workshop. The staff then gave instructions about how to use the cameras, directing participants to personalize their photographs to convey what was meaningful to them to share with those in Poughkeepsie.[97] When they ran out of 35mm film cameras, staff members bought disposable color film cameras for the participants. The HRHCare staff recalled how taken the participants were with having a camera, indicating that many had never used one.[98]

Although the emphasis of the workshop in Oaxaca was quite different than the one in Poughkeepsie, the pictures that participants produced also drew on family, snapshot, and documentary photography. However, while Garcia-Nuñez focused on composition, framing, and lighting in the Poughkeepsie workshop, HRHCare staff placed less of an emphasis on aesthetics in La Ciénega. In La Ciénega HRHCare staff did not present a slideshow highlighting documentary photographers, other than the work of the Communities without Borders participants in Poughkeepsie. This was partially due to the time frame of the workshop, which was much shorter than the workshop in Poughkeepsie. HRHCare also chose not to limit the participants to 35mm cameras or black-and-white film. While the choice of black-and-white documentary-style photography enabled Bread and Roses to relate Unseen America with truth claims associated with the social documentary photography tradition, HRHCare valued photographs more for their content—that participants represent personal aspects of their daily lives, for family and friends.

The photographs produced by participants in Oaxaca portray the individuals left behind—women, children, and the elderly. These images represent the lives of community members without those who had migrated (mostly young and adult men). Many of the participants' images are of individuals performing everyday activities—women cooking, selling, buying, and socializing at the market and children playing with animals, toys, and in the streets. These images are untitled and include photographs of girls cooking by Maria Asunción Celaya Sosa, a woman at a market by

Francisca Cruz Arellanes, a woman working in a store by Margarita Castellanos Bautista, and a woman outside a house by Laura Ramírez Castellanos (Figure 14).[99] Here, women and girls are portrayed performing their everyday tasks in the absence of men. With these images, participants also drew upon documentary aesthetics as well as elements of family and snapshot photography.

The HRHCare staff's goal for expanding this project into La Ciénega was to gain the trust of workshop participants, so they would feel assured that their family members' health-care needs would be met at the Poughkeepsie community health-care center. During their week in La Ciénega, staff members listened to participants talk about family members in the United States, including many children who had migrated and whom they had not seen in years.[100] HRHCare staff member Wilfredo Morel remarked that the La Ciénega workshop participants "felt so separated from their family members that we became substitutes for their family

Figure 14. This photograph of a woman outside a house was taken by Laura Ramírez Castellanos as part of Hudson River HealthCare's Communities without Borders project in La Ciénega, Oaxaca. Courtesy Hudson River HealthCare.

members."[101] As a result, workshop participants in La Ciénega invited HRHCare staff not only into their homes, but also to a wedding.

Although HRHCare's emphasis was on creating a "photographic bridge" between individuals in Poughkeepsie and La Ciénega, some participants in La Ciénega saw this translocal project as a way to respond to conditions caused by a global economic system, neoliberal trade policies, and militarized national borders. As such, there was a tension between the different audiences addressed by the participants in their work—members of their translocal community or a broader audience. HRHCare's intention was to join these two communities through photographs, yet some participants in La Ciénega wanted their images to reach audiences beyond their translocal communities. For these individuals, participation in the Communities without Borders project was not motivated only by their interest in sharing photographs with family members in the United States, as they saw the project as a way to communicate the impact of migration on their lives to a broader audience.

This tension is narrated in *Unseen America: Seeking Health through Art*, HRHCare's video about the Communities without Borders project. Some participants in La Ciénega who were interviewed for the film explained that their photographs were directed toward family members in the United States, while others spoke about how they wanted a broad audience beyond their translocal community to view their images. A teenager in the video explained that she wanted migrants from La Ciénega who now live in the United States to see her photographs. In the film she stated that she became involved in the workshop because of her interest in photography, but also to create images for community members who "no he vuelto desde hace tiempo" (have not been back in a while). She hoped these images would influence them to come back.[102]

Other Communities without Borders participants in La Ciénega addressed the difficulties faced both by those who stayed in La Ciénega and by those who migrated, exposing the effects that neoliberal trade policies, U.S. immigration policies, and increased enforcement along the U.S.–Mexico boundary have had on the town. In *Unseen America: Seeking Health through Art*, a middle-aged woman stated that the Communities without Borders project enabled them "para mostrar al mundo las costumbres de nuestra comunidad, la forma en que vivimos, como somos capaces de salir adelante, el trabajo que hacemos para seguir adelante" (to show the whole world the customs of our community, the way that we live, how we're able to get ahead, the work we do to keep going forward). This woman situated her comments in relation to the effects of migration on her town. In the video, she spoke directly to the camera, explaining how migration led to the disintegration of families in her community, as fathers and sons migrated to the United States, leaving women, children, and the elderly behind. However, she also explained that, in 2003—the year of her interview—there were no other options. Since there were few jobs in La Ciénega, her town survived thanks to those who migrated and sent money back home. She stated, "Uno no puede avanzar, no se puede lograr una vida mejor, o al menos una vida donde los parientes de uno, los hermanos, los hijos, los esposos no tengan que salir de casa" (One can't move forward, one can't achieve a better life or at least a life where one's relatives, one's brothers, one's children, one's husbands didn't have to leave home). She acknowledged that members of her community had limited choices—either to remain in La Ciénega and be unemployed or to "leave and suffer."[103]

This woman addressed the main concerns of those in La Ciénega— that leaving home was inevitable for some in their community. Lynn Stephen, who conducted interviews in the town of San Augustín Atenango, Oaxaca, noted that the concerns of those left behind "are part of the emotional political-economy of migration linking transborder communities together in multiple sites."[104] The photographs produced by workshop participants in La Ciénega narrate the loss of their family members who moved to the United States. The loss of those left behind relates to what Alicia Schmidt Camacho describes as the "narration of migrant sorrows."[105] The absence of family members in the photographs intimately registered with viewers in La Ciénega and Poughkeepsie. In the video, this woman's critique of the effects of migration on her town— and address to a broader audience conceived of as viewers outside the translocal community—went beyond the parameters of the Communities without Borders project as established by HRHCare.[106]

Although the Oaxacan migrants in Poughkeepsie and their family members in La Ciénega have been caught in a predicament produced by transnational capitalism, neoliberal policies, and economic restructuring,

HRHCare's emphasis for the Communities without Borders project was to connect a translocal community. The images produced by participants in Poughkeepsie and La Ciénega, however, also narrate a critique of the global economic system that fosters the need for low-paid workers and for people to migrate across national borders in search of economic security.

"People Can't Travel, but Photographs Do": Communities Divided by Borders

The exhibitions of photographs displayed in Poughkeepsie and La Ciénega portray the daily lives of this translocal community in two locations—one in Poughkeepsie and the other in La Ciénega—yet the positioning of these photographs next to one another in the context of these exhibitions speaks to both the translocal connections of these communities as well as to their physical separation from each other. While the photographs can be placed next to one another, those portrayed in the photographs cannot. The images from the Communities without Borders workshops became freighted with different meanings in their distinct contexts of reception in Poughkeepsie, La Ciénega, as well as in Oaxaca City where the images were also exhibited. These personal photographs could be understood and appreciated by many members of this translocal community, and yet the exhibitions had different effects on workshop participants in Poughkeepsie and La Ciénega. These exhibitions also had outcomes that had not been anticipated by HRHCare staff, such as increasing connections among migrants from La Ciénega living in Poughkeepsie, which led to their involvement in political events outside HRHCare, such as the "A Day without an Immigrant" boycott, march, and rally held on May 1, 2006. Further, as noted above, participants used the Communities without Borders project not only as a means to share personal images with family members, but also as a critique of the circumstances that force Oaxacans and other Mexicans to migrate to the United States in order to help support their family members, and the difficulties they encounter as low-wage workers in the United States.

The exhibition of these photographs in Poughkeepsie and Oaxaca had different effects. In Poughkeepsie and La Ciénega, these images were viewed primarily by family and community members, while in Oaxaca

City they were seen by individuals who had no connection to those portrayed in the photographs. After the workshop in La Ciénega, participants in Poughkeepsie selected photographs from both workshops to include in the first exhibition of the project, which was held at Poughkeepsie's Family Partnership Center on October 19, 2003.[107] Workshop participants in Poughkeepsie also developed titles or captions for their photographs, all of which were identified by the names of the photographers. Although Poughkeepsie workshop participants were initially concerned about posting their names with the photographs because of their undocumented status, over time they became more comfortable with the idea. This first exhibition was attended by local politicians; staff from the Dutchess County Art Council, Bread and Roses, Hudson River HealthCare, and the Family Partnership Center; and workshop participants and their friends and family. According to HRHCare staff members Vilma Velez, Wilfredo Morel, and Nick Cannell, community members—especially those from La Ciénega living in Poughkeepsie—enjoyed the show tremendously, pointing out familiar places and faces in the photographs to one another.[108] The exhibition in Poughkeepsie affirmed Mexican—and specifically Oaxacan—migrants' senses of identity and belonging, bringing them together as a group.[109] The exhibition also contributed to the migrants' involvement in political events in Poughkeepsie.

After the show in Poughkeepsie, some HRHCare staff members returned to Mexico to set up exhibitions of these photographs at the Cultural House in La Ciénega and Los Danzantes Restaurante in Oaxaca City.[110] Similar to the Poughkeepsie exhibition, La Ciénega's *Un puente fotográfico: Conectando dos comunidades* (A photographic bridge: Connecting two communities) brought together images of the daily lives of family members in Poughkeepsie and La Ciénega. The exhibition was attended by local politicians, such as Carmelo Ortiz Castellanos, as well as by the broader community. Since many family members in La Ciénega had not seen their relatives in the United States for years, viewing these photographs gave them some sense of their families' daily lives in Poughkeepsie.[111] As such, these exhibitions of photographs in Poughkeepsie and in La Ciénega functioned in ways that were similar to the viewing of family photographs.

In Oaxaca City, however, these pictures appeared before audience members with little or no connection to this community, and thus, the photographs had different resonances for these viewers. Patricia Holland has argued that insiders' experiences of personal or family images are quite distinct from those of outsiders.[112] Elizabeth Druback-Celaya attended the exhibition in Oaxaca City, noting that it was quite different from the Poughkeepsie and La Ciénega exhibitions. The photographs were displayed at Los Danzantes Restaurante, an upscale restaurant catering to tourists visiting Oaxaca. Druback-Celaya noted that in this context the exhibition "was appealing to people on an artistic level."[113] However, this was not a goal for the participants in La Ciénega, some of whom wanted to show the effects of migration on the town to those outside this community. What only migrants in Poughkeepsie and La Ciénega residents could see was the absence of those who had migrated. Viewers outside of this translocal community could only see *what was photographed*, as opposed to what was *not present* in the image.

HRHCare organized exhibitions in Poughkeepsie and La Ciénega as a means to connect this translocal community, yet there were other outcomes of the exhibition, especially for individuals from La Ciénega living in Poughkeepsie. The photographs of life "back home" had an effect not only on the workshop participants, but also on attendees of the exhibition who were from La Ciénega. In 2003 almost 85 percent of the Mexican migrants living in Poughkeepsie were from La Ciénega, but they had not previously felt that they were part of a group.[114] As a result of the exhibition, the workshop participants and other migrants living in Poughkeepsie began envisioning themselves as part of a community of Oaxacans living in Poughkeepsie.[115] For those from La Ciénega, the photography project cemented their identity as the core of the Mexican community in Poughkeepsie.[116] Also, after the workshop some participants began to take up leadership roles at HRHCare. For example, Roberto became a board member of HRHCare's health-care facility in Poughkeepsie, and Hortensia, who began as a volunteer, became a community representative for the center.

The involvement of Oaxacan, as well as Mexican, migrants in the photography workshop contributed to their sense of connection as a community in Poughkeepsie, which encouraged some to take up leadership roles within HRHCare and Comité Latino, and also to participate in political events related to migrant rights. After the workshops and exhibitions had ended, HRHCare staff members fulfilled their plan to create a Comité Latino in Poughkeepsie to support access to health care for Latinas/os. The group was comprised of the promotores and promotoras de salud who shared information about HRHCare's center with the Latina/o community in Poughkeepsie. While members of the Communities without Borders project began to take up leadership positions within HRHCare, some individuals also began organizing around broader issues that concerned Latina/o migrant communities throughout the United States.

In 2006, some participants became involved in planning "A Day without an Immigrant" boycott, march, and rally in Poughkeepsie. Following nationwide protests in March 2006, organizing began across the country for "A Day without an Immigrant"—a one-day boycott of businesses by Latina/o migrants and their allies—to show migrants' collective impact on the U.S. economy. "A Day without an Immigrant" boycott, march, and rally was part of a national response against HR 4437, the Border Protection, Antiterrorism and Illegal Immigration Act (or the Sensenbrenner-King Act).[117] This bill would have made residing in the United States without immigration documents a felony, and it would have criminalized anyone who aided undocumented migrants. Communities without Borders participants worked with other local groups—including the Asociación Hispana de Benito Juárez, the Worker's Rights Law Center of New York, and Vassar College's May 1 Planning Coalition—to organize the "A Day without an Immigrant" events in Poughkeepsie.[118]

The involvement of some participants in the Communities without Borders project in planning events around "A Day without Immigrant" enabled them to connect with a broader network of individuals in Poughkeepsie in an effort to challenge a federal bill that would have particularly punitive effects on undocumented Latina/o migrants.[119] Their participation in this action was an example of what Jonathan X. Inda and Julie Dowling refer to as "migrant counter-conducts," which contest the criminalization of undocumented migrants in the United States.[120] Poughkeepsie's "A Day without an Immigrant" boycott on May 1, 2006, was successful in demonstrating the impact that Latina/os and Latina/o businesses had on the city's economy. Many Latina/o-owned businesses shut down on the day of the boycott, including La Amistad bakery, the Pancho Villa grocery, Los Compadres restaurant, and Paco's barbershop.[121] Closing Latina/o-owned businesses in Poughkeepsie was significant, since they dominate a section of Main Street. During the march and rally, Latina/o migrants and their supporters articulated their concerns about HR 4437, particularly the way in which undocumented migrants would be treated as felons. However, these events were organized not only to protest HR 4437, but also to pressure politicians to reform immigration laws and to grant amnesty to undocumented migrants. Although the rally in Poughkeepsie was small compared to those in other U.S. cities, it was believed to be the largest in the city in over twenty years.[122] Further, the national protests and boycotts held in the spring of 2006 increased Latina/o participation in public political activity in Poughkeepsie and throughout the United States.[123]

The Communities without Borders project is an example of the ways in which Mexican migrants have been "locat[ing] political and cultural agency beyond the sanctioned boundaries of liberal nationalism" by claiming local and translocal forms of belonging.[124] The exhibition of these photographs led to conversations among workshop participants and other Oaxacan migrants regarding their positions as community leaders. As a result, some became involved in HRHCare—specifically Comité Latino—as well as in political events in Poughkeepsie, including the 2006 protests against HR 4437. Communities without Borders is thus an example of how, as Lynn Stephen describes, undocumented Oaxacan migrants in the United States are asserting their political presence "outside the framework of U.S. immigration law and within the framework of border-crossing transnational communities."[125] In this case, workshop participants used photography to connect with members of their translocal community. In going beyond the frame of Communities without Borders, some also challenged policies that contributed to the migration of their family members, including neoliberal trade policies, as well as the enactment of restrictive and punitive U.S. immigration laws that prevented them from returning home.

Conclusion

In recognizing the translocal ties of Oaxacan migrants in Poughkeepsie, HRHCare went beyond the national frame of Unseen America to organize a photography workshop in La Ciénega. In Communities without Borders, HRHCare transformed their Unseen America project into a translocal Unseen *Americas* project—what the organizers described as a "photographic bridge" between these communities—to build connections between the organization and workshop participants. Although the initial goal of Communities without Borders was to identify individuals to serve as promotores and promotoras de salud, the staff also developed a translocal component to prompt those from La Ciénega to encourage their family members in Poughkeepsie to use HRHCare's services.[126] HRHCare's decision to set up another photography workshop in La Ciénega challenged the most basic framework of Unseen America—that the projects be situated within the United States. In expanding their Unseen America project, HRHCare emphasized the connections among members of a translocal community who were separated because of neoliberal economic and restrictive U.S. immigration policies.

What differentiated the Communities without Borders project from other Unseen America projects, including the one organized by the Workplace Project in Long Island, was its translocal focus. The photographs that the Poughkeepsie migrants produced represented their everyday lives—what I refer to as the *undocumented everyday*—while the mixed-genre aesthetic they developed related to the translocal address of their images, producing a *translocal aesthetic*. Participants in La Ciénega also developed a translocal lens, as they addressed their photographs to family members in Poughkeepsie, while knowing their images would also be viewed by those in La Ciénega. Even beyond the translocal mode of address that informed this photography, some participants in La Ciénega directed their photographs to a broader audience to call attention to the effects of migration on their town. However, while family members in Poughkeepsie would be able to envision their own absence in the photographs, an audience of outsiders could not view these images in the same way.

Communities without Borders was a translocal response to the conditions produced by transnational capitalism, neoliberal trade policies (including NAFTA), and the militarization of the U.S.–Mexico border. Although the project fostered the translocal connections among Oaxacan migrants in Poughkeepsie and members of their communities of origin in La Ciénega, it also highlighted the separation between these communities. While it was not the intention of the organizers of the Communities without Borders project, the exhibitions of photographs by Oaxaca migrants in Poughkeepsie and their family members in La Ciénega visualized the impact of harsh U.S. immigration laws on translocal communities. These exhibitions were a response to the juridical limitations imposed upon undocumented Mexican migrants during the early 2000s, which made it difficult, if not impossible, for these individuals to visit their family members if they wanted to return to the United States.

The Communities without Borders project narrates how migrants imagine local and translocal "ways of belonging," as opposed to formalized national membership through citizenship or other "legal" statuses.[127] In this sense, this photography project was a response and a challenge to the U.S. state's construction of belonging and citizenship. In Poughkeepsie, this project contributed to the involvement of Communities without Borders participants in organizing against HR 4437, the Border Protection, Antiterrorism and Illegal Immigration Act (or the Sensenbrenner-King Act). Although participants in the Communities without Borders project in Poughkeepsie believed that the photographic workshops brought them together as a community, La Ciénega participants were also reminded of their separation from their family members in Poughkeepsie. As a result, the participants in La Ciénega were interested in directing their photographs not only to family members in Poughkeepsie, but also to broader audiences in order to bring attention to the effects of policies that compel their family members to live across national borders. Although the photographs produced by the workshop participants in Poughkeepsie and in La Ciénega enabled them to connect across national boundaries, they were also symptomatic of the obstacles faced by these community members, who are divided by a global economic system, neoliberal trade policies, and militarized national borders.

PART TWO

Documentary, Self-Representation, and "Collaborations" in the U.S.–Mexico Borderlands

CHAPTER THREE

Visible Frictions

The Border Film Project and the "Spectacle of Surveillance"

In April 2005, the Minuteman Civil Defense Corps Project, an off-shoot of the Minuteman Project, a nativist, anti-immigrant group, planned an action in Tombstone, Arizona, with the goal of attracting media attention to "illegal" immigration in the U.S.–Mexico borderlands. The self-proclaimed "Minutemen" were attempting to influence politicians considering reform of U.S. immigration policy during President George W. Bush's second term, when tensions had become increasingly fraught. Scholars including Leo Chavez have suggested that the Minutemen created a spectacle that "demarcate[d] power positions" in ways that "emphasiz[ed] the power and privileges of citizenship," while casting "illegal aliens" as "the subjects of this spectacle."[1] The Minutemen surveilled undocumented Mexican and Central American migrants using visual technologies—such as night vision cameras and unmanned aerial drones—and photographed them after they had been "caught."[2] The Minutemen's use of visual surveillance demonstrates one way in which, as Chavez argues, the Minutemen's "policing noncitizens is an act of symbolic power and violence that defined their own citizen-subject status."[3]

Also in 2005, three friends—Brett Huneycutt, Victoria Criado, and Rudy Adler—initiated the Border Film Project, which they described as a "collaborative art" project to address conflicts over U.S.–Mexico border policy.[4] The three organizers of this documentary photography project distributed disposable cameras to Mexican and Central American migrants in northern Mexico, en route to the United States, and later to members of the Minuteman Project positioned at "observation sites" along the U.S. side of the U.S.–Mexico boundary.[5] In creating the Border Film Project, these organizers focused on the perspectives of undocumented migrants and Minutemen to represent what they considered "both sides" of the immigration debate.[6] Arguably, the Border Film Project participated in the spectacle of surveillance taken up by the Minutemen and U.S. state agents in the U.S.–Mexico borderlands, perpetuating a form of social violence against undocumented Latina/o migrants.

The migrants' and Minutemen's photographs first circulated as part of an exhibition in galleries, and they were subsequently the basis for the book *Border Film Project: Photos by Migrants and Minutemen on the U.S.–Mexico Border* (2007), as well as a website. The *Border Film Project* contains photographs by undocumented migrants and by members of the Minuteman Project, and it also features excerpts from interviews with some of these individuals. The Border Film Project is one of many documentary photography projects produced over the last decade that has focused on representing migrants traveling from Mexico and Central America, but there are two qualities that differentiate it from other works.[7] The first is the project's emphasis on self-representation. The second is that the organizers featured not only migrants, but also members of the Minuteman Project, who were one of the most visible anti-immigrant groups in the United States at that time. How the organizers frame the photographs of migrants and Minutemen as self-representation—considering the mediation and curation of the exhibitions, the book, and the website—as well as their construction of a visual equivalence between these two groups is significant for understanding the inadequacies of visibility for early twenty-first-century politics of U.S. immigration.

The organizers of the Border Film Project privileged photographic self-representation as capable of transcending differences between migrants and Minutemen, as well as revealing other hidden truths. Despite the organizers' presumption that the perspectives of migrants and Minutemen needed to become more "visible" in U.S. society, undocumented Latina/o migrants were already quite perceptible in the eyes of U.S. state agents during the project's production. Indeed, the legal and political consequences of this visibility speak to the differences between these two groups. The organizers viewed their act of giving cameras to migrants and Minutemen as humanitarian, because they believed that it enabled their subjects to visually portray elements of their lives. In doing so, however, the Border Film Project reproduced the Minutemen's "national" gaze, aligned with those of the state agents patrolling the U.S.–Mexico boundary.[8] These images also relate to a longer history of the U.S. state's production of photographs "for repressive and often racialized purposes of criminal identification," as Anna Pegler-Gordon describes.[9] This chapter explores the implications of using photography to *document* Mexican and Central American migrants' *"illegal"* passage into the United States within the context of the federal government's emphasis on national security in the post-9/11 era.

The images produced by migrants and Minutemen are informed by the technology of the disposable camera as well as by the photographers' positions as visitors to the areas they document. In addition to documentary, personal, and snapshot photography, the images by migrants and Minutemen also employ elements of landscape and portrait photography. Unlike the participants in Unseen America workshops, the photographers (migrants and Minutemen) who participated in the Border Film Project took photographs to record "significant" events, rather than aspects of their "everyday" life. These events include the Minutemen's "guarding" of the U.S. side of the U.S.–Mexico boundary and Mexican and Central American migrants' documenting their journey through remote areas in the U.S.–Mexico borderlands.

While the Minutemen's images mix documentary and snapshot aesthetics, they do not employ snapshot aesthetics in their photographs of migrants, which would have necessitated the migrants' acquiescence. Instead, their photographs of migrants relate to the U.S. state's history of using documentary photography for "managing populations" that perpetuates a state-aligned and surveillance-oriented gaze.[10] In the migrants' own photographs, they combine documentary and snapshot aesthetics to represent their journeys, which also narrate the effects of U.S. immigration law and U.S. border militarization. The migrants' images make visible the effects of these laws—specifically U.S. border policies as forms of structural and institutional violence. In addition, they photograph themselves crossing the U.S.–Mexico border, which are visual forms of "migrant counter-conducts," in which they contest their exclusion and criminalization. In taking these photographs, they also counter the spectacle of surveillance that marks undocumented migrants as "illegal aliens."

Although the Minutemen's photographs of migrants relate to repressive purposes, Mexican and Central American migrants' images challenge representations of unauthorized migrants in the mainstream media, in which the cameras are aligned with the perspective of state agents. Jodie Lawston and Ruben Murillo note that two images of undocumented Latina/o migrants have been widely disseminated in the mainstream media in recent years: the first "portrays a group of dark, shadowy figures sneaking across the U.S.–Mexico border," while the second shows "undocumented immigrants in detention, handcuffed or shackled, being escorted into the back of the Border Patrol truck." In both of these images, migrants are viewed "through the lens of criminalization."[11] The images produced by migrants as part of the Border Film Project counter the spectacular coverage of migrant apprehension as portrayed in the mainstream media, as well as by state agencies policing the false specter of undocumented Latina/o migrants through inflated claims of danger. The conventions of mainstream news coverage and the lens of state power articulate two modes of representation—one sensationalized, the other a method of visual apprehension and capture. As opposed to these dominant forms of looking relations, the migrants' images center their points of view as forms of counter-knowledge and counter-representation.

This chapter studies how photographic representations of undocumented migrants and Minutemen are framed through exhibitions as well as in the *Border Film Project* and how they are shaped by unequal relations of power. For example, this chapter analyzes the efforts of the organizers to provide supposedly equal representation and to construct a pictorial equivalence between migrants and Minutemen in the *Border Film Project*. These visual arrangements appear to be intended to convey a parallel between these groups. The artifice of equality and equivalence deployed visually relates to the liberal humanist perspective that informs the work of the *Border Film Project* in the construction of an ostensibly neutral "middle ground" between these two groups, as it disavows the curatorial logic of the project's organizers. In order to make an equivalence between images of migrants and Minutemen the organizers disappear the terms through which the images operate. However, the migrants' images unsettle this emphasis of the *Border Film Project* through an implicit critique of its normative terms. The cumulative effect of the migrants' photographs is to make visible their political and material circumstances as well as the structural violence produced as a result of U.S. border policy.

In analyzing the *Border Film Project*, I focus on the ways in which the organizers attempt to represent their position as the rational center in the U.S. border policy debate, at the same time that they also take up a particular perspective—one that resembles what Nicholas De Genova describes as "an effect of the nativist presuppositions of U.S. nationalism."[12] As opposed to John Higham, who characterized nativism as "intense opposition to an internal minority on the ground of its foreign (i.e., 'un-American') connections," De Genova defines this perspective as a "preoccupation with the 'native-ness' of U.S. citizens, and the promotion of the priority of the latter—exclusively on the grounds of being 'native.'"[13] In the *Border Film Project,* the organizers take up a "nativist point of view" by glossing over power differentials between U.S. citizens and undocumented Latina/o migrants. This is also illustrated in the organizers' portrayal of the migration of Mexicans and Central Americans to the United States as related to "illegal" immigration, and in the organization of images in the exhibitions, in which migrants are represented as moving through space. This contrasts with the Minutemen's portrayal of themselves as "citizens" guarding the border and as "authentic" Americans through their association with the land.

I begin by historicizing the rise in U.S. border militarization in the 1990s, as well as by contextualizing the work of the Border Film Project during George W. Bush's second term, when groups like the Minuteman Project became increasingly influential. The organizers' decision to include migrants and Minutemen (and not others) speaks of their choice

to represent these groups as furthest out on the political spectrum on
U.S. border policy, making absent the role of the U.S. state. In the remainder of the chapter I analyze the inclusion of photographs produced
by migrants and Minutemen in an exhibition at the Scottsdale Museum
of Contemporary Art (SMoCA) and the development of the Border Film
Project as a book and website. Part of the larger issue in the production
of the *Border Film Project* is that rather than pointing to the conditions
that contribute to migration, the organizers reproduced the spectacle of
the U.S. state's (and the Minutemen's) surveillance of migrants by representing them through the lens of criminality.[14] However, I also contend that the migrants' photographs confront the "border spectacle"
deployed by the Minutemen as well as state agents by offering alternative "ways of seeing" that make visible the effects of U.S. border policy
on undocumented migrants. As I argue in the conclusion of this chapter, unfortunately, in the context of the exhibition, the *Border Film Project*
book, and website, the migrants' "ways of seeing" are circumscribed by
the logic of the project.

The Rise of Militarized Policing in the U.S.–Mexico Borderlands

The increased militarization of the U.S.–Mexico border and criminalization of undocumented migrants during the turn of the twenty-first century is a critical context for analyzing the self-representation of migrants
and Minutemen in the Border Film Project. Starting in the 1990s, the
Immigration and Naturalization Service (INS) established a number of
policies, including "Hold the Line," "Gatekeeper," "Lower Rio Grande,"
and "Safeguard," on the southern boundaries of the U.S. border states.
According to Roxanne Lynn Doty, these operations—which placed Border Patrol agents in the places where Mexican and Central American
migrants crossed most often—emerged as the "'immigration problem'
was gaining consensus across the political spectrum."[15] Joseph Nevins
relates the increase in militarized policing in the U.S.–Mexico borderlands that began in the 1990s to "new ways of seeing."[16] In his book
Operation Gatekeeper, Nevins questions "why unauthorized immigration
became a 'problem' of crisis proportions":

This nation-state-building project, and its associated process of what we might call the "illegalization" of unauthorized entrance, required the conquest of territory and the pacification of populations on both sides of the U.S.–Mexico boundary. . . . In doing so, the state helped to create new ways of seeing among the populations affected by these developments, involving perceptions of territory and social identities as well as associated practices. These new ways of seeing were inextricably tied to evolving and hierarchical notions and practices regarding race, class, gender, and geographical origins—especially as they related to the American "nation."[17]

Numerous scholars have written about the militarization of the U.S.–Mexico boundary in the 1990s, which included what Gilberto Rosas has referred to as "spectacular displays of state power," including increases in surveillance cameras and in Border Patrol personnel, causing undocumented migrants to cross in more dangerous and remote areas.[18] Since the late 1990s, southern Arizona has been the center of unauthorized migration and border enforcement.[19] Migrants were forced to travel through isolated stretches of the desert in Cochise County, the Altar Valley in Arizona, and the Tohono O'odham Nation. Between 1994 and 2009, over five thousand migrants died en route to the United States, including many who journeyed through these remote desert areas.[20]

The post-9/11 context—and specifically the ways in which "migrant illegality" has been represented—is central to understanding the Border Film Project.[21] As De Genova notes, "With the advent of the antiterrorism state, the politics of immigration and border enforcement in the US have been profoundly reconfigured under the aegis of a remarkably parochial US nationalism and an unbridled nativism, above all manifest in the complete absorption of the INS into the new Department of Homeland Security."[22] Alicia Schmidt Camacho adds that the "security mandates" of the Department of Homeland Security "have made antiterrorism a new discourse for the surveillance of migrants and management of the southern boundary."[23] As I noted in the introduction to this book, the 2006 Secure Fence Act (HR 6061) was created during George W. Bush's second term in office in efforts to stop terrorism and "illegal" immigration, and it led to the construction of 700 miles of fencing along sections of the U.S. border with Mexico.[24] The Bush administration also doubled the size of the Border Patrol in 2006, making it the largest U.S. law enforcement agency.

The Minuteman Project—and the group's influence on the U.S. government during Bush's second term in office—is also essential to understanding the Border Film Project. During this time, the Minutemen received support not only from the Department of Homeland Security and the Border Patrol, but also from members of Congress, most notably Republican Tom Tancredo of Colorado, the head of the congressional Immigration Reform Caucus.[25] Jane Juffer argues that the figure of the Minuteman became "mainstreamed" during these years, appearing as a helpful citizen "volunteering" to guard the border, rather than as a vigilante who would "take the law into his own hands and punish the 'illegal aliens' who can be easily lumped together with terrorists."[26] Roxanne Doty has related the success of the Minutemen's legitimating activities to their influence on federal governmental agencies.[27] In May 2005, when the U.S. House Committee on Government Reform held a hearing on border security, the national president of the Border Patrol Council lauded the work of the Minutemen along the border.[28] In addition, Doty suggests that the Minutemen Civil Defense Corps Project cofounder Chris Simcox's announcement that the group would build a border security fence unless the White House positioned military reserves or the National Guard there led to President Bush's plan to deploy six hundred National Guard troops to the border.[29] In 2005, both New Mexico governor Bill Richardson and Arizona governor Janet Napolitano adopted the anti-immigrant discourse of the Minutemen regarding the "crisis" on the border.[30]

The influence of nonstate actors on the state exemplifies what Doty terms "statecraft from below." Doty argues that this challenges our understanding of how "sovereign authority and power work, and where or in whom they are located."[31] In her analysis of anti-immigrant groups like the Minutemen, Doty focuses on the central theme of sovereignty, one element of which is the politics of exceptionalism. She argues, "*Exceptionalism* refers to those political situations in which individuals and groups are turned into an *exception* by the exercise of sovereign power, resulting in their exclusion from basic rights guaranteed by the law or the constitution." In addition to being enacted at different levels of government—local, state, and federal—she contends that "citizens [such as the Minutemen] can engage in a politics of exceptionalism that feeds into official government action."[32] Doty suggests that the politics of exceptionalism are practiced by anti-immigrant groups in coordination with the U.S. state, in such a way that has "resulted in widespread and focused attention on distinctions between citizens and noncitizens, which in turn legitimates the exclusion and marginalization of some and quite often entails the demonization of noncitizens."[33] Further, Gilberto Rosas has argued that "the racism embedded in 'immigrant' exceptionality becomes increasingly transparent" in groups such as the Minuteman Project, Ranch Rescue, and American Border Patrol.[34] However, it should be noted that the practices of these anti-immigrant groups were in line with those of state agents, including Sheriff Joe Arpaio and his deputies in Maricopa County, Arizona.[35]

In 2005, when the Border Film Project was being produced, anti-immigrant vigilante groups were using a range of state surveillance technologies to track undocumented migrants whom they detained, placed under armed guard, and photographed while waiting for the Border Patrol.[36] The Minutemen and members of other anti-immigrant groups used photography both as a form of surveillance and—like hunters or fishermen—as a way to document their "catch" as trophies. Undocumented migrants had little recourse if the Minutemen or other groups photographed them. The migrants often believed that the Minutemen were agents of the U.S. state, since they typically dressed in uniforms that were similar to those of Border Patrol agents. The Minutemen's use of cameras was sometimes more directly abusive, such as when members of the group (including a man named Bryan Barton) forced the Mexican migrant they were detaining to hold a T-shirt that read, "Bryan Barton caught an illegal alien and all he got was this lousy T-shirt."[37] In this context, using cameras to surveil migrants functioned as an extreme form of objectification. However, the Minutemen's use of cameras both to track and to document migrants is more acceptable to the public than their history of physically assaulting undocumented migrants, legal residents, and U.S. citizens of Latina/o descent.[38] Since this relationship of Minutemen and undocumented migrants existed previous to the development of the Border Film Project, it informs the way in which these images can be interpreted.

Marking Boundaries: Migrants, Minutemen, and the U.S.–Mexico Borderlands

The Border Film Project was conceived by three friends in their mid-twenties—Brett Huneycutt, Victoria Criado, and Rudy Adler—during the summer of 2005. Huneycutt and Adler had grown up together in Phoenix, and they envisioned creating a documentary film that would "shed light on the issue of 'illegal' immigration," primarily on the U.S.–Mexico boundary.[39] Both Huneycutt and Criado were recent graduates of Boston College. Huneycutt studied economics, and Criado majored in political science. Adler had recently graduated from University of Arizona, from which he received a finance and entrepreneurship degree. Previous to his involvement with the Border Film Project, Huneycutt had received a Fulbright to research migration from El Salvador. According to Huneycutt's biography on the Border Film Project website, he also "organized seminars on the U.S.–Mexico border, an immersion experience to a Zapatista refugee camp in Chiapas and dental clinics in two rural Salvadoran villages." Criado also led immersion trips to Tijuana, Mexico, that focused on immigration and the U.S.–Mexico border. Prior to her involvement in the Border Film Project, Criado worked as a Latin American market analyst for Deutsche Bank in New York. Meanwhile, Adler had been an intern at W+K 12, an ad agency within Wieden + Kennedy, where he worked on "ad campaigns, films and art shows for companies with a social conscience."[40] The Border Film Project—which cost around $10,000—was self-funded: the organizers drew from their savings accounts as well as credit cards.[41]

Huneycutt, Criado, and Adler began their work on the film by visiting border towns in Mexico and interviewing migrants and human rights workers. Over time, they also interviewed Border Patrol agents, members of the Minuteman Project, and politicians, such as Senator John

McCain, who were focused on immigration issues. Once they had compiled about sixty hours of footage, they were unsure what to do with it. Instead of editing this footage into a documentary film, they imagined a project modeled on one Adler had worked on at an advertising agency. This project entailed giving disposable cameras to people all over the world and instructing them to "take pictures of things you think are perfect."[42] Huneycutt, Criado, and Adler's project involved distributing disposable cameras to migrants in Mexico before they crossed the U.S.–Mexico boundary who could "document the border" through their own eyes.[43] Criado noted in an interview, "We realized that we were lacking the perspective of the people who are living this reality every day."[44] The organizers believed that the project would "simplify the complexities of immigration and the U.S.–Mexico border and show the reality on the ground."[45] The organizers stated in an interview that they developed the project because their "journey is something we can't document," and they believed that "migrants can best document [it] themselves."[46] They initially titled the project "Documenting the Undocumented," and their stated goal was "to show the journey without it being tainted by our own perspective and by just our presence there."[47]

To distribute the cameras, Huneycutt, Criado, and Adler visited migrant shelters and humanitarian organizations in Altar, Sonora, and other towns in northern border states in Mexico.[48] (Altar is one of the main locations to which migrants travel before heading to the United States.) Some of these individuals had previously been deported and they were attempting to make the trip again. The organizers taught migrants how to use disposable cameras and explained how to mail them back once they were in the United States. They told migrants to document anything that they found significant, the people with whom they traveled, and "the challenging parts of the trip, the obstacles and the victorious moments."[49] However, they also included instructions that informed them: "No saque fotos de la patrulla fronteriza ni ningún policía" (Do not take pictures of border patrol or any police). During their first attempt at this project, the organizers handed out one hundred cameras but received only one back. After the fact, they realized that asking migrants to provide their addresses in Mexico or the United States might have deterred them from participating.[50] The next time the organizers handed out cameras, they did not ask for the migrants' addresses. Instead, in exchange for mailing back their disposable cameras, the organizers gave out $25 gift cards for Walmart. Criado noted that the migrants "seem[ed] really interested in the political ramifications this [the project] could have."[51] Some migrants could not participate, however, because their smugglers would not allow it, which speaks to the dangers of documenting their journey.

The organizers' initial purpose for the film and photography project was "to raise awareness about what migrants go through to come to this country," yet by including the Minutemen in what became known as the Border Film Project, the organizers transferred some of their ideas about "re-humanizing" migrants to members of the Minuteman Project.[52] Approximately six weeks after Huneycutt, Criado, and Adler distributed cameras to migrants, they spent a few weeks giving them to members of the Minuteman Project along the U.S. side of the border. In an interview that addressed the organizers' decision to include the Minutemen, Criado noted that both migrants and Minutemen "are the groups that are living this reality and who better to tell the history of the border but the people who are living it?"[53] The organizers distributed cameras at the Minutemen's "observation sites" near the U.S.–Mexico boundary in Arizona, New Mexico, and California. They told the Minutemen that if they mailed back their cameras, they would receive a $25 Shell gift card. The Minutemen were asked to fill out a card with the camera, which included their names, addresses, ages, phone numbers, e-mail addresses, hometowns, and observation sites. These individuals could also indicate if they wanted copies of the pictures and were asked whether the organizers could display their first name, age, and hometown when they exhibited the images.

Although including photographs by migrants and Minutemen seems to be an unlikely combination (and according to the organizers, was opposed by both groups), the organizers justified their decision by connecting the ways in which migrants and Minutemen were both portrayed in the media. Specifically, Huneycutt noted, "Both the Minutemen and migrants are often caricatured. . . . The Minutemen are caricatured as gun-toting vigilantes. The migrants are caricatured as people who come to take advantage of welfare or steal American jobs."[54] Huneycutt stated in another interview, "The migrants are really just hard-working people who are coming to help out their families . . . and the Minutemen are concerned citizens who are worried about national security and saving American jobs."[55] Making connections between the experiences of migrants and those of the Minutemen informed the Border Film Project's exhibitions, book, and website.

By 2007 the organizers had received seventy-three cameras—thirty-eight from migrants and thirty-five from Minutemen—that held around two thousand photographs.[56] Both the migrants and the Minutemen were constrained by the technological limitations of the disposable camera, which produced a different aesthetic than that of professional documentary photographers. For example, the absence of an adjustable lens prevented the participants from taking close-ups or wide-angle shots. Also, since they returned the cameras to the organizers before processing, the participants could not further shape the images after they had taken the photographs. They could not crop or retouch the photographs, nor could they select particular images and dispose of others. As a result, some of the photographs appear much like informal snapshots. Catherine Zuromskis notes that the snapshot genre is generally viewed as "innocent or naïve," and this notion is "further reinforced by the understood documentary truth of the photographic image."[57] Both the form of self-representation and the presumably unselfconscious "snapshots" of migrants and Minutemen are intended to signify "reality" to the viewer.

Although the organizers were interested in presenting both the migrants' and Minutemen's views of "the border," these photographs do not represent the participants' "everyday" lives, but rather their engagement in *significant* events. These included the Minutemen's participation as "volunteers" guarding the U.S.–Mexico boundary and the migrants' journeys through the U.S.–Mexico borderlands. Individuals who live in the U.S.–Mexico borderlands, in the towns, colonias, cities, and reservations—including those from the Tohono O'odham nation—were not included in this project. Unlike those who live in the U.S.–Mexico borderlands, the migrants and Minutemen were transient. These migrants moved through the borderlands, and the Minutemen were temporary visitors "stationed" on the U.S. side.[58] In other words, the Minutemen's photographs do not document their daily lives, but rather their involvement in surveilling migrants' movements.

The Minutemen's photographs of migrants are distinct from snapshots that require the subject's consent. These photographs feature a "national gaze," as the Minutemen aligned themselves with the point of view of state agents, documenting migrants' "crimes" of attempting to enter the United States without immigration papers.[59] For example, a sequence of photographs starts with what looks to be a landscape photograph, but by the second image, it is clear that the Minuteman is documenting and surveilling migrants (Figure 15). The first image in the sequence features a figure across the road in the distance. Because the figure is so far away, it appears to be a landscape shot. In the second photograph, however, the Minuteman has approached someone who faces away from the camera but is still identifiable as a young man waiting by the road. The third photograph includes a member of the Border Patrol (at a distance) who has pulled up to the young man in his vehicle and appears to be questioning him. The final photograph is a medium shot, taken from behind the Border Patrol agent who is arresting the young man. Also visible in the frame is part of the Border Patrol's vehicle, which reads "Call Us Toll-Free 24 hours / 1–877–USBP–HELP," which relates to the Minuteman's role in contacting the Border Patrol that led to the arrest of this migrant. Although the Minuteman's images of the migrant being arrested by the Border Patrol depict the unequal power relations between the migrants and the Minutemen, his role is made absent, partly because he is not included in the photographs. This relationship between migrants and Minutemen—in which the latter attempts to make the former's "illegality" visible—is also eclipsed in the organizers' statements about the Border Film Project, to which I will return later.

As opposed to the Minutemen, undocumented Mexican and Central American migrants had a lot at risk in photographing themselves, as their main goal in crossing the U.S.–Mexico boundary was to evade detection by state agents. Unlike tourist travel, which involves the elective movement of people with the intention to return home, Mexican and

Figure 15. This series of photographs of a man on the side of the road who is apprehended by a Border Patrol officer was taken by Rick, a Minuteman. (Camera 081, distributed in Boulevard, California.) According to Rick's description of the image in *Border Film Project: Photos by Migrants and Minutemen on the U.S.–Mexico Border* (2007), he "reported migrant on highway to the Border Patrol and photographed the encounter."

Central American migrants' journeys to the United States are often motivated by desperation. Further, due to border militarization and the risks of dying en route, this journey does not always include a return home.[60] The experiences of undocumented migrants can be related to groups with little control over their movements.[61] The journeys of Mexican and Central American migrants involved moving from the "familiar to the foreign," which Alicia Schmidt Camacho has described as "a process of conversion, effected *through* violence—the sanctioned interdiction of the state, which may seize and remove migrants by its use of force or by the extralegal, informal aggressions of nonstate actors like the Arizona Minutemen."[62] Although it is generally not emphasized within the Border Film Project, here Schmidt Camacho articulates the relation of migrants and Minutemen to one another.

Both the Minutemen and migrants take up the aesthetics of snapshot and documentary photography, although for very different purposes. Migrants and Minutemen use snapshot aesthetics to photograph the members of their groups. The snapshot form is associated with documentary, and thus photographic truth, but it also involves a performance, as its aesthetic conventions include frontal images in which subjects pose for the camera. These images are generally staged, but sometimes they portray candid or intimate moments. The Minutemen's photographs of one another resemble snapshots, including Minutemen posed together, looking at the camera (Cameras 035, 071), or one in which a man wears a T-shirt that reads "Innocent Bystander" (072) and smiles for the camera.[63] In creating these photographs for the Border Film Project, the Minutemen knew that people outside the group would see them. Considering that, they did not take images that would be unacceptable to a broad audience, especially during a time when the organization was attempting to "whitewash" its image. The migrants employ conventions of snapshot photography in representing other migrants, as in photographs where their travel companions wave and smile at the camera (170, 367). However, the Minutemen did not take "snapshots" of migrants or vice versa, as one of the form's criteria involves the subject acquiescing to being photographed.

The Minutemen mix aesthetics of documentary and snapshot photography when they portray themselves performing the work of state agents. They frequently photograph one another in military garb, which suggests that they view themselves as fighting a war (072). This perspective is supported by the many photographs of Minutemen carrying weapons—especially guns—engaging in target practice, looking through binoculars, communicating with one another on walkie-talkies or CB radios, surveilling from portable towers, and "tracking" migrants (035, 051, 052, 072). Examples of the latter photographs include Minutemen surveilling migrant movement (074), reporting migrants to the Border Patrol (081, 097), or tracking migrants by their footprints or objects they left behind (051, 097).

The Minutemen's photographs of both themselves and migrants relate to how nonstate actors have assumed the state's role in an age of neoliberalism.[64] Jane Juffer argues that "the vigilante in neoliberal times functions not as a complete renegade but rather in conjunction with, or at least alongside, the government, both entities acting outside the law, in the name of the law, in order to enforce the law."[65] The Minutemen are well aware of this role. For example, the back of the commemorative T-shirt for the April 2005 Minutemen action read: "Americans doing the job government won't do."[66] Juffer views the Minuteman as a "neoliberal vigilante" who "perceives himself to be a solid citizen," as opposed to someone who operates outside the law.[67]

By relating the mainstreaming of the Minutemen to neoliberalism— as well as to President Bush's post-9/11 call on Americans to become volunteers—Juffer argues, "Volunteers operate in the territory between the state and the free and amoral exchange of the market, supplying the 'compassion' in conservatism."[68] She relates the notion of compassionate conservatism, which was dominant during the George W. Bush administration, to the Minutemen's "code of ethics," including their belief that they are performing a civic duty. The Minutemen represent themselves as patriotic "solid citizens" by volunteering on the border, where they "supply the 'compassion' in conservatism."[69]

The documentary photographs that the Minutemen take of migrants are aligned with more repressive uses, as a tool of surveillance, relating to the work of state agents. Thus, their images of migrants can be situated in a broader political context, in which members of anti-immigrant groups use imaging and surveillance technologies to harass unauthorized migrants and to make them visible to the state. The Minutemen portray the migrants as committing the crime of "illegally" crossing the U.S.–Mexico boundary, photographing migrants either being detained by a Minuteman or being apprehended by the Border Patrol (081, 097). The Minutemen do not include themselves in the photographs in which they are detaining migrants. Thus, there is no opportunity to visualize the relationship between the two groups. Instead, the Minutemen use their cameras as weapons to intimidate, and visually apprehend migrants waiting for the Border Patrol. The Minutemen's use of cameras is a form of what Justin Akers Chacón describes as "low intensity terrorism," which is similar to the ways that anti-immigrant activists use cameras to harass Latina/o migrants in public places by threatening to show the photographs to state agents.[70]

The Minutemen's photographs of themselves and undocumented migrants in the U.S.–Mexico borderlands attest to the way in which they participate in creating what De Genova refers to as the "border spectacle."[71] The Minutemen's surveillance of migrants relates to the state's role in the "legal production of Mexican/migrant illegality," which, De Genova contends, "requires the spectacle of enforcement at the U.S.–Mexico border in order for the spatialized difference between the nation-states of the U.S. and Mexico to be enduringly inscribed upon Mexican [and Central American] migrants in their spatialized (and racialized) status as 'illegal aliens.'"[72] During the early 2000s, the Minutemen, Sheriff Joseph Arpaio of Arizona, and others created a spectacle around border enforcement that was disseminated by the mainstream media.[73] This spectacle—which involved the media's taking up a "law and order" frame—emphasized "discourses of legality to target racialized immigrants," which criminalized undocumented migrants.[74] Thus, undocumented migrants have been represented as lawbreakers entering the United States illegally.[75] These perspectives, which influenced Republican politicians, led to more Border Patrol agents being stationed on the U.S.–Mexico border.[76]

The migrants and Minutemen who participated in the Border Film Project portray the landscape of the borderlands in distinct ways.[77] The Minutemen's photographs participate in the "spectacle of enforcement," which, as noted by De Genova above, emphasizes the "spatialized difference between the nation-states of the United States and Mexico."[78] Further, Joseph Nevins suggests that "frontiers, borders, and boundaries are not merely social phenomena, in a material sense they are also 'ways of seeing': metaphors for and manifestations of how we perceive the world and act within it."[79] The Minutemen shot the majority of their photographs in U.S. Southwest desert landscapes, which are characterized by open spaces. The Minutemen position themselves in these landscapes, but they exclude elements representing human presence, other than trash, which they associate with the movements of migrants. Considering Leo Chavez's point that the Minutemen's "dramatics were an attempt to reaffirm the contours of the nation-state," it is interesting that they infrequently portray border barriers in their photographs, except for the Minutemen's border fence (065, 069, 079).[80] Instead, most of their photographs focus on the U.S. border regions that they patrol.

The Minutemen's landscape photographs of the U.S. Southwest narrate anti-immigrant sentiments, referencing a longer history of the ways in which nativist movements have used images of the natural environment to gain support for their cause. Although these photographs represent Minutemen "tracking" migrants by the trash they leave behind, they also link migration and trash in the U.S.–Mexico borderlands, a trope that was common in mainstream media representations in the 1990s.[81] Sarah Hill argues the media portrayal of the U.S.–Mexico borderlands during this time was "an extreme portrait of 'matter out of place,' implicitly borne by the movement of people out of place: Mexican immigrants."[82] This emphasis on the borderlands environment was not as prominent in 2005 as it was during the 1990s, yet Hill argues that "the border and its presumed porosity and Mexican immigration have become even more exploited by nativists; in recent years 'pollution' continues to appear in the litany of offenses committed by immigrants who breach the border with their 'assaults.'"[83] This association between "trash" and migration informs the Minutemen's photographs of the borderlands.

The Minutemen associate migrants with the trash they leave behind as "matter out of place."[84] These photographs focus on the garbage left by migrants as they moved through the desert, highlighting items of refuse—such as water bottles (081, 247) or discarded deodorant (051)— in an otherwise "natural" environment. In the latter photograph, a man wearing a cowboy hat, moccasins (with a knife stuck in them), and a handstitched buckskin jacket smiles at the camera, while squatting and pointing to the deodorant left in the desert scrub. The image draws upon conventions of documentary photography, particularly the use of the camera to surveil migrants and provide evidence of their presence where they are not "allowed." The picture also contains elements of snapshot photography, as this man's smile (or smirk) indicates that he knows the photographer. Specifically, his facial expression suggests an intimate exchange between two people with a similar understanding of this piece of "trash" as providing "evidence" of the unwanted presence of migrants in the landscape.

In the migrants' photographs, they portray objects such as water bottles not as refuse but as necessities that they need in order for them to survive. Due to the increase in border militarization in the ten years prior to the Border Film Project, migrants had to travel by increasingly dangerous routes to evade detection, and they frequently lacked water and food. One major problem was staying hydrated, and a leading cause of death during the migrants' journey was dehydration. Some of the migrants' images include their travel companions drinking from water stations left for them by humanitarian groups (189) or from water troughs intended for animals (238). In the latter case, their drinking from a trough attests to their desperation and the extreme conditions they faced on their journey. They also document other migrants carrying gallons of water through the desert, as well as children holding water bottles (606) and a Pedialyte bottle on the ground (247), attesting to the young age of some who make this perilous journey.

While Nicholas De Genova argues that "the elusiveness of the law, and its relative invisibility in producing 'illegality,' requires this spectacle of 'enforcement' at the border," in their photographs, migrants represent alternative "ways of seeing" the effects of U.S. immigration law on undocumented migrants, and as such make the violence of the law visible.[85] In documenting their journey through the desert, migrants provide evidence of the effects of border policing and militarization, which led to their traveling dangerous routes, risking injury and death.[86] Migrants portray themselves in landscapes that are both open and "littered" with obstacles through which they must move. Many of the migrants' photographs depict their movement around these obstacles, including fences or walls, over which they have to climb (170, 363, 601, 602, 121). Migrants photograph signs indicating that trespassers will be prosecuted (361), and they portray their walking for miles through remote areas (238), climbing over barbed-wire fences, scaling walls (601), and sustaining injuries while doing so (152). Some migrants also photograph official government signs indicating their entry into the United States, including one that reads "Bienvenidos a Douglas, AZ" (367), as well as a banner outside a post office that advertises the availability of passport applications (379).

The migrants' photographs make visible the effects of U.S. border policy and policing and represent visual forms of migrant counter-conducts. Their images exemplify what Catherine Zuromskis refers to as "alternative snapshot practices," in which migrants document their "surreptitious" travels through the U.S.–Mexico borderlands.[87] Along with representing migrants' movement, their images document more sedentary moments, as well as instances when their journeys were interrupted. These photographs portray migrants with serious injuries (121) or who encounter state agents, including one image of a Border Patrol helicopter descending near the migrant who documented it overhead (202) (Figure 16). The image of the helicopter—which, according to the organizers, was the last one on the roll—represents "something that cannot be seen," specifically migrant apprehension near the U.S.–Mexico boundary from

Figure 16. This photograph of a Border Patrol helicopter in close range was taken by a migrant in the U.S.–Mexico borderlands. (Camera 202, anonymous, distributed in Agua Prieta, Sonora.) From *Border Film Project: Photos by Migrants and Minutemen on the U.S.–Mexico Border* (2007).

the point of view of an undocumented migrant. This image shows a migrant returning the gaze of the state, rather than being surveilled from the state agents' point of view. Portraying the experience of migrant apprehension from the perspective of an undocumented migrant—rather than from the state agent's point of view—is a visual form of a migrant counter-conduct, as it contests the exclusion of undocumented migrants from the United States, as well as the ways in which they are criminalized. Although this photograph documenting the surveillance of state agents was returned to the Border Film Project organizers, it raises questions about the limits of undocumented migrants' using cameras against the "state's gatekeepers and surveillance systems."[88]

Further, the migrants' photographs narrate what Alicia Schmidt Camacho calls the "melancholic aspect of the journey north," which she argues has "put the tale of the enterprising migrant 'seeking a better life' in crisis."[89] For example, their images portray other migrants waiting at shelters (189), anxiously waiting for rides (207, 210), or in a Border Patrol bus after being apprehended (145). One migrant's photograph focuses on an impediment, a barbed-wire fence, which has a carcass of a small animal entangled in it (377). The photograph was taken at an angle, so the fence and image are not parallel, making the photograph appear askew. Beyond the fence is the United States, represented by an American flag waving in front of some buildings. The bottom of the flagpole touches the very top of the barbed-wire fence that connects them to one another. What is distinctive about this photograph is that the migrant took it standing behind the wire fence, which separated this individual from the United States. The mangled carcass relates to the risks that migrants take to get to the United States, but also fears regarding what they might encounter in the United States.

The migrants' photographs make the effects of U.S. border policies visible by representing those who perished while attempting to reach the United States. Although "photography is the medium of appearance," as Peter Osborne has noted, migrants depict the U.S.–Mexico borderlands as a site of *disappearance* for undocumented migrants.[90] In fact, the term *desaparecido* (disappeared) is what is used to describe "those who set up to cross the border but are never heard from again."[91] Migrants portray other migrants' deaths through images of crosses. Many took photographs of handmade crosses at border towns including one of a cross on the border fence (120). These images included statements—like "Van más de 2,500. ¿Cuántos Más?" (There are more than 2,500. How many more?)—that challenge the conditions that lead to migrant death. Although many migrants photographed crosses marking where other migrants perished, the majority of these images were not exhibited or included in the book.[92] These images of crosses represent an alternative "way of seeing" the effects of border militarization and the policing of migrants by the Border Patrol and the Minutemen, which led to more migrant deaths.[93] These photographs, in which migrants represent the disappearances of other migrants and bear witness to their deaths also "constitute a political act" that confronts the border spectacle produced by the Minutemen as well as U.S. state agents by exposing its effects on undocumented migrants.[94]

Curating the "Border Film Project: El Proyecto Fronterizo Fotográfico" at SMoCA

While Huneycutt, Criado, and Adler were waiting to receive the cameras back from the migrants, they began to contact galleries and museums about exhibiting these photographs in a show they titled *Documenting the Undocumented*. Although it was not intentional, the title implicitly references the organizers' involvement in mediating these photographs. The title does not indicate that the undocumented are "documenting" themselves, but instead that the organizers "document the undocumented" through their distribution of the cameras and their collection of the images. The title also aligns the organizers with state agents who document the undocumented. This project appealed to galleries and museums because of its emphasis on the self-representation of migrants. In speaking about the interest shown in the photography project, Adler stated that "it's been an easy sell. . . . It's amazing how just the simple idea of passing out cameras to migrants seems to capture everyone's imagination."[95] Further, the project acquired another appealing dimension in its representation of "both sides," when the organizers began to distribute cameras to Minutemen.

The emphasis on representing "both sides" was important to the curators at SMoCA, which held the first major exhibition of this work. As Huneycutt, Criado, and Adler were developing the images by migrants and Minutemen, they imagined their audience as comprised of those on the "left" and the "right," as well as individuals who had no opinion about undocumented migrants or anti-immigrant organizations.[96] SMoCA curator Marilu Knode commented that "being more open, allowing conflicting opinions to exist is important for all of us in this complex world."[97] This viewpoint informed many aspects of the project, including how the photographs were framed in exhibitions, in the *Border Film Project* book, and on the Border Film Project's website.[98] Over time, however, the organizers began to focus more on emphasizing the similarities between migrants and Minutemen.

After Huneycutt, Criado, and Adler received a substantial number of cameras back from the migrants and the Minutemen, they selected which photographs would be exhibited. The Border Film Project held numerous exhibitions in galleries, bookstores, museums, and universities across the United States. The first major exhibition of the Border Film Project was held at SMoCA, which was titled *Border Film Project: El Proyecto Fronterizo Fotográfico*. The exhibition traveled to other sites, including DiverseWorks in Houston, Texas.[99] Although it was unusual for SMoCA to create an exhibition based on an unsolicited proposal, museum staff members were interested in the Border Film Project, due to its relevance for Arizona residents.[100] As curator Cassandra Coblentz explained, "More undocumented migrants cross the border into Arizona than any other state in the country, and it's an issue that's a priority for many people."[101] The installation was designed by Ibarra Rosano Design architects in Tucson, in consultation with the museum staff, and it was "inspired by the border shadows—both literal and metaphoric."[102] The photographs and the video—which the organizers compiled based on interviews they conducted—were positioned within the inner spaces, while the outer walls served as a divider, similar to a border fence. Toward the exit, the curators included an interactive element to the exhibition, posing questions to viewers on a wall, including: "What commonalities did you notice in viewing the photographs taken by Minutemen and the migrants?" "If the border is broken, how can it be fixed?" "How might you answer this question differently if you were born on the other side?"[103] In addition, the curators indicated that viewers could share their own immigration stories and write their comments on notecards that were posted on a magnet board.[104] The curators positioned quotations from migrants and Minutemen on the outer wall of the exhibition. All of the quotations were paired (one migrant, one Minuteman) and were presented in both English and Spanish.

Although the organizers selected the photographs that would be shown in the exhibition, it was the curators who arranged them in the installation. Of the 2,000 color photographs that the organizers received from migrants and Minutemen, they chose around 250 to include in the exhibition. These images were mounted as four-by-six-inch prints, without accompanying names or descriptions, and were displayed in the middle circle of the room. Coblentz explained that they did not enlarge the majority of the photographs because the scale reminded the audience about the source of the images—as snapshot photographs taken from disposable cameras.[105] The curators did enlarge a few of the photographs, including one portrait of a Minuteman's face against the blue sky and one of a migrant climbing over a fence, which they positioned around the walls of the installation space. These curatorial decisions—including the lack of text accompanying the images—relate to the organizers' perspective that the project "allows the migrants and the Minutemen to speak for themselves."[106] However, the exhibit narrates the organizers' view that, as Huneycutt stated, "there is truth on both sides of the immigration issue, and the solution undoubtedly lies somewhere in the middle."[107] In addition to the photographs, the video that was included in the exhibition featured interviews with migrants and Minutemen, but unlike a conventional documentary, it had neither a voice-over narrating the film, nor any interviews with "experts."

What gets obfuscated in displaying these photographic forms of self-representation is the role of the Border Film Project organizers and the SMoCA curators in shaping the exhibition. Although the Border Film Project highlighted the perspectives of migrants and Minutemen because they took the photographs, these individuals did not select, nor did they arrange, the images. The organizers developed the Border Film Project from an archive of two thousand photographs taken by migrants and Minutemen, which reflects Allan Sekula's statement that "archives . . . constitute a *territory of images*; the unity of an archive is first and foremost that imposed by ownership."[108] By exchanging their disposable cameras for Shell or Walmart cards, the migrants and Minutemen relinquished their ownership of the photographs and their control over the organization and circulation of those images.

Further, in their acquisition of these images, the Border Film Project organizers made invisible the specific uses and meanings of these images for these groups. As Sekula argues, "In an archive, the possibility of meaning is 'liberated' from the actual contingencies of use," and this "abstraction from the complexity and richness of use, a loss of context," certainly applies in the case of the Border Film Project.[109] The "uses" of the Minutemen's photographs—which are related to their surveillance and policing of undocumented migrants—are made absent in the Border Film Project, as are the meanings associated with the migrants' images of crosses documenting migrant death.

The organizers chose which of the two thousand images from the Border Film Project archive would be included in the exhibition, but the curators arranged the images, directing audience members through the exhibition by grouping photographs of migrants and Minutemen, while mostly separating them from one another. The curators' decision to set the images of migrants apart from those of the Minutemen relates to the organizers' emphasis on representing "both sides," while failing to make a connection between these two groups or to address the broader issues that contribute to migration. Some reviewers of the exhibition criticized the arrangement of images, specifically the photographs' isolation from one another. Chris Kraus related this decision to the ways in which the "work's creators cautiously cast their endeavor in the pseudo-neutrality of humanism," which prevented the organizers and curators of the exhibition from presenting an analysis of the causes of migration.[110] Although neither migrants nor Minutemen inhabited the areas that they photographed, the curators represent Mexican and Central American migrants' images in such a way that these individuals are portrayed as *moving through* the borderlands, while they envision the

Minutemen as "*settled*" on the U.S. side of the border. Even though these characteristics emerge from the photographs, the curators also *emphasize* these elements through their display.

The curators' arrangement of photographs by migrants relates to what Alicia Schmidt Camacho has described as "the tale of the enterprising migrant 'seeking a better life,'" by focusing on migrants' successful travels to the United States.[111] Some of the migrants' images were displayed as a photo collage, so viewers could see the specific journeys of the photographers. These collages were comprised of images that document migrants' trips, which started where they received their cameras in northern Mexico border towns, through the desert landscapes of the U.S.–Mexico borderlands, with some ending up at the U.S.–Mexico boundary or in towns in the U.S. Southwest. For example, the curators reconstructed the journey of two migrants walking through the desert and ending up in a border town, presumably in the United States (Figure 17). Re-created in this way, this grouping of photographs visualizes the journey in a way that individual photographs could not. However, while elements of the migrants' journeys were assembled in the form of photo collages, both the organizers and the curators deemphasized other possible outcomes of migrants' journeys, specifically migrant death. Although migrants sent back many photographs of crosses marking the places where migrants had died, few of them were included in the exhibitions or in the book or website.[112] The decision not to include these images may be related to curatorial preferences, but it also speaks to the Border Film Project's emphasis on making absent the role of the U.S. state in causing migrant deaths, as well as the actual relationships of migrants and Minutemen.

The issues concerning the display of photographs in the Border Film Project are similar to those of the Unseen America workshops that I analyzed in the first two chapters. However, in every exhibition of the Border Film Project, these images were addressed to an audience beyond the communities of those who took the pictures.[113] These photographs were taken with disposable cameras, which are associated with forms of photography that normally would dictate inclusion in a personal album, to be viewed by an "intimate public." By being exhibited, included in a book and on a website, these images became available to a broader

Figure 17. Installation view of "The Border Film Project: El Proyecto Fronterizo Fotográfico" on view at the Scottsdale Museum of Contemporary Art (SMoCA), September 16, 2006–January 28, 2007. Copyright SMoCA.

audience. As Patricia Holland has argued, "insiders'" experiences of personal images can be distinguished from those of "outsiders."[114] These differences become apparent in these photographs that are characterized by the amateur quality of snapshots, which associates them with personal use, when they appear in a museum context where they are on display for aesthetic purposes.[115] In this in-stitutional context both the Minutemen and migrants fall within the category of "naïve" artists, which also exposes the differences between the social class and cultural capital of the photographers as opposed to those of the Border Film Project organizers.

Although the exhibition of the Border Film Project at SMoCA was directed toward a general audience, in interviews the organizers stated that they would like members of both groups to see these images on display. The organizers believed that bringing the migrants and Minutemen together would allow the members of these groups to "be in the same room together" and to "come together to see each other's perspectives."[116] Since the organizers had not asked for the addresses of the migrants—

only those of the Minutemen—it was not possible for them to reach out to the migrants. It does not appear as if the organizers recognized the accessibility issues for migrants in attending the exhibition. Of the two groups, only Minutemen were reported as seeing the exhibition.

The organizers' statements imply that if migrants and Minutemen attended the exhibition, they would understand each other's views.[117] In envisioning viewership in this way, the Border Film Project organizers failed to account for the antagonistic gazes of migrants and Minutemen. Just as the Minutemen could look at migrants' photographs and see "illegal" immigrants entering "their" country, migrants could see the Minutemen's photographs and feel threatened by their performance of "native-ness"—as U.S. citizens acting in the name of the state. Thus, in their display of images from the Border Film Project archive the organizers do not account for what Allan Sekula has referred to as the "radical antagonisms" between gazes, in this case of migrants and Minutemen.[118]

Although there were critical reviews of the Border Film Project exhibitions, the theme—to represent "both sides" of the debate on U.S. border policy—was positively referenced in numerous reviews.[119] In the show at SMoCA, this element was frequently related to attendees' comments. For example, one review included a statement made by a visitor to the museum who noted that "the images—which range from blistered migrant feet to people standing in the desert to Minuteman volunteers on patrol—make it an important exhibit that represents both sides of the issue."[120] In interviews, both the organizers of the Border Film Project and curators at SMoCA highlighted commonalities between the images of the migrants and those of the Minutemen.[121] Some reviews of the exhibition noted that the photographs of migrants and Minutemen had similar characteristics.[122] This theme—to emphasize the shared characteristics of the migrants and Minutemen—was further developed in the *Border Film Project* book and website.

Truth-Claims of the Visible and the Artifice of Equality

During the exhibition at SMoCA, the organizers were at work on a book, the *Border Film Project*, which was published in 2007. There are numerous similarities between the book and the exhibition, including the organizers' emphasis on the transparent meanings of photographic self-representation and their downplaying of their curatorial imprint on the book's production. Similar to the SMoCA exhibition, of the two thousand photographs from migrants and Minutemen, they used less than 10 percent in the *Border Film Project*. However, unlike the exhibition, which had no names attached to the images, the book's images are numbered and correspond to a table in the center of the book that contains information about the people who took the photographs, including names and the locations where they picked up their cameras. The organizers also paired some photographs with short quotations from interviews they conducted with migrants and Minutemen.[123] In addition to the quotations from interviews, the organizers included two statements—one on the "Project Background" of the Border Film Project and the other on the topic of "The U.S.–Mexico Border"—both of which are positioned in the center of the book.

The *Border Film Project*, published only in English, is an art photography book composed of the work of migrants and Minutemen. The book was sold at museum gift shops, at retail stores including Urban Outfitters, American Apparel, and elsewhere, and directed toward a U.S. middle-class audience. The address to a U.S. audience is evident in the organizers' statement that the book represents the "human face of immigration," in order to "challenge *us* to question *our* stereotypes" (emphasis added), which in turn will enable the viewer of these images "to see through new and personal lenses."[124] The organizers' goals for the *Border Film Project* rested on the belief that representing the embodied perspectives of undocumented migrants and Minutemen to a broader audience would contribute to a reasoned and balanced approach to reforming U.S. border policy.

The cover of the *Border Film Project*, which includes an image of a Minuteman and one of a migrant, narrates the address of the book to an outside audience as well as the relation between the viewer and these "naïve" artists (Figure 18). Both of these photographs are framed by circular holes cut into the cover, which are divided by a line symbolizing the boundary between the United States and Mexico. The cover deemphasizes the Minutemen's role as surveilling migrants, instead positioning

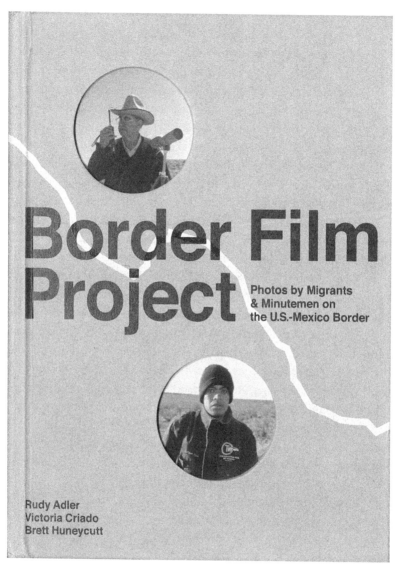

Figure 18. Cover Image of *Border Film Project*. The cover of the *Border Film Project* juxtaposes photographs of a Minuteman and a migrant. [Camera 010 (top) Wayne, Minuteman, 55, distributed in Hachita, New Mexico; and Camera 238 (bottom), Armando, 38, and Javier, 24, migrants, distributed in Agua Prieta, Sonora.] According to the "notes" in the *Border Film Project*, Armando and Javier traveled "from Mexico City and Hermosillo. Crossed New Mexico desert on Christmas. Camera mailed from Deming, New Mexico."

us (the viewers) as surveilling both migrants and Minutemen. We (the viewers) look through the lens-shaped holes in the cover to view photographs of the main subjects of the *Border Film Project*—an undocumented migrant and a Minuteman. The intended audience for the book is similar to that of many social documentary photography projects—individuals who are sympathetic to the plight of the less fortunate and who are positioned higher up the social ladder than those whose representations are on display. In framing their subjects through the lens of self-representation, the organizers present the project as unconstrained by policing and coercion, which are themselves the conditions of possibility for its visual economy of images. Thus, the book is complicit with both the Minutemen's and the U.S. state's surveillance of undocumented migrants in the U.S.–Mexico borderlands.

By taking images of migrants and Minutemen and arranging them without consultation with either group, the *Border Film Project* organizers ideologically subjugated both groups. As Allan Sekula contends, the meaning of photographs "is always directed by layout, captions, text, and site and mode of presentation."[125] In the *Border Film Project*, the organizers' choice of images, the ordering of images, the positioning of quotes from interviews, and the insertion of a description of the project in the center of the book all work to construct a visual equivalence between migrants and Minutemen. At the same time, the organizers take up a nationalist or "nativist point of view" in their statements framing the images by migrants and Minutemen.

The organizers' arrangement of images in the book is similar to a form of ordering frequently found in photographic archives.[126] Sekula argues that photographic archives prioritize an "empiricist model of truth," in which "pictures are atomized, isolated in one way and homogenized in another."[127] The *Border Film Project* organizers replicate this type of ordering by choosing to arrange the images in two ways. Their first approach was to separate the photographs by migrants from those of the Minutemen, similar to the curators' decision at the SMoCA exhibition. Although there were exceptions, the organizers generally positioned images of or by migrants across from one another on full-page spreads, isolating them from images of or by Minutemen, which were also placed across from one another on full-page spreads. The captions—which are quotes from interviews with migrants and Minutemen—are situated next to many, although not all, of the images. The ordering of the captions is similar to that of the images. Quotations from migrants are generally placed next to their pictures, and those from Minutemen are positioned next to their images. Arranged in this way, the captions appear to correspond to the specific image with which they are paired. The organizers' second approach was to pair images of migrants and Minutemen with similar visual elements on full-page spreads. Although I have examined the effects of isolating the images by migrants and Minutemen from one another in my analysis of the SMoCA exhibition, I now turn to the effects of emphasizing the similarities between the images of migrants and Minutemen in the book.

The Border Film Project's focus on self-representation is related to the organizers' attempt to present the "truth" of the migrants' and Minutemen's experiences, yet in constructing a parallel between these two groups in their ordering of the images in the book, they decontextualize the relationship between migrants and Minutemen. Further, by placing visually similar images by migrants and Minutemen together on full-page spreads, they relegate these photographs "to 'purely visual' concerns," establishing what Sekula has described as a "relation of *abstract visual equivalence* between pictures."[128] This homogenizing of the images of migrants and Minutemen appears related to the organizers' linking of these two groups by their supposed class position and their marginality in relation to the U.S. state. The organizers share the views of "sectors of the progressive left," which Lisa Duggan argues "reproduce within their own debates Liberalism's rhetorical separation of economic/class politics from identity/cultural politics."[129] In doing this, the *Border Film Project* organizers align themselves with a liberal nativist position that Nicholas De Genova argues "deracialize[s] the figure of immigration in a manner that abdicates any responsibility for analyzing the racial oppression of migrants of color."[130] The organizers thus deemphasize issues of race or racism within the Minuteman Project, which parallels the statements of leaders who, as Robin Dale Jacobson contends, "while adamantly denying the role of race . . . [in their organization] focus on the schemas of invasion."[131] In the book the organizers did nothing to expose the way in which the Minuteman Project attempted to conceal their organization's role as an extension of white supremacist national formation.[132]

Although the organizers position most of Minutemen's and migrants' images on separate pages, in some cases, they place visually similar images of migrants and Minutemen on full-page spreads, to gesture toward a more substantial comparison between the two groups. One of these spreads contains a photograph of a migrant couple on one side with a photograph of an Anglo man and woman (members of the Minuteman Project) on the other (103/006). The organizers placed one interior shot taken by a migrant next to another by a member of the Minuteman Project to emphasize the comparable living conditions of these two groups (134/016). The pairing of these two sets of images appears to be related to an emphasis on the similar class positions of those portrayed as well as to heteronormativity and domesticity, as represented by the images of the two heterosexual couples and of domestic space. As Zuromskis notes, snapshots are "a means of linking private symbols of domestic harmony to explicitly public ideas of social conformity and American nationalism."[133] The Minutemen's use of snapshot aesthetics relates to their attempt to make themselves (and their ideas) more palatable to a mainstream audience.

Similar photographic juxtapositions appear in the book and on the website, where the images are organized under three categories—"Migrants," "Minutemen," and "Similarities"—referring to photographs by migrants and Minutemen that share elements of composition or subject matter. The categories "Migrants," "Minutemen," and "Similarities" speak to the ways in which the organizers both isolate the two groups from one another, while they also lump images by Minutemen and migrants that resemble one another into a third category by making absent the different contexts in which these photographs were taken.

The photographs organized under the "Similarities" category on the website are supposed to represent the shared visual elements of these images, yet they appear to emphasize the migrants' and Minutemen's different "ways of seeing" both their environments and themselves. The photographs paired under the "Similarities" category include portraits of a migrant and a Minuteman taken from low camera angles, looking up at a blue sky. Other images feature shadows of a migrant and a Minuteman, a migrant and Minuteman sleeping, and areas where migrants have camped, both of which focus on a Coke bottle.[134] Although these images share some visual elements, they are actually quite distinct. In the first set of images, a migrant's photograph appears to be a self-portrait, one in which the migrant is looking down at the camera, whereas the portrait of the Minutemen has been taken by someone else, and the eyes of the Minuteman do not engage the viewer. The low camera angle monumentalizes the image of the Minuteman, whereas the migrant's eye contact with the camera forges a relation between himself and the viewer. In the photographs of shadows of a migrant and a Minuteman, again the former looks as if it is a self-portrait, while the latter appears to be shot by someone else. These images are also quite different visually—the shadow of the Minutemen is sharply outlined and has an iconic cowboy quality, whereas the shadow of the migrant is blurry, cast in desert grasses. Further, the Minuteman's shadow connects him with iconic images of cowboys in the "natural" setting of the U.S. West. As Lisa Cartwright and Marita Sturken argue, images of cowboys are "part of the ideology of U.S. expansionism and frontier," in which they represent ideologies of "rugged individualism," as well as the "romantic ideal of freedom," which contrasts with the "confined lives of everyday working people."[135] This cowboy image also associates the Minutemen with the vigilantes of the "Wild West" who handed out "cowboy justice" in towns like Tombstone, Arizona, where the Minutemen were based.[136]

What is apparent with these and other photographs in the "Similarities" category is the way that the Border Film Project organizers' pairing of certain images conceals the differences between them. The organizers' ideas about self-representation are similar to those of traditional social documentary photography, in which images "transmit immutable truths," yet as Sekula argues, "Photographic meaning depends on context."[137] In one pairing, a Minuteman sleeps on a cot, presumably resting for a day of surveilling migrants, whereas the image of a migrant woman sleeping accentuates her feet, blistered and bleeding from walking through the desert. This contextual difference also applies to two images—one taken by a migrant, the other by a Minuteman—of a desert area where migrants have chosen to stop. In one image, a migrant photographs others as they all rest. In the other, a Minuteman portrays a campsite used by migrants that he found while "tracking" them. In these photographs, the locations look similar, yet the migrant and the Minuteman have a different relationship to the places they photograph. The migrant represents this space as an area that migrants move through, while the Minuteman portrays this area as a space that must be surveilled and guarded. The deliberate pairing of these images speaks to the "depoliticization of photographic meaning" in archives described by Sekula, which is an inherent feature of the Border Film Project.[138]

The organizers' use of quotations as captions places the project in a "law and order" frame, as they chose quotes that situate the Minutemen as upholding the law by guarding the border. They contrast this with undocumented migrants, who speak about crossing the border through what the organizers represent as "illegal" means. The "law and order" frame taken up in the *Border Film Project* presents undocumented migrants through a lens of criminalization.[139] In the "Project Background" section of the book, the organizers refer to the Minutemen as "volunteers" rather than vigilantes, thus employing the same terms that the Minutemen use to describe themselves.[140] As "volunteers" who "are by and large concerned Americans," the organizers construct the Minutemen as *ethical* subjects.[141] By inversion, the organizers represent undocumented migrants as *unethical* subjects, and as "bad" immigrants, who undermine "the democratic sovereignty of 'the nation' through their circumventions of 'the rule of law.'"[142] While the organizers represent the Minuteman as a U.S. citizen who "volunteers" to enforce the law, the undocumented migrant is understood to be what Bonnie Honig refers to as the "bad immigrant, the illegal alien who undermines consent in two ways: he or she never consents to American laws and 'we' never consent to his presence on 'our' territory."[143] By constructing the *Border Film Project* through a "law and order" frame, the organizers present the Minutemen as ethical subjects. This supports the mainstreaming of the group, which involved Republican politicians in Washington, the leadership of the Minuteman Project, and the mainstream media.[144]

The decisions made by the organizers in constructing the *Border Film Project* make them complicit in the mainstreaming of the Minutemen, which included an effort to contain elements of vigilante behavior and racism by members of the group, a number of whom were active in the right-wing militia movement.[145] For example, the organizers never reference the Minutemen's "extralegal enforcement techniques," in which their actions go beyond the law.[146] The quotations from the Minuteman Project members in the *Border Film Project* are selective, in that they represent the views of those who supported the group's move toward gaining broader acceptance nationally. None of the quotations in the *Border Film Project* includes statements from the leadership prior to their efforts to mainstream the organization, or from rank-and-file members of the group whose views countered those of the current leadership.[147]

Although the *Border Film Project* organizers present their perspective as the moderate center between two "extreme" viewpoints, they adopt a form of liberal nativism in their book that shares qualities with a racially inflected conservative nativism, aligning them with the Minutemen, rather than with the migrants. The organizers espouse a point of view, by which, De Genova argues, both liberals and conservatives articulate "what a native *we* should do with a foreign *them*." As De Genova explains, "The answers are defined around a variety of contending interpretations of what might be best for 'the nation' (*our* nation) and its citizens (*us*)."[148] In their statement on the subject of the "U.S.–Mexico Border," the organizers assert, "A large immigrant population has both benefits and costs. Cheap labor means lower prices for goods and services, a benefit for all Americans."[149] As indicated in the second sentence, their focus is on benefitting "Americans," referring to U.S. citizens. These are examples of what Linda Bosniak refers to as "cost arguments," which focus on the economic impact of immigration for U.S. citizens and "the nation" and "are rarely treated as normatively suspect—or 'nativist.'"[150] Bosniak argues that the "national priority thesis" inherent in cost arguments clearly privileges the interests of U.S. citizens in immigration policies.[151] However, by focusing on the "benefits" of an undocumented workforce as well as the "costs" of so-called illegal immigration for working-class "Americans," the organizers presume the logic of U.S. national "interest."

The Border Film Project organizers invoke cost arguments because they are viewed as an acceptable means to restrict immigration. They also avoid what are (generally) considered unacceptable race-based arguments. However, there is frequently a racial subtext in cost arguments. Although the organizers may not have intended their comments to be a cover for race-based arguments, by taking up the Minutemen's position, they make absent the racist motivations behind the organization, which include preventing (what they believe will be) an "invasion" of Mexicans in the United States. (The Minutemen camouflage their race-based agenda by aligning themselves with the state against the "illegal" migration of people from Mexico.) David Michael Smith notes in a review of the *Border Film Project*, "The Minutemen are never able to explain why they view illegal immigrants as a grave danger to the United States. Moreover, the authors may be too quick to dismiss a description of Minutemen as vigilantes," as "immigrant rights advocates would dispute the authors' contention that many Minutemen are simply continuing the public service they began in the military service or law enforcement."[152] In the *Border Film Project* the organizers do not contextualize these photographs in relation to the history of U.S. immigration law or U.S.–Mexico border enforcement. Instead, they situate the project within the more limited sphere of mainstream immigration politics. An alternative approach would have acknowledged the significance of the colonization of the U.S. nation-state or globalization in determining U.S. border and immigration policy.

Conclusion

The idea behind the Border Film Project was to use photography—and specifically the conventions of self-representation—to convey the experiences of undocumented Mexican and Central American migrants and the Minutemen, yet the mediation and curation of these photographs significantly influenced how these images were viewed within exhibitions, in the *Border Film Project* book, and on the website. Although the organizers state that the project allowed the migrants to represent their own experiences, they construct the migrants' journeys through the U.S.–Mexico borderlands as "illegal." This perspective is evident in the organizers' adopting what De Genova refers to as a "nationalist conceptual framework premised on the coherence of a self-contained national economy," in which they present migration to the United States as if it "had no relation whatsoever, either historically or in the present, with U.S. imperialism and U.S. global hegemony."[153] The organizers do not contextualize the ways in which U.S. border policies have led to the increased militarization of the border, which has contributed to the growth of vigilante groups, while also simultaneously producing the "illegality" and increased vulnerability of Mexican and Central American migrants.[154]

Although the organizers of the Border Film Project and the curators of the exhibitions downplay their role in creating the meaning of these images, they made crucial decisions regarding the selection and organization of these amateur photographs in exhibitions, in the book, and on the website. In the *Border Film Project*, the organizers construct a visual and textual parallel between migrants and Minutemen, which erases the power differentials between U.S. citizens and undocumented migrants. In doing this, the organizers evade the specific ways in which the Minutemen have taken part in the government's policing of undocumented migrants' movement from Mexico into the United States, and they do not address the question of vigilante violence conducted by groups and individuals against undocumented migrants in the U.S.–Mexico borderlands. As Nicholas De Genova argues, during a "historical period of heightened nativism and anti-immigrant racism," if one is not "taking stock of these constitutive inequalities [between U.S. citizens and undocumented migrants] and also critically destabilizing the conceptual presuppositions that accompany them," this work could potentially become what Janice Radway has referred to as "just another technology of nationalism."[155] In the *Border Film Project*, the organizers align themselves with the Minutemen's "national gaze," which is further supported by a "nativist point of view."

The organizers foreground a "national gaze" in the construction of the Border Film Project, and yet the migrants' images disrupt the ways in which migrant "illegality" is produced by making visible the effects of border militarization and border policing (by both state agents and the Minutemen) on undocumented migrants. The migrants who participated in the Border Film Project center their experiences traveling through the U.S.–Mexico borderlands as counter to the contrived spectacle of the threat of undocumented migrants and the state gaze as a means to apprehend, capture, and immobilize them. The photographs taken by migrants, which combine documentary and snapshot aesthetics, thus represent alternative "ways of seeing" the effects of U.S. immigration law and U.S. border militarization. In this way their images resemble visual forms of "migrant counter-conducts," in that they counter how undocumented migrants are viewed through the lens of criminalization by state agents, the Minutemen, and the mainstream media. Instead, they present an alternative perspective from which to view how state and nonstate actors mobilize their power. Their photographs also narrate the disappearance of other migrants, implicating the role of the U.S. state in producing migrant death. Even as the migrants' images potentially unsettle the curatorial logic of the Border Film Project, they are not simply disruptive or counter to the reasoning behind this photography project. When taken out of this context, the images gesture toward other horizons. Their alternative ways of envisioning are conscripted and partially subsumed by the logic of the project. The Border Film Project demonstrates the limitations of self-representation, which is always mediated through the context of presentation. In the next chapter I further examine issues of mediation within artistic and filmic works produced in collaboration with women maquiladora workers in Tijuana, Mexico.

CHAPTER FOUR

Refusing Disposability

Representational Strategies in Maquilápolis: City of Factories

In the early 2000s, filmmaker Vicki Funari and artist Sergio De La Torre began to collaborate with a group of women maquiladora workers in Tijuana, Mexico, who were training to become *promotoras* (community activists) on a film tentatively titled "The Maquila Project."[1] As part of this collaboration, Funari and De La Torre led a fourteen-week workshop on video production for the promotoras, who were at that time affiliated with Casa de la Mujer/Grupo Factor X, an *asociación civil* (AC, civil association) that focused on the health and labor rights of women maquiladora workers.[2] During the workshop Funari and De La Torre had numerous conversations with the promotoras about how to represent their work in the maquiladoras in the film. One of their first conversations was with promotora Vianey Mijangos, who, as De La Torre noted later, "started doing these hand movements (what they do at work, but without the machinery)" while they were talking.[3] From their interaction with Mijangos, Funari and De La Torre contemplated a way to "show how their [women maquiladora workers'] bodies are conditioned to function as machines," while also representing "the impact of the *maquiladora* system on women's daily lives and on their interior lives."[4] During the workshop, each woman demonstrated one part of the industrial process that they performed in the maquiladoras, some of which they included in extended choreographed sequences in the opening credits and in other sections of the film.

In the first half of this book, I examined projects developed by labor unions and social service organizations as well as other groups that involved undocumented Mexican and Central American migrants in representing elements of their lives in photography. In the second half of the book, I shift my focus to collaborations between U.S.-based filmmakers, artists, and activists and Mexican and Central American migrants in the production of film, video, and audio projects. In studying these collaborations, I consider the relation between political and aesthetic forms of self-representation, including elements associated with the documentary genre.

Similar to what I have argued about self-representation in photography, self-representation in film and video has been viewed as less mediated and as more "truthful" than conventional documentary projects. Although an emphasis on self-representation in documentary film developed in the United States during the 1960s and 1970s, this form was not widely used until the 1990s, when the camcorder was released into the consumer market. During the 1990s, public television stations started to develop programming—such as the Public Broadcasting Service (PBS) series *POV* (*Point of View*)—featuring nonfiction work that was "self-authored" and, as Keith Beattie argues, "openly subjective."[5] Patricia Aufderheide contends that the videos broadcast on *POV* can be characterized by their "first-person voice in testimonial" as well as "by the bringing of the viewer into the world of the storyteller's experience."[6] In addition to first-person documentaries, Aufderheide notes that *POV* also included "collaborative efforts between artists and otherwise disenfranchised voices, drawing on a long history of social activism through documentary."[7]

This chapter examines *Maquilápolis: City of Factories* (2006), a film directed by Vicky Funari and Sergio De La Torre, in collaboration with a group of women maquiladora workers. The film was coproduced by the Independent Television Service (ITVS) and broadcast on *POV*. At the time of the film's production, these women, the majority of whom were migrants to Tijuana, were being trained as promotoras by the staff at Casa de la Mujer/Grupo Factor X.[8] The collaborative process used in making *Maquilápolis* contributed to a film that privileges the subjectivity of the promotoras. The women who were involved in the film's production created representations of themselves that were distinct from how maquiladora (maquila for short) owners and the Mexican media viewed them—as a cheap and disposable workforce. In this film, these women presented themselves as engaged in activism, offering critical perspectives on both the maquila industry and the Mexican government's neoliberal economic policies. Through their involvement in *Maquilápolis* the promotoras used and revised forms of documentary media as part of their counter-representational practices.

What distinguishes *Maquilápolis* from conventional documentary film is that the collaborative process taken up by Funari, De La Torre, and the promotoras prioritizes the latter as political actors and emphasizes their role as agents in their political organizing. Aspects of *Maquilápolis* are similar to documentary films in which the filmmakers attempt to incorporate the subjects' perspectives in the film, yet there is a different relationship between the subjects of *Maquilápolis* and their primary audience. *Maquilápolis* is not a project in which the U.S.-based filmmakers represent the lives of the promotoras for an outside audience, but rather one in which the subjects of the film are its coproducers, addressing their core constituency of women maquila workers. Through the distribution of the film, the promotoras share and publicize their activist campaigns with workers both within and outside the maquiladoras. At the same time that *Maquilápolis* was a part of the workers' activist campaigns, the film contests documentary's claim to "unmediated" representation.

Although the film centers on the promotoras' subjectivity, the juxtaposition of different aesthetic elements—including video diaries, documentation of their involvement in activist campaigns, as well as choreographed sequences, in which the women "perform" factory labor—disrupts the ways in which self-representation in documentary film is usually presented as unmediated. *Maquilápolis* defies some key conventions of documentary film by crossing stylistic conventions and by emphasizing its use of multiple genres. Along with more conventional documentary mise-en-scène, for example, the opening credits also incorporate video diary and staged sequences. The film starts with a segment from promotora

Carmen Durán's video diary, followed by a sequence that includes aerial shots of the U.S.–Mexico boundary with voice-over narration, in which the promotoras historicize the development of the maquiladoras. After the shots of the U.S.–Mexico boundary, the aesthetics of the film shift during a sequence in which the promotoras perform the monotonous movements of assembly work—not inside on the actual line, but outdoors in a dirt lot with maquiladora factories punctuating the surrounding landscape (Figure 19).[9] Here, staged performances denaturalize their classification as manual laborers, accentuating the tension between repetitive mechanized movement and the women as subjects in excess of their capacity to labor. The concerted artificiality of the performance underscored the discrete generic sequences as representational strategies. Including performance elements in the film reframes and contextualizes the aesthetic logic of the documentary genre itself.

In this chapter, I investigate how artists' and filmmakers' distinct approaches to collaboration in works produced with women maquiladora workers influenced forms of self-representation. Although their collaborative process of working with the promotoras shaped the production of the film, Funari and De La Torre initially had difficulty convincing these women to work with them on *Maquilápolis*. This was partly due to their experiences on another "collaborative" art project, *Tijuana Projection*, which was performed at inSite 2000–2001, a binational art event between Tijuana and San Diego.[10] As part of *Tijuana Projection*, artist Krzysztof Wodiczko projected previously recorded videos of promo-toras from Grupo Factor X onto the Centro Cultural in Tijuana (CECUT), intercutting them with live performances in which the promotoras spoke about the difficulties they experienced in their lives. Although both *Tijuana Projection* and *Maquilápolis* involve interlocutors in presenting the perspectives of women maquila workers for an audience, *Maquilápolis* explicitly sets out to critically reconfigure and call attention to these dynamics, while Wodiczko's *Tijuana Projection* replicates precisely the most problematic dynamics of power and representation common to the documentary genre.

The different processes by which Wodiczko and Funari and De La Torre collaborated with the promotoras produced fundamentally different

Figure 19. Factory workers perform the motions of a maquiladora production line. From *Maquilápolis: City of Factories* (2006). Directed by Vicky Funari and Sergio De La Torre. Photograph by Daniel Gorrell.

projects. Although the promotoras' testimonies were central in *Tijuana Projection*, Wodiczko did not incorporate them into the artistic process of creating his work. Further, he limited which aspects of the women's lives would be included in the performance, and his preconceptions about their lives ultimately constrained the project. In creating *Maquilápolis*, Funari and De La Torre consciously integrated the perspectives of the promotoras in Grupo Factor X into the film's production, and they treated the women as coproducers. Their collaborative approach was modeled on the promotoras' training as community activists. The promotoras—who were involved with *Maquilápolis* from preproduction through distribution—also helped organized a "Binational Community Outreach Campaign" during which they screened the film at community centers and nonprofits in the U.S.–Mexico borderlands. As such, the promotoras became part of the artistic process in the production of *Maquilápolis*.

This chapter's first section contextualizes the production of *Maquilápolis* by foregrounding the development of the Border Industrialization Program (1965), which led to the establishment of maquiladoras in Mexico's northern border cities and drew migrants from all over the country. I also examine the effects of neoliberal policies—such as the North American Free Trade Agreement (NAFTA)—in Mexico, as well as how women maquila workers organized in response. I then analyze the collaborative processes and representational strategies in *Tijuana Projection* and *Maquilápolis*. In *Tijuana Projection*, Wodiczko literally turned the promotoras into objects, referring to them as "projectors" who cast images and stories onto CECUT, at the same time that he presented this self-representation as unmediated. This was a denial of Wodiczko's own "projection" of their lives, which structured the film. *Maquilápolis*, by contrast, narrates a critique of women workers as producers of commodities in the maquilas, while disrupting the way that the film—in prioritizing the form of self-representation—could be viewed as more candid and authentic. At the close of the chapter, I examine the film's "afterlife" in the continuing collaboration among Funari, De La Torre, and the promotoras on a "Binational Community Outreach Campaign" and related projects.

Redefining Development:
Neoliberalism, Maquiladoras, and Promotoras

In this section, I provide a broader historical context for the development of maquiladoras, leading up to the production of *Tijuana Projection* and *Maquilápolis* in the early 2000s. During this period, the experiences of women maquila workers were shaped by the growth of neoliberal policies in Mexico. The development of export-processing industries—known as maquiladoras in Mexican border cities such as Tijuana and Ciudad Juárez—followed the establishment of the Border Industrialization Program (BIP), an agreement between the United States and Mexico, in 1965. The BIP offered incentives to multinational corporations, including tax breaks and cheap labor. The Mexican government hoped the maquiladoras would offer jobs to male workers returning to the country following the end of the Bracero Program in 1964.[11] Once the BIP was put into place, however, the multinational corporations who ran the maquiladoras did not employ returning braceros; instead, they primarily hired young women, whom they believed would work for less pay.[12] During the early years of the BIP (1960s and 1970s), the maquiladoras hired more women than men, leaving high rates of male unemployment unresolved.[13] Many women employed in the maquilas had migrated from other parts of Mexico to northern border cities, most notably Tijuana.[14] Although this gender imbalance changed by the mid-1980s, the maquiladoras remained gender segregated, with women frequently working in different industries and in lower-level positions than men.[15]

The development of maquiladora industrialization occurred as the Mexican government began to loosen its laws for regulating foreign investment in the country, which included moving from an import substitution industrialization (ISI) model of development to a neoliberal developmental model.[16] Although the Mexican state has financially supported the infrastructure of the maquiladoras for the multinational corporations, it has failed to do the same for the maquila workers, who live in substandard housing with limited services.[17] The liberalization of Mexican laws governing foreign investment eventually contributed to the development of NAFTA in 1994, which established a free trade zone among the United States, Mexico, and Canada. Mexico's neoliberal economic model has reduced government spending on social services, shifting responsibilities to local communities.

This rise of neoliberal free trade agreements like NAFTA has also negatively affected workers' rights in Mexico. Legal scholars, including Joshua Kagan, have suggested that many of the maquilas' workplace issues since NAFTA do not result from an *absence* of labor laws within Mexico, but rather a *lack of enforcement* of existing laws.[18] As Kagan notes, some of the most significant problems in the maquilas are the substandard working conditions.[19] He cites numerous reports that trace the maquila workers' high levels of exposure to chemical substances to a lack of available safety equipment.[20] Other work-related problems included long hours and high production quotas, which contributed to serious workplace injuries, such as musculoskeletal disorders.[21] Women's workplace issues include their pay rate, since they frequently work in lower-level positions than men and are paid less for their work. Further, women must endure mandatory pregnancy testing.[22] Many multinational corporations require pregnancy testing for female workers to avoid hiring them, as Mexican law requires companies to pay women their full salary during the six weeks before and after the birth of a child.[23]

Although the Mexican government's lack of interest in enforcing existing labor laws or creating new ones to regulate the multinational corporations that run the maquiladoras has negatively affected the lives of maquila workers, these workers have also organized to challenge their working conditions.[24] In response to their substandard working conditions, maquila workers established independent unions, asociaciones civiles, and NGOs to assist them in asserting their rights.[25] Further, specific organizations for women workers also developed, including Centro de Orientación de la Mujer Obrera (COMO, or Woman Worker's Orientation Center) and Casa de la Mujer/Grupo Factor X in Tijuana.[26] Carmen Valadéz, the former director of Grupo Factor X, stated that "from the beginning of the *maquilas* there have been struggles by women."[27] COMO, which was founded in 1968, integrated former maquila workers into the administration of the organization through a training program of *promotores externos* (workers acting as community organizers and labor activists) in the early 1980s.[28] As part of their training, the promotores externos attended the *tronco común*, which Devon Peña describes as a "six-month-long promotional course focusing on consciousness-raising, critical analysis of the *maquiladoras*, study of transnational capitalism, and workers' recognition of their history-making and social change capacities."[29] As Peña contends, this training aided women maquila workers both in their labor struggles and in their community organizing.[30]

By deciding to organize within autonomous organizations, women maquila workers in COMO and other groups in northern Mexico privileged their communities' concerns over those of the multinational corporations that ran the maquilas. Peña suggests that this perspective challenges how multinational corporations have objectified maquiladora workers:

> The subjectivity of *maquila* workers, as members of a socially constituted and historically located community, was channeled through COMO in an increasingly antagonistic relation to the "objectivity" of transnational capitalist accumulation. Capital's pretensions at possessing universal models of development, especially in the organizational form of the *maquiladoras*, were challenged by the refusal of Mexican working-class women to acquiesce in the reduction of their lives to mere cogs and assembly lines.[31]

Peña mentions that the women maquila workers' "refusal of capitalist *mal*development" was facilitated not only by their participation in COMO, but also through their "development of oppositional identities." For example, Peña describes how women maquila workers defy the ways in which "capital seek[s] to impose 'abstract labor'; that is, [by] trying to reduce humans to interchangeable and substitutable units of labor time." He argues that the promotoras in COMO redefined "development" by working to fulfill their communities' needs, instead of those of capitalist development, suggesting that this struggle has been "revolutionary," because these needs are "collectively articulated in the community as autonomous forms of self-development and self-valorization."[32]

Both the emphasis and structure of COMO were taken up by other "civil associations" composed of women maquila workers in Mexico's northern border cities, including Casa de la Mujer/Grupo Factor X in Tijuana. Grupo Factor X grew out of the feminist group called Emancipación, the members of which were women maquila workers, political activists, union members, and journalists in Tijuana during the 1970s and 1980s. Members of Emancipación founded Factor X in 1989. Originally, Factor X activists focused on health issues, including access to abortion. Eventually, they expanded their agenda to include the health and labor rights of women maquila workers.[33] Some of the organization's concerns included the effects of working conditions in the maquilas on women workers, as well as issues regarding domestic violence. Factor X provided a range of programs at its women's center, Casa de la Mujer, including workshops on sexual harassment and labor organizing, as well as classes on reproductive, sexual, and workplace health issues. Workshop participants became promotoras, assisting community members with their problems and concerns. Factor X also sponsored groups for survivors of domestic violence, medical and legal clinics for workers, and assistance with documenting human rights violations in the maquilas.[34]

Due to institutional reforms dismantling the welfare state and "structural adjustment" in Mexico, nongovernmental organizations like Grupo Factor X increasingly tried to fill in gaps left by the neoliberal state. Further, while global restructuring negatively affected women workers in Mexico, Doreen Mattingly and Ellen Hansen also contend that the "privatization of social services has created space for binational cooperation and for women to take on new roles as activists and community leaders."[35] Although much of the organizing of maquila workers is based in Mexico, there are also binational (U.S.–Mexico) and transnational activist networks involved, due to the proximity of the maquilas to the U.S.–Mexico boundary. Carmen Valadéz, the former director of Grupo Factor X, noted that these organizations are "constructing networks of action, empowerment and solidarity—local, national and international— between women."[36] Local organizations in Tijuana include El Centro de Información para Trabajadoras y Trabajadores, Acción Communitaria (CITTAC, Worker's Information Center), which informs maquila workers of their rights, and Red de Tijuana de Trabajadoras y Trabajadores de la Maquila (Maquiladora Workers' Network).[37] There are also U.S.-based organizations, such as the San Diego Maquiladora Workers' Solidarity Network, which lead tours of the maquiladoras to create awareness of maquila workers' low wages and substandard working conditions.[38]

While binational organizing networks focused on maquila workers' rights have emerged in response to neoliberal economic policies in the United States and Mexico, neoliberalism has also promoted the growth of binational art events, such as inSite, organized in Tijuana and San Diego between 1992 and 2005.[39] inSite, similar to other international art events established since the early 1990s, has focused on "site-specificity," as well as what Grant Kester refers to as a "growing interest in collaborative or collective approaches in contemporary art," including a "movement towards participatory, process-based experience." Kester situates this emphasis in the context of a "neoliberal economic order dedicated to eliminating all forms of collective or public resistance (institutional, ideological, and organizational) to the primacy of capital."[40] George Yúdice is critical of who benefits from the "cultural capital" produced from U.S.–Mexico border art events like inSite, stating that "when 'culture' is made to happen at the border, the effects exacerbate the inequalities there, especially if the cultural capital derived therefrom accrues to those who already have plenty of it: the sponsors, directors, curators, artists and art going publics."[41] Building on Kester's and Yúdice's comments, I will now analyze the production of a "collaborative" art project, *Tijuana Projection* by Krzysztof Wodiczko, that was performed at inSite during 2000 and 2001 and that involved women workers training to become promotoras at Factor X.

"Community Engagement" and Artistic Production at inSite, 2000–2001

The binational art event that became inSite has a contested history. The staff at La Jolla Museum of Contemporary Art first conceived of it in the late 1980s. However, as George Yúdice notes, the museum's proposal was criticized by members of the Border Arts Workshop/Taller de Arte Fronterizo (BAW/TAF), a collective that created community-based activist art in the U.S.–Mexico borderlands for over two decades. BAW/TAF members accused the organizers of appropriating their work in a grant proposal to the National Endowment for the Arts (NEA) and the California Arts Council in 1989.[42] A few years later, the Installation Gallery in San Diego, which showcased the work of local and regional artists, collaborated with Mexican cultural institutions in the creation of inSite to foreground the binational art community of San Diego and Tijuana.[43] The organizers conceived of inSite as both a residency and exhibition program, in which local and international artists could develop new site-specific work.[44] inSite's emphasis on "community engagement" developed during the 1997 exhibition as a partial response to critiques of inSite by members of BAW/TAF, as well as to the increased interest of U.S. art funders in community-based public art during the 1990s.[45]

There are numerous issues that have arisen from inSite's emphasis on "community engagement" projects. In *The Expediency of Culture*, Yúdice historically situates "community engagement" art projects, which developed "as neoliberalism took root and responsibility for the welfare of the population has increasingly shifted onto 'civil society.'"[46] Kester has critiqued community projects by artists working with disenfranchised groups, focusing on the unproblematized relation between the artists who initiate the projects and the community that they involve in their creation.[47] In *Conversation Pieces*, Kester describes different collaborative art projects between artists and specific communities, highlighting those that engage in "modes of dialogical production," which includes "sustained involvement over time with a specific community in order to deepen knowledge and build trust."[48] Kester characterizes this art practice as a form of "dialogical interaction," which, he suggests, "requires a reciprocal openness, a willingness to accept the transformative effects of difference, on the part of both the artist and his or her collaborators."[49] Kester also differentiates dialogical projects that are concerned with "creating a critically reflexive consciousness among viewers," with "counter-hegemonic projects." Counter-hegemonic projects "are premised on the production of a critical community consciousness," which is achieved "through an extended process of collaborative exchange rather than through the creation of an avant-gardist spectacle."[50] I relate Kester's understandings of the issues that arise in collaborations between artists and members of "specific" communities—along with his distinguishing between different approaches to dialogical art projects—in my analysis of Krzysztof Wodiczko's *Tijuana Projection*.

When he was asked to commission an artwork for inSite 2000, Krzysztof Wodiczko—who was at that point known for his ephemeral projections onto monuments and his work on homelessness in New York City—had not decided which "community" he would collaborate with.[51] Wodiczko did imagine this project as the first of many that would include live interventions to "testify regarding democracy's failures."[52] According to correspondence with inSite codirector Cecilia Garza Bolio, he was deciding between working with women maquila workers or with men imprisoned in San Diego's jails.[53] He wrote in his proposal that the participants would "be asked to evoke personal situations rarely addressed in the media."[54] While doing so, their faces and voices would be projected and amplified onto CECUT in real time. During his June 2000 visits to San Diego and Tijuana, Wodiczko decided to collaborate with women maquila workers on *Tijuana Projection*. inSite curators helped him locate two organizations—Grupo Factor X and Yeuani—with whom he could develop his project.[55]

Although Wodiczko had never created an artwork with live testimony before, certain themes from his previous works reemerge in *Tijuana Projection*. According to Wodiczko, his goal for *Tijuana Projection* was to "give visibility and voice, through the use of advanced media technologies, to women who work in Tijuana's *maquiladora* industry."[56] This emphasis is similar to Wodiczko's *Homeless Vehicle Project*, in which he brought visibility to New York City's homeless population. In both cases, Wodiczko positioned himself as the agent who could bestow visibility and voice to disenfranchised people. However, in the context of creating artwork based on the testimony of women maquila workers, emphasizing "visibility" could sometimes contribute to the vulnerability experienced by these women, some of whom were victims of domestic abuse.[57]

Tijuana Projection was contained and constrained by what George Yúdice argues was Wodiczko's vision of the women maquila workers as the "defeated."[58] During his visits to Tijuana in 2000–2001, Wodiczko met with promotoras from Factor X and recorded them reflecting on the challenges they faced in their lives. In the transcripts of these and other recordings, the promotoras spoke about working in the maquiladoras. A few referred to workplace accidents or unfair labor practices, in addition to abusive or oppressive relationships outside of the workplace.[59] A number of other themes arise in the transcripts. One is related to the women's decisions to leave abusive relationships and to move themselves and their children to Tijuana, where they could work and become financially independent.[60] Some spoke of their work as promotoras and about how Factor X not only campaigned on their behalf, but also trained them to confront factory managers who broke Mexican labor laws.[61] These women noted how the organization enabled them to assist other women while they also helped themselves. Others mentioned their efforts to improve their neighborhoods, which lacked running water, electricity, and telephone lines, by finding ways to get the streets paved and to steal electricity.[62] As they discussed elements of their lives, some of the promotoras addressed other women, whom they also encouraged to speak about the issues that concerned them and to contact the organizations available to help them.[63]

During the performances of *Tijuana Projection* at CECUT on February 23 and 24, 2001, Wodiczko oversaw which aspects of the promotoras' statements were heard, as well as what parts were silenced.[64] The women took turns wearing a special headset with a camera and microphone, which was connected to projectors and loudspeakers that transmitted their faces and voices onto CECUT in real time. The headset was awkward, claustrophobic, and reminiscent of a futuristic torture device.[65] The camera was positioned at a low angle, looking up at the women's faces, so their projections onto CECUT were distorted and disfigured. Wodiczko worked with a number of assistants to intercut the women's live testimony with prerecorded video. In the actual performance of *Tijuana Projection*, the participants' testimony accentuated their experiences as victims, rather than more fully representing their activism. To some extent, *Tijuana Projection* can be characterized as what Wendy Hesford and Wendy Kozol describe as "reproducing the spectacle of victimization."[66]

Tijuana Projection highlights issues surrounding the meaning of collaborative art projects for members of disenfranchised communities. In conducting research on *Tijuana Projection*, George Yúdice raised concerns about what happened after the show, specifically what responsibility the artist and staff might have to these women once the project and exhibition were over.[67] Yúdice questioned the benefits for the "publics and communities who invest their col*labor*ation in the success of a 'project,' social issues transformed into 'art?'" and asked what exactly the "local population" received in return for its participation.[68] Fiamma Montezemolo raised a similar point in an interview with Néstor García Canclini, who participated in a panel, "Image Power: Cultural Interventions as Public Memory in Postmodern Spaces," with George Yúdice, Krzysztof Wodiczko, and Susan Buck-Morss following the *Tijuana Projection* performance at inSite. In the interview, Montezemolo acknowledges the unequal "returns" from collaborations between artists and "communities." She suggests that while the artist "leaves, taking his or her success away," the community returns to "its daily situation of uncertainty."[69]

Some of these issues raised by Montezemolo and Yúdice were addressed in the panel featuring Canclini, Yúdice, Wodiczko, and Buck-Morss. In the transcript of the question-and-answer session following the panel, an "unidentified female" asked the panelists a question that directly addressed the relations between artists and "communities" in the production of works like *Tijuana Projection*:

My question is in response to the role of the women in Krzysztof's piece and the role of other community participants and other projects throughout inSite and responds somewhat to what Susan [Buck-Morss] said when you mentioned the artists who had been involved in these projects are not just the artists that were invited by the curators but the collaborators. And my question I think to anyone on the panel but maybe to Krzysztof in particular is at what point does a collaborator become a coauthor? And I ask this question because of my concerns, which are probably shared by many people here, of how to avoid the problem of so-called collaborators becoming exploited persons who are utilized for those of us who are coming from a more privileged place in the art world. And that's so therein is my question about how do these, again when, when do collaborators, do they ever become coauthors. And if they do, at what point?[70]

Wodiczko did not directly answer the question about when a collaborator becomes a coauthor. Instead, he noted that the promotoras were "using this project as a continuation or an enhancement of what they already do, that is, speaking out and actually teaching workers how to speak out and fight for their rights."[71] Here, he suggests that *Tijuana Projection* was a means for the promotoras to forward their own political agenda. Since the project was addressed to an art-going audience of inSite attendees, rather than other maquila workers, the promotoras' involvement in this project did not directly help them in their organizing. Wodiczko's address to an audience beyond maquila workers became evident when Maria Hinojosa interviewed him a number of years later. He stated that his goals for the project were "to turn those of whom we know nothing, who are hidden, invisible residents of our cities into projectors so that they can project themselves on a large scale and open up to a large number of people and learn . . . how to find words, metaphors, and expressions to convey difficult experiences."[72] Wodiczko's emphasis on the audience not knowing anything about the lives of these women suggests that he envisioned that those who would attend the performance would not be maquila workers.

Wodiczko's control over the production of *Tijuana Projection* limited what the promotoras received in return for their involvement in the project.[73] Although they shared numerous aspects of their lives with Wodiczko, he emphasized the violence they experienced, rather than the organizing work that they had done with Grupo Factor X.[74] The women's inability to control their self-representation in *Tijuana Projection* was directly opposed to their training as promotoras. This disjuncture between Wodiczko's view of *Tijuana Projection* and that of the promotoras did not emerge publicly during its production, however. The gap between these perspectives was enabled by what Kester calls "the institutional authority of the artist and his or her privileged relationship

to channels of legitimate discourse about the project," which "can con-
spire to create the appearance of a harmony of interest even where none
may actually exist."[75]

Although one reviewer did describe the women as "disempowered
by their experiences [of abuse]," most of the reviews of *Tijuana Projection*
in the United States and Mexico were not critical of the artwork.[76] In
fact, the reviews presented different perspectives from those of some of
the participants, one of whom contended that the promotoras' involvement in *Tijuana Projection* disrupted the organizing they were doing as
promotoras-in-training at Factor X.[77] The unequal power relations between Wodiczko and the promotoras were absent in the performance
of *Tijuana Projection*, reflecting the issues that arise when projects do
not incorporate community members as "coauthors." What would have
happened if Wodiczko had asked the promotoras what they wanted to
accomplish with the project? If they were included in the decision making the women's testimony may have been quite different, and may have
been addressed to an entirely different audience.

The difficulties that emerge from artists' collaborations with specific
"communities" are often structural. For example, the lack of coauthor-
ship in *Tijuana Projection* reveals the broader issues that arise when
community-based projects involve itinerant artists in their production.
Kester writes about the necessity for a dialogical interaction between artists and community members, claiming that this involves "a sustained
relationship in time and space."[78] Kester also suggests, however, that
"the nature of contemporary art patronage and production works against
this kind of sustained commitment," in part due to most people's pref-
erence for well-known "international" artists instead of "local" artists.[79]
Problems also arise when itinerant artists work on collaborative art projects with specific "communities" they do not know. These projects are
generally short term, which prohibits a more extensive engagement
between artists and "communities." This makes it difficult, as Kester suggests, "to develop the kind of insights that result from extended dialogical
interaction (or to evaluate the long-term impact of a given intervention)."[80]
Although inSite had emphasized that artists involve themselves in "community engagement" projects for at least one year, *Tijuana Projection*

demonstrates the issues that emerge from collaborative art produced by itinerant artists working with "local" community members with whom they have had little or no previous interaction.

Wodiczko's decision to take up a "normative" set of conventions—rather than a more collaborative and relational approach—had implications for the production of *Tijuana Projection*. Similar to his earlier works that could be characterized as "avant-gardist spectacles," Wodiczko appeared to be focused on "creating a critically reflexive consciousness among viewers," which as Kester argues can be "seen as an end in itself."[81] Wodiczko represents *Tijuana Projection* as an artwork that gives women "visibility" and "a voice," and yet he deemphasizes their agency as promotoras who have organized against the multinational corporations that run the maquilas and worked to improve the conditions in their colonias. *Tijuana Projection* does not acknowledge the unequal power relations between the artist and the promotoras, which privileges Wodiczko's view of the workers, rather than their view of themselves.

Another "normative" set of conventions that serves Wodiczko's *Tijuana Projection* is how he represents the artwork as a project of self-representation for the maquila workers. His statement on the project, which was published in the inSite 2000–2001 catalog, recounted:

> For the projection, six women from various generations sought to voice the difficulties of their personal situations—domestic and sexual abuse, exploitation in the workplace, police violence. They tried to find words for life events rarely addressed either in their private or social cultures or in the public media. *Each of them projected her face onto the central sphere and amplified her voice via a specially designed head-mounted camera microphone and wearable transmission equipment* [emphasis added].[82]

Although the project's legitimacy appears based on its claim to present unmediated self-representations of the promotoras, more than anything it narrates Wodiczko's perspective on their lives. In an interview with Maria Hinojosa, it is telling that Wodiczko identifies himself as the agent ("projectionist") in *Tijuana Projection*, referring to the women as objects ("projectors").[83] By positioning the promotoras as objects—both in this statement and within *Tijuana Projection*—Wodiczko subsumes their own subjectivity. This relationship affected the form of *Tijuana Projection*, in which Wodiczko effaced his own role in the performance at the same time that he represented *Tijuana Projection* as illuminating the "truth" of these women's experiences. In many ways, he was "projecting" his views on the lives of the women workers, rather than allowing them to represent themselves. Thus, Wodiczko's *Tijuana Projection* draws upon both meanings of "collaboration," which, according to Grant Kester, include a primary meaning—"to work together"—and a secondary meaning—"a form of betrayal."[84]

While Wodiczko objectified the promotoras in *Tijuana Projection*, in *Maquilápolis*, the promotoras worked with filmmaker Vicky Funari and artist Sergio De La Torre to address their position as commodities in the eyes of artists and as producers of commodities in the maquila sector. In the remainder of this chapter, I examine how the promotoras' involvement in *Tijuana Projection* affected the production of *Maquilápolis*, in which Funari and De La Torre worked together with promotoras from Factor X to create a film about their lives and activist projects. Funari and De La Torre based their collaboration on the promotoras' training with Factor X, which led to a film that is formally distinct from a conventional documentary. In making *Maquilápolis*, Funari, De La Torre, and the promotoras created a film that employs a range of formal elements— including video diary, cinema verité, and staged sequences—to highlight each as representational strategies, and to disrupt the way that the film, in emphasizing self-representation, could be viewed as unmediated.[85]

Performative Acts

The promotoras' lack of control over their self-representation in *Tijuana Projection* was opposed to their work as promotoras-in-training at Grupo Factor X. In *Maquilápolis*, they collaborated with Funari and De La Torre in the creation and production of a film that complemented their organizing skills. In this sense, *Maquilápolis* disrupts the way in which *Tijuana Projection* and some conventional documentary films portray women maquila workers as "disempowered victims of globalization."[86] *Maquilápolis* narrates a critique of the way that multinational corporations view women workers solely as producers of commodities in the maquilas. This critique—which is evident both in the form and content of the film—draws on the promotoras' knowledge of working in the maquilas, but it is also based on their training as community activists at Factor X. The film focuses on the promotoras' growing awareness of the broader structural forces shaping their work in the maquilas and the living conditions in their colonias.

Vicky Funari and Sergio De La Torre began "The Maquila Project" in 2000. They were inspired by conversations with Carmen Valadéz and other organizers from Grupo Factor X, who suggested that a film would allow the promotoras to share their struggles and their work experiences in the maquilas.[87] Funari and De La Torre had met a number of years earlier at a screening of Funari's film *Paulina* (1997) for Grupo Factor X.[88] Originally from Tijuana, De La Torre previously worked with promotoras in Grupo Factor X on an installation when he was a member of Los Tricksters, an artists' collective.[89] According to Funari, "The Maquila Project" began when the organizers of Grupo Factor X invited all the women training to become promotoras to participate in a video workshop, which was coordinated by Funari and De La Torre.[90] Initially, not all the women workers wanted to take part in the workshop. Possibly referencing *Tijuana Projection*, among other projects, De La Torre noted, "These factory workers had previously worked with artists in Tijuana, and had expectations, ideas, and demands about our practices. Some of them said, 'No, we're not interested in this project,' and some of them said yes."[91]

Although some of the women maquila workers were initially reticent about participating in a video workshop led by Funari and De La Torre, most of those in training to become promotoras eventually decided to become involved in "The Maquila Project."[92] In their meetings with the promotoras, Funari and De La Torre emphasized that the women would be intimately involved with the production of the film, suggesting that it could help them with their organizing and outreach efforts. Funari stated: "We wanted to give the women a chance to express themselves and tell their stories. To use the process as a furthering of their own self-organizing," also noting, "What's important about the film . . . was that it came out of a collaborative process and is a completely subjective account."[93] Funari and De La Torre modeled their collaborative process on the promotoras' training with Factor X. They not only wanted to work with the promotoras on a film, but also to train them to make their own films. De La Torre describes *Maquilápolis* as more than a film, noting, "It's a project that involves working with factory workers directly in the process of making a film."[94] In an interview with Rosa-Linda Fregoso, De La Torre adds that the film is "more of a social art practice, a direct dialogue with the subjects."[95] This collaboration was relational, and Funari and De La Torre prioritized the political projects and multiplicity of social relations with which the promotoras were engaged.

De La Torre and Funari wanted the process of making the film to be useful to the promotoras in documenting and publicizing their struggles and campaigns, and as a model of organizing for other women maquila workers. They developed their process by collaborating with the activists on the training that they received to become promotoras at Factor X. By the time that Funari and De La Torre led the video workshop, Factor X had developed a fourteen-week course, focusing on occupational health, labor rights, and gender issues. This course provided an overview of toxins in the workplace at the same time that it trained the women workers to become promotoras, so they could both educate and organize members of their communities about their rights.[96] According to De La Torre, "When Vicky and I found out about Factor X and their process with the factory workers, we wanted to borrow and mimic what they were doing. So we worked with Factor X, using some of their already-established resources to develop the film, which not only included the stories, but also the structure of collaborating with the workers."[97] Similar to the training they received as promotoras in which they learned about occupational health issues and their rights as workers, Funari and De La Torre instructed a group of sixteen promotoras in basic video techniques, including how to use a video camera and edit footage, in addition to teaching sound recording and how to tell stories in film form.[98] During these workshops, the promotoras analyzed how women maquila workers had been portrayed in the media, which helped them to envision alternative ways to represent themselves.[99] Following the workshops, the promotoras started to record video diaries and to document their activism.

Funari and De La Torre returned to Tijuana periodically to watch and discuss the promotoras' video diaries, as well as their documentation of their activist campaigns, including interviews they conducted. Funari and De La Torre consulted with the promotoras on other aspects of the film, including the narration, which they cowrote with Lupita Castañeda, one of the promotoras in the workshop. The process of making the film took many years, partly due to the filmmakers' other commitments. This enabled the promotoras to document the effects of factory flight and layoffs in the maquila industry due to the economic recession of the early 2000s, as well as various stages of their activist campaigns.[100] The promotoras were involved in all aspects of the film's production, and also organized a Binational Community Outreach Campaign to distribute the film to specific audiences, which I describe in the conclusion of this chapter.

Funari and De La Torre approached the making of *Maquilápolis* differently than if they had been interested in producing a conventional documentary film. In their collaboration with the promotoras, they created a film that analyzed the effects of globalization on Mexican women as workers in the maquilas and as promotoras. Much of the film was created by the promotoras, from their video diaries to reports and interviews on conditions in the maquilas and the colonias to the narration of the film.[101] Funari and De La Torre also collaborated with the promotoras on performance sequences and incorporated the aesthetics of the maquiladoras into the film.

The film's emphasis on the labor disputes and activist campaigns is evident from its opening scenes, which include segments from Carmen Durán's video diary, as well as the promotoras' narration. Following a brief sequence from Durán's video diary, we hear the voice-over narration of one of the promotoras who states:

En los años 60s, escuchamos por primera vez la palabra "maquiladora." La maquila venia a cambiar todo. Porque ofrecían salarios mejores que en otras partes del país. Eso es lo que veníamos buscando los migrantes a esta tierra.

[We first heard the word "maquiladora" in the 1960s. The maquiladora changed everything because they paid better wages than in the rest of Mexico. That's what we migrants came looking for.][102]

The promotoras narrate the history of the development of maquilas, from the BIP, which established these factories, to the 1994 NAFTA agreement, which increased the number of maquila workers in the region.[103] In describing the BIP and NAFTA, the promotoras highlight the benefits of these policies for multinational corporations that receive tax breaks while employing cheap labor. In their narration, the promotoras challenge how multinational corporations represented the benefits of the maquiladoras to the Mexican government and the Mexican people, specifically that they would boost the Mexican economy and alleviate immigration to the United States.

Voice-over narration is common in documentary film; however, in *Maquilápolis,* it is the promotoras who narrate the film, not an outsider "observing" their world. But even these narrations do not float freely through some omniscient space outside the film and are instead always situated in a specific site of enunciation. The narration describes the changes in the promotoras' perceptions, from their initial awareness of the maquilas, which drew many to migrate from all over Mexico to the northern border city of Tijuana, to their position as women workers within the context of globalization, which they developed in their training as promotoras with Factor X.[104] Through their narration, the promotoras explain the multinationals' interest in employing women workers, whom they claim have "agile hands," as well as being "cheap and docile." Although the promotoras contend that most of the women (like themselves) who come to work in the maquilas are unaware of what they will encounter, by becoming activists, they learned to, in their words, "make changes in our daily lives, in our communities, in our workplaces, and within ourselves."[105] In writing about *Maquilápolis,* Lisa Lowe argues that "this transformation of perspective occurs in both aesthetic form and thematic content; the women record the shift from being objects viewed as commodities, yet disposable labor, to becoming subjects who depict themselves as analysts of these conditions and as activists working against them."[106] The promotoras' involvement in *Maquilápolis* contributed to their agency as filmmakers, which paralleled and extended their activism.

In their narration, video diaries, and interviews, Lupita Castañeda, Carmen Durán, Lourdes Luján, and the other promotoras contest their treatment by the multinational corporations who view them as "disposable Third World wom[e]n."[107] In this sense *Maquilápolis* is a direct response to their position as women workers within the legal construction of the maquilas as deterritorialized nonstate spaces deregulated for outsourcing and manufacturing.[108] As such, the promotoras demonstrate how the maquilas are part of a context whether or not they are legally disentangled from the regulatory structure of nation-states. The interviews conducted with Castañeda and Vianey Mijangos reveal how multinational corporations violate Mexican labor laws by erecting "ghost unions" (unions in name only, which protect employers, not employees) and fire individuals who attempt to establish independent unions. In bringing attention to these policies the promotoras ground their analyses of the maquiladoras' impact on women in Tijuana against the multinationals' perception of women maquila workers as cheap and docile. The promotoras thus present *Maquilápolis* as part of their broader campaigns to oppose how the Mexican government allows multinationals to exploit the Mexican workforce.

The promotoras at Grupo Factor X who were working on specific struggles and activist campaigns were featured prominently in the film. These individuals included Carmen Durán, who was part of a legal battle against Sanyo for closing a maquila without paying its workers severance. Maquila worker Lourdes Luján also appeared in the film. She, along with other members of the binational organization Colectivo Chilpancingo Pro Justicia Ambiental (Chilpancingo Collective), collaborated with the Environmental Health Coalition in San Diego to pressure the Mexican Environmental Protection Agency—known as Procuraduría Federal de Protección al Ambiente (PROFEPA)—and the U.S. Environmental Protection Agency (EPA) to clean up Metales y Derivados, an abandoned lead-recycling plant in Tijuana's Otay Mesa Industrial Park.

Maquilápolis documents Carmen Durán's battle against Sanyo, which she claims harassed its workers, exposed them to toxic chemicals before relocating its factory to Indonesia, and then failed to pay severance. In her narration Durán explains that although the Mexican government has strong labor laws, these laws are not adequately enforced. In the film, Durán files a labor claim against Sanyo, claiming the company was breaking Mexican labor law. Although the law dictates that Durán and her coworkers were required to receive legal counsel, they were advised that their assigned lawyer would side with Sanyo. Consequently, they contacted Jamie Cota from CITTAC to represent them instead.[109] The film documents their hearing with the Labor Arbitration Board, which was supposed to work with both parties to settle the dispute. Cota informs Durán and her coworkers that since Sanyo has broken the law, they will win their case and set a precedent for similar legal disputes.

The film also focuses on the Mexican government's collusion with the multinational corporations that run the maquilas. Durán mentions other multinational corporations' violations of Mexican labor law, and she charges Mexican government agencies with disregarding the health and well-being of maquila workers. Specifically, Durán describes working with dangerous materials at maquilas owned by Panasonic, Sanyo, and other corporations, without adequate safety protection. She also explains her severe health conditions, some of which resulted from lead contamination.

Maquilápolis situates Durán's and Luján's lives and experiences in their colonias, while challenging the way in which they are represented by agents of the Mexican government. For example, neither the local government nor the maquilas provide public services (electrical, sewage, and water) in Tijuana's colonias, where the majority of maquiladora workers live. As Kathryn Kopinak has discussed, maquiladora industrialization in Tijuana has passed "many of the costs associated with constructing a competitive labor force onto workers and their communities, especially migrant workers and their families."[110] Although Durán speaks with pride about the house she constructed out of recycled garage doors, she also explains the difficulties and dangers of living without running water or electricity. In these sequences the promotoras use their involvement in the film as a means to educate members of their communities, such as when Durán informs her neighbors that they are

entitled to public services. In another sequence, Durán and Luján participate in a "border tour" with U.S. activists, who together visit the Office
of Economic Development of Baja, California, in Tijuana. During that
visit, the U.S. activists ask Director Manuel García Lepe about the infrastructure of Tijuana and the "quality of life" for maquiladora workers
living in the colonias. Lepe responds that maquila workers have a "good
standard" of living. However, this perspective is countered by Luján's
video diary, in which she explains that their salaries do not cover basic
living expenses, and by Durán, who questions if Lepe has ever visited the
maquiladora workers' neighborhoods.

Unlike Durán's case against Sanyo, which was based on Mexican
labor law, there were no environmental laws in Mexico at the time that
the BIP was established in the mid-1960s.[111] Thus, the film documents
the difficulties for activist campaigns that focus on the environmental
consequences of maquiladora industrialization in Tijuana's colonias,
such as Chilpancingo. In her video diary, Luján documents her involvement in a binational campaign to clean up lead contamination from
Metales y Derivados in Chilpancingo. Most of those who live in Chilpancingo are long-term residents whose community existed before the
arrival of the maquiladoras in the 1970s.[112] Some like Luján remember
when people could wash and swim in Arroyo Alamar, before it was
polluted. These workers have thus been eyewitnesses to the increasing
contamination of the Arroyo Alamar, as well as to the effects of environmental pollutants on the health of their family, friends, and neighbors.

Due to the limitations of Mexican environmental law, Luján cofounded
the Colectivo Chilpancingo, which collaborated with a U.S.-based organization, the Environmental Health Coalition, in an attempt to get NAFTA,
the United States, and the Mexican government to clean up the site. Luján
explains that she decided to become a promotora after taking a health
survey by the Environmental Health Coalition of San Diego, which was
examining the effects of environmental pollutants on the health of those
living in her colonia. In her video diary, Luján explains that while PRO-
FEPA shut down Metales y Derivados in 1994, the lack of proper storage
containers at this former recycling plant contaminated the surrounding soil and water. Sociologist Kathryn Kopinak has described Metales y

Derivados as "the most dangerous brownfield site of abandoned hazardous waste on the border."[113] In 1998 the Colectivo Chilpancingo, which Luján cofounded, worked with the Environmental Health Coalition to file a petition with NAFTA's environmental agency, the Commission for Environmental Corporation (CEC), asking it to clean up the site. The lack of response to their petition demonstrates what the film's collaborators call the "failure of NAFTA to live up to its negotiation's promise to protect public health and the environment."[114] However, the Colectivo Chilpancingo and the Environmental Health Coalition's organizing led to international media coverage and an eventual agreement in 2004 between U.S. and Mexican environmental agencies to clean up Metales y Derivados.

In *Maquilápolis* the filmmakers center the subjectivity of the promotoras in part through the inclusion of their video diaries. The aesthetics in the video diaries can be characterized by the promotoras' use of consumer video cameras, which, as Keith Beattie argues, conveys a "visual language of authenticity" that "is articulated within effects which bear the traces of amateurism."[115] Durán's video diary opens with her filming inside the maquila. The first shot focuses on women working in a maquila, after which she films herself by holding the camera at arm's length. The camera is positioned from a low angle and has a closely cropped frame. Durán introduces herself by speaking directly to the camera. This kind of filmmaking creates "high levels of identification with the filmmaker," which, as Beattie argues, provides "a different form of connection with the viewer than is achievable in traditional representational techniques."[116] In the following segments, Durán introduces her three children, the family home, and her colonia, which she situates in relation to the maquiladoras—including Sony—located up the hill. Lourdes Luján also filmed her sons, her husband, her home, and her colonia, focusing on the arroyo. The video diaries, which are a form of self-produced low-resolution video, focus on familiar relations that reinforce a connection between amateur video and subjectivity.

Although *Maquilápolis* represents the grassroots campaigns of these promotoras, it is not solely a "document" of their struggles. Rather, the film combines multiple conventions, including documentary and staged sequences, which are not "reenactments" (commonly used in documentary film), but rather performances. Through the filmmakers' use of various aesthetic elements—including video diaries, documentation of activist campaigns, and choreographed sequences—*Maquilápolis* contests how self-representation in documentary film is viewed as unmediated. Although the video diaries draw on some of the conventions of self-representation in film and video—for example, unmediated access and claims to the "real"—this is complicated by the juxtaposition of the diaries with performative sequences. Durán's video diary is followed by overhead and aerial shots of the U.S.–Mexico boundary and a sequence during which the promotoras "perform" repetitive motions of industrial labor. Lourdes Luján's video diary is bookended by two staged sequences. The first features images of a maquiladora's empty interior, accompanied by voice-over narration in which the promotoras state what work they do (i.e., "I assemble flybacks"). Next, Luján's video diary begins with her introducing herself in a voice-over narration, with an image of her shadow in the grasses near the Arroyo Alamar. In the following interview, Luján and a neighbor discuss the effects of contaminants on the arroyo, their families, and community members—the same issues that motivated Luján to become a promotora. Following the interview, the promotoras are portrayed in different environments in Tijuana using a time-lapsed filmmaking technique while one of the promotoras provides a voice-over narration, explaining the women's roles as community activists.

Many of the choreographed sequences focus on the hands of the promotoras. The visual representation of the maquiladora workers' hands directly references the multinational corporations' interest in employing women workers, whose bodies are disassembled, objectified, and instrumentalized. These images include the promotoras' hands performing motions of repetitive industrial labor, holding the products that they have produced in the maquilas, and knitting, as in the closing credit sequence. This emphasis on the women's "hands" contrasts with the U.S. agricultural industry's interest in the "arms" of male workers from Mexico. The industry referred to these men as braceros, which means those who work with their arms. In emphasizing the hands of the women maquila workers, Funari, De La Torre, and the promotoras draw on a form of abstracted labor similar to the one used by filmmaker Alex Rivera in *Why Cybraceros?* (1997) and *Sleep Dealer* (2008). Hands are also mentioned by some of the promotoras, including Carmen Durán, who referred to Sanyo's "runaway" factory by explaining, "they depart with their hands full and leave us with our hands empty."

Some of the film's other performative sequences narrate women workers' positions as producers of commodities in the maquilas. In drawing on the promotoras' analyses of their roles within the maquilas—specifically articulated by Lupita Castañeda—Funari and De La Torre worked with the promotoras to visualize how maquila workers were positioned in a global economic system. For example, *Maquilápolis* features a sequence during which a television created in the maquiladoras rotates on a stand, as if it were a precious commodity. Funari and De La Torre show its internal components, including the "flyback," which Durán assembled in the maquiladoras. In the next scene, Durán rotates as she holds the component in her hands (Figure 20). Later in the film, this same technique is used with head shots of the women, in which they rotate as the promotoras state the names of the companies that have employed them. In representing the women the same way that they present the objects they produce, Funari and De La Torre and the promotoras capture what Melissa Wright describes as the "internal contradiction" of the "myth of the disposable Third World woman."[117] In other words, while multinational corporations view these women as disposable, they are also indispensable to the global production process, to the extraction of value added, and to the capitalist accumulation of wealth.

In *Maquilápolis*, the women's performances critique the positioning of workers as "objects of labor," as well as the conventions of documentary film. The juxtaposition of multiple filmic conventions calls attention to the conscious use of genre as a deliberate representational strategy by Funari, De La Torre, and the promotoras. The scenes in which the promotoras act as performers—staging the repetitive movements of their assembly work—critically reframe the multinational corporations' treatment of them as replaceable automatons. These performances also foreground the women's participation in a way that denaturalizes the video

Figure 20. Carmen Durán, a factory worker and promotora holds a "flyback," a television component she assembled. From *Maquilápolis: City of Factories* (2006). Directed by Vicky Funari and Sergio De La Torre. Photograph by Daniel Gorrell.

diary and documentary film segments. Performing their own objectification problematizes the women's roles in the film and their relationship to the audience. Thus, it becomes difficult for the documentary sequences or even the video diaries to appear in their conventional role, where the subjects of the film speak the "truth" to the viewers. Not only do these fissures of representational convention disrupt any sense of a singular or seamless diegesis, but, ironically, the very artificiality of the performance sequences allows for the activists to circumvent their cinematic enclosure.

In *Maquilápolis,* Funari, De La Torre, and the promotoras from Factor X specify the environmental and social consequences of the "export processing zone" on the working-class population of Tijuana. Durán's visual documentation of her and her coworkers' severance claims against Sanyo—and later claims against Hansenmex, a company that left Tijuana to avoid paying taxes—serve as a compelling critique of the multination-als' treatment of maquiladora workers as temporary and expendable. Lourdes Luján's documentation of Colectivo Chilpancingo's campaign against Metales y Derivados provides another illustration of the mate-rial consequences and costs of so-called free trade. *Maquilápolis* is a proj-ect that strengthened the workers' campaigns to convince the Mexican government to apply its labor laws to multinational corporations, and—along with the U.S. government—to clean up areas contaminated by the maquiladoras.

Following the release of *Maquilápolis* in 2006, Funari, De La Torre, and the promotoras continued their collaboration. As previously men-tioned, *Maquilápolis* was created to aid the promotoras in Factor X with their organizing. As such, the filmmakers and promotoras developed a Binational Community Outreach Campaign to screen *Maquilápolis* for community groups and NGOs based in the U.S.–Mexico borderlands.[118] The film's "afterlife" following postproduction can be differentiated from that of *Tijuana Projection* as well as conventional documentaries. Funari and De La Torre have described their collaboration with the promotoras as one that broke with the "traditional documentary process of dropping into a location, shooting and leaving with the 'goods,' which would only repeat the pattern of the maquiladora itself."[119] In addition to the Bina-tional Community Outreach Campaign, *Maquilápolis* was broadcast on public television in the United States; screened at film festivals in Mexico, the United States, Europe, and Asia; and shown in communities across the United States and Mexico.[120] Many of the screenings included public appearances by Funari, De La Torre, and the promotoras featured in the film, including Carmen Durán.[121]

Funari and De La Torre envisioned the distribution of *Maquilápolis* beyond the usual documentary film festival route, which is why they worked with the promotoras to develop a Binational Community Out-reach Campaign to target specific audiences.[122] This campaign was driven by the promotoras' goal to share the film with other maquila workers to inspire further activism. Funari, De La Torre, and the promotoras saw the campaign as a means "to get people involved and mobilized for change and to support cross-issue and cross-border activism."[123] The campaign presented the film "to create meaningful social change around the issues of globalization, social and environmental justice and fair trade."[124] The campaign's binational focus was directed at individuals and organizations in the United States and Mexico, encouraging collaboration on issues such as those pertaining to labor and the environment, which affect both countries. As Lisa Lowe has argued, the experiences of the promotoras in *Maquilápolis* "give rise to political practices that cannot be remedied through rights-based citizenship and whose strategies necessarily reach beyond traditional state channels."[125] This binational emphasis developed out of the promotoras' experiences in the film—including Durán's and Lujan's participation in a "border tour" with activists from the United States and Mexico and Lujan's collaboration with U.S. and Mexican groups to clean up Metales y Derivados—both of which attest to the importance of transnational organizing.

Some of the promotoras involved in the production of *Maquilápolis* organized the Binational Community Outreach Campaign, from its planning to its execution.[126] Colectivo Chilpancingo, CITTAC/Worker's Information Center, the Colectivo Feminista Binacional (Binational Feminist Collective), and the Environmental Health Coalition comprised the binational coalition. As part of the 2007 Street Cinema Border Tour, Lupita Castañeda served as outreach campaign coordinator, which involved traveling with *Maquilápolis* to cities, towns, and colonias along the U.S.–Mexico boundary. Other promotoras who participated in the Street Cinema Border Tour included Teresa Loyola and Lourdes Luján.[127] During the July 2007 tour, Funari, De La Torre, and the aforementioned promotoras spoke at screenings coordinated with NGOs located in the U.S.–Mexico borderlands. At these events, the promotoras described their activist campaigns and answered questions about the film. As part of the Binational Community Outreach Campaign, the organizers developed a *Discussion Guide* in both English and Spanish, which was distributed at film screenings.

In part by modeling their collaboration on the promotoras training with Factor X, Funari and De La Torre envisioned both the video workshop and the production of *Maquilápolis* as enabling the promotoras to learn how to produce videos and promote their activist campaigns. Following the production of *Maquilápolis*, Funari and De La Torre applied for grants to give the promotoras two cameras to produce their own videos. In addition, they used grant funding to purchase editing equipment and to offer the promotoras a video-editing workshop. Carla Pataky, a member of Tijuana's Bulbo collective and a teacher at the Autonomous University of Baja, California (UABC), led the workshop. Pataky taught the promotoras how to use digital video–editing equipment, which—along with their training from Funari and De La Torre—allowed them to make videos from pre- to postproduction.[128] In the workshop, the promotoras created short videos on topics including sexual harassment, illegal pregnancy tests in the maquilas, and updates on Metales y Derivados. Lupita Castañeda said the workshop "has allowed us to reflect upon ourselves and to give ourselves the role of protagonists, as creative women."[129]

Conclusion

In returning to George Yúdice's question regarding the return for "publics and communities" who engage in collaborative projects with artists, I contend that *Maquilápolis* prioritizes the promotoras' political projects, challenging the multinational corporations' positioning of these workers as disposable. Similar to what Alicia Schmidt Camacho argues about *Sangre joven: Las maquiladoras por dentro* (1986) by Sandra Arenal, which contains *testimonios* of women maquila workers, the distribution of the film as part of a Binational Community Outreach Campaign, and specifically as part of the Street Cinema Border Tour, adds value as it circulates, not for the "value added" for multinational capital by exploitation and low wages in the maquiladoras, but specifically for the way in which the film places value on the perspectives of women maquiladora workers and provides a model for the ways in which maquila workers can effect change.[130] The promotoras' involvement in the making of *Maquilápolis* played a significant role in the formation of their identity as activists. This is a film in which the promotoras' role as activists passing on knowledge of their constituencies parallels their sense of agency as filmmakers.

In this chapter I have argued that the aesthetic interventions of Funari, De La Torre, and the promotoras in *Maquilápolis* deemphasize the positioning of the promotoras as authentic "raw material" who are transformed by the filmmakers' "processing."[131] In this context Lupita

Castañeda's comment about being an "object of labor" takes issue with the promotoras being viewed solely as producers of commodities in the corporate sector as well as being regarded as commodities in the eyes of some artists. There are numerous parallels between *Sangre joven: Las maquiladoras por dentro* and *Maquilápolis*, including the ways in which the women workers' perspectives are made central, as well as how they "contest the state's authority."[132] Through their involvement in *Maquilápolis* and their work as promotoras, these women workers further galvanized oppositional identities, providing an alternative representation of themselves and of the Mexican government's neoliberal economic policies. Specifically, in *Maquilápolis*, the promotoras work to denaturalize their classification as manual laborers, as in the scenes when they perform the repetitive movements of physical labor, which are shown at the beginning, middle, and end of the film. This performance, similar to Schmidt Camacho's descriptions of women workers in *Sangre joven*, "enacts a form of oppositional consciousness that opposes the materiality of the body, its debility, to the abstractions of economic rationality and scientific management."[133]

In *Maquilápolis* a group of promotoras helped to create a film that serves as a site of strategic negotiation. By working both within and beyond conventions of documentary filmmaking, these activists constructed images that intervened in contexts characterized by unevenly distributed relations of power, where they were positioned as expendable. Further, through their involvement in the production of the film the promotoras passed on their knowledge to their constituencies both in and outside of the maquiladoras of Tijuana. Tarek Elhaik relates the film's focus on the promotoras' subjectivity to "the question of technologically mediated self-representation as a form of counter-narrative and redemption of desubjectivized and disembodied selves."[134] As part of the promotoras' counter-representational practice, *Maquilápolis* contains forms of situated knowledge as well as strategic acts of representation. Further, through their involvement in the film, Funari, De La Torre, and the promotoras sustain a long-term commitment to particular places and people even as they develop their capacity for political and social change through networks of affiliation.

PART THREE

Counter-Optics

Disruptions in the Field of the Visible

Disappearance and Counter-Spectacle in *Sanctuary City/Ciudad Santuario,* 1989–2009

The year 2006 was a watershed for immigrant rights organizing in the United States. Millions of supporters participated in marches against HR 4437, the Border Protection, Antiterrorism, and Illegal Immigration Control Act, which would have criminalized undocumented migrants and anyone who assisted them.[1] A day laborer, speaking at a meeting of the San Francisco Day Laborer Program at La Raza Centro Legal that spring, said that HR 4437 "doesn't just affect Mexicans or Central Americans, documented or undocumented"; "this is against us—this is against Latinos."[2] This statement addresses both the conception and implementation of federal immigration policies, and it identifies the broader ramifications of HR 4437, which include the racial profiling of Latinas/os, regardless of their residency status. Tomás Summers Sandoval relates this "refrain of mutuality" to an earlier moment in December 1985 when Mayor Dianne Feinstein signed a resolution to make San Francisco a "sanctuary city" for refugees from Central America, including El Salvador and Guatemala. This policy was intended to help Central American refugees; a 1989 sanctuary ordinance broadened protection to all undocumented migrants in the city.[3]

This chapter examines how artists envisioned the disjuncture between this local ordinance and federal immigration policies following momentous immigrant rights marches. Leo Chavez suggests that Latina/o migrants took part in these marches as a "spectacular display of belong-ing."[4] In contrast, there was a significant rise in the number of Immi-gration and Customs Enforcement (ICE) raids following the spring of 2006, many of which targeted Latina/o migrants.[5] I examine the effects of the ICE raids in San Francisco, in large part because it is a place where conflicts between local and federal immigration policies were most perceptible, focusing on how an art installation both visualized and made audible the disjuncture between local policies and federal immigration law.

The exhibition *Sanctuary City/Ciudad Santuario, 1989–2009* was a collaboration between artist Sergio De La Torre and a small group of art students, and directly commented on San Francisco's sanctuary ordi-nance.[6] The ordinance was initially drafted in the 1980s, as refugees fled U.S.-supported state and extralegal violence in Central America. The municipal legislation prohibits city employees from aiding federal immi-gration agents, unless they are required to do so by federal or state law or a warrant.[7] The art exhibit focused on issues of safety and security for undocumented Latina/o migrants following a series of ICE raids in the Bay Area. Although De La Torre wanted to collaborate with undocu-mented Latina/o migrants, he was unable to find willing participants due to the perceived personal risk.[8] However, he did develop the show with the support of nonprofit organizations in the Mission District that served Latina/o migrants. Latina/o migrants also permitted him to record and present their verbal testimony about the effects of ICE raids in the Bay Area. These testimonials were given at joint hearings orga-nized by San Francisco's Human Rights Commission (HRC) and Immi-grant Rights Commission (IRC). De La Torre incorporated elements of these hearings into the exhibition.

Sanctuary City/Ciudad Santuario, 1989–2009 opened at Queen's Nails Project, a gallery in the Mission District, in the spring of 2009. Posi-tioning the art exhibit within a gallery in the Mission District was a means for these artists to address Latina/o viewers in the neighborhood. The exhibition featured audio testimonies given during public hearings on the effects of federal immigration enforcement policy in San Fran-cisco playing in the "sound" room; a stop-motion video that involved two artists' performance and counter-surveillance of police officers on Mission Street; and a text-based twenty-year timeline of city, state, and federal immigration laws and policies. The following year, De La Torre and one of the art students projected text onto a building in the Mission District near where ICE raids had taken place in 2008. This text included sections of transcripts from the audio testimonies, as well as quotations from local politicians' speeches.

The artists' use of audio rather than video testimony of Latina/o migrants—and their projection of text from these testimonies rather than images of migrants—was a means to challenge the way that the Department of Homeland Security (DHS) attempted to make undocumented Latina/o migrants "visible" through strategies of "fugitive apprehension" during this time period. These operations, which included raids, detentions, and deportations, were part of federal immigration officials' emphasis on what Nicholas De Genova refers to as "*targeted* policing, and its predictable capacity for generating a spectacle of law enforcement 'results.'"[9] The spectacle of ICE raids followed the 2006 mass immigration mobilizations, during which undocumented Latina/o migrants were very visible within public space.[10] The raids attempted to make undocumented migrants' "illegality" visible, while rendering them physically absent within public space. The absence of migrants arose from the fear—or actual experience—of detention and deportation, returning to an era previous to the spring of 2006—when both pro- and anti-immigrant activists discussed the "immigration problem"—"confident that," as Claudio Lomnitz recognizes, "immigrants themselves could not or would not speak up in public."[11]

In this sense, *Sanctuary City/Ciudad Santuario* is characteristic of artwork that relates to what Yates McKee describes as the "paradoxical aesthetics of disappearance articulated by [a] cluster of practices that resonates with Judith Butler's call for a 'critical image.'"[12] According to Butler, the critical image "must not only fail to capture its referent, but *show* this failing."[13] In not visually presenting the Latina/o migrants who testified in the "sound" room, the artists cut against the grain of the expected resolution in representation—countering the expectation of desire for the voices to correspond to visual representation. The audio documentation of these hearings does not have the same kind of refer-entiality as documentary film and video, which Meg McLagan contends is dependent upon "the indexical bond that exists between the photo-graphic image and the object in the historical world to which it refers."[14] With the use of audio without a visual counterpart, De La Torre and his artistic collaborators call attention to these expectations and disrupt the desire of the audience for the realization of the promise of documenta-tion. At the same time, the absence of visual images in the sound room enabled viewers to listen closely to the audio testimony, underscoring the *aural* presence of Latina/o migrants.

In the exhibition, there was a distinction between the gallery audi-ences' experiences of "hearing" the hearings and of reading the text. *Sanctuary City/Ciudad Santuario* thus highlights both the competing narratives and sensorial registers between politicians who refer to San Francisco as an ostensibly safe haven from state coercion and Latina/o migrants who testified to an increase in immigration raids, detentions, and deportations. In the exhibit, the quotations by city officials are rep-resented in text form, while the Latina/o migrants' testimonies at the joint hearings—organized by San Francisco's HRC and IRC—are pre-sented in audio form. As McLagan argues, testimonies "are performa-tive and work on an affective level."[15] The aural tone of the testimony given by Latina/o migrants, in which they described the effects of federal immigration policies, registered on an affective level, while the excerpts from newspaper articles and government documents included as wall text did not.

As opposed to visually representing undocumented Latina/o migrants, the artists used aesthetic strategies that made them audible and pres-ent, yet also narrated their disappearance through detention and depor-tation. Further, by projecting excerpts from migrants' testimony and quotations from politicians in public spaces in the Mission District—specifically, on a building near where ICE agents conducted immigra-tion raids and where city police officers profiled Latina/o migrants—the artists highlighted the contradictions between migrants' experiences and the statements given by politicians. Thus, the *Sanctuary City/Ciudad*

Santuario projections occupied spaces in the Mission District as "counter-spectacles."[16] These counter-spectacles amplify the practices of state surveillance and illuminate the disjuncture between the effects of ICE raids and racial profiling on Latina/o migrants, and local politicians' statements about the sanctuary ordinance.

In the chapter's first section, I address the tensions between San Francisco's sanctuary ordinance and the federal government's post-9/11 national security agenda. *Sanctuary City/Ciudad Santuario* cites two decades of immigration policies and their effects on Latina/o migrants in San Francisco. It also emphasizes events after 9/11, including the failure to pass comprehensive federal immigration reform in the 2000s; the mass rallies for immigrants' rights in 2006; and new immigration enforcement programs, such as Secure Communities (S-COMM). I examine how the changing relationship between federal and local immigration enforcement put pressure on local officials in San Francisco even as the multilayered structure of the U.S. nation-state created possibilities for local actors to advocate on behalf of undocumented migrants through recourse to the sanctuary ordinance. The remainder of the chapter examines *Sanctuary City/Ciudad Santuario* and various art projects that developed out of this exhibition. Specifically, I focus on how the installation and projections underscore the ways in which local and federal forces both converge and conflict in the enforcement of immigration legislation. I argue that this artistic work deconstructs the rhetoric of safety taken up by city police whose job it is "to serve and protect," as well as ICE's Secure Communities program, which involves local law enforcement agencies in the policing and reporting of the immigration status of city residents.

Frictions and Disjunctures

In 2007 when Sergio De La Torre was developing *Sanctuary City/Ciudad Santuario*, he was interested in questioning *who* is safe and *who* is secure at a time when federal immigration authorities, specifically ICE agents, were conducting raids in workplaces and residences in San Francisco. The city had had a sanctuary ordinance since 1989, based on a 1985 resolution that prohibited San Francisco's police, schools, and health and social service agencies from assisting the Immigration and Naturalization Service (INS) in investigations and arrests of Salvadoran and Guatemalan refugees. Both the resolution and the subsequent ordinance forbid city employees from helping immigration agents with investigations and arrests, unless required by law.[17]

The resolution and ordinance in San Francisco were outcomes of activist organizing by the sanctuary movement, which worked nationwide in the 1980s to push for municipal sanctuary policies that would limit local resources for federal immigration enforcement, while also protesting U.S. policies in Central America.[18] Members of the sanctuary movement put forward municipal sanctuary policies in cities across the United States to protest that Central Americans from El Salvador, Guatemala, and Nicaragua rarely qualified for asylum in the United States under the 1980 Refugee Act. As María Cristina García notes, the United Nations High Commission for Refugees (UNHCR) accused the United States of "not living up to its responsibilities as a signatory to the UN protocol," but the administration of President Ronald Reagan did not view violence in Central America as justifying asylum for refugees.[19] This administration also failed to acknowledge the role that its own foreign policy played in creating Central American refugees. In addition, the Reagan administration developed policies in the early 1980s that led to the detention and deportation of undocumented migrants. During these years, members of the sanctuary movement believed that the United States had a moral obligation to assist refugees, since U.S. military intervention in Central America had created them. In the Bay Area and beyond, churches became sanctuaries for refugees.[20]

As noted earlier, the 1989 sanctuary ordinance in San Francisco was originally developed for refugees from Central America, but it was later extended to protect all undocumented migrants in the city. As opposed to post-9/11 federal immigration policies, San Francisco's 1989 ordinance presents what Jennifer Ridgley calls "an alternative vision of security and political membership" for undocumented migrants.[21] The ordinance prompts city officials to protect undocumented migrants from federal immigration agencies and encourages these officials to view undocumented migrants as residents, rather than as criminals.

Sanctuary City/Ciudad Santuario addresses the post-9/11 relationship between federal and local immigration enforcement. Although the Illegal Immigration Reform and Immigrant Responsibility Act (IIRIRA, 1996) empowered state and local enforcement agencies to implement immigration laws through association with the federal government, none signed a 287(g) Memorandum of Understanding before 9/11. As Monica Varsanyi notes, after 9/11 a classified memo written by Attorney General John Ashcroft "affirming the authority of state and local police to enforce civil immigration law . . . opened the door to the devolution of immigration policing powers." As a result, "numerous sub-federal governments developed agreements with the federal government to enforce immigration law at the state and local level."[22] Since at least the mid-2000s, the frictions among multiple legal immigration regimes on the local, state, and national levels have occurred around myriad issues, including proposed legislation, such as Arizona's "Support Our Law Enforcement and Safe Neighborhoods Act," otherwise known as Arizona Senate Bill 1070 (SB 1070); the distribution of municipal and state ID cards; and "sanctuary" ordinances.[23]

The process by which the federal government "opened the door" for local governments to establish their own policies created conflicts between federal immigration agencies (including ICE) and local politicians in cities like San Francisco. San Francisco's sanctuary ordinance treated undocumented migrants as city residents, while ICE developed the 2003 National Fugitive Operations Program (NFOP), which criminalized undocumented migrants and initiated programs that focused on their detention and deportation.[24] ICE declared this program part of "national security," created to "protect" U.S. citizens from the "dangers" associated with "aliens," who were sometimes referred to as criminals. However, ICE's quota system—involving raids, detentions, and deportations—mostly targeted nonfugitives (those who had never been charged in an immigration court but were instead arrested based on ICE's suspicion that they were in the country unlawfully).[25] As Julie Myers, assistant secretary of ICE and DHS, stated at a June 2006 Senate Judiciary Committee hearing on immigrants in the workplace, "By careful coordination of our detention and removal resources and our investigative operations, ICE is able not only to target the organizations unlawfully employing illegal workers, but to detain and expeditiously remove the illegal workers encountered."[26] To justify the positioning of undocumented workers as "criminals," government officials, including DHS secretary Michael Chertoff, configured their workplace raids, which were part of campaigns with names like Operation Wagon Train, around document fraud and identity theft. These violations brought criminal charges, rather than merely administrative immigration violations. In December 2006—the day after a raid on six Swift & Company meatpacking plants in six states, which affected over twelve hundred workers—Chertoff characterized undocumented migrant workers as criminals for purchasing Social Security cards or other forms of identification to work in the United States. Chertoff cast Operation Wagon Train as part of the DHS's mission, which Myers stated at the hearings on "Immigration Enforcement of the Workplace" was "to protect our nation and the American people by targeting the people, money, and materials that support terrorist and criminal activities."[27] In the case of workplace raids, Nicholas De Genova argues, "migrants came to be easy stand-ins for the figure of terrorism."[28]

At the same time that Operation Wagon Train was being developed, undocumented migrants in the San Francisco Bay Area and beyond became the targets of numerous raids by ICE agents, as part of Operation Return to Sender. During these raids, over twenty-one hundred undocumented migrants from thirty-four states and Washington, D.C., were arrested during three weeks in May and June 2006. The majority of them were from California.[29] Operation Return to Sender, which was part of ICE's National Fugitive Operations Program, located undocumented migrants with deportation orders or criminal records and returned them to their countries of origin.[30] According to ICE's records, however, the Operation Return to Sender raids demonstrated that the majority of undocumented migrants who were arrested had no criminal records.[31] Although there were very few "criminal fugitives" located during the 2006 raids, some of those who were arrested were classified as "immigrant fugitives." These individuals had previous deportation orders but no criminal records. It should be noted that due to the lack of accurate information in the ICE database, undocumented migrants rarely received deportation notices.[32] In San Francisco, ICE agents who were part of Fugitive Operations Teams went to the homes of migrants with deportation orders or criminal records and arrested any undocumented migrants present—even if they had no deportation orders or criminal records.[33] The Migration Policy Institute stated that NFOP's arrest quota system caused ICE agents to "fail to distinguish between the different priority levels of immigration violators, encouraging the agency to direct scarce resources towards apprehending the easiest, rather than the most dangerous targets."[34]

Although Operation Wagon Train and Operation Return to Sender were distinct campaigns, both included well-publicized raids, detentions, and deportations of undocumented migrants. De Genova argues that these initiatives subjected undocumented migrants "to excessive and extraordinary forms of policing, denied any semblance of supposedly fundamental 'human rights' or 'civil liberties' . . . often with little or no recourse to any semblance of protection from the law."[35] Local journalists in the Bay Area, such as David Bacon, wrote about some of the abusive practices associated with Operation Return to Sender. For example, Bacon reported that ICE agents were stationed at an elementary school in Richmond, California, stopping people and asking for immigration papers, but only those who "looked Latino."[36] In 2007 the ACLU of northern California submitted a Freedom of Information Act (FOIA) request for documents from ICE about the raids associated with Operation Return to Sender. The people affected accused ICE agents of abusive practices, including "racial profiling, questioning children and conducting raids near schools, entering residences without a warrant, and misidentifying ICE agents as local police officers."[37] The ACLU was concerned that ICE was "breaking laws that protect civil rights," so it filed a lawsuit against the agency. Despite the lawsuit, ICE continued to conduct raids in the Bay Area as part of Operation Return to Sender.

Local officials and migrant rights supporters also responded to the ICE raids that were conducted as part of Operation Return to Sender. In 2007 Berkeley and Oakland, California, adopted sanctuary city ordinances that were similar to San Francisco's ordinance.[38] The city of Richmond also developed a bill with a sanctuary ordinance to prohibit city workers from cooperating with federal immigration agents.[39] In addition, there were numerous immigration rallies in San Francisco, San Jose, and Oakland, which, while smaller than those assembled in 2006, involved protests against the ICE raids. The smaller size of the marches was noted by migrant rights supporters and linked with the effects of the raids in 2006 and 2007. Anna Dorman, who managed La Clínica de la Raza's health education program in Oakland, commented that the 2007 turnout was smaller than 2006 because "the raids were an attempt to scare people." Dorman also noted that the 2007 raids might have been an attempt to intimidate migrants from demonstrating again in large numbers.[40] Local activists also made the connection between the spring 2006 immigrant rights marches and the ICE raids. Larissa Casillas of the Bay Area Immigrant Rights Coalition said the raids were an "intimidation tactic" used to pressure immigrants against "speak[ing] out for their rights and com[ing] out of the shadows."[41]

Along with Operation Return to Sender, which targeted "fugitive aliens" in residential areas, ICE also conducted mass raids on San Francisco area workplaces. One of the largest raids was at the restaurant chain Taquería El Balazo. The raid occurred on May 2, 2008, the day after the immigrant rights march in San Francisco. During these raids—which took place at eleven restaurants—over sixty workers were detained.[42] ICE agents entered Taquería El Balazo without arrest warrants, and they questioned workers without legal representation. Most of the workers had no criminal record, although ICE claimed that it targeted individuals involved in criminal activity. Sixty were arrested, and five were minors. After being released from jail all of these workers were placed under monitoring programs, wherein they were required to wear electronic ankle bracelets and remain at home twelve hours a day, in addition to required visits to San Francisco's ICE office three times a week. One local journalist argued that the raids "were part of a massive round up designed to intimidate immigrant workers."[43] However, the raids also led to protests and local challenges to federal law.[44]

In contesting ICE and its policies, city politicians used San Francisco's sanctuary ordinance as their first line of defense. Responding directly to the ICE raids at Taquería El Balazo restaurants throughout the Bay

Area, San Francisco's IRC drafted a resolution on May 12, 2008, to denounce the raids. The resolution first referred to the sanctuary ordinance, acknowledging that San Francisco City and County "values the dignity of all of its residents, regardless of immigration status, and will make every affirmative effort to ensure that all San Franciscans live in safety and free from discrimination," and ended by calling for a meeting between the San Francisco district director of ICE, members of San Francisco's HRC, the IRC, and local community-based immigrant organizations.[45]

However, contradictions between the sanctuary ordinance and federal immigration law appeared to be irreconcilable. In statements made following the ICE raids that occurred a few months later, Jamal Dajani, the chairman of San Francisco's IRC, contended that the arrests were "a total violation of the sanctuary ordinance," noting that "this is exactly why the sanctuary ordinance was created." In response, Lori Haley, a spokesperson for ICE, argued that "sanctuary doesn't affect ICE's efforts to enforce immigration law. ICE officers are sworn to enforce federal law."[46] The statements of Dajani and Haley demonstrate the disjuncture between the local ordinance and federal immigration law.

The conflicts between San Francisco's sanctuary ordinance and federal immigration law also led to clashes between city officials regarding the city's cooperation with federal immigration agencies. Although the sanctuary ordinance has been in place since 1989, its enforcement has fluctuated with the positions of San Francisco politicians. While city officials used the ordinance to denounce the Taquería El Balazo raids, Mayor Gavin Newsom attempted to change the ordinance when a wrongful death lawsuit was brought against the city. In 2008, around the time of the ICE raids at Taquería El Balazo, Edwin Ramos, a twenty-two-year-old undocumented migrant from El Salvador, was accused of murdering three members of the Bologna family. This case was used by both state and federal authorities to attack San Francisco's sanctuary ordinance. Politicians argued that the sanctuary ordinance failed because city officials had not transferred Ramos—who had committed felonies as a juvenile—to federal immigration officials. State and federal authorities contended that city officials should contact ICE in these cases, so they could deport undocumented migrants who had committed felonies. This case exemplifies what Susan Bibler Coutin describes as the "transnational conjunction of immigration and criminal justice policies," which "constitutes 'criminal aliens' or émigrés as expendable."[47] Following this case, Newsom attempted to retract aspects of the sanctuary ordinance, indicating that city officials would not shield juvenile migrants convicted of felonies from federal immigration officials. After immigration advocates protested this, Board of Supervisors member David Campos proposed an amendment that would restrict *when* city police could report the immigration status of juvenile offenders to the period *after* they had been convicted of a crime.[48] However, Mayor Newsom stated that he would not implement the Board of Supervisors' amendment, arguing that it contradicted federal law.[49]

The debates over San Francisco's sanctuary ordinance brought to the surface tensions between local and federal immigration law and among local officials. The disagreement between Board of Supervisors member David Campos and Mayor Newsom in 2008 highlighted the likelihood that the sanctuary ordinance was in violation of the Illegal Immigration Reform and Immigrant Responsibility Act of 1996 (IIRIRA) 8 USC. § 1373, "Communication between Government Agencies and the Immigration and Naturalization Service," among other federal laws.[50] As Rose Cuison Villazor has noted, "Related to this preemption argument is the view, recently validated by a state court, that the San Francisco sanctuary law violates California law's requirement of reporting the immigration status of persons who have committed crimes to federal authorities."[51] However, Villazor argues that there were other implications in the confrontation between Mayor Newsom and David Campos over the sanctuary ordinance as well, such as that it "conferred rights to undocumented immigrants" and "recognized undocumented non-citizens as members of the community."[52]

Although San Francisco's sanctuary ordinance accepts undocumented migrants as members of the city, this diverges from the federal government's understanding of who is a member of the national polity. Villazor understands San Francisco's sanctuary ordinance as providing a form of local citizenship or membership for undocumented migrants.

As she further argues, while citizenship is usually thought of as a legal status granted by the nation-state, there are alternative ways to construct citizenship, and she suggests that cities are locations where local citizenship or membership has been "articulated, constructed, or contested."[53] Sanctuary ordinances, which are inclusionary of undocumented migrants, provide what Varsanyi refers to as "grounded citizenship," which is based on residence in a place.[54] Miriam Wells also argues that this "grounded experience of common life" brings undocumented migrants into "the protected 'we' of state and local jurisdictions."[55] Although undocumented migrants may experience a form of local citizenship or membership in "sanctuary" cities, this conflicts with their status as undocumented, according to federal immigration law.

These issues, regarding the position of undocumented migrants within cities like San Francisco, are the focus of *Sanctuary City/Ciudad Santuario*. *Sanctuary City/Ciudad Santuario* was created in the midst of intense conflicts between local politicians and federal officials in San Francisco regarding policies toward undocumented migrants. Although there were protests and other responses by local migrant rights organizations to Operation Return to Sender, this period could be characterized by the withdrawal of undocumented migrants from some public spaces due to fears of being arrested, detained, and deported from the United States. This political context significantly affected the production of *Sanctuary City/Ciudad Santuario*, changing De La Torre's initial plans to collaborate on the project with undocumented Latina/o migrants in San Francisco.

Confronting Regimes of Legality in *Sanctuary City/Ciudad Santuario*, 1989–2009

In 2007, one year after the momentous immigrant rights marches, San Francisco Art Institute (SFAI) curator Hou Hanru invited Sergio De La Torre to work with SFAI students, community groups, and nonprofit organizations on a project about the city. De La Torre was chosen to lead this project because of his background collaborating with nongovernmental organizations on projects like *Maquilápolis: City of Factories* (2006). In a 2007 grant application submitted to the Creative Work Fund, De La Torre indicated that he planned to collaborate not only with students at

SFAI, but also with young Latina/o migrants affiliated with the Instituto Familiar de la Raza, a Chicana/o and Latina/o mental health center located in the Mission District, on a video project that addressed issues of "safety" and "security" for Latina/o migrants in San Francisco.[56] This emphasis was especially relevant at a time when ICE raids targeting undocumented Latina/o migrants in San Francisco were prevalent.

De La Torre's decision to collaborate on a project with Latina/o migrants while ICE raids were ongoing in the Bay Area was in many senses ill fated. In his grant application, titled "Agit-Van," De La Torre stated he would include young Latina/o migrants as creative participants in the production of the video that would be projected by a traveling cinema truck equipped with a video projector and sound system.[57] De La Torre tried to reach out to migrants to collaborate with him through the Instituto Familiar de la Raza and other nonprofit organizations in the Mission District, including Dolores Street Community Services, La Voz Latina, PODER (People Organizing to Demand Environmental and Economic Rights), and the Central American Resource Center (CARECEN), but he was not able to identify individuals who were interested in participating in the project. As he recalled, "People were afraid back then. They didn't want to talk to anyone."[58] De La Torre commented further, "What we found was, even after prompting, no one was willing to share their experiences. The lack of conversation we experience[d] was . . . the biggest hurdle we faced with this project."[59] Thus, instead of working with young Latina/o migrants, De La Torre collaborated with a group of SFAI students, including Wenhua Shia, Rosario Sotelo, Karla Claudio, Dina Roumanstieva, and Chris Treggiari, to address Latina/o migrants and to develop participatory elements within the exhibition to engage them as viewers.

The creation of the art installation *Sanctuary City/Ciudad Santuario* was similar to the preproduction of a documentary film. De La Torre and his collaborators first conducted research on San Francisco's sanctuary ordinance. In addition to staff at the nonprofit organizations in the Mission District whom they contacted, the artists also compiled information from the Migration Policy Institute, the Pew Hispanic Trust, the ACLU,

ICE, and other nonprofits and government agencies in the United States and Mexico. The artists investigated the costs of border enforcement, the remittances in dollars that were sent by undocumented Latina/o migrants to their families in their home countries, the number of deportations of Mexicans and Central Americans, and the number of individuals who died trying to cross the U.S.–Mexico boundary undetected.[60] The artists also researched stories in local newspapers and recorded public hearings that were organized by social service agencies in the Mission District and San Francisco's HRC and IRC. Although De La Torre could not collaborate with undocumented Latina/o migrants in the making of *Sanctuary City/Ciudad Santuario*, he did attend public hearings on the effects of federal immigration enforcement in San Francisco. With permission, he recorded the testimony of Latina/o migrants who spoke. During these hearings individuals affected by the ICE raids testified about their experiences and those of family or community members. Thus, the artists were able to include the perspectives of Latina/o migrants in the art installation. The artists recorded and edited these testimonies into an audio piece that was exhibited in the "sound room." The testimony was a form of "migrant counter-conduct" in which those who testified contested state agents' criminalization of undocumented migrants.

Although direct collaboration with undocumented Latina/o migrants was not possible for the artists, their decision to exhibit *Sanctuary City/ Ciudad Santuario* at Queen's Nails Project in the Mission District foregrounded an effort to reach a Latina/o audience and claimed a public space within that neighborhood in order to challenge the surveillance of Latinas/os by city police and ICE agents. The exhibition—which could be viewed from May 28 to June 21, 2009—was installed in two rooms at Queen's Nails Project. The main room of the exhibition featured maps of the Mission and the nearby Excélsior Districts; the year 2000 census's information about the Latina/o population in San Francisco; a stop-motion video addressing the police surveillance and racial profiling of Latina/o migrants driving on Mission Street; wallpaper made from U.S. immigration forms; and a twenty-year timeline of U.S. immigration laws enacted at the city, state, and federal levels. The wall of the main room had a sign that read, "grab a Sharpie and ladder and join in" so that migrants who visited could write about their own experiences on the timeline.[61] Playing in a separate "sound room" were the audio testimonies, which were spoken in Spanish (and translated into English) and taped at a joint hearing organized by San Francisco's HRC and IRC in 2009.[62] In addition to the testimonies that played in the sound room, the artists included an art piece comprised of an electronic ankle bracelet rotating on a lazy Susan, lit by a small spotlight. De La Torre and his collaborators used the ankle bracelet to reference the experiences of undocumented migrants who had no deportation orders but were still swept up in ICE raids, detained, and later released under house arrest.[63]

Sanctuary City/Ciudad Santuario was addressed to viewers in the Mission District, an area that has historically been home to a significant Latina/o population.[64] Queen's Nails Project, an artist-run gallery that presented collaborative, site-specific, and experimental projects by artists and curators, was located on Mission Street right in front of a bus stop where many Latina/o migrants waited to commute downtown for work.[65] The position of these migrants as commuters suggests their integration into the city as workers, but still, these individuals had been surveilled and excessively scrutinized in this area by city police. The artists attempted to engage commuters by having information about San Francisco's sanctuary ordinance printed on the front window of the gallery in both Spanish and English. In one window, the artists included a brief description of the sanctuary ordinance, as well as information about its historical beginnings as part of the 1980s sanctuary movement. The text on the window was an important intervention into the policing of Latina/o migrants on Mission Street, a place where individuals were regularly arrested by the city police and handed over to ICE, in complete disregard of the sanctuary ordinance. In the other window, the artists included a question, printed in a larger font: "What Rights Does an Immigrant Have?"/"¿Qué derechos tiene un/a inmigrante?" (Figure 21). This question—directed at passers-by—was a means for the artists to draw in viewers for the exhibition and to intervene in the policing of

Figure 21. Front window of Queen's Nails gallery during the exhibition of *Sanctuary City/Ciudad Santuario, 1989–2009,* May 28–June 21, 2009. Photograph by Sergio De La Torre.

Latina/o migrants in the Mission. The artists also publicized their exhibition at the 2009 May Day march and rally in San Francisco.

The contradiction between local policies and federal immigration laws was a major theme in *Sanctuary City/Ciudad Santuario.* This theme developed from the artists' conversations with staff at nonprofit organizations, including those at Dolores Street Community Services, who directed them toward the most pressing issues for undocumented Latina/o migrants. Although the artists could not directly collaborate on the project with undocumented Latina/o migrants, they did include migrants' testimonies from the joint HRC/IRC hearings in the exhibition. The artists audiotaped—rather than videotaped—this testimony, since Latina/o migrants in the Mission District told De La Torre that they "did not want their faces to be shown" because of their fear of being targeted by immigration agents, and as De La Torre explains, "We wanted to respect that."[66] The artists edited down the audio testimony into a twenty-minute segment that played in a smaller sound room at

Queen's Nails Project. Most of the testimony in the audio recording was spoken in Spanish, although it included English translations given at the hearings for some of the testimonies.

The artists' decision to include audio rather than a video of Latina/o migrants' testimony regarding their experiences being targeted by local police and federal immigration agents relates not only to the specific context of the ICE raids but also to broader issues about race, representation, and subjection. Jennifer González argues that "race discourse produces an economy of visibility—and simultaneous invisibility—by which group members are subject to a disciplinary gaze that operates to fix their position within a given social or political landscape through techniques of exhibition (in museums, on the street, on the screen, etc.)."[67] In *Sanctuary City/Ciudad Santuario,* the artists brought attention to the disciplinary gaze of local police and federal immigration authorities who contributed to migrants' experiences of being racially profiled on the street, leading to arrests, detentions, and deportations. The artists included the audio testimony in the exhibit to engage gallery visitors as witnesses to the migrants' experiences.

Although the artists' decision to forgo accompanying images might frustrate the audience's desire to see the people who testified, the sound of the migrant's voices conveys a distinct and material physicality of the speakers. The sound room was a small, enclosed space that positioned the gallery viewer as a witness to the testimonies of Latina/o migrants at the hearing. The artists' choice to work primarily with audio in the sound room underscores the simultaneous aural *presence* and the visual *absence* of Latina/o migrants, which is characteristic of what McKee describes as an aesthetics of disappearance. Exhibiting the testimony in the form of an audio piece meant that the hearings were in fact "hearings," which Catherine Cole describes as "something that can be listened to, a sonic experience that communicated through orality: the cadence, inflections, rhythms, volume, accent, and grain of the voice."[68] Through listening to the testimony the audience can hear what Roland Barthes refers to as the "grain"—which is the body in the voice—in this case representing the embodied performance of Latina/o migrants.[69]

Even though the audience could not see the facial expressions or hand gestures of those who testified, the "grain" of their voices contributed to what they were saying and thus what the audience heard. The testimonies included in the audio recordings that played in the sound room were restricted to those given by Latina/o migrants.[70] In their testimonies, which were limited to two minutes each, Latina/o migrants emphasized the effects of ICE raids and racial profiling on themselves, their families, and their communities. Although some of the testimony was spoken matter-of-factly, other individuals who testified were audibly emotional. Erika gave the first testimony to HRC/IRC in Spanish:

La Raza recibe 400 familias a la semana para solicitar comida, para solicitar despensas de emergencia por al razón de tantas redadas producidas. ¿Qué es lo que está pasando? Estas familias no tienen ingreso, estas familias han sido separadas por una causa que quizás sea injusta.

[La Raza receives 400 families a week; these families come to solicit food and emergency kits as a result of the raids. What is happening? These families don't have income and are being separated, something that to me sounds like injustice.][71]

In other testimonies, individuals noted the dire effects of ICE raids, which impacted workers more than employers, since workers frequently lost their property or housing as a result. In addition, one speaker who was not identified in the recording described how he was profiled by ICE agents:

Ese día yo estaba buscando un puesto de trabajo cuando los agentes de ICE tomaron fuerza y agresivamente me detuvieron. Al regresar a mi apartamento me preguntaron si yo vivía allí, les dije que sí. Después de entrar a el apartamento, nos tiraron al piso (había cinco personas en la casa en ese momento), nos pidieron nuestros nombres sin que nos mostraran sus carnet o que se identificaran.

[That day I was looking for a job when ICE officers forcefully and aggressively took hold of me. Upon returning to my apartment they asked me if I lived there, I told them yes. After entering the apartment they threw us to the floor (there were five people in the house at that time), asked us our names without showing us their badges or identifying themselves.][72]

This man's testimony describes a procedure characteristic of Operation Return to Sender, where ICE agents would force entry into an undocumented migrant's home, asking not only for his personal information, but also that of others living in the same house or apartment building.[73] Young people also testified regarding their fear of losing their parents due to the raids. In her testimony, Karina, a high school student, stated, "Hay veces que llego a mi casa pensando que si mis padres van a estar allí. Hay veces que salgo con miedo. A veces me da miedo ir, ni quiero ir a la tienda" (There are times when I arrive at my house wondering if my parents will be there. There are times that I am scared to go out. There are times that I'm afraid to even go to the store).[74] Karina's statement speaks to the particular challenges faced by young people who are undocumented.

By only presenting audio testimony of Latina/o migrants and specifically reaching out to Latina/o migrants as viewers of the exhibition, the artists appeared to be positioning them as the primary witnesses for the testimonies. The construction of Latina/o migrants as witnesses relates to a point made by Janet Walker and Bhaskar Sarkar that in these kinds of contexts "the art of bearing witness helps politicize consciousness, stirring members of affected communities towards acts of resistance."[75] However, the artists also knew that the installation in the sound room would be heard by non-Latina/o audiences. In writing about the documentary film *The Sky: A Silent Witness* (1995), in which some women interviewed were not portrayed visually, Wendy Hesford notes, "The primary motive for the testifier's anonymity may have been protection, but her refusal to become a visual text also places the viewer in a curious relation to this rhetorical refusal." Similar to the film *The Sky*, the artists who created *Sanctuary City/Ciudad Santuario* do "not permit the viewer to appropriate trauma or the suffering of others through the spectacle of visual identification."[76]

The artists' inclusion of audio testimony in the sound room is characteristic of what Meg McLagan refers to as "'documentary rhetoric'—realist forms of representation and conventions of documentary," yet the use of audio also challenges the notion of visibility as "unmediated" that is so much a part of "documentary rhetoric."[77] McLagan notes that the use of testimony has "proliferated in multiple genres and arenas," starting in the 1990s, "from written texts to film and video documentaries to live performances and face-to-face encounters in activist meetings, NGO forums, and governmental hearings," and yet Ann Cvetkovich argues that "there is no transparent representation of trauma nor any straightforward context of reception."[78] This is further complicated when interlocutors present this testimony in audiovisual or written form.[79] Although many differences exist between written and spoken text, what is similar between the (written) testimonio described by John Beverly, drawing from a genre that has been used in Latin America against political repression and state violence, and the oral testimony included in *Sanctuary City/Ciudad Santuario* is that, in both cases, oral forms are addressed to a broader audience through interlocutors.[80]

In the sound room, migrants' oral statements accentuated the absence of their physical bodies. Accompanying the recordings of the Latina/o migrants' testimonies was an electronic ankle bracelet rotating on a lazy Susan, in which the artists drew attention to competing sensorial registers—vision versus sound—and between the effect of the migrants' oral testimonies and the material object that stood in for federal immigration agents' "techniques and modes of subjection."[81] The absence of visual representations in the sound room makes reference to the end result for many people who have disappeared through detention or deportation from the United States.[82] Inherent in artistic projects such as *Sanctuary City/Ciudad Santuario* are what McKee describes as the challenges of making "disappearance appear as such, which is to say, as an intolerable governmental practice premised on the dismembering of particular subjects from the realm of both legal protection and public memory."[83] At the same time, the absence of a body attached to the bracelet separates it from the "crime" to which it is assigned—namely, being an undocumented migrant.[84]

The artists' emphasis on documenting the presence of the undocumented migrant community and displaying the disciplinary artifacts of government agencies was also evident in the exhibition's main room. Here, the artists included the 2000 census data on Latinas/os in San Francisco; maps of neighborhoods where Latinas/os reside; government documents, such as the immigration forms that they used as wallpaper; and a wall-mounted timeline of immigration laws from 1989 to 2009. Five tables stood in the main room, each containing a piece of the map of the Mission and Excélsior Districts. When the tables were put together, they created a map of the entire area. Displayed on the five tables with maps placed upon them were plastic sleeves that contained census data, including the percentages of Latina/o migrants from Latin America, Central America, Mexico, and the Caribbean living in the Mission and Excélsior Districts since the 1980s.[85] The tables with maps and sleeves demonstrated the historical presence of Latinas/os in the Mission and the Excélsior Districts.[86] The artists' inclusion of this census data was also a comment on the gentrification of the Mission District, particularly through evictions and the general displacement of Latinas/os. This related to the theme of the exhibition, which as mentioned earlier was to address issues of "safety" and "security" for Latina/o migrants in San Francisco.

During 2008 and 2009—the years when *Sanctuary City/Ciudad Santuario* was being developed and exhibited—the Mission District was going through demographic changes similar to those in the late 1990s and early 2000s, when tech companies moved into the area. Karl Beitel details the dot-com boom and the community organizing against gentrification in the Mission District, noting: "Rents were skyrocketing, and the housing stock of the Mission was coming under intensifying pressure from a younger, primarily white, group of newly arriving urban immigrants drawn by the dot-com boom, which led to the evictions and displacement of many Latina/os from the Mission District."[87] Beitel also mentions that a coalition of community groups formed the Mission Anti-Displacement Coalition (MAC) to protest gentrification.[88] Within a few years, MAC formed the Mission Anti-Displacement Project (MAP), which developed the People's Plan to pressure city officials to protect low-income and migrant community members from eviction.[89] Although many issues around gentrification continued to plague low-income and migrant communities in the Mission District when *Sanctuary City/ Ciudad Santuario* was being exhibited, what had changed from the late 1990s were post-9/11 immigration policies. These led to what Tomás Summers Sandoval describes as "one of the most frightening periods of mass incarceration and deportation" in U.S. history.[90]

While the tables provided information on Latinas/os in San Francisco during a period of increased gentrification, the walls displayed immigration documents, as well as a timeline that showed fluctuations in immigration law on the local, state, and federal levels; the rise of militarized policing on the U.S.–Mexico border and its effects on migrant crossing; and other issues pertaining to U.S. immigration (mostly from Mexico) over a twenty-year period between 1989 and 2009. Through the *Sanctuary City/Ciudad Santuario* exhibition, the artists intervened in broader political discourses related to U.S. immigration policies by focusing on the discriminatory actions of local police and federal immigration agencies, the disjuncture between federal and local immigration policies, and the conflicts between local politicians. The artists also included information about local policies meant to protect undocumented migrants. In fact, one of the reoccurring elements of the timeline was its focus on the support of San Francisco's politicians for migrants' rights. According to the timeline, San Francisco was among the first cities to develop a sanctuary ordinance (1989) and the first to establish an Immigrant Rights Commission (1997). It was also the first city to accept the *matrícular consular*, a card issued by the Mexican consulate to Mexicans with birth certificates and proof of local residence, as a valid form of identification (2001). San Francisco was also the first large city to provide municipal ID cards to migrants (2009).[91]

As a result of this arrangement of information, viewers confronted a disjuncture between the testimony of undocumented Latina/o migrants, who described their experiences as targets of ICE raids and racial profiling, and textual information, including quotes from city officials displayed on the timeline, who stated that San Francisco's sanctuary ordinance protected undocumented migrants. The wall text included a 2007 statement by San Francisco mayor Gavin Newsom that indicated he would "discourage federal authorities from conducting immigration raids in San Francisco." The timeline also referenced Newsom's Sanctuary City Public Awareness campaign to promote San Francisco's sanctuary ordinance for undocumented migrants. The campaign emphasized that no one who accessed city services would be handed over to federal immigration authorities.[92] Mayor Newsom claimed that undocumented migrants should feel comfortable contacting city officials, including reporting crimes. During the HRC/IRC joint hearing, however, numerous individuals testified that city police profiled Latina/o migrants and in some cases impounded their cars. For example, Guillermina—whose voice could be heard in the sound room—testified: "Yo vivo en la 20 y Mission, y trabajo en la 16 y Mission, y es increíble como 4 policías están quitando carros al mismo tiempo" (I live at 20th and Mission and I work on 16th and Mission and it's incredible to see that in that area there are 4 policemen taking cars at the same time).[93] De La Torre discovered during the hearings that after their cars were taken away, some of these individuals were arrested, with city police notifying ICE agents who would have them transferred to a detention center and put in deportation proceedings.[94]

De La Torre and his collaborators also created a stop-motion video composed of photographs that he and Rosario Sotelo took from their front car window while driving on Mission Street, in an area where police were stationed (Figure 22).[95] The stop-motion video was the end product of De La Torre's and Sotelo's "performances" of "driving while Latina/o," during which they turned the tables on city police by surveilling them. De La Torre had learned at the IRC/HRC hearing that city police stationed on Mission Street stopped individuals who "looked Latina/o" for minor traffic violations and then requested their identification as well as proof of citizenship. This correlates with Philip Kretsedemas's contention that "local police often develop racial-ethnic profiles of 'illegals' that are based on broad generalizations of how the typical

Figure 22. Still from a stop-motion video by Sergio De La Torre and Rosario Sotelo that was on display as part of the *Sanctuary City/Ciudad Santuario, 1989–2009* exhibition at Queen's Nails gallery, May 28–June 21, 2009.

immigrant looks, acts and sounds."[96] By hanging a rosary in the rearview mirror as they drove around Mission Street, De La Torre and Sotelo made reference to the "racial-ethnic profiles" developed by police officers and ICE agents, who tried to identify undocumented Latina/o migrants by the *objects* with which they adorned their vehicles.[97]

This stop-motion video piece challenges what Gilberto Rosas calls Latina/o migrants' "policeability," which Marta María Maldonado, Adela C. Licona, and Sarah Hendricks describe as "a state of constant surveillance predicated on the hyperregulation of routine activity, evident in displays of state power, vigilantism and the informal management of everyday life."[98] Although many undocumented Latina/o migrants do not have access to drivers' licenses—which, according to Maldonado, Licona, and Hendricks, "create conditions of forced immobilizations"—they can apply for them in places like San Francisco. However, as testified to during the HRC/IRC hearings, driving does make undocumented Latina/o migrants more susceptible to police surveillance. Through the artists' counter-surveillance, this piece could be an artistic example of what Maldonado, Licona, and Hendricks characterize as "transgressive Latin@ altermobilities."[99]

Although the artists employed an aesthetics of disappearance in the sound room, in their stop-motion video they adopt an *aesthetics of mobility*. The aesthetics of the stop-motion video—which creates the appearance of motion by rapidly sequencing still images—resembles a Google map feature. However, what distinguishes the stop-motion video from the Google map feature—during which the viewer has the virtual experience of moving through space—is that the video represents Latinas/os documenting their experiences of driving on Mission Street. While Avery Gordon argues that photography has been used as a "tool by which modern states can survey and control their populations," the photographs taken by De La Torre and Sotelo instead represent the viewpoint of the Latinas/os watching for police and are thus a form of counter-surveillance.[100] The stop-motion video also references the technologies of surveillance at work in Google maps as linked to practices of control, displacement, and gentrification, but for different purposes. The aesthetics of the Google map feature relate to the fact that as Latinas/os were being racially profiled by city police and ICE agents while driving in their own neighborhoods, the Google bus shuttled their employees from expensive apartments in the Mission District to the corporate offices in Silicon Valley, a service that encouraged more of their employees to live in the neighborhood.[101] This piece thus draws connections between the effects of gentrification in the Mission District and the racial profiling of Latina/o migrants leading to detention and deportation. These linkages are significant as the San Francisco Board of Supervisors held public meetings in which residents gave testimony opposing a development proposal in the Mission District months before the hearing recorded by the artists on the effects of federal immigration enforcement.[102]

The artists provided Sharpie pens at the gallery so visitors could write about their own experiences of migration on the timeline. Although De La Torre had hoped that Latina/o migrants would participate, not many engaged in the interactive elements of the exhibition. De La Torre explained that at this time undocumented Latina/o migrants were not comfortable sharing personal information in public. Although some Latina/o migrants from the neighborhood did come to see *Sanctuary City/Ciudad Santuario*, perhaps because it was an area where police surveilled Latina/o migrants, it never became a truly participatory project involving Latina/o migrants, according to De La Torre.[103] Thus, the exhibition did not include the perspectives of undocumented Latina/o migrants to the extent that De La Torre had initially planned.

In order to circulate information presented in *Sanctuary City/Ciudad Santuario* outside of the gallery space, the artists created a limited-edition poster that was available to anyone who attended the exhibition. The poster contained a condensed version of the timeline on display in the exhibition. Similar to the timeline, the poster illustrated the fluctuations in immigration policies and enforcement at the local, state, and federal levels. This historical perspective is a significant feature of the poster, which provides the context in which city policies such as the sanctuary ordinance were developed in response to changes in federal immigration laws. The poster is not only a resource in terms of the information it presents, it also enables the viewer to reflect on immigration policies that have been established in the past as a means to respond to those developed in the present. Following the exhibition, De La Torre noted that the poster was displayed in the offices of local politicians, including Board of Supervisor member David Campos, who represented the Mission and Excélsior Districts.[104]

The Afterlives of *Sanctuary City/Ciudad Santuario*

Following the exhibition of *Sanctuary City/Ciudad Santuario*, two of the artists developed other projects, bringing elements of the exhibition into public spaces in the Mission District. The first project was El Centro de Recursos Santuario SF (SF Sanctuary Resource Center), a mobile resource center, created by Chris Treggiari, which contained information about the sanctuary ordinance. De La Torre developed the second project with Treggiari, which brought together elements of the installation, specifically the migrants' testimony and quotes from local politicians, into public space. They projected this text onto a building in the Mission District near where ICE raids had taken place. The concept of a mobile projector developed from De La Torre's original proposal, which included the "Agit-Van," a truck that would screen videos produced by young Latina/o migrants in locations across the Bay Area.

This approach, to bring artwork out of the gallery and into public space, is reminiscent of artists and arts collectives that were engaged in public and community-based work during the 1980s and 1990s. These include Gran Fury, REPO-History, and the collaborative art projects of David Avalos, Louis Hock, and Liz Sisco, who were members of the Border Arts Workshop/Taller de Arte Fronterizo (BAW/TAF).[105] These artists created projects to transform public spaces; to mark the forces of state power and corporate privatization, to highlight uneven development or racialized gentrification that overdetermines particular locations, or to reclaim spaces for local residents by creating alternative or oppositional histories. Similar to the artists whose work Jennifer González discusses in *Subject to Display*, with the *Sanctuary City/Ciudad Santuario* projections, De La Torre and Treggiari "employ a radical or critical situational aesthetics concerned with exploring how public and private spaces are imbedded with the history of race discourse and related forms of subjection," by "re-creating or infiltrating public spaces . . . in order to articulate those signs and spaces that play a central role in the process of subjection."[106] The projections were an intervention into the public space of the Mission District as a means of bringing attention to the forces of state power, including ICE, as well as the effects of racialized gentrification.

De La Torre and Treggiari's emphasis on infiltrating public spaces with the *Sanctuary City/Ciudad Santuario* projections also resembles the public artwork of Krzysztof Wodiczko, especially his large-scale slide and video projections on monuments and buildings.[107] As mentioned earlier, Wodiczko was influenced by the Situationists, such as Guy Debord, who wrote that their "central idea is that of the construction of situations."[108] According to Debord, "The construction of situations begins in the ruins of a modern spectacle." Thus "situations" challenge the authority of the spectacle, which he described as "a social relationship between people that is mediated by images."[109] Yates McKee contends that part of post-9/11 government practice has been to remove certain subjects from public memory, and yet the *Sanctuary City/Ciudad Santuario* projections make visible the experiences of Latina/o migrants who were not protected by the sanctuary ordinance, rather becoming targets of the U.S. federal immigration agencies.

Although De La Torre had not been able to collaborate with undocumented Latina/o migrants on *Sanctuary City/Ciudad Santuario*, he did rework the "Agit-Van" concept to bring aspects of the exhibition into public view. Through the projections, De La Torre could reach a broader group of viewers, including Latina/o migrants. Instead of using a mobile film truck, De La Torre and Treggiari created a mobile projector, from which they projected text from the exhibition. De La Torre wanted to make the projections interactive, so he imagined that including a tablet would enable viewers (notably Latina/o migrants) to write about their own experiences, as well as their responses to the testimonies and the statements from local politicians, which would also be projected onto the building. Unfortunately, due to lack of funds, De La Torre and Treggiari were not able to include this interactive element in the projections. Although the Latinas/os who saw the projections were not able to include their perspectives in the piece, the artists did interact with passers-by and could therefore gauge their responses to the projections.[110]

The *Sanctuary City/Ciudad Santuario* projections that took place in July 2010 functioned as a public intervention into a space in the Mission District near where the ICE raids had occurred. De La Torre planned to project text onto a building (located on Mission Street and 23rd Street) near where an ICE raid of a Taquería El Balazo location had taken place. With the projections, the artists juxtaposed quotations from the migrants' testimonies with statements made by city officials (Figures 23 and 24). The text was projected in this order:

We will stand up and fight for people so they live their lives out loud in the light of day with dignity and respect.

A los niños nos da miedo volver a casa pensando si nuestros padres estarán ahí. [The kids, we are afraid to go home wondering if our parents will be there.]

City residents should feel safe when they visit a public health clinic, enroll their children in school, report a crime to the Police Department, or seek out other city services.

Our action is to stand strong in opposition to these ICE raids to make sure that we are not contributing in any way, shape, or form.

Pedimos que la ciudad continúe siendo un santuario. [We ask that the city remains a sanctuary.]

This is a city of refuge.

Hagamos una reforma migratoria justa. [Let's make a just immigration reform.]

Estamos viendo familias destrozadas. [We're seeing families torn apart.]

La policía nos ha quitado nuestros vehículos. [The police have taken away our vehicles.]

Not in my city.

Queremos que las familias tengan una reunión con el alcalde. [We want families to have a meeting with the mayor.]

No es un crimen venir a otro país. [It is not a crime to come to another country.]

Cuando salgo a la calle salgo con miedo. [When I go out I go in fear.]

Agentes de migración me esposaron y, me tiraron al piso, dentro de mi casa, sin identificarse. [Immigration agents handcuffed me and threw me on the floor, inside my house, without identifying themselves.]

Detuvieron a mi hijo con la excusa de que llevaba basura en el carro. [They (ICE agents) arrested my son with the excuse that he had trash in the car.]

La ciudad no agradece nuestros sacrificios. [The city is not grateful for our sacrifices.]

Si la ciudad nos castiga, ¿cuál debe ser nuestra actitud? [If the city is punishing us, what should be our attitude?]

I will act responsibly.

Although the *Sanctuary City/Ciudad Santuario* projections were partly drawn from the audio testimony in the sound room, these two works differed in their affective tones. The audio testimony that played in the gallery had an emotional resonance that was distinct from the textual projections. The affective quality of the testimony can be distinguished from the projections, which included textual excerpts from the statements of those who testified. At the same time, the projections were a form of what Walker and Sarkar refer to as "situated testimony," which is "delivered in situ from the very place where catastrophic events occurred and, in some cases, while the situation continues to unfold."[111] Both in the gallery and as part of the projections, however, the presence of migrants' statements also accentuated the absence of their physical bodies.

In choosing the text for the *Sanctuary City/Ciudad Santuario* projections, the artists assumed a bilingual audience. These projections—like other images and text—have "a certain acoustic dimension," as Yates McKee argues, in that they "address, call out to, and make claims on others."[112] Similar to the artwork that González examines in *Subject to Display*, the projections offer "a disorienting environment in order to invite the viewer to identify (or disidentify) with a specific subject position."[113] The text, which was in English and Spanish, was not translated, and consequently, these projections "address, call out to, and make claims" on different viewers. English-speaking viewers read text that conveyed local officials' support for the sanctuary ordinance, while Spanish-speaking

Figure 23. Sergio De La Torre and Chris Treggiari projected this statement, made by a politician in San Francisco following ICE raids, onto a building in the Mission District in July 2010. Photograph by Jessica Watson. Courtesy of Sergio De La Torre.

Figure 24. This text is drawn from testimony on ICE raids in San Francisco, which Sergio De La Torre and Chris Treggiari projected onto a building in the Mission District in July 2010. Photograph by Jessica Watson. Courtesy of Sergio De La Torre.

viewers read text about Latina/o migrants' experiences as targets of ICE raids, the criticism of city officials for not enforcing the sanctuary ordinance, and the condemnation of federal officials for their unjust immigration policies. Only the bilingual viewers of the projections could access the contradictions between the statements of politicians (in English) and those of Latina/o migrants (in Spanish).

De La Torre noted that Latina/o and non-Latina/o viewers seemed to have different responses to the projections. According to De La Torre, "We had multiple Latino men and women watch the entire cycle of the quotes we displayed . . . thanking us and asking more about the project." He also noted, "We did get some interaction with some non-Latino viewers, but in general they would stay for a minute or two and move on. . . . Some specific questions I got from these viewers dealt more with the art component of this . . . the projection, the cart, etc." Overall, he found that "Latino viewers were much more engaged with the content." De La Torre noticed that mainly Latinas/os stopped and read the text or conversed with the artists about the project. He recalled that these viewers "had questions about the 'Sanctuary City' ordinance. A majority of our viewers at this event . . . had no idea about the ordinance. . . . For the most part we spoke with people who were positive about the ordinance."[114] De La Torre also had conversations with local business owners, including a white woman who owned the bar near where he had positioned the projector. According to De La Torre, this woman was concerned that the projections would negatively affect her business. She remained hostile toward him, even after he explained the project. This bar—which catered to newer residents—demonstrates the changing streetscape of the Mission due to gentrification, which led to fewer Latina/o-owned businesses.[115] In confronting the artists about the projections, the bar owner was attempting to police the Mission's commercial space, which could be an effort toward the "redefinition of communities and neighborhoods on the basis of whiteness," which, as Nancy Raquel Mirabal argues, also involves "creating spaces where white bodies and desires and, most importantly, consumption, dominate and shape the neighborhood."[116] The projections' broader intervention responded to the increasing gentrification in the Mission District by bringing the recent memories of Latina/o migrants into public space.

Part of the effect of the *Sanctuary City/Ciudad Santuario* projections is that viewers who read the excerpts of migrants' testimony and statements from politicians might view this space differently following the event. The artists' decision to project the text onto a Giant Value store on Mission Street served as a metaphor for Latina/o migrants as low-wage workers, and the projections transformed this building into an ephemeral billboard, a form of alternative publicity. Although "ephemerality" is a key component of such projections, Wodiczko has also suggested that "the absence of the image is often more powerful than when it was there."[117] Projections transform a space, giving it a different meaning. Similar to the work of photographer Christina Fernández, the *Sanctuary City/ Ciudad Santuario* projections "make visible what is already part of the city or the culture but that is unseen or unheeded by society at large."[118]

The *Sanctuary City/Ciudad Santuario* projections served as a public response to the ICE raids, by underscoring the dialectics of presence and absence, documented and undocumented, safety and vulnerability. The projection of migrants' testimony onto buildings in the Mission functions as a form of "counter-spectacle" to what De Genova calls the "spectacle of security" in the post-9/11 era.[119] This spectacle of security included ICE raids, which were "well-publicized," highlighting "the more menacing figure of 'criminal aliens' with pending arrest warrants."[120] As a "counter-spectacle," the projections make visible events like the ICE raids, which are typically unseen by the broader public, as well as their effects on undocumented Latina/o migrants. The size of the text in the projections amplified these statements, making them all the more visible as markers, and as a means to claim space within the context of the streetscape. The artists' choice to project text—rather than images—from the testimony challenged how Latina/o migrants were made visible in public spaces. Although ICE raids were not taking place in San Francisco during the projections, the testimony of Latina/o migrants was a reminder that the city had not adequately enforced its sanctuary ordinance. The texts insist that it do so in opposition to more recent federal immigration initiatives, such as ICE's Secure Communities program.

Although the projections were part of the artists' attempt to make visible the effects of the ICE raids on Latina/o migrants, as well as the discrepancy between the statements and actions of local officials, they served another purpose in a neighborhood facing gentrification that threatened to decrease the Latina/o presence in the Mission. That the testimony was projected onto a Giant Value store, which catered to lower-income residents of the Mission but has since been demolished to make room for high-rise apartments, speaks to the effects of the encroaching influx of tech wealth into the Mission District. In the context of the Mission District, which historically has had a significant population of Latina/o residents, Mirabal notes, "By casting gentrification as primarily an economic byproduct of a growing economy, dot-com or otherwise, it is possible to avoid, even ignore questions of difference and the role they play in the disposability of certain populations and the privileging of others."[121] Tomás Summers Sandoval argues in the context of a public meeting organized by the Board of Supervisors on a development proposal in the Mission in 2007 that "the Latino community of San Francisco today is struggling for survival" due to the effects of gentrification.[122] The *Sanctuary City/Ciudad Santuario* projections are thus an artistic intervention that brings attention to the displacement of Latina/o migrants from the Mission District as the effect of both ICE raids and racialized gentrification. The projection of testimony onto the Giant Value building connects the ICE raids to a longer history of gentrification within San Francisco.[123]

The connection between the ICE raids and racialized gentrification in the Mission District was also apparent in *No Vacancies*, another artwork created by De La Torre, which was exhibited at West Wall gallery. The sixty-foot-long accordion-style book includes photographs of Bay Area residential buildings where ICE raids took place between 2007 and 2009 (Figure 25). In developing this artwork De La Torre drew on information about the locations of ICE raids in the Mission District that he and his collaborators had received from nonprofit organizations, including the Dolores Community Center and CARECEN. Although he was not able to get specific addresses where the ICE raids had occurred, he did photograph buildings in the area where they had taken place. When *No Vacancies* was exhibited, the photographs were accompanied by wall text, which specified the blocks where the ICE raids happened.[124]

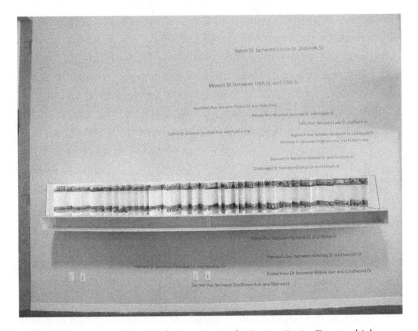

Figure 25. Installation view of *No Vacancies* by Sergio De La Torre, which was on view at the West Wall gallery in San Francisco, April 2010–December 2011. Courtesy of Sergio De La Torre.

In *No Vacancies* De La Torre underscores that the raids could have taken place at any of these locations, while also drawing upon and deconstructing the conventions and constraints of documentary photography as an aesthetic practice.

No Vacancies references the effects of arrests, detentions, and deportations on undocumented Latina/o migrants and their families, many of whom lost their housing. Although some undocumented Latina/o migrants were evicted as the result of ICE raids or gentrification, *No Vacancies* indicates that these buildings are already occupied. In his artist statement on *No Vacancies*, De La Torre noted the influence of Ed Ruscha's *Every Building on the Sunset Strip* (1966), in which he photographed all the buildings on the strip in Los Angeles, compiling an artist book with the photographs. However, De La Torre differentiates his project from that of Ruscha, whom he suggests takes up a formalist approach by flattening out the buildings as a means to reference their architectural histories. Instead, De La Torre states that with *No Vacancies* he is "play[ing] with the idea of preserving memories that go beyond the building's appearances."[125] Similar to the *Sanctuary City/Ciudad Santuario* projections that publicize Latina/o migrants' testimony on ICE raids, *No Vacancies* also references these events, which had previously been hidden from the public eye.

Conclusion

De La Torre and his collaborators posed the questions "Who is safe?" and "Who is secure?" in post-9/11 San Francisco, focusing on the multiple regimes of legality governing immigration on the local, state, and federal levels. In the exhibition and the projections, the artists highlighted what Monica Varsanyi calls "a patchwork of immigration-related policies" in San Francisco, particularly the effect of federal immigration policing and the weak enforcement of the sanctuary ordinance.[126] As mentioned earlier, federal immigration enforcement policies and programs like ICE's NFOP contributed to the removal of undocumented migrants through detention and deportation, which the artists referenced through an aesthetics of disappearance. Elements of *Sanctuary City/Ciudad Santuario*, including the projections, operated as a form of "counter-spectacle" that functioned as a way to both claim space for Latina/o migrants and to challenge their surveillance, arrest, detention, and deportation by law enforcement officials in the Mission District. Further, various artworks within the *Sanctuary City/Ciudad Santuario* exhibition, including the stop-motion video, employ an aesthetics of mobility that counters the ways in which federal immigration policy can physically limit the movement of undocumented migrants who can be taken away (arrested/detained) or removed (deported) from the United States against their will.[127]

In *Sanctuary City/Ciudad Santuario,* the artists did not visually depict the undocumented Latina/o migrants testifying during the joint HRC/IRC hearings in April 2009, but they did represent the presence of these individuals in the context of the hearings as part of the audio piece in the sound room. The act of testifying before these committees relates to these migrants' "politics of presence," what Anne McNevin refers to as "an embodied taking-up of public space." Through their participation in events like the IRC/HRC hearings, undocumented Latina/o migrants form "new subjectivities," which, as McNevin argues, include "expressions of belonging to local communities."[128] Further, providing testimony at these hearings exemplifies an act that McNevin argues "may morph into others which build new kinds of communities for certain kinds of purposes, establish new modalities of membership across formal/informal lines and connect in transitory or fundamental ways with social ties in other places."[129] In the following chapter, I relate the "politics of presence" to what Amalia Pallares and Gabriela Marquez-Benitez describe as a "politics of motion," in which "undocumented immigrant activists and their allies feel the need to challenge their criminalization in more explicit and confrontational ways."[130]

Although the undocumented Latina/o migrants who testified before the HRC/IRC joint hearings did not want to be represented visually within *Sanctuary City/Ciudad Santuario,* some became involved in very public forms of organizing as part of the National Day Labor Organizing Network's (NDLON) No Papers, No Fear campaign that took place in the summer of 2012. Presenting testimony at the joint HRC/IRC hearings in a more inclusive context (San Francisco) provided a model for those who, while not invited, also appeared before a U.S. Commission on Civil Rights (USCCR) field briefing in Birmingham, Alabama, which focused on state immigration laws (SB 1070 and SB 1070 copycat laws) passed after the *Arizona v. U.S.* decision in 2012. As I describe in the next chapter, undocumented youth and migrant activists began to shift their tactics in 2010, after which being publically visible as undocumented while engaged in forms of direct action became a key strategy within one sector of the movement that focused on protesting migrant deportations.

CHAPTER SIX

Reconfiguring Documentation

Mobility, Counter-Visibility, and (Un)Documented Activism

In 2012 the National Day Labor Organizing Network (NDLON) and the Puente Movement of Arizona organized the No Papers, No Fear Ride for Justice, which included a group of forty undocumented youth and migrant activists who rode on the "undocubus" from Phoenix, Arizona, to Charlotte, North Carolina. As part of the Ride for Justice, these activists stopped in locations where undocumented migrants were most surveilled and policed—specifically those that had 287(g) agreements or states with Arizona Senate Bill 1070 (SB 1070) copycat laws in place—in order to organize against these laws. As noted in the introduction, 287(g) agreements "allow a state and local law enforcement entity to enter into a partnership with ICE, under a joint Memorandum of Agreement (MOA)," and thus, "the state or local entity receives delegated authority for immigration enforcement within their jurisdictions."[1] Arizona SB 1070, the Support Our Law Enforcement and Safe Neighborhoods Act, which was proposed in 2010, required police to determine the immigration status of anyone arrested or detained, whenever law enforcement officials had a "reasonable suspicion" that they were not in the United States legally.[2] In addition to organizing workshops during the Ride for Justice, activists planned and recorded their actions and later circulated the videos on activist websites and on YouTube. The activists' documentation of these actions exhibited how undocumented youth and migrant activists have forged a politics based on reconfiguring self-representation and visibility.[3]

At one stop on the Ride for Justice, in Birmingham, Alabama, four activists participated in an action at a U.S. Commission on Civil Rights (USCCR) field briefing that focused on the effects of state immigration laws after the *Arizona v. U.S.* decision. Gerardo from the Puente Movement in Arizona was the first activist to speak, which he did during SB 1070 coauthor Kris Kobach's presentation. Gerardo declared that he was "undocumented and unafraid," as he held up a sign that read "UNDOCUMENTED." This action resonated with the statement "indocumentada y sin miedo" (undocumented and without papers) chanted by migrants during the spring 2006 marches against HR 4437, the Border Protection, Antiterrorism, and Illegal Immigration Control Act of 2005, when, as Nicholas De Genova notes, "there was an enthusiastic and recalcitrant affirmation of migrant mobility and a veritable embrace of de facto 'illegality.'"[4] Through his physical presence at the USCCR briefing, Gerardo directly challenged Kobach's legislative efforts of "attrition through enforcement" to create fear in undocumented migrants so that they would "self deport."[5] In a blog post Gerardo described his experience listening to Kobach's testimony and wrote about how it differed from his own perception of how SB 1070 had affected undocumented migrants in Arizona, where he lived. In the context of anti-immigrant state laws, Gerardo commented that "people [are] without freedom to move around freely in their own neighborhoods."[6] As Gerardo explained, the overall effect of these laws is a limit placed on the physical presence of undocumented migrants and the freedom that comes with their mobility. In arguing that the No Papers, No Fear campaign utilized mobility as a political strategy, I refer to Dimitris Papadopoulos and Vassilis Tsianos's understanding that mobility is "not just about movement, but is about the appropriation and remaking of space."[7] Although the Ride for Justice challenged the ways in which the U.S. state attempted to limit the movement of undocumented migrants, it also served as a means for activists to appropriate spaces and places where immigration laws were most punitive and restrictive by training other undocumented migrants in those locations to challenge these laws.

In this chapter I analyze documentary videos created by activists in NDLON and the Puente Movement, as well as those in the National Immigrant Youth Alliance (NIYA). These videos were produced before, during, and after acts of civil disobedience, at which time the activists risked being arrested, detained, and deported.[8] These political actions arose from an approach to organizing taken up by migrant activists who, as Amalia Pallares and Gabriela Marquez-Benitez argue, "disrupt the normalization and naturalization of disciplining and criminalizing" undocumented migrants.[9] These activists developed more confrontational tactics to respond to the Obama administration's immigration policies, which intentionally concealed or minimized publicity around its policing, detention, and deportation of undocumented migrants.[10] Undocumented youth and migrant activists made their actions public to counter this concealment. Further, activists use everyday technologies— such as cell phone cameras and social media—to engage in the counter-surveillance of state agents. Although state agents use surveillance to monitor Latina/o migrants, the activists' counter-surveillance exemplifies how, as Kevin Haggerty argues, "traditional hierarchies of visibility are being undermined and reconfigured."[11]

In examining these videos, I focus on the connections between political and cultural forms of self-representation. Specifically, I analyze how undocumented youth and migrant activists use and revise documentary forms to represent their performances of unauthorized acts, which defy the machinations of the U.S. state. Through strategies of *counter-visibility*, these activists publicize their political actions to shield themselves from detention and deportation. Through the production of *counter-documents*, these activists draw upon modes of documentary practice to challenge the state's ability to determine the parameters of political inclusion and to mobilize other undocumented migrants. The video excerpts that activists circulate through social media have analogous functions to elements of traditional documentary film, such as testimony or vérité-style sequences. The politics of visibility for these activists is at once similar to the traditional reformist ethos of documentary making public, but put in the service of more far-reaching agendas, which challenge the meaning of political inclusion. Counter-documents strategically protect, confront, and mobilize.

These videos serve as a means for these activists to frame their depictions, to elaborate forms of counter-documentation, and to make public political claims. These activists' emphasis on the production and circulation of visual media is specific to the context of state and federal immigration policies that can render visibility a form of surveillance linked to detention and deportation. It is part of a strategy to publicize the actions of these activists who engage in direct action and is not geared toward reaffirming the norms of inclusion.[12] These tactics respond to how U.S. governmental agencies, including Immigration and Customs Enforcement (ICE), an arm of the Department of Homeland Security (DHS), threatened or deported undocumented migrants. At the same time, these activists invert the visual terms of surveillance to shield themselves from possible detention and deportation.

In producing counter-documents these activists employ documentary aesthetics, but also include performative elements in which they demand social justice for undocumented migrants. These actions are performances, which activists—like "artivists" (artist-activists)—use "to intervene in political contexts, struggles and debates," as Diana Taylor contends.[13] In addition, Taylor argues that while performance "is usually perceived as the antithesis of the 'real,'" in her understanding of the term she notes that it "does not suggest artificiality; it is not 'put on' or antithetical to 'reality.'"[14] In the videos that they produce before their direct actions, activists perform to "appear natural" and to create a "real" aesthetic. In some of their videos they record performances in which they are engaged in acts of counter-surveillance. In these and other contexts, activists present themselves as being oppositional to the state and challenge normative notions about "deserving" versus "undeserving" migrants.

Although their actions involve performance, these undocumented activists largely distanced themselves from the performances of exceptionalism that emerged from what Amalia Pallares refers to as the "neoliberal frame that has shaped the advocacy for the DREAM Act and the representations of DREAM Act eligible youth."[15] Further, undocumented migrant activists represent themselves in ways that are distinct from portrayals that surface in the "migrant melodrama," which Ana Elena Puga argues is a growing subgenre in a variety of media, including documentary film.[16] Although the counter-documents produced by undocumented youth and migrant activists are influenced by these performances, they largely reject these representations, since they are counter to the goals of their political activism. For example, prior to a civil disobedience action in North Carolina in 2011, Martin, an undocumented youth activist, was quoted in a press release stating that he chose neither "to present another emotional testimony," nor to "ask for sympathy," instead asserting, "We ask for justice. Mere justice!"[17] Martin's declaration functions as a disruption, since he refuses to take part in a performance of exceptionalism that was central to the strategies of DREAM activists. Further, Martin does not participate in what Puga calls "the political economy of suffering," which involves an "exchange of affect—migrant suffering for spectator empathy."[18] Martin's focus on demanding social justice can also be found in videos produced by activists in NIYA and NDLON, which recorded how these activists "stand up to power" against anti-immigrant laws.

These activists' circulation of videos of their actions through digital and social media is linked to their emphasis on the political mobilization of undocumented migrants. These actions were performances that, Taylor suggests, offer "a way to transmit knowledge by means of the body."[19] However, in the case of the activists' videos, knowledge is transmitted through virtual space, as opposed to "real" space. Migrant activists used the videos to frame their own depictions and to make public political claims.[20] I consider how these videos are distributed through digital media as counter-documents, and thus, they are meant to reach other undocumented migrants to be engaged by these politics and further mobilized. The circulation of these videos exemplifies how activists use digital and social media to publicize their political actions and to connect with other undocumented migrants.

In this chapter, I examine how undocumented youth and migrant activists use documentary media to disrupt how U.S. immigration laws and policies create disorder in their everyday lives. Similar to antideportation activists in Australia and Europe—as described by Peter Nyers—migrant activists in the United States also "burrow into the apparatuses and technologies of exclusion to disrupt the administrative routines, the day-to-day perceptions and constructions of normality," including the "normality" of deportation.[21] My arguments focus on the relationship between the activists' production and circulation of counter-documents and their organizing against localized forms of policing, such as Arizona SB 1070 and copycat laws, as well as the localization of federal immigration policies and programs, including 287(g) and Secure Communities (S-COMM). As noted in the introduction, S-COMM involved local law enforcement in policing and reporting on migrants' immigration status, leading to huge increases in the detentions and deportations of undocumented migrants.[22] This activism combines social media counter-documents and place-based political actions across regional networks, in which undocumented youth and migrant activists adopt mobility both as a political strategy and a means of mobilization. Their assertion of migrant mobility thus counters detention—of being punitively fixed in place—which is narrated in their actions and given further capacity to circulate by the distribution of these actions in documentary form through digital and social media that radiate outward to audiences, including other undocumented migrants.

The first section of this chapter focuses on the political strategies of undocumented youth and migrant activists in the 2000s, leading up to when some broke their affiliations with mainstream immigrant rights groups and instead began to form their own organizations. Next, I examine the ways in which undocumented youth activists have used counter-documents as part of their broader political strategies. First, I analyze the work of NIYA activists who produced documentary videos of their protesting and participating in acts of civil disobedience, during which they risked arrest, detention, and deportation. The following section focuses on the video *Si No Nos Invitan, Nos Invitamos Solos: No Papers, No Fear Protest in Alabama*, filmed at a USCCR field briefing in Birmingham, Alabama. This video was produced as part of the No Papers, No Fear campaign, which was organized by NDLON and the Puente Movement. In addition to migrant activists' disruption of a USCCR field briefing and its representation in the form of a video, these activists distributed the video by embedding it within various online media platforms.[23] The tactics deployed by undocumented migrant activists include utilizing documentary media to record performances of their unauthorized acts, which they circulate as a means to mobilize other undocumented migrants. As such I contend that these activists deliberately countered policing and attempts at state surveillance of undocumented migrants in the United States through strategies of circulation, mobility, and mobilization.

Undocumented Youth Activism in the Early Twenty-First Century

The political strategies regarding undocumented youth changed significantly from 2001, when the image of the "DREAMer" was developed by mainstream immigrant rights associations that attempted to get the DREAM Act passed. In creating the DREAMer, these organizations, Walter Nicholls argues, specified that "these youths were exceptionally good immigrants and particularly deserving of legalization."[24] By the end of the decade, some undocumented youth activists challenged the normative ways in which the DREAMer was initially conceptualized by mainstream immigrant rights organizations. Instead, they worked to create their own organizations and develop their own political strategies, which they believed could better represent their priorities. These strategies included "coming out" as undocumented, which prompted young, undocumented migrants to declare their immigration status and to speak on behalf of the issues that concern them.

Undocumented youth activists who founded the Immigrant Youth Justice League (IYJL) in Chicago organized the first National Coming Out of the Shadows Day, held on March 10, 2010, four years after the 2006 Immigrant Rights March.[25] (The campaign slogan of the event was "Undocumented and Unafraid.")[26] A number of undocumented youth leaders within the IYJL identified as queer, and they modeled their coming-out strategies on those of LGBT activists.[27] In Chicago, these actions included a march and press conference at Federal Plaza, during which seven young people announced their first names, stated that they were undocumented, and voiced their support for the DREAM Act. By coming out as undocumented, these young people signaled that they were not afraid of letting the public know about their immigration status.[28] Coming out as undocumented became an important strategy, as increasing numbers of undocumented youth activists participated in actions and protests, publicizing their activities through digital and social media.

In the years following 2010, when this strategy first emerged, announcing one's immigration status became central to the self-representation and visibility of undocumented youth activists. Undocumented youth also began to create videos in which they stated their names and shared their stories of how they found out that they were undocumented on activist websites and on YouTube. Producing videos allowed these youth activists to reach out to a broader audience.[29]

Undocumented youth also started to participate in acts of civil disobedience in 2010, which Amalia Pallares and Gabriela Marquez-Benitez note was a way that they put themselves "at the center of their own struggle."[30] In preparation for incorporating civil disobedience into their actions, undocumented youth activists spoke with immigration attorneys about possible risks—such as arrest, detention, and deportation—that could occur if they participated. In planning these actions activists developed response teams to support their participation in civil disobedience and to oversee campaigns and petition drives.[31] The first civil disobedience action involving undocumented youth took place on May 1, 2010, in Washington, D.C. One hundred people—including members of Congress—were arrested. Following that event, activists organized a civil disobedience action on May 17, 2010, the fifty-sixth anniversary of *Brown v. Board of Education*. A group known as the DREAM Act 5 held a sit-in at the Arizona office of Senator John McCain, during which they called on him to support the DREAM Act. Four of the activists were arrested and sent to the Pima County jail. The next day, three of these activists were transferred to an ICE processing facility. After eight hours in the facility, they were released with no explanation. At the time *New York Times* reporter Maggie Jones noted that "while the Obama administration is deporting a record number of immigrants convicted of crimes, the Department of Homeland Security has so far spared undocumented youth who have been arrested during DREAM Act protests."[32] By publicizing their actions, these undocumented youth activists found that they could evade detention or deportation. Mohammad, an activist, explained at the time that "the more public we are with our stories, the safer we are."[33] Thus, coming out as undocumented could serve as a form of protection for undocumented youth who wanted to participate in direct actions.

Walter Nicholls argues that the DREAMer concept led to tensions within the immigrant rights movement by creating a category ("DREAM eligible") with "restrictive eligibility criteria," which contributed to the division between who is a "deserving" or an "undeserving" migrant. Nicholls also suggests that the concept of the "DREAMer" led to divisions over who should be developing strategies for the immigrant rights movement, and thus undocumented youth activists began "to question not only the strategy but also the representational hierarchies within the 'movement.'"[34] Undocumented youth activists formed organizations such as NIYA that focused on direct action and were also critical of "traditional DREAMer discourse."[35]

Further, some undocumented youth activists began to shift their focus from efforts toward legalization to the decriminalization of undocumented migrants, and to work with migrant-led organizations to protest state and federal immigration laws and policies. In 2010 undocumented youth collaborated with local and national migrant-led organizations to protest SB 1070, both before and after Governor Jan Brewer signed it into law. In 2010 NDLON helped coordinate the ¡Alto Arizona! (Stop Arizona!) campaign against SB 1070, with the assistance of NIYA and the Puente Movement, among other groups. This organizing involved more undocumented migrants in the struggle—specifically those who would be directly affected by SB 1070. The Puente Movement created community defense courses, so undocumented migrants could learn to defend themselves against ICE and the local police who collaborated to arrest, detain, and deport them.[36]

After the DREAM Act failed to pass the Senate in December 2010, more youth activists redirected their focus to broader issues that concerned all undocumented migrants. As activist Tania Unzueta Carrasco has argued, "This legislative failure forced us to more publicly challenge the nation-state and its definitions of citizenship and deportability."[37] In 2010 there was a significant increase in the number of undocumented migrants who had been arrested, detained, and deported due to the effects of federal immigration policies, such as 287(g) and S-COMM.[38] In making the shift, undocumented youth activists rejected the hierarchies within mainstream immigrant rights organizations that supported the

DREAM Act and represented undocumented young people as "innocent," while U.S. immigration law viewed their parents as criminals. In 2011 undocumented youth activists planned actions that drew attention to the effects of federal immigration programs—including S-COMM—and they collaborated with NDLON and other organizations to challenge anti-immigrant state laws—including SB 1070—as well as copycat laws in Alabama, Georgia, and elsewhere.

The undocumented youth and migrant activists' desire to organize against anti-immigrant state laws, as well as federal policies such as 287(g) and S-COMM, was a response to the localization of federal immigration policy. Monica Varsanyi and other scholars of immigration policy have written about the devolution of federal immigration powers to states, counties, and municipalities, which began with the Illegal Immigration Reform and Immigrant Responsibility Act (IIRIRA) in 1996.[39] Although some states, counties, and municipalities have developed policies that are inclusive of migrants, including sanctuary laws, allowing undocumented migrants to obtain drivers licenses or municipal ID cards, others have passed anti-immigrant laws that emphasize "attrition through enforcement," in addition to enforcing federal immigration laws by participating in the 287(g) program and S-COMM. In response, undocumented youth and migrant activists challenged both local immigration policies and local law's enforcement of federal immigration programs.

Walter Nicholls has pointed out that the localization of federal immigration policy contributed to the decentralized structure of the undocumented youth movement and some parts of the migrant rights movement. Unlike mainstream immigration rights organizations, which function through a centralized "top-down" structure, these undocumented youth and migrant activists developed a decentralized infrastructure. As Nicholls argues, the migrants' rights movement "has drawn resources up and out from the grassroots . . . and circulated these resources horizontally to other DREAMers operating at local, statewide, and national scales."[40] This strategy involves networks in which undocumented youth activists located in states with more support for migrant rights organize with activists in states with anti-immigrant laws—including Arizona, Alabama, and Georgia—as well as in counties with 287(g) agreements. In the spring of 2011, for example, activists involved in IYJL traveled from Chicago to Georgia to join local activists to protest against SB 1070 copycat law HB 87: the Illegal Immigration Reform and Enforcement Act. On June 28, 2011, these activists collaborated with local groups to stage a civil disobedience action at the state capitol.[41] The action was streamed on-line, and supporters watched from across the country. Although undocumented youth involved in civil disobedience risked being arrested, detained, and deported, they still chose to participate.[42] These activists believed that making their political action visible would inspire other undocumented migrants to act.

This action at the Georgia state capitol reflects some major shifts in the undocumented youth movement. Although the DREAM Act was developed by politicians and nonprofit organizations and sometimes used in efforts to get comprehensive immigration reform passed, more undocumented youth activists began to organize with other undocumented migrants in order to challenge federal and state anti-immigration policies.[43] The "targeted audiences" for the activists' campaigns shifted as well, from politicians who could put through comprehensive immigration reform to other undocumented migrants with whom the youth could organize.

Undocumented Activists, Documentary Media, and the Politics of Visibility

Even before youth activists were leading their own organizations, they included digital media technologies as part of their political mobilizing. Specifically, Hinda Seif contends that "digital media allows [undocumented students] to network nationally and internationally and express themselves with less peril."[44] Undocumented youth activists also trained each other in media and communication skills. Sasha Costanza-Chock explains that undocumented youth activists "engage in their own forms of 'transmedia mobilization,' by providing multiple entry points to a larger narrative that extends across platforms into face-to-face space and encourages participation."[45] "Transmedia mobilization" thus involves undocumented youth activists communicating through digital and social media, so they can organize and strategize.[46]

In this section, I examine the counter-documents that undocumented youth activists produced as part of their broader political strategies. These counter-documents were created by activists affiliated with NIYA, which was formed in 2011 by undocumented youth activists interested in deploying more confrontational tactics. NIYA members filmed themselves prior to their protests, partly because by participating in civil disobedience they risked not only arrest, but also detention and deportation. Their videos, which included personal narratives, could be used as part of antideportation campaigns. The first examples that I analyze include undocumented youth videotaping themselves before they were arrested for participation in a civil disobedience action in North Carolina. These activists produced the videos as a means of protection, and to contest the limits of the Obama administration's policy of prosecutorial discretion.[47] The second example is a video recorded on a cell phone by an undocumented youth activist as he was being arrested by Border Patrol agents in Alabama during his attempt to infiltrate an immigration detention center. His video, which was streamed live on the Internet, documented how state agents were failing to exercise prosecutorial discretion when they encountered undocumented youth. These videos were uploaded onto activist websites—in addition to appearing on YouTube and blogs—to publicize these actions and arrests in order to mobilize other undocumented youth and as part of campaigns to release these activists. In these videos activists used documentary media as a form of protection to counter policing and attempts at the state's surveillance of undocumented migrants. As counter-documents, these videos portray activists and actions in ways that are deliberately oppositional.

In September 2011, to prepare for a protest of the discriminatory policies toward undocumented students at Central Piedmont Community College, NIYA activists Marco and Mohammad traveled to Charlotte, North Carolina, to coordinate the action with Viridiana, the cofounder of the North Carolina Dream Team. The event took place in Charlotte because the Democratic National Convention would meet there in 2012, and the protest was directed toward the Obama administration and the Democratic leadership in Congress. Although North Carolina did not have an SB 1070 copycat law in place, since Charlotte was located in a

287(g) county, undocumented youth risked arrest, detention, and deportation. Assuming that they would be arrested, undocumented activists
in North Carolina made video recordings of themselves before the civil
disobedience action, which took place on September 6, 2011.[48]

By this time, undocumented youth activists had learned that they
could lessen their chances of being detained or deported by publicly
declaring their immigration status and publicizing their actions. During the protest in North Carolina, a group of activists declared that they
were undocumented; they spoke about discriminatory policies toward
undocumented students at Central Piedmont Community College; and
they explained the effects of the federal government's programs—such
as S-COMM and 287(g)—on undocumented migrants. Following the
rally, activists staged a civil disobedience action at an intersection near
the college. Ten activists were arrested.[49] While these activists were in
jail, ICE put holds on them, thus initiating their transfer to an immigration detention center in Georgia. In the end, however, not one of the
undocumented youth was detained. The activists attributed this decision
to the "bad publicity" it would generate for the Obama administration if
their detention was reported in the media.[50]

This action by undocumented youth activists tested the Obama administration's announcement on August 18, 2011, that ICE was ignoring
"low priority" cases to focus on deporting undocumented migrants convicted of serious crimes.[51] Young, undocumented migrants, many of
whom came to the United States as children, appeared to be among
those who would benefit from this change. Some politicians and immigrant rights activists applauded this announcement, but these were not
the changes that many undocumented youth and migrant activists had
been advocating for—such as stopping any action against undocumented
migrants, including those *not* currently facing deportation. Nor did President Barack Obama's announcement have any effect on federal policies
and programs, such as 287(g) or S-COMM, by which ICE agents continued to arrest, detain, and deport undocumented migrants. Instead of
changing immigration laws, the Obama administration attempted to
make the current laws less harsh through prosecutorial discretion, which
delays the deportations of undocumented migrants but does not grant

them permanent residency status.[52] The administration was trying to deflect criticism by attempting to make immigration laws more palatable.

Discretion is a historically fraught concept, which is based on interpretation and has allowed for decisions rooted in institutional racism.[53] The Obama administration's announcement about prosecutorial discretion needs to be situated within the historical context of U.S. immigration law. In her book *Impossible Subjects*, Mae Ngai writes about the use of administrative discretion in the 1930s, which was defined as "discretionary relief from deportation in meritorious cases." She argues that discretion "gave rise to an oppositional political and legal discourse, which imagined 'deserving' and 'undeserving' illegal migrants and, 'just' and 'unjust' deportations."[54] She notes that "unjust" deportations were mostly applied to European migrants and only occasionally to Mexican ones. In the current context, discretion was held up as a positive change, one that was given to those who truly "deserve" it. For undocumented migrants in removal proceedings, discretion also reinscribed the authority of the state to evaluate migrants on an individual basis. Discretion is thus an administrative technology of individuated subjection, which is also based on the exclusion of those who are deemed to be "undeserving."

NIYA activists wrote a press release in advance of their action in North Carolina, in which they critiqued the limits of prosecutorial discretion, arguing that the Obama administration was using it to pacify undocumented youth. As mentioned earlier, Martin, one of the activists involved in the action, issued a statement as part of the press release in which he defied the authority of the state to evaluate individuals on a case-by-case basis by saying that he would not "present another emotional testimony" nor "ask for sympathy."[55] In this context Martin's statement functions as a form of disruption as he resists abiding by these same limits set forth by the Obama administration in cases of discretion. In their press release, NIYA activists contest how discretion involves working within the constraints of the current political context, to restrict or partially undo current immigration laws. Prosecutorial discretion does not account for the shifting ground of immigration policies, which can change with a new administration. These activists questioned the force of discretion within the broader context of punitive U.S. immigration policies.

The press release emerged out of what Tania Unzueta Carrasco and Hinda Seif describe as the "context of shifting deportation and 'prosecutorial discretion' policies and enforcement measures affecting categories of who is deemed deportable and who is not."[56] It was also influenced by changes in strategies put forward by NIYA and undocumented youth activists. Undocumented youth whom ICE had placed in deportation proceedings had been advised by activists involved in the Education Not Deportation (END) campaign to create videos to both draw in and mobilize a broader public to pressure ICE to stop their deportation.[57] Information about the production of videos was included in *Education Not Deportation: A Guide for Undocumented Youth in Removal Proceedings*, a publication developed by NIYA, the Asian Law Caucus, Educators for Fair Consideration, and DreamActivist.org. Because the governmental joint task force overseeing potential removal cases considered the migrant's pursuit of education in the United States, circumstances of arrival in the country, and length of stay, an undocumented youth's story was important to his or her case. Consequently, the *END Guide* encouraged undocumented youth to tell their personal stories, which included their names, ages, places of residence, educational histories, involvement in community activities, and immigration statuses.[58]

In addition to helping undocumented youth create narratives that would "inspire others to act," the *END Guide* also directed these young people to represent themselves in specific ways. The authors of the *END Guide* advised those in removal proceedings to mobilize feelings of identification to appeal to a broad audience. Undocumented youth were told to speak about their personal lives and to include photographs of themselves within the videos, which would encourage viewers to empathize with them. As the *END Guide* notes, "By using pictures you intend to show the public that you are just like them."[59] In addition to "making . . . personal connection[s]," the authors of the *END Guide* also suggested that these individuals *perform* their stories.[60] Although the instructions for the video component appear simple—including the writing and recording of a public narrative—-the guide's authors advise that their stories should appear "natural," and thus, individuals should avoid reading their narratives to the camera. This approach was intended to produce a "real" aesthetic, although the appearance of "naturalness" involves a carefully rehearsed performance.

The approaches recommended by the *END Guide* have their limitations. For example, in order to convince ICE to use discretion, the *END Guide* suggests that undocumented youth make their narratives "compelling" and "worthy of discretion." There were repercussions to this strategy, as noted by activist Tania Unzueta Carrasco, who argues that while activists attempted to "challenge the label of 'criminality' as a qualifier for deportability, we were doing so by emphasizing other hegemonic characteristics."[61] Directing undocumented youth to highlight their "worthiness" implicitly diminishes that of others who have not attained this "success." Thus, the END videos involve crafting a kind of performance of exceptionalism. This performance reaffirms the state's prerogative to determine worthiness, and it supports the presumption that most undocumented migrants are unworthy of discretion. This public narrative is quite different from the counter-documents produced by undocumented youth, which serve as a form of disruption.

The END campaign's focus on the videos created by undocumented youth to prevent their deportation appealed for inclusion within the nation, which differed from the counter-documents produced by activists in North Carolina. These activists drew upon the aesthetic elements of these videos, while also challenging their approach.[62] Similar to the videos produced for the END campaign, the activists in North Carolina included first-person narratives in their videos, during which undocumented youth speak directly to the camera. Each video features a single person, closely cropped, and shot in a simple, straightforward way. Although the aesthetics of these videos are similar, the activists in North Carolina aimed to repurpose these first-person, conventional forms to challenge the terms of discretion.

Some of these distinctions in the approach to these videos are related to their different purposes and the specific audiences to whom they were addressed. Undocumented youth were in deportation proceedings when they created their videos based on the *END Guide*, whereas the activists in North Carolina produced their videos ahead of their direct action. Although the *END Guide* suggested that videos be directed to John Morton, director of DHS/ICE—as well as to the politicians from the individual's state and district—those produced by the activists in North Carolina were addressed to at least three different audiences: government agents reviewing cases for discretion, their family members, and other undocumented youth.

The distinction between using a personal narrative as a case for inclusion in the nation-state and as a means of more fundamentally challenging the terms of political inclusion is evident in the videos produced by undocumented youth activists in North Carolina. Some activists recorded these videos as a precaution, in case they were put in deportation proceedings.[63] These videos included information such as the activist's name, age, educational history, and how he or she came to the United States. Although these undocumented youth activists included information about themselves in their videos that was conventionally deployed as support for discretion, they often represented themselves in ways that failed to conform to normative characteristics, such as how the DREAMer had been scripted by mainstream immigrant rights organizations.[64]

The videos made by activists prior to their arrests, however, served other purposes, too. These videos were produced in order to mobilize other undocumented youth to become involved in the struggle against restrictive anti-immigrant laws. As opposed to gaining the support of politicians and leaving the repressive structure of immigration laws in place, in their videos these activists directly challenged these laws by referring to the effects of racism and discrimination against people of color in the United States, which led to racial profiling of Latina/o migrants, while referencing their own privilege, especially in relation to their parents. The aesthetics of the videos produced by the END campaign and those created by activists in North Carolina are similar, conveying direct address and emphasizing a lack of televisual mediation. However, the former is an appeal to the state on its own terms, while the latter challenges these terms as a counter-document.

In their videos, undocumented youth challenge how U.S. immigration law criminalizes undocumented migrants—including their parents—while also critiquing the limits of prosecutorial discretion. The videos produced by the activists in North Carolina presented a counter-narrative to how the U.S. state deemed their parents—as undocumented migrants—

to be deportable. By getting arrested, these activists were testing the Obama administration's policies, as well as contesting how these policies made some groups eligible for discretion, but not others. Unlike the videos featured in the *END Guide*, these activists did not create "compelling" personal narratives to represent themselves as "worthy of discretion." Instead, their videos challenged how politicians and state agents treated undocumented migrants. For example, Angelica stated in her video that she was tired of all the politicians' lies and the ways that local officials treated undocumented migrants as criminals.[65] Other activists' videos portrayed how undocumented youth challenged U.S. immigration policy on behalf of their parents. In Santiago's video, he noted that he was "standing up to power," with the hope that his parents could also do so someday, without the risk of deportation.[66] As opposed to referring to their parents' actions as "illegal" (due to the way in which they crossed the U.S.–Mexico boundary), they stated that their parents were brave to travel to the United States to improve their family's lives. Instead of criminalizing their parents, these activists chided politicians for failing to act on behalf of undocumented migrants.[67]

Rather than appealing to the U.S. nation-state for inclusion, the videos produced by undocumented youth were a means to motivate other young migrants to join their cause. In their videos, the activists represented themselves as models for other undocumented youth to effect real political change. For example, Santiago stated that undocumented youth should not "assimilate to a system that oppresses us and try to belong to that system," declaring that "we need to challenge that system and create a real movement, a movement where we are fighting for human rights for all."[68] Martin also spoke directly to undocumented youth, encouraging them to mobilize on their own behalf. Specifically he stated that, "It's time to step up and do something—we will no longer be placed on hold." He also asserted, "Doing nothing—waiting to get deported is a horrible idea. You have to do something about what's going on. No one is going to take care of our issues—we have to take responsibility now to do something about this injustice. So get involved—do something now—there's no time to wait."[69] In creating these counter-documents, undocumented youth activists challenge how some migrants were not considered to be "deserving" of discretion. They also encourage undocumented youth to become active in protesting anti-immigrant laws.

Moreover, these videos convey a specific, strategic visibility. After the videos were produced, they were uploaded onto activist websites, as well as onto social networking sites such as Facebook, YouTube, and blogs.[70] Numerous scholars have argued that digital and social media have shaped how social movements have publicized their campaigns in recent years. Similar to the human rights activists whom Meg McLagan writes about, undocumented youth activists have also produced "a new kind of media activism," which "not only makes sophisticated and innovative use of techniques of celebrity and publicity through a wide range of forms . . . but that also involves the creation of new organizational structures that provide a kind of scaffolding for the production and distribution of these media."[71] Activists' distribution of these counter-documents does a certain kind of political work. In addition to challenging hierarchies established by the U.S. state and reaffirmed by mainstream immigrant rights groups, the activists' circulation of their videos through social media are also a means to protect and mobilize other undocumented migrants.

In the context of undocumented youth activists' online presence, their websites, such as one developed by the undocumented-led online organization DreamActivist.org, function as "portals into activism."[72] Following the arrest of these undocumented youth activists in North Carolina, DreamActivist.org circulated a petition to President Obama and Janet Napolitano, the secretary of the Department of Homeland Security, to end 287(g) and S-COMM. The authors of this petition note the contradiction between Obama's August 2011 announcement on discretion and the fact that the activists arrested were "put on the fast track to immigration detention."[73] The actions of these undocumented activists highlighted federal laws and policies that continue to place undocumented migrants in detention and deportation proceedings. Their videos also addressed a core constituency of supporters and claimed a digital space for challenging U.S. immigration policy.

The protest by the North Carolina Dream Team was a direct challenge to the Obama administration's announcement about prosecutorial discretion, since their arrests and near placement in deportation proceedings exposed the inconsistencies in state agents' use of discretion. That ICE started the process of placing activists into detention centers following the White House's announcement demonstrates the weakness of the concept of "discretion." The activists were arrested for "civil" disobedience, but ICE agents attempted to place them into deportation proceedings, which contradicted the Obama administration's announcement that DHS/ICE would prioritize penalizing those who had committed criminal—rather than civil—violations. Although a joint task force between the DHS and the Department of Justice (DOJ) was gearing up to review all three hundred thousand cases in deportation proceedings, ICE agents continued to arrest, detain, and deport undocumented migrants for civil violations.

In their videos, youth activists in North Carolina represented themselves as disruptive, and refused to abide by the constraints of discretion. While undocumented youth had focused on lobbying politicians to support the DREAM Act from the early 2000s through 2010, in these videos activists also direct themselves toward other undocumented youth in order to enlist them to act on behalf of all undocumented migrants. Although the END campaign advised activists to represent themselves within the terms of discretion, many in these videos refused to abide by those limitations. Through their public actions and their videos, these activists mobilized other undocumented migrants to challenge punitive U.S. immigration laws and policies—such as 287(g) and S-COMM— that have contributed to the increased number of migrants who have been detained in or deported from the United States.

Soon after the action in North Carolina, NIYA activists escalated their political strategies beyond acts of civil disobedience. The activists arrested in North Carolina were not transferred to an immigrant detention center, but most undocumented migrants with ICE holds who were in the jail at that time were brought to the Stewart Detention Center in Georgia. By conversing with "low priority" undocumented migrants in the jail, NIYA activists developed a new strategy to infiltrate immigration detention centers to inform undocumented migrants of their rights, as well as to gather information to help release those detained.[74] The production of counter-documents was central to this strategy. These activists wanted to demonstrate that when the media was not there, "low priority" un-documented migrants were being arrested, put in detention centers, and then in deportation proceedings. The activists focused on the inconsistencies in the implementation of the guidelines for discretion. This type of action could only be performed by undocumented migrants. As Marco wrote, "We the undocumented . . . have become in effect perfect soldiers to tackle the architects and structures of our detention."[75] Marco was noting that undocumented migrants could get into detention centers in efforts to release those who were detained, and beyond that, Mohammad stated that NIYA members should also use their undocumented status to "flip the power of those who think they are in charge."[76] Thus, although government agents believed they had the upper hand, Mohammad's comment demonstrated that the activists could use their undocumented status to infiltrate detention centers in order to illustrate the inconsistencies between who was being detained and deported and how this information was being "officially" reported by the Obama administration.[77]

The first activists to document the inconsistencies in the enforcement of the guidelines for discretion were Jonathan and Isaac, two NIYA-affiliated activists from Southern California. Jonathan and Isaac were arrested in November 2011 at a Border Patrol office in Mobile, Alabama, and were detained at the South Louisiana Correctional Center in Basile, Louisiana. At the time, Jonathan and Isaac were members of the San Gabriel Dream Team who traveled from Southern California to Alabama to join activists to protest HB 56: the Beason-Hammon Alabama Taxpayer and Citizen Protection Act. Activists organized rallies and actions in Montgomery, Alabama, to protest HB 56, an SB 1070 copycat law based on "attrition through enforcement," which criminalizes undocumented migrants, prompting many to leave the state. What differentiated the actions in Alabama from those previously organized by undocumented youth activists was that it was the first time that they engaged in civil disobedience along with their parents or with activists of their parents' generation.[78] All the undocumented migrant activists who were involved in civil disobedience in Alabama were arrested. Due to the publicity surrounding these actions, everyone—including the adults—was released, avoiding detention centers or deportation proceedings.

The activists' strategy to infiltrate immigration detention centers was part of a broader campaign to highlight how federal and state agents were not consistently abiding by the terms of discretion as they continued to arrest, detain, and deport undocumented migrants who were considered "low priority." The jail-to-detention-center pipeline was enabled by ICE's S-COMM program, which connected local police to federal immigration authorities through the use of integrated databases that used biometric technologies—including fingerprinting—to determine the immigration status of the individuals who were arrested.[79] The S-COMM program provided the infrastructure for taking an undocumented migrant who had committed a minor crime—such as a traffic violation—to a detention center or to be put in deportation proceedings. As part of the campaign against the S-COMM program, undocumented youth activists held civil disobedience actions at ICE offices nationwide. For example, Jonathan and Isaac participated in a civil disobedience action against ICE in Los Angeles in October 2011, during which young activists blocked a van full of undocumented migrants who were about to get deported.[80] These undocumented youth activists also took part in an act of civil disobedience at one of the ICE offices, located next to the immigration detention center. These actions were recorded by undocumented youth activists, including the sit-in at the ICE office, which was filmed on the camera of a cell phone and circulated on activist websites, YouTube, and blogs.[81] By holding a civil disobedience action in front of a van of undocumented migrants who were about to be deported and in the middle of an ICE office, undocumented youth activists attempted to disrupt the "processing" of undocumented migrants by the ICE "machine."[82] These actions included recording the activities of government agents, which were largely unseen by the broader public, specifically the ways in which ICE detains undocumented migrants and then systematically deports them. The activists' use of documentary media functioned as a tactical weapon.

Jonathan and Isaac engaged in counter-surveillance, as they attempted to infiltrate an immigration detention center. To document what federal agencies were doing behind closed doors—making visible what the state wanted to keep invisible—Jonathan and Isaac performed as "ordinary" undocumented migrants, so that their actions did not receive the attention of the news media. Jonathan and Isaac described this infiltration as a "silent action," in which they declared their immigration status before federal immigration agents without the presence of the media.[83] The strategies of these activists—including the "silent action"—developed in response to the Obama administration's predilection for "silent raids" and its more veiled approach to detention and deportation, which stands in contrast to the spectacle associated with ICE workplace raids during the Bush administration.

During their action, Jonathan was the first to enter the office, and he used the video camera on his cell phone to live stream his interaction with the Border Patrol.[84] He put his cell phone in a jacket pocket with the camera lens directed at the Border Patrol personnel. In watching the video on a live stream, the viewers see the Border Patrol staff, but they only hear Jonathan. After entering the Border Patrol office, Jonathan speaks to a receptionist, acting as if he is lost. The camera is shaky, and the aesthetics resemble that of cinema verité, making it appear similar to a journalistic exposé. Later, when Jonathan interacts with the Border Patrol agents, he breaks character and starts to question what they are doing. When the agents explain they are "enforcing immigration law," Jonathan accuses them of deporting people, noting as well that he is "undocumented," a term they do not understand. (Jonathan then translates the term, stating that he is "illegal.") Jonathan continues to film the Border Patrol agents as they ask him questions regarding his entry into the United States. Within a short time after his arrival at the Border Patrol office, the agents decided that Jonathan—considered "low priority" by the terms of prosecutorial discretion—would be moved to an immigration detention center. The documentary video serves as evidence that exposes how state agents failed to follow the guidelines for discretion.

Jonathan's cell phone camera documented what happens when there is not publicity around the case of a "low priority" undocumented migrant. Consequently, he provided evidence that undocumented migrants—like himself—who met the terms of discretion were being detained. Jonathan used his cell phone camera as part of a strategy of counter-surveillance, as, in his words, "we knew people like us were being deported and we wanted to create a scenario where that could be seen in the public sphere."[85] The video exposes that state agents were not abiding by ICE's policy regarding prosecutorial discretion in their "processing" of undocumented migrants, and it documents this *not-so-silent-action*, as Jonathan's words were heard during the live stream. His interaction with Border Patrol agents was posted on YouTube, under the title *Undocumented Youth vs. Border Patrol Round 1—Mobile, Alabama*, while Jonathan and Isaac were still being held at the South Louisiana Correctional Center (Figure 26).[86] This action involved counter-surveillance and also created a counter-narrative to the story provided by the Obama administration: that state agents were exercising prosecutorial discretion.[87] The video served as a counter-document, as a means to circulate Jonathan's interaction with state agents, revealing the limits of the Obama administration's policies around discretion, and to demonstrate the ways in which he and Isaac directly challenged the work of the Border Patrol, DHS, ICE, and the Obama administration.

One of the main strategies of undocumented youth activists at this time was to publicize their actions through digital and social media, to bring attention to how U.S. immigration policies affect undocumented

Figure 26. This still is from the video *Undocumented Youth vs. Border Patrol Round 1—Mobile, Alabama*, which was shot by Jonathan while he was being questioned in a Border Patrol office in Mobile, Alabama, in November 2011.

migrants, which also serves as a form of protection against their detention and deportation. These strategies, which I refer to as a form of
counter-visibility, are a response to the Obama administration's emphasis on minimizing publicity around its policing of undocumented youth
migrants. However, Jonathan's video also reveals the limitations in representing state agents from the perspective of undocumented migrants.
After a few minutes of filming the Border Patrol with a cell phone camera, the Border Patrol agents arrested Jonathan, limiting his ability to
document what they were doing after their initial interaction.

While detained in the South Louisiana Correctional Center, Jonathan
and Isaac collected information from migrants who should have been
"low priority," yet had been placed into deportation proceedings.[88] They
also heard stories about the personal risks that migrants—including
some who should have qualified for asylum—confronted on their journey to the United States.[89] After ten days in the South Louisiana Correctional Center, ICE agents discovered that Jonathan and Barrera were
activists, and they were released.[90] On the day they left the detention
center, Mohammad circulated a press release about the activists' infiltration, which he related to the work of undocumented youth activists
who wanted to challenge anti-immigrant state laws.[91] NIYA activists
engaged in this work by participating in the No Papers, No Fear Ride
for Justice.

I now turn to the collaboration between undocumented youth and
migrant rights activists on the No Papers, No Fear Ride for Justice, organized by NDLON. The tour took place in the summer of 2012, to mobilize undocumented migrants, particularly in states with anti-immigrant
laws and in counties with 287(g) agreements. This campaign built on
NDLON's previous efforts working with migrant rights activists in states
with anti-immigrant laws, such as Arizona, Georgia, and Alabama.[92] One
goal of the No Papers, No Fear campaign was to draw on the strategies
of undocumented youth activists, including their organization of direct
actions against ICE, which they publicized through digital and social
media. Undocumented youth activists coordinated the No Papers, No
Fear media campaign, which involved publicizing these direct actions.[93]
Migrant rights activists involved in NDLON and the Puente Movement

viewed these tactics as successful, and consequently, they employed some of the same strategies as part of the No Papers, No Fear tour.

Si No Nos Invitan, Nos Invitamos Solos:
No Papers, No Fear Protest in Alabama

As mentioned in the introduction to this chapter, activists in NDLON, the Puente Movement, and other migrant-led organizations coordinated the No Papers, No Fear Ride for Justice in the summer of 2012. This tour included a multigenerational group of almost forty activists, ranging from nineteen to sixty-five years old, traveling on a bus (called the "undocubus"), through eleven states from Arizona to North Carolina.[94] The participants were protesting the spread of SB 1070 copycat laws, U.S. immigration laws and policies, and the presence of the Obama administration at the Democratic National Convention, held in Charlotte, North Carolina, in September 2012. The campaign was named No Papers, No Fear to challenge state laws like SB 1070, Alabama's HB 56, and Georgia's HB 87, which allowed police to ask for the immigration papers of anyone whom they believe is undocumented. According to the organizers, the campaign was intended to "bring national attention to the consequences of this country's immigration policy through carefully planned acts of civil disobedience, publicized through social media."[95] This campaign drew upon initiatives from the Turning the Tide summit, held in New Orleans in 2010, which emphasized what activists call a "trans-local" approach to organizing.[96] Activists focused on counties with 287(g) agreements and states with SB 1070 copycat laws. This trans-local approach challenged mainstream immigrant organizations that focused on national organizing in support of the DREAM Act and comprehensive immigration reform.

The No Papers, No Fear campaign continued the work of undocumented migrant activists in Arizona, Alabama, and Georgia, all of whom planned protests involving civil disobedience. Some of these activists had created *comités populares* (people's committees) to organize against anti-immigrant state laws, while emphasizing the cooperation between local law enforcement and federal immigration officials in detaining and deporting undocumented migrants.[97] They also highlighted the consequences of anti-immigrant state laws by organizing protests and workshops to address issues faced by undocumented migrants, such as how to defend themselves in deportation proceedings.[98] In protesting the effects of state and federal immigration policies on their communities, these activists were disruptive and represented themselves in ways that were oppositional.

The No Papers, No Fear campaign emphasized mobility and mobilization through the Ride for Justice, as well as by the circulation of videos of their actions, which were also forms of publicity and visibility. The campaign had its own volunteer media crew comprised of individuals who documented these actions through photography and video.[99] While these media makers filmed many actions, in the remainder of the chapter I will concentrate on two videos that contain highlights of an action at a U.S. Commission on Civil Rights (USCCR) field briefing in Birmingham, Alabama, that focused on the effects of anti-immigration state laws after the *Arizona v. U.S.* decision.[100] These videos are titled *Ganando el derecho de hablar por nosotros mismos: Winning the Right to Speak for Ourselves* and *Si No Nos Invitan, Nos Invitamos Solos: No Papers, No Fear Protest in Alabama*. Both were produced by media makers and migrant activists—including Jorge and filmmaker Barni Axmed Qaasim—on the "undocubus."[101]

When this action at the USCCR field briefing took place in August 2012, Alabama's anti-immigrant law (HB 56) was considered to be the "toughest in the nation."[102] As mentioned earlier, HB 56 was based on Arizona's SB 1070, which promotes "attrition through enforcement." Prior to the briefing, the members of the USCCR, described as an "independent, bipartisan agency charged with monitoring federal civil rights enforcement," determined who would speak.[103] Consequently, individuals who were not on the agenda were not allowed to share their perspectives with members of the commission.[104] Those who *were* on the agenda included politicians, educators, and directors of organizations, including the Federation for American Immigration Reform (FAIR) and the Center for Immigration Studies. Although the USCCR invited speakers from the Mexican American Legal Defense and Education Fund (MALDEF), not a single individual directly affected by these laws was included on the agenda. This absence reflects how undocumented migrants are treated as permanently criminalized people in the United States and, as Lisa Marie Cacho argues, as members of groups who are "subjected to laws but refused the legal means to contest those laws . . . [and] denied both the political legitimacy and moral credibility necessary to question them."[105] Although undocumented migrants were not invited to speak, a group of activists from the No Papers, No Fear tour interrupted the briefing, sharing how they had been negatively affected by anti-immigrant laws.

Previous to their interruption of the USCCR briefing, activists with the No Papers, No Fear campaign held a protest outside the building that included a performance by a group of migrant activists. In the tradition of political street theater, these activists drove up in a white van and parked in front of the building. About ten activists stepped out of the van wearing prisoners' uniforms that were made of black garbage bags with white stripes spray-painted on them. As they shouted "¿Quién tiene el poder? ¡Hacemos! Sin papeles, sin miedo" (Who has the power? We do! No papers, no fear), they ripped off their prison garb to reveal campaign T-shirts underneath that featured an image of a butterfly. They also threw handcuffs onto the ground and draped a banner for the No Papers, No Fear campaign over the van. The activists then opened a cardboard box filled with live butterflies, which they set free. Following this part of the action these activists marched into the building where the USCCR briefing was taking place while shouting "No papers, no fear. Dignity is standing here."

Once inside the building, four of the activists challenged the dictates of whom the USCCR considered acceptable speakers. This action involved what artist and activist Rozalinda Borcilă refers to as "interventionist tactics," which are used as a means to "disrupt . . . spaces where social conflict was rendered invisible."[106] As noncitizens who were essentially barred from speaking, each activist had "to interrupt the dominant political (speaking) order not just to be heard but to be recognized as a speaking being as such."[107] This group chose to address the effects of these anti-immigrant laws on undocumented migrants during the testimony of Kris Kobach, the Kansas secretary of state, and the so-called legal mind behind SB 1070.[108] Through their testimonies and presence at the field briefings, these activists contributed to a discussion that initially depended on their absence. Their action and the video they produced are examples of the activists' strategies of disruption, counter-visibility, and counter-documentation.

The activists who interrupted the briefing include Gerardo and Mari Cruz from the Puente Movement in Arizona, Juan José from Teatro Jornalero sin Fronteras (Day Laborer Theater without Borders) in Los Angeles, and María H. from Mujeres Unidas y Activas in San Francisco. All of them stood up to speak individually, holding signs indicating that they were "undocumented."[109] As part of this action, the activists emphasized their undocumented status—by both their signs and their statements. This information brought added significance to their physical presence at the briefing, drawing attention to the risks they faced to speak out against these laws.

Although the USCCR tried to make the perspectives of undocumented migrants absent in the briefing, these activists emphasized their presence in many ways, including speaking out against these anti-immigrant state laws. Jackson Miller notes that within the context of protests, including those by undocumented migrants, "presence is created through embodied practices," including the "capacity to establish control of some space and maintain the attention of some audience."[110] The activists established their presence not only by physically being there, but also by what they said and how they said it, and by their signs and the organized actions of the group. Following Gerardo who spoke first, Mari Cruz (who identified herself as María) stood up and started shouting in Spanish:

My name is María [last name] y vengo de Phoenix, Arizona. Han violado nuestros derechos como seres humanos. Aquí estoy! Aquí estoy levantando la voz por mi comunidad, por mis hijos, por todas las familias que han sido separadas. Aquí estoy!! Y quiero . . . presentar esto para que lo vea! Para que vea que soy una madre! Una madre responsable! No soy una . . . no soy una criminal! No soy! No soy criminal! Aquí estoy! Estoy defendiendo mis derechos!

[My name is María {last name} and I am from Phoenix. They have violated my human rights. Here I am! I am here to lift up my voice on behalf of my community, my children, and all those families that have been separated. I am here! And I would like . . . to present this so that you can see it! To see that I am a mother, a responsible mother! I am not . . . I am not a criminal! I'm not! I am not a criminal! I am here to defend my rights!]

María H. also stood up, moved toward the aisle, and shouted angrily in Spanish (Figure 27):

Ya basta! Bola de corruptos! Mi nombre es María [last name]. Soy madre de familia. He recibido mucha discriminación. Soy María [last name]. Indocumentada y sin miedo! No tengo miedo! Aquí estoy! Deben respetar nuestros derechos! Son derechos civiles! Esto es una basura! Allí se la dejo, quédense con ella. No saben respetar el dolor humano. A mis hijos le han quitado la troca dos veces! Tienen que pagar dos mil dólares . . . para sacar aquel vehículo! Hace un año, perdimos nuestra casa. No hay derechos humanos!

[Enough! You are all corrupt. My name is María {last name}. I am the mother of the family. I am facing powerful discrimination. I am María {last name}. I am undocumented and unafraid. I do not have fear. Here I am! You are supposed to respect my civil rights! They are civil rights! This paper (commission briefing) is trash. I will leave it here! You can keep it. You don't know how to respect human suffering. They have taken the truck from my sons, twice. They have to pay $2,000 . . . to get this vehicle out. One year ago, we lost our house. There are no human rights.][111]

By declaring "Aquí estoy" (Here I am), these women claimed their presence during the hearings, at which anti-immigrant state laws were discussed without the input from people affected by them. The statement "Aquí estoy" is reminiscent of "Aquí estamos" (Here we are), part of the migrants' chants during the marches in spring 2006. Nicholas De

I am here and you are supposed to respect my civil rights.

Figure 27. Still from a video *Si No Nos Invitan, Nos Invitamos Solos*, which was filmed by Barni Axmed Qaasim during a U.S. Commission on Civil Rights briefing in Birmingham, Alabama. This action was part of the No Papers, No Fear: Ride for Justice Tour in August 2012.

Genova suggests that this statement "affirmed the theme of presence—the profound and extricable presence of migrants, and especially that of the undocumented, within the U.S. social formation and within the space of the state."[112] In enacting what Anne McNevin characterizes as a "politics of presence—an embodied taking-up of public space,"[113] these activists could "constitute themselves as political agents under new terms, taking different positions in the social space than those in which they were previously positioned," as Engin Isin suggests.[114]

In testifying that immigration laws and policies—such as SB 1070 and the ICE raids—had violated their civil and human rights, these women emphasized their roles in their families and communities. Both Mari Cruz's and María H.'s affect could be characterized primarily by anger, as they shouted loudly at Kobach and at the USCCR staff in Spanish. Their statements—in which they spoke on behalf of family and community members—exemplify how, as Amalia Pallares argues, narratives of family "serve as a site of collective identity" within migrant activism.[115] As Lisa Marie Cacho notes, however, migrant activists "unintentionally reify other legally vulnerable, legally constructed categories," such as when they counter-pose their familial roles—that is, mothers—against criminality, as if these two identities were incompatible.[116] Further, Ana Elena Puga analyzes the figure of the undocumented migrant as "embedded in a network of roles or 'cast' in the language of theater," which can be "recast" when roles become contested.[117] She notes that, while "characterizations, plot, and spectacle can sometimes win rights," they can also "lead to artificial resolutions about who belongs and who does not belong in the borders of the nation-state."[118]

In addition to their disruptions, these activists performed unauthorized acts that challenged the format of the USCCR briefing. Since there was no space made for undocumented migrants to speak at the briefing, security guards escorted these activists out of the room following their action. As Peter Nyers suggests, "Not surprisingly, representatives of the sovereign order display a striking anxiety whenever the abject foreigner takes on the status of a political activist engaged in acts of self-determination (e.g., stopping their deportation)" as "the dominant order of speaking beings cannot tolerate the sights or sounds of noncitizens acting as political agents."[119] As such, the very structure of the briefing—specifically the USCCR's terms of exclusion—preempted any immediate policy impact of the action.

However, members of the USCCR were not the only audience for this action. The undocumented migrant activists used documentary media to capture their performances of unauthorized acts, which they distributed as counter-documents on activist websites. The action was a form of disruption within the briefing, but the video *Si No Nos Invitan, Nos Invitamos Solo* also had an afterlife, as it circulated through activists' websites. Although activists were addressing Kobach and members of the USCCR during the briefing, the video documentary was directed toward those who were absent—specifically, other undocumented migrants—as a means of political mobilization.[120] The activists' decision to upload the video on the No Papers, No Fear website and on YouTube publicized the action to other undocumented migrants.

This video was more than the recording of the disruption of a briefing; rather, it was purposely shaped for circulation through the staging of the protest, the location of the cameras, and the process of editing.

The video also has its own formal elements, as well as what McKee and McLagan refer to as "its own capacities for circulation and remediation, its own affectual address to a spectator"—in this case, other undocumented migrants.[121] The circulation of these counter-documents is thus part of the way in which undocumented migrant activists create what Alicia Schmidt Camacho refers to as "alternate subnational or transnational spheres of communication and politics."[122] Although very few people could witness the action live during the USCCR hearings, many people could watch it after the video was uploaded onto various websites.

This action was also a form of protection for the activists in case of legal action by the state. The strategy for publicizing the Alabama protest was modeled on one that was used after an earlier civil disobedience action as part of the No Papers, No Fear Ride for Justice in Knoxville, Tennessee. As a result of that action, undocumented migrant activists had been arrested and faced deportation. However, activists from the No Papers, No Fear campaign posted videos of the undocumented migrants' arrests, along with a message for viewers to call ICE to release them.[123] Organizers of the campaign built an e-mail list, a Facebook page, and a Twitter following, and they were thus able to mobilize migrants and allies on behalf of those arrested. As a result of this organizing, all of those arrested were eventually released.[124] This approach was seen as a model for actions that followed—including the one in Alabama—since organizers believed that if these actions were publicized, the activists could avoid arrest or deportation.

The use of media in the No Papers, No Fear campaign—including forms of social media—was a significant aspect of undocumented migrant activists' political organizing. The recording and circulation of *Si No Nos Invitan, Nos Invitamos Solos* on a range of media platforms brought attention to the ways that these anti-immigrant laws affect undocumented migrants as well as the deliberate exclusion of migrant activists from the briefing. Strategies employed by undocumented youth activists—and by previous campaigns organized by NDLON, such as ¡Alto Arizona! (Stop Arizona!)—were incorporated into the No Papers, No Fear campaign.[125] No Papers, No Fear developed its own website, which described the organization and provided information for activists about how to "engage," "endorse," and "converge" with the campaign. The website became an archive of counter-documents, providing visibility for the campaign and enabling activists to contribute to counter-networks composed of undocumented migrant activists and their supporters.[126]

Thus, in the context of the action in Alabama, the No Papers, No Fear website was a platform for political action. Similarly, *Si No Nos Invitan, Nos Invitamos Solos* served as a counter-document that represented the ways in which activists were performing unauthorized acts as well as challenging anti-immigrant state and federal laws. The activists also mobilized in support of the No Papers, No Fear campaign and protected the undocumented migrants who took part in the action from being detained or deported. These undocumented activists disrupted the goings-on of the state and represented themselves in ways that were oppositional. Further, by being present at the briefing and sharing representations of this action through digital media, undocumented migrant activists defied state agents' attempts to limit their physical movement, both within and across national boundaries.

In large part due to the organizing work of undocumented youth and migrant activists, President Barack Obama enacted two executive orders between 2012 and 2014—DACA and Deferred Action for Parents of Americans and Lawful Permanent Residents (DAPA). On August 15, 2012, during the No Papers, No Fear tour, DACA was instituted nationally. DACA allows undocumented youth to apply for "deferred action," which enables them to remain in the United States for two years and to apply for work permits.[127] DACA builds on policies developed during the Obama administration such as "prosecutorial discretion," which was put in place to eliminate "low priority" cases, so ICE could focus on deporting undocumented migrants convicted of crimes. Some undocumented youth activists—such as Tania Unzueta Carrasco—have critiqued DACA, noting the ways in which "it further bolsters the categorization of immigrants as 'worthy' or 'unworthy.'"[128] Following DACA, undocumented youth and migrant activists involved in NDLON and NIYA continued to organize against policies that led to the deportation of undocumented migrants through the #Not1More campaign.[129] In November 2014, President Obama announced that by executive action he would expand the terms of DACA in order to provide relief to a broader group of undocumented migrants through DAPA.[130] Similar to DACA, DAPA did not create a path to citizenship for undocumented migrants; rather, it provided a stay of deportation for three years. Further, as indicated by its title, this executive action was limited to parents of U.S. citizens and lawful residents who had lived in the United States for at least five years and did not have a criminal record.[131]

Those who had advocated for administrative relief—including activists, lawyers, and scholars—supported this executive action but some were also critical of how Obama—through his rhetoric of felons and families, children and criminals—continued to maintain a hierarchy between "deserving" and "undeserving" migrants.[132] Activists challenged this by interrupting the president's speeches, including one that he gave in Chicago in December 2014 in which he said that federal agencies would focus on deporting "felons, not families."[133] B. Loewe, the former communications director for NDLON, who worked on the #Not1More campaign, noted that these activists were involved in "disrupting the President's rhetoric and inserting reality into his publicity events."[134] In performing these unauthorized acts, Unzueta Carrasco and Seif contend that "these activists disrupt the power of the nation-state to make these determinations and expand the debate about and boundaries of citizenship."[135] These disruptions, as well as the direct actions mentioned earlier, are examples of the "impossible" activism of undocumented migrants.[136]

Conclusion

Through the production of counter-documents, undocumented youth and migrant activists have created alternatives to liberal tropes of "visibility" and the state's differentiation between "deserving" and "undeserving" migrants. These activists reworked visibility from an *abstract* form of empowerment to a more *specific* political strategy, which involved publicizing actions that challenged U.S. immigration laws and policies. Further, the videos produced by activists in NIYA, NDLON, and the Puente Movement are examples of how undocumented migrants are asserting their political presence in ways that transcend liberal nationalism.[137]

In *Migrant Imaginaries*, Alicia Schmidt Camacho argues that undocumented migrants' "demand for a different framework of governance doubles as a search for political and aesthetic forms that can perform the work of representation in all its senses."[138] From the statements provided by activists involved in NIYA, NDLON, Puente, and other groups, this "different frame of governance" would be one in which undocumented migrants were free to move around within the United States and between the United States and other countries without the fear of deportation. Through emphasizing undocumented migrants' mobility and mobilization, the No Papers, No Fear campaign challenged what scholars have referred to as the "dominant politics of mobility."[139] Vicki Squire suggests that it is important to consider how "mobilizing politics means to render politics mobile through exploring how the 'irregular' movement of people entails a shift in what it means to be political."[140] Further, Peter Nyers and Kim Rygiel argue that this accent on "mobility as an analytic disrupts the dichotomy of noncitizen/citizen."[141] The No Papers, No Fear campaign brought attention to the limits placed on the physical presence of undocumented migrants, as well as the ways in which they were able to push past those boundaries.

In the early 2010s, undocumented youth and migrant activists developed innovative political strategies and aesthetic forms with which to represent themselves. These activists reconfigured their self-representation through their political activism and their production of counter-documents that challenged the state's ability to determine the parameters of political inclusion. Further, activists' recording of their actions—in which they test the terms of prosecutorial discretion as well as contest anti-immigrant laws—relates to their strategies to mobilize other undocumented migrants. Circulating videos that represent their performing unauthorized acts through digital and social media enabled activists to provide a model of organizing. The documentation and circulation of activist interventions allows undocumented migrants to view what is possible and for scholars and writers to integrate these ephemeral actions into a broader history of migrant activism.

In this chapter, I have examined how Mexican and Central American migrants are revising forms of documentary media for political purposes.

Specifically, I have argued that these activists mix elements of performance with documentary realism to represent their actions, which they circulate through social media to other undocumented migrants. The role of counter-documents is central to the organizing work of undocumented youth and migrant activists, yet the distribution of these forms of media changes not just the context of documentary, but also what this genre of media production can do. Meg McLagan argues that "new media refashions previous media forms . . . and this process of 'remediation' upends old ideas about subjects and participants, producers and texts that underpin theories of how media work."[142] Similar to other kinds of media that are distributed through digital and social media, counter-documents have the ability to "define the terms of political possibility and create terrain for political acts," as McKee and McLagan suggest.[143] As such, counter-documents strategically assemble evidence, disrupt, and mobilize.

Counter-Representational Acts

The case studies in chapter 6 speak to a particular convergence of migrants' documentary media and activism that emerged in the early 2010s. The role of "artivists" and the combining of art and activism have also been key elements of contemporary migrant activism, from ¡Alto Arizona! and No Papers, No Fear to the more recent #Not1More campaign. As Gabriela Marquez-Benitez and Amalia Pallares argue, activists involved in #Not1More employ strategies that "highlight enforcement practices and render the violence of the state visible."[1] Their actions include civil disobedience in which they have attempted to close Immigration and Customs Enforcement (ICE) offices.[2] Further, activists have chained themselves to buses holding detained undocumented migrants in efforts to stop their deportations, and have organized marches to detention centers. In April 2014, antideportation activists planned events related to "2million2many" in which one hundred actions were held in eighty cities to protest the increased number of deportations of undocumented migrants that occurred during President Barack Obama's terms in office.[3] Antideportation actions were organized by groups all over the United States, including artivists involved in the No Name Collective, which, as part of the Moratorium on Deportations Campaign (MODC) in Chicago, performed an action called "Shut Down ICE," in which they organized a march across Chicago with a one-hundred-pound block of ice for a protest at ICE's headquarters.[4] Rozalinda Borcilă, who is a member of the No Name Collective, notes that "for us, this shift or slip-page between ICE and ice, between the symbolic and the 'real' was a way of dealing with the political as aesthetic through engaging performative practice."[5] In addition to "Shut Down ICE," Borcilă notes that the group "developed a series of actions and formalized a set of practices—some self-consciously performative—that articulate a set of shared critiques of, and a desire to experiment with, dominant forms of organizing and social movement work."[6] Activists documented some of these actions, which they circulated on activist websites and on YouTube.

While the final chapter of this book concludes in 2012, migrant activ-ists' use of documentary media continued with the #Not1More campaign, which was founded in 2013. As part of the campaign, activists recorded their actions and uploaded videos to the #Not1More website to create an interactive timeline of antideportation actions on their website.[7] The time-line serves as an archive of direct actions and important political events between the founding of #Not1More in 2013 and President Obama's November 2014 announcement regarding DAPA. The circulation and archiving of videos of ephemeral actions on activist websites—such as those of the #Not1More campaign—provides a "restaging and repetition of these acts," which also "form part of a broader critical space of *coun-termapping*" and "political resistance" that Imogen Tyler argues "creat[es] an unravelable fabric of political resistance across borders."[8] In writing about Mexican and Central American migrants' use and revision of doc-umentary forms, this book also participates in a broader critical space of "countermapping" and "political resistance."

This book has been an effort to understand the particular salience of self-representation as a common trope in documentary projects involv-ing Mexican and Central American migrants in the United States and U.S.–Mexico borderlands during the early twenty-first century. These projects emerged out of the context of the War on Terror and the way that migrant "illegality" has been reconfigured since 9/11. Since the early 2000s, new laws and policies in the United States have both racial-ized and criminalized undocumented migrants, without allowing them the space or place to contest them. In their documentary projects these migrants narrate their exclusion from citizenship and belonging by U.S.

immigration policies and everyday ideologies, as well as how they are affected by neoliberal economic policies. In producing these photographs, films, and videos, these individuals emphasized their subjectivity, while also visualizing their presence within the United States and in the U.S.–Mexico borderlands. Those who participated in these documentary projects created a mixed-genre aesthetic in their photographs, films, and videos. These aesthetic strategies are not secondary to politics, but are inextricably connected with them. These migrants' photography, film, video, and audio work demonstrates their centering of their perspectives in response to state violence and repression.

Through their use of documentary media Mexican and Central American migrants have visualized alternative ways of belonging that do not rely upon notions of citizenship. I have also argued that in these projects migrants utilize documentary media as part of strategies with which to respond to the conditions they face and that oppose liberal conceptions of representation as a means of inclusion and recognition. In their documentary work these undocumented migrants contest the policing of inclusion and exclusion within the nation-state. Further, through the production of these photographs, films, and videos, they resist state forms of documentation and make the violence of the law visible. Some of this work was produced by undocumented youth and migrant activists who, as Tania Unzueta Carrasco and Hinda Seif have noted, are "disrupting citizenship paradigms by calling into question citizenship, as recognized by the state, as a determining factor for whether a person has a right to live, work, and participate in the nation-state."[9] The work of these activists thus serves as a means to challenge the U.S. state's construction of belonging and citizenship, including how it positions undocumented Mexican and Central American migrants as *not* belonging within the United States.

Further, in their use of documentary forms of self-representation Mexican and Central American migrants have created alternatives to liberal tropes of visibility. As opposed to linking visibility with empowerment, in their use of documentary media migrants deploy strategies of visibility and invisibility within specific contexts. The politics of visibility for migrant activists entailed an argument against the terms of political inclusion—specifically normative notions regarding "deserving" and "undeserving" migrants.[10] Instead, they have used documentary media to frame their own depictions, to make public political claims, and to create forms of protection. In their rejection of liberal claims to the transformative capacity of visibility, the strategies practiced by these migrant activists defy conventions of representation that demand inclusion as a normative imperative.

In visualizing alternative modes of social existence and ways of belonging, Mexican and Central American migrants remake the form and function of documentary media, producing a mixed-genre aesthetic that is partly related to their mode of address. Their combining documentary and other photographic genres, including personal, family, and snapshot, narrate local and translocal ways of belonging, as opposed to formalized national membership through citizenship or some other official "legal" status. Their images—such as those that portray the *undocumented everyday*—call attention to their address to local audiences. Some photographs feature a *translocal aesthetic*, which connects the migrants' translocal mode of address to their families and communities living across national boundaries, and it relates their simultaneous belonging to multiple locations. Further, some images combine elements of documentary, personal, and snapshot photography to provide alternative "ways of seeing" the effects of U.S.–Mexico border policing on undocumented Mexican and Central American migrants. The aesthetics of documentary realism shift from their photographic work to their film, video, and audio projects, which include documentary elements but also incorporate performance. In these latter works, artists and activists use affective and performative elements to center both their lives and their political projects, while transforming the genre of documentary itself.

In their documentary photography, film, and video works, migrants represent their "counter-conducts," including their everyday struggles, as well as the effects of neoliberal economic and U.S. immigration policies. In their photographs, they portray themselves engaging in both organized and everyday forms of migrant counter-conducts, such as protesting or attempting to enter the United States surreptitiously. In this work, these migrants challenge the way in which the state attempts to restrain their mobility.[11] Some images envision the effects of U.S. immigration law and U.S.–Mexico border policy on undocumented migrants, including photographs depicting crosses that mark migrant death in the borderlands. Further, activists visualize the violence of neoliberal trade policies and restrictive immigration laws in their film and video work. To organize against these laws and policies, they circulated these films and videos through a variety of outlets—such as a Street Cinema Border Tour in the U.S.–Mexico borderlands—as well as through digital and social media, including activists' websites.

Artists and activists also developed a mixed-genre aesthetic as part of film, video, and audio projects that include elements of disruption or interruption in public spaces. This extends their documentary work to serve as an intervention in public spaces, to make visible practices that both the U.S. and Mexican governments want to keep hidden. Some of this work involves taking up an aesthetics of disappearance in not representing undocumented migrants visually or in ways that mark traces of their absence, while in other work artists create counter-spectacles to highlight state practices. Artists also employ counter-surveillance as well as an *aesthetics of mobility* to challenge state surveillance of undocumented migrants that can physically limit their movement. The use of performance in this work draws out the implications of documentary in certain spaces—both personal and political—for those involved in its creation. Activists use documentary media to record their performances, in which they surveil state agents or interrupt the activities of the state as part of their political actions. Through strategies of *counter-visibility*, migrant activists publicize their actions to shield themselves from detention and deportation. They also create *counter-documents* as a form of evidence that challenges official forms of documentation and state policies on immigration. The activists' distribution of counter-documents connects to their activism and their use of mobility as a political strategy—to appropriate and remake space, to counteract detention, and to mobilize politically.

The undocumented migrants who created these forms of documentary media have developed innovative political strategies and counter-representational practices. They have reconfigured their self-representation through mixed-genre aesthetic works that challenge both neoliberal economics and the U.S. state's ability to define the parameters of political inclusion. Their recording and circulating of these representations on digital and social media recalls Imogen Tyler's point that it is the "proliferation of acts of resistance *within* their many documentary afterlives that allows for a weaving of alternative political imaginaries with which to perceive differently the state we are in."[12] This study has focused primarily on how Mexican and Central American migrants have used and revised documentary projects of self-representation to respond to specific contexts in the United States and U.S.–Mexico borderlands as part of their efforts to create "communities of struggle that question the inclusive/exclusive logic of citizenship, the economics of illegality and the global marketization of migration."[13] These projects are not about migrants "documenting" elements of their lives, but in emphasizing their own subjectivity, their work narrates the ways in which they challenge citizenship, neoliberal globalization, and the role of undocumented people in the U.S. economy. As such, their photographs, films and videos emphasize the importance of their *subjectivity, presence, and mobility.*

Rather than separating discussions of aesthetics and politics, this book has focused on how Mexican and Central American migrants involved in various forms of counter-conducts and activism create forms of visual culture, while also examining the involvement of artists in migrant activism. Part of this book's intervention relates to methodology, and specifically to the approach utilized to analyze migrants' documentary work of self-representation. Yates McKee and Meg McLagan contend that scholars must push visual culture analysis to "argue for the recognition and interpretation of the image complex," which "allows us to take realms, often treated separately—aesthetics, mediation, political movements—and see them as mutually constitutive."[14] This approach is especially relevant for studies of the work of migrant activists. As Rozalinda Borcilă argues, "The kind of collective theorizing and articulation" by artists in the anti-deportation movement "seems to gesture towards a possibility of dissolving art and activism into a more generalized social process of oppositional learning and being."[15] Future scholarship on Mexican and Central American migrants' political and artistic work can build upon these approaches, which entails both listening for and seeing the connections between their aesthetic and political strategies.

Acknowledgments

I am grateful to the many individuals who helped me in the process of researching and writing this book. Special thanks go to Esther Cohen, the former executive director of the Bread and Roses Cultural Project, who told me about Unseen America's collaboration with the Workplace Project in Hempstead, Long Island, New York, in 2000. Carlos Canales from the Workplace Project and photography teacher Matthew Septimus shared invaluable information about the workshop with me. I thank members of the Bread and Roses staff, including Shaila George, Judith McCabe, and Bonita Savage, for helping me with my research on Unseen America. Staff members at Hudson River HealthCare (HRHCare) were incredibly generous with their time and materials, letting me comb through their files while discussing the Communities without Borders project. I am particularly grateful to Anne Nolon, Vilma Velez, Wilfredo Morel, Nick Cannell, Elizabeth Druback-Celaya, and the participants in the Communities without Borders project. Thanks also to Barbara Hill, Juan Garcia-Nuñez, and Quito Ziegler. I am especially appreciative that the HRHCare staff re-created the *Communities without Borders* exhibition during my visit.

I have appreciated the many conversations I have had with artist Sergio de la Torre over the years. I thank him for sharing photographs and materials related to the *Sanctuary City/Ciudad Santuario, 1989–2009* exhibition. Filmmaker Vicki Funari gave me critical information about the making of *Maquilápolis: City of Factories* and forwarded stills from the film. I would also like to thank Diana Arias and Sylvia López Estrada for sharing their perspectives on projects involving Grupo Factor X.

I would like to acknowledge the work of activists who participated in the "Everyday Forms of Popular Power: Art, Media, and Immigration" symposium that Irene Vásquez and I co-organized at University of New Mexico (UNM) in November 2012. My sincerest thanks go to Nicolas González-Medina, Jonathan Perez, Isaac Barrera, Nadia Sol Ireri Unzueta Carrasco, Viridiana Martínez, and Jesus Barrios for sharing their perspectives with UNM students and faculty. I would also like to thank both former and current staff members from the National Day Labor Organizing Network (NDLON), including B. Loewe and Chris Newman, for our conversations about NDLON's organizing work. Further, I am grateful to Barni Axmed Qaasim for discussing her experiences as a media maker on the No Papers, No Fear Ride for Justice tour and to Jonathan Alvira for allowing me to use his photograph in this book.

Without the expertise of archivists, museum professionals, and librarians, this project would not have been possible. Special thanks go to Heather Smedberg of Mandeville Special Collections Library at University of California, San Diego, for her assistance with the inSite collection. I am also grateful to the Scottsdale Museum of Contemporary Art's (SMoCA) registrar Pat Evans for locating materials related to the *Border Film Project: El Proyecto Fronterizo Fotográfico* exhibition. I appreciate the help of curator Cassandra Koblenz, who discussed the exhibition with me. Thanks also to Victoria Criado for allowing me to include images from the *Border Film Project* in this book. I also acknowledge the efforts of the interlibrary loan staff at Zimmerman Library, UNM, for helping me locate and retrieve much-needed materials.

I am thankful to have received vital financial assistance to research and write this manuscript. At UNM, the Research Allocation Committee awarded me two grants to conduct research on this book. I am also appreciative of the Dean's Office of the College of Arts and Sciences for a Career Advancement Semester, which enabled me to finish writing the manuscript, as well as subvention funds to cover the costs of image rights and indexing.

Numerous colleagues provided valuable feedback on this manuscript. Comments by two readers, Claire F. Fox and Ramón Rivera-Servera, significantly shaped my revisions to the chapters and helped me refine my overall arguments. I am grateful to have had the opportunity to present this work to a broader audience. In particular, I would like to thank students and faculty associated with the Transnational Americas Working Group and the Department of African American Studies at University of California, Berkeley; the Center for Ideas and Society, Immigration Research Group, Culver Center for the Arts, History Department, and Department of Media and Cultural Studies at University of California, Riverside; and the Center for the Study of Race, Indigeneity, and Transnational Migration at Yale University for their feedback. This work has been significantly enhanced by conversations with scholars at the "Feeling Photography" symposium, University of Toronto; the "Looking at Arts, History, and Place in the U.S.–Mexico Borderlands" symposium, University of Arizona; the Newberry Library's Series in the U.S.–Mexico Borderlands; and "The Latino Midwest," Obermann-International Programs Humanities Symposium, University of Iowa. I would especially like to thank Leigh Raiford, Monica Huerta, Cathy Gudis, Molly McGarry, Steve Pitti, Alicia Schmidt Camacho, Elspeth Brown, Thy Phu, Laura Briggs, Franny Nudelman, Wendy Kozol, Gerry Cadava, Benjamin Johnson, Kathleen Belew, Katherine Morrissey, Sarah Moore, John-Michael Warner, Sandy Soto, Amelia Malagamba, Laura Gutiérrez, Alicia Arrizón, Frank Galarte, Larry La Fountain, Jane Juffer, and John Nieto-Phillips. I am grateful to the following individuals who collaborated on organizing panels for the American Studies Association's annual conference: Rosa-Linda Fregoso, Alejandro Lugo, Claudia Sadowski-Smith, Kirsten Silva Gruesz, Gloria Melissa García, Claire F. Fox, José David Saldívar, Ricardo Dominguez, Sasha Costanza-Chock, Curtis Marez, Cristina Beltrán, Gilberto Rosas, and Sandy Soto. My thanks also go to colleagues—specifically those affiliated with the Latin American and Iberian Institute and the Transnational American Studies Lecture Series—for their feedback on presentations that I gave at UNM.

I am grateful to Claire F. Fox, Omar Valerio-Jiménez, and Santiago Vaquera-Vásquez for the invitation to participate in a weeklong summer seminar on "Teaching the Latino Midwest" at the Obermann Center at the University of Iowa. I would like to thank other members of the seminar, including Aidé Acosta, Frances Aparicio, Carolyn Colvin, María

Cotera, Theresa Delgadillo, Lilia Fernández, Felipe Hinojosa, Mike Innis-Jiménez, Marta María Maldonado, Louis Mendoza, Amelia Montes, and Ramón Rivera-Servera, for their comments on an earlier version of the final chapter.

I benefited tremendously from feedback offered by numerous scholars, including Marita Sturken, Claudia Sadowski-Smith, Joseph Entin, Sara Blair, Franny Nudelman, Katherine Morrissey, John-Michael Warner, Omar Valerio-Jiménez, Andy Urban, and Amy Tyson. Thanks to Roxanne Willis for her editorial assistance, as well as to Diego Bustos and Susan Walter, who helped with copyediting the Spanish-language text, and Sarah Soliz, who prepared the final manuscript. I could not have written this book without the assistance of George Luna-Peña, Rafael Martínez, María López, Lara Hayner, Raquel Madrigal, Naomi Ambriz, and Christina Juhasz-Wood. At the University of Minnesota Press, working with Danielle Kasprzak and Anne Carter has been a delight. I also thank Richard Morrison for his encouragement and interest in this project.

I thank my past and present colleagues in the American Studies department at UNM, who offered their encouragement of this project: Amy Brandzel, David Correia, Jennifer Nez Denetdale, Laura Gómez, Kathleen Holscher, Alex Lubin, Gabriel Meléndez, Vera Norwood, Sandy Rodrigue, Shanté Smalls, Tony Tiongson, Michael Trujillo, and Irene Vásquez. I also express my appreciation to the many students who have been part of lively graduate seminars on migration and immigration, transnational American studies, and visual culture. I am grateful to UNM colleagues and friends Jesse Alemán, Judy Bieber, Susan Dever, Szu-Han Ho, Liz Hutchison, Dominika Laster, Leila and Jeremy Lehnen, Mary Quinn, Suzanne Schadl, Jason Smith, Bill Stanley, Susan Tiano, Melina Vizcaino-Alemán, and John Whitlow. I so enjoyed the time I spent with UNM colleagues Brian Herrera, Holly Barnet-Sánchez, and Tey Diana Rebolledo while planning the "Latina/o Literary Imagination" symposium. In recent years, I have had great conversations with scholars and filmmakers visiting UNM, including George Yúdice, Mary Louise Pratt, Renato Rosaldo, Alex Rivera, Cristina Ibarra, Barni Axmed Qaasim, and Monica Varsanyi.

The Transnational Americas Research Cluster has provided a supportive context in which to share work, and I thank the participants in these discussions, including Irene Vásquez, Bárbara O. Reyes, Patricia Rosas Lopátegui, Joseph Garcia, Kency Cornejo, Raquel Z. Rivera, Susana Martínez Guillem, Adán Ávalos, Rafael Martínez, María Eugenia López, Froilan Orozco, Moises Santos, Raquel Madrigal, Naomi Ambriz, and Summer Abbott. I so appreciate fellow members of the Sanctuary Campus Working Group, including Irene Vásquez, Rafael Martínez, Jenny Moore, Felipe Gonzales, Greg Martin, Rebecca Kitson, Justin Remer-Thamert, Myrriah Gómez, Brenna Gómez, Jennifer Tucker, José Orduña, Caitlin Roach Orduña, Kathryn Wichelns, Ruth Trinidad Galván, Ernesto Longa, and Damián Wilson for their organizing efforts at UNM. Thanks also to students and staff affiliated with the New Mexico Dream Team and El Centro de la Raza at UNM. For their leadership on immigrants' rights in New Mexico, I gratefully acknowledge the work of state representative Javier Martínez, Rachel LaZar of El Centro de Igualdad y Derechos in Albuquerque, and Marcela Díaz of Somos un Pueblo Unido in Santa Fe. Thanks also to Gilberto Rosas, Naomi Paik, Jason Ruiz, Elliot Young, Mae Ngai, and Lourdes Gutiérrez Nájera for strategizing and sharing information.

On a more personal note, I would like to thank friends and family, including Enrique Aguilar, Aliyah Baruchin, Sophie Bell, Cristina Beltrán, Jayna Brown, Ronda Brulotte, Matt Budman, William Fowler Collins, Rosemary Cosgrove, Erin Debenport, Joseph Entin, Laurel George, Malcolm Goldstein, Marin Goldstein, Oisin Goldstein-Dea, Pilar Goldstein-Dea, Cathy Gudis, Brian Herrera, Adrian Johnston, Blaine Keesee, Jacob Keesee, Alex Ku, Stephanie and Stuart Lipkowitz, Carol Marcy, Zachary Morgan, Erik Nauman, Carmen Nocentelli, Tey Marianna Nunn, Sarah Putnam, Walter Putnam, Michael Quanci, Jim Roeber, Scott Saul, Sarah Schulman, Julia Talbot, Sam Truett, Mary Tsiongas, Claudia X. Valdes, Kathryn Wichelns, Jane Yeomans, Cynthia Young, and Yoko Ziegler. I also recognize my parents, Carol and Sanford Schreiber, and my sister, Madeline Schreiber, for their ongoing support. Most of all I would like to thank Alia and Alyosha. I am very fortunate to have two such amazing people in my life.

Notes

Preface

1. I follow the terminology developed by other scholars who have written about undocumented Mexican and Central American migrants in the United States during the late twentieth and early twenty-first centuries. My use of the word *migrant* draws from the work of Mae Ngai, who argues that the term does not "privilege permanent settlement before other kinds of migration." See Ngai, *Impossible Subjects: Illegal Aliens and the Making of Modern America* (Princeton, N.J.: Princeton University Press, 2004), xix. Further, Nicholas De Genova uses the term *migrant* "to serve as a category of analysis that disrupts the implicit teleology of the more conventional term 'immigrant,' which is posited always from the standpoint of the 'immigrant-receiving' nation-state." De Genova, "The Legal Production of Mexican/Migrant 'Illegality,'" *Latino Studies* 2 (2004): 160n1. Alicia Schmidt Camacho notes that migrant "also references a subordinate position with respect to that of the 'citizen.'" Schmidt Camacho, *Migrant Imaginaries: Latino Cultural Politics in the U.S.–Mexico Borderlands* (New York: New York University Press, 2008), 5.

2. The USA PATRIOT Act is the acronym for "Uniting and Strengthening America by Providing Appropriate Tools Required to Intercept and Obstruct Terrorism." For the text of the act, see http://www.justice.gov/archive/ll/high lights.htm. As María Cristina García notes, the USA PATRIOT Act "expanded the powers of law enforcement agencies to search, monitor, and detain suspected criminals and terrorists; allowed the indefinite detention of noncitizens suspected of a crime and facilitated their deportation for a number of activities." García, *Seeking Refuge: Central American Migration to Mexico, the United States, and Canada* (Berkeley: University of California Press, 2006), 161–62; see also David Cole, *Enemy Aliens: Double Standards and Constitutional Freedoms in the War on Terrorism* (New York: New Press, 2003).

3. Nicolas De Genova, "Conflicts of Mobility and the Mobility of Conflict: Rightlessness, Presence, Subjectivity, Freedom," *Subjectivity* 29 (2009): 450. Emphasis in original.

4. Ibid., 451. Emphasis in original.

5. In this book, I use the term *undocumented* to refer to migrants without legal status as permanent residents or naturalized citizens.

6. Quito Ziegler, telephone conversation with author, March 5, 2010.

7. As Lisa Marie Cacho contends, "Anxieties over undocumented immigration following September 11 generated a new kind of crisis over 'illegal' immigration." Cacho, *Social Death: Racialized Rightlessness and the Criminalization of the Unprotected* (New York: New York University Press, 2012), 101.

8. Specifically, Stuart Hall suggests that participants in a culture give meanings to things based on how we "integrate them into our everyday practices." Hall, "Introduction," in *Representation: Cultural Representations and Signifying Practices*, ed. Stuart Hall (London: Sage, 1997), 3.

9. Wendy Hesford, *Spectacular Rhetorics: Human Rights Visions, Recognitions, Feminisms* (Durham, N.C.: Duke University Press, 2011), 57–58.

10. Ibid, 58; Patricia Pace, "Staging Childhood: Lewis Hine's Photographs of Child Labor," *Lion and the Unicorn* 26 (2002): 326, as quoted in ibid.

11. Hall, "Introduction," 9–10.

12. Ibid., 8.

13. Sonia E. Alvarez, Evelina Dagnino, and Arturo Escobar, "Introduction," in *Cultures of Politics/Politics of Cultures: Re-visioning Latin American Social Movements* (New York: HarperCollins, 1998), 7. Further, as Pablo Alvarado, the executive director of the National Day Labor Organizing Network, explains, "There is no movement without culture." See http://leadershipforchange.org/awardees. As quoted by Cecilia Menjívar, "Immigrant Art as Liminal Expression: The Case of Central Americans," in *Art in the Lives of Immigrant Communities in the United States*, ed. Paul DiMaggio and Patricia Fernández-Kelly (New Brunswick, N.J.: Rutgers University Press, 2010), 186.

14. Lynn Stephen, *Transborder Lives: Indigenous Oaxacans in Mexico, California, and Oregon* (Durham, N.C.: Duke University Press, 2007), 65.

15. I am drawing the idea of the "gift" of citizenship from Mimi Thi Nguyen's notion of "the gift of freedom," which she defines "as the workings of liberalism in its imperial form and as a metaphor and a medium for grasping continuities and innovations between operations of power and violence." Nguyen, *The Gift of Freedom: War, Debt, and Other Refugee Passages* (Durham, N.C.: Duke University Press, 2012), 6.

16. For more information, see http://altotrump.com/.

17. Liz Robbins, "Immigrants Head to Washington to Rally While Obama Is Still There," *New York Times*, January 11, 2017, A28.

18. Due to the current political context, I have chosen to include only the first names of individuals who may be undocumented in this book. "Immigrant Leaders from across New Mexico Head to Washington D.C. to Join Rally

ahead of Inauguration, Showcase Local Sanctuary Policies That Defend Immigrants from Looming Trump Administration," January 12, 2017, http://www.somosunpueblounido.org/january-12%2c-2017.html.

19. See https://www.whitehouse.gov/the-press-office/2017/01/25/executive-order-border-security-and-immigration-enforcement-improvements.

20. As I explain in the introduction, 287(g) agreements were established as part of the 1996 Illegal Immigration Reform and Immigrant Responsibility Act (IIRIRA), which allows Immigration and Customs Enforcement (ICE) to develop partnerships with local and state law enforcement.

21. See section 5d of "Enhancing Public Safety in the Interior of the United States," https://www.whitehouse.gov/the-press-office/2017/01/25/presidential-executive-order-enhancing-public-safety-interior-united; Brian Bennett, "Not Just 'Bad Hombres': Trump Is Targeting up to 8 Million People for Deportation," *Los Angeles Times*, February 4, 2017.

22. There were approximately 2.5 million deportations during President Obama's two terms in office.

23. See https://www.whitehouse.gov/the-press-office/2017/01/25/presidential-executive-order-enhancing-public-safety-interior-united.

24. Quoted in Matthew Reichbach, "Immigrants, Supporters Vow to Fight Trump's Immigration Order," *New Mexico Political Report*, January 25, 2017, http://nmpoliticalreport.com/147060/immigrants-supporters-vow-to-fight-trumps-immigration-order/.

25. During the legislative session, Javier Martínez introduced a bill to prohibit the "use, transfer, or selling of state land to aid in the construction of a border wall." Somos un Pueblo Unido press release, "Hundreds Rally at State Capital against Trump's Immigration Executive Orders; Push for Joint Memorial Urging Legislature and Congress to do the Same," February 6, 2017.

26. See quote from Natalia in Robbins, "Immigrants Head to Washington."

27. Amalia Pallares defines "impossible activism" as referring to the way that undocumented migrants' "political rights are not recognized as legitimate." Amalia Pallares, *Family Activism: Immigrant Struggles and the Politics of Noncitizenship* (New Brunswick, N.J.: Rutgers University Press, 2015), 1–2.

Introduction

1. This day marked the "National Day of Action to Shut Down ICE," in which activists attempted to both bring attention to and stop the deportations of undocumented migrants held in immigration detention facilities. These actions were part of the #Not1More campaign, which, as noted on the website, "builds collaboration between individuals, organizations, artists, and allies to expose, confront, and overcome unjust immigration laws." See http://www.notonemoredeportation.com/about/. Day laborers involved in worker centers founded NDLON in 2001 to advocate for migrant rights. Janice Fine, *Worker Centers: Organizing Communities at the Edge of the Dream* (Ithaca, N.Y.: ILR

Press and Cornell University Press, 2006). While NDLON formed in response to the problems of day laborers, allowing them to organize as workers, it also collaborates with undocumented migrants when they are being denied basic rights and risk being arrested, detained, and deported due to their immigration status. The Puente Movement is a grassroots migrant justice organization based in Phoenix, Arizona. According to their website, they "develop, educate, and empower migrant communities to protect and defend our families and ourselves in order to enhance the quality of life of our community members." See http://puenteaz.org/about-us.

2. The week previous activists chained themselves to the wheels of a bus that held migrant detainees who were facing convictions as part of Operation Streamline.

3. See http://www.notonemoredeportation.com/2013/10/14/protest-closes -phoenix-ice-office-prevents-deportations/.

4. These signs and posters are also archived online as part of galleries on activist websites, such as one for the #Not1More campaign. See http://www .notonemoredeportation.com/.

5. Specifically, these images have been used as a means to encourage individuals to empathize with undocumented migrants in deportation proceedings. For example, the authors of *Education Not Deportation* note that "by using pictures you intend to show the public that you are just like them." *Education Not Deportation: A Guide for Undocumented Youth in Removal Proceedings*, http:// www.e4fc.org/images/E4FC_DeportationGuide.pdf, 35.

6. Pallares, *Family Activism*, 131. According to the National Immigration Law Center, "A 'mixed-status family' is a family whose members include people with different citizenship or immigration statuses." See https://www.nilc .org/issues/health-care/aca_mixedstatusfams/.

7. While the majority of these documentary projects have been produced by undocumented Mexican and Central American migrants, in chapter 4 I examine the work of Mexican migrants in northern Mexico. Further, in the final chapter I include the work of undocumented youth activists, some of whom are either not Latina/o or who are Latina/o, but not Mexican or Central American.

8. Keith Beattie, *Documentary Screens: Non-fiction Film and Television* (New York: Palgrave, 2004), 107.

9. Allan Sekula, "The Body and the Archive," *October* 39 (Winter 1986): 3–64; and John Tagg, *The Burden of Representation: Essays on Photographies and Histories* (London: Macmillan, 1988).

10. Anna Pegler-Gordon, *In Sight of America: Photography and the Development of U.S. Immigration Policy* (Berkeley: University of California Press, 2009), 10.

11. Coco Fusco, "Racial Time, Racial Marks, Racial Metaphors," in *Only Skin Deep: Changing Visions of the American Self*, ed. Coco Fusco and Brian

Wallis (New York: International Center of Photography and Harry N. Abrams, 2003), 39. At the time that the Real ID Bill was being developed, the federal government started to gather biometric data, such as digital fingerprints and photographs, from all visitors to the United States through the US-VISIT program. See http://www.immihelp.com/visas/usvisit.html. As Sekula has argued, "Bertillion survives in the operations of the national security state, in the conditions of intensive and extensive surveillance that characterizes both everyday life and the geopolitical sphere." Sekula, "The Body and the Archive," 62.

12. Dimitris Papadopulos and Vassilis Tsianos, "The Autonomy of Migration: The Animals of Undocumented Mobility," in *Deleuzian Encounters: Studies in Contemporary Social Issues*, ed. Anna Hickey-Moody and Peta Malins (New York: Palgrave, 2008), as quoted in Katarzyna Marciniak and Imogen Tyler, "Introduction: Immigrant Protest; Noborder Scholarship," in *Immigrant Protest: Politics, Aesthetics, and Everyday Dissent*, ed. Katarzyna Marciniak and Imogen Tyler (Albany: SUNY Press, 2014), 13.

13. Cacho, *Social Death*, 8.

14. Pallares, *Family Activism*, 12.

15. Ibid. Pallares notes that while undocumented migrants are denied formal citizenship, "they have access to certain social and labor protections on the basis of their territorial presence and personhood, as conveyed in the equal protection clause of the 14th amendment." Ibid., 4.

16. Marciniak and Tyler, "Introduction," 9.

17. Cacho, *Social Death*, 144.

18. For example, Claire F. Fox argues that "Lynn Stephen's study of undocumented Mexican workers in the United States deemphasizes the objective of claiming liberal citizenship rights by exploring the ways in which undocumented Mexican people in the United States assert political presence, even without access to the rights conferred by U.S. citizenship." Fox, *Making Art Pan-American: Cultural Policy and the Cold War* (Minneapolis: University of Minnesota Press, 2013), 313n107. See also Stephen, *Transborder Lives*, 241.

19. For example, in writing about contemporary migrant activism, Anne McNevin suggests that while activists "disrupt citizenship norms," their approach is "not aimed at gaining legal or conventional citizenship status," and thus it "leaves open the possibility of opting out of citizenship as a mode of resistance." McNevin, "Undocumented Citizens? Shifting Grounds of Citizenship in Los Angeles," in *Citizenship, Migrant Activism and the Politics of Movement*, ed. Peter Nyers and Kym Rygiel (New York: Routledge, 2012), 178–79. Further, Schmidt Camacho suggests that "migrant social movements define justice in terms that surpass the sovereignty of nations or the logic of capital accumulation." Schmidt Camacho, *Migrant Imaginaries*, 5.

20. Schmidt Camacho, *Migrant Imaginaries*, 5.

21. Ibid., 12. Schmidt Camacho is drawing upon Charles Taylor's *Modern Social Imaginaries* (Durham, N.C.: Duke University Press, 2004).

22. As Cacho contends, "Anxieties over undocumented immigration following September 11 generated a new kind of crisis over 'illegal' immigration." Cacho, *Social Death*, 101.

23. See TRAC, "Secure Communities and ICD Deportation: A Failed Program?" April 8, 2014, http://trac.syr.edu/immigration/reports/349/.

24. Monica W. Varsanyi and other scholars have written about the engagement of municipal and city governments in immigration enforcement. See Varsanyi, *Taking Local Control: Immigration Policy Activism in U.S. Cities and States* (Stanford, Calif.: Stanford University Press, 2010); and Doris Marie Provine, Monica W. Varsanyi, Paul G. Lewis, and Scott H. Decker, *Policing Immigrants: Local Law Enforcement on the Front Lines* (Chicago: University of Chicago Press, 2016).

25. Jonathan X. Inda and Julie A. Dowling, "Introduction: Governing Migrant Illegality," in *Governing Immigration through Crime: A Reader*, ed. Jonathan X. Inda and Julie A. Dowling (Stanford, Calif.: Stanford University Press, 2013), 23.

26. According to ICE's website, S-COMM was a "comprehensive plan to identify and remove criminal aliens," which involved the use of "biometric identification technologies." S-COMM also provided state and local law enforcement agencies with the equipment to perform record checks of both the criminal history and immigration status for people in their custody. The results of these screenings were then disseminated to ICE and state and local law enforcement agencies. See ICE's website for S-COMM: www.ice.gov/pi/news/factsheets/ secure_communities.htm.

27. U.S. citizens who are Latina/o face discrimination for "looking like" undocumented Latina/o migrants. McNevin, "Undocumented Citizens?" 165. Marta María Maldonado, Adela C. Licona, and Sarah Hendricks note that "U.S.-born Latin@s are also affected by the rhetorics and practices of the regime of deportability, because . . . being 'read' as Latin@ immediately renders one 'suspect' of illegality." Maldonado, Licona, and Hendricks, "Latin@ Immobilities and Altermobilities within the U.S. Deportability Regime," *Annals of the American Association of Geographers* 106, no. 2 (2016): 323.

28. Hesford, *Spectacular Rhetorics*, 18.

29. Jodie M. Lawston and Ruben R. Murillo, "Policing Our Border, Policing Our Nation: An Examination of the Ideological Connections between Border Vigilantism and U.S. National Ideology," in *Beyond Walls and Cages: Prisons, Borders, and Global Crisis*, ed. Jenna Loyd, Matt Mitchelson, and Andrew Burridge (Athens: University of Georgia Press, 2012), 182.

30. Susan Jeffords, *Hard Bodies: Hollywood Masculinity in the Reagan Era* (New Brunswick, N.J.: Rutgers University Press, 1996), 6.

31. Guy Debord, *The Society of the Spectacle* (New York: Zone Books, 1994), 4; and Diana Taylor, *The Archive and the Repertoire: Performing Cultural Memory in the Americas* (Durham, N.C.: Duke University Press, 2003), 13.

32. Diana Taylor, *Disappearing Acts: Spectacles of Gender and Nationalism in Argentina's "Dirty War"* (Durham, N.C.: Duke University Press, 1997), 119.

33. Nicholas Mirzoeff, *The Right to Look: A Counterhistory of Visuality* (Durham, N.C.: Duke University Press, 2011), 282.

34. Although the vast majority of participants in these projects were migrants, a couple of the promotoras were longtime residents of Tijuana.

35. Tania A. Unzueta Carrasco describes the "1.5 generation" as "immigrants, born abroad yet raised and educated in the United States." She contends that the "1.5 generation lives and organizes by navigating a complex relationship with the nation-state, which places us as both as criminal and legitimate subjects." Unzueta Carrasco and Hinda Seif, "Disrupting the Dream: Undocumented Youth Reframe Citizenship and Deportability through Anti-Deportation Activism," *Latino Studies* 12, no. 2 (2014): 287.

36. Michael Cooper, "Laborers Wanted, but Not Living Next Door," *New York Times*, November 28, 1999.

37. According to the website for the Southern Poverty Law Center, while FAIR "maintains a veneer of legitimacy," some of the individuals who run the organization "have ties to white supremacist groups." The organization was founded by John Tanton, who advocated for the United States to have a "majority white" population and to limit the number of nonwhites allowed into the country. See the Southern Poverty Law Center's website, www.splcenter.org.

38. Jennifer Ridgley, "Cities of Refuge: Immigration Enforcement, Police, and the Insurgent Genealogies of Citizenship in U.S. Sanctuary Cities," *Urban Geography* 29, no. 1 (2008): 55.

39. Schmidt Camacho, *Migrant Imaginaries*, 199. Other scholars, such as Rinku Sen, have also written about the act's effects on migrants. See Rinku Sen with Fekkak Mamdouh, *Accidental American: Immigration and Citizenship in the Age of Globalization* (San Francisco: Berrett-Koehler, 2008), 59.

40. Nicholas De Genova, *Working the Boundaries: Race, Space, and "Illegality" in Mexican Chicago* (Durham, N.C.: Duke University Press, 2005), 206. According to De Genova, these acts "were truly unprecedented in the severity with which they broadened the qualitative purview and intensified the ramifications of migrant 'illegality.'" Ibid., 242. De Genova also notes that the IIRIRA's language was "replete with references to 'the' border, a tell-tale sign that could only portend a future disciplining of Mexican migration." Ibid.

41. Jonathan X. Inda, *Targeting Immigrants: Government, Technology, and Ethics* (Malden, Mass.: Blackwell, 2006), 176–77.

42. Rebecca J. Hester, "Bodies in Translation/Health Promotion in Indigenous Mexican Migrant Communities in California," in *Translocalities/Translocalidades: Feminist Politics of Translation in the Latin/a Américas*, ed. Sonia E. Alvarez, Claudia de Lima Costa, Verónica Feliu, Rebecca J. Hester, and Norma Millie Thayer (Durham, N.C.: Duke University Press, 2014), 173.

43. Lisa Duggan, *The Twilight of Equality? Neoliberalism, Cultural Politics, and the Attack on Democracy* (New York: Beacon Press, 2004).

44. Pallares, *Family Activism*, 6. She is referencing Leo Chavez, *The Latino Threat: Constructing Immigrants, Citizens, and the Nation* (Stanford, Calif.: Stanford University Press, 2008), among the work of other scholars.

45. Cacho, *Social Death*, 22.

46. Muneer Ahmad, "Developing Citizenship," *Issues in Legal Scholarship* 9, no. 1 (October 2011): 6. The approach was also used by mainstream immigrant rights organizations to advocate for the DREAM Act in the early 2000s. Pallares, *Family Activism*, 100.

47. Pallares, *Family Activism*, 102–3.

48. I use the term *undocumented youth* to distinguish them from migrant activists who are not eligible for the DREAM Act or Deferred Action for Childhood Arrivals (DACA) due to their age. However, I am aware that it is problematic to use the term *youth* to describe individuals whose ages span from teenagers to young adults.

49. Inda and Dowling, "Introduction," 3. Inda and Dowling's concept of "migrant counter-conducts" draws on Michel Foucault's notion of "counter-conduct," which he describes as "the sense of struggle against the processes implemented for conducting others." Foucault, *Security, Territory, Population: Lectures at the Collège de France, 1977–1978*, trans. Graham Burchell (New York: Palgrave Macmillan, 2007), 201. Expanding on Foucault's definition of "counter-conduct," Inda and Dowling explain that this concept indicates that there is a "strategic reversibility to power relations such that any governmental effort to shape the conduct of individuals and populations is interwoven with dissenting counter-conducts." Inda and Dowling, "Introduction," 24. These counter-conducts can be contrasted with "citizenship scripts," which are related to the state's regulation of conduct. Pallares, *Family Activism*, 4–5; and Engin F. Isin, *Citizens without Frontiers* (London: Bloomsbury, 2012), 148.

50. Inda and Dowling, "Introduction," 24n32.

51. Nicholas De Genova et al., "Migrant Struggles," in special section, "New Keywords: Migration and Borders," special issue, "Marking Time: Cultural Studies and Communication," *Cultural Studies* 29, no. 1 (2015): 26. Emphasis in original.

52. NIYA was "an undocumented youth-LED network of grassroots organizations, campus-based student groups and individuals committed to achieving equality for all immigrant youth, regardless of their legal status." See NIYA's Facebook page.

53. De Genova et al., "Migrant Struggles," 26.

54. Rozalina Borcilă with Katarzyna Marciniak and Imogen Tyler, "The Political Aesthetics of Immigrant Protest," in *Immigrant Protest: Politics, Aesthetics, and Everyday Dissent*, ed. Katarzyna Marciniak and Imogen Tyler (Albany:

SUNY Press, 2014), 56; Lauren Berlant, *Cruel Optimism* (Durham, N.C.: Duke University Press, 2011), 262.

55. Yates McKee, "'Eyes and Ears': Aesthetics, Visual Culture and the Claims of Nongovernmental Politics," in *Nongovernmental Politics*, ed. Michel Feher, Gaëlle Kirkorian, and Yates McKee (New York: Zone Books, 2007), 339.

56. Ibid., 334.

57. Martha Rosler, "Post-Documentary, Post-Photography?" in *Decoys and Disruptions: Selected Writings, 1975–2001* (Cambridge, Mass.: MIT Press, 2006), 228.

58. Stephen defines translocal as "the movement of place-specific culture, institutions, people, knowledge, and resources within several local sites and across borders—national and otherwise." Stephen, *Transborder Lives*, 65.

59. See Hesford, *Spectacular Rhetorics*, 57–58; and Abigail Solomon-Godeau, *Photography at the Dock: Essays on Photographic History, Institutions, and Practices* (Minneapolis: University of Minnesota Press, 1994), 178–79.

60. Ramón Rivera-Servera and Harvey Young, "Introduction: Border Moves," in *Performance in the Borderlands*, ed. Ramón Rivera-Servera and Harvey Young (New York: Palgrave, 2011), 3.

61. Taylor, *The Archive and the Repertoire*, 18.

62. Their representation of the *undocumented everyday* challenges what Rosas refers to as "policeability," which Maldonado, Licona, and Hendricks describe as "a state of constant surveillance predicated on the hyperregulation of routine activity, evident in displays of state power, vigilantism, and the informal management of everyday life." Maldonado, Licona, and Hendricks, "Latin@ Immobilities and Altermobilities," 323; and Gilberto Rosas, "The Managed Violences of the Borderlands: Treacherous Geographies, Policeability, and the Politics of Race," *Latino Studies* 4, no. 4 (2006): 401–18.

63. Stephen, *Transborder Lives*, 65.

64. McKee, "Eyes and Ears," 332.

65. While *Maquilápolis* could be considered what Bill Nichols calls a "performative documentary," it does not neatly fit within this genre. Nichols, *Blurred Boundaries: Questions of Meaning in Contemporary Culture* (Bloomington: Indiana University Press, 1994).

66. McKee, "Eyes and Ears"; Judith Butler, *Precarious Life: The Powers of Mourning and Violence* (London: Verso, 2004), 146, as quoted in McKee, "Eyes and Ears," 339. Emphasis in original.

67. Chon Noriega refers to the "cine-testimonio" as a form of "counterdocument," which is "intimately tied to the need to legitimize the postrevolutionary nation or struggles against state terror." Chon Noriega, "Talking Heads, Body Politic: The Plural Self of Chicano Experimental Video," in *Resolutions: Contemporary Video Practices*, ed. Michael Renov and Erica Suderberg (Minneapolis: University of Minnesota Press, 1996), 211.

68. De Genova et al., "Migrant Struggles," 26.

69. Schmidt Camacho, *Migrant Imaginaries*, 290; and Douglas Massey and Jorge Durand, eds., *Crossing the Border: Research from the Mexican Migration Project* (New York: Russell Sage Foundation, 2006).

70. In 2013 there were an estimated 11.3 million undocumented migrants, which was an increase from 8.4 million in 2000, but down from a high of 12 million in 2007, before the recession. Jeffrey S. Passel and D'Vera Cohn, "Unauthorized Immigrant Population Stable for Half a Decade," Pew Research Center Report, July 22, 2015, http://www.pewresearch.org.

71. See Jie Zong, and Jeanne Batalova, "Central American Immigrants in the United States," Migration Policy Institute, September 2, 2015, http://www.migrationpolicy.org; and Ana Gonzalez-Barrera, "More Mexicans Leaving Than Coming to the U.S.," Pew Research Center Report, November 19, 2015, http://www.pewhispanic.org.

72. Wil S. Hylton, "The Shame of America's Family Detention Camps," *New York Times Magazine*, February 8, 2015, 26. After CAFTA-DR was enacted, fifty thousand jobs in the textile industry were lost, since 122 textile companies left the nations that were part of the agreement. Stop CAFTA Coalition, "Monitoring Report: DR-CAFTA in Year One," September 12, 2006, 30–32, as referenced in Cacho, *Social Death*, 122.

73. See Arturo Arias, "Central American–Americans: Invisibility, Power, and Representation in the U.S. Latino World," *Latino Studies* 1, no. 1 (2003).

74. García, *Seeking Refuge*, 162.

75. Arias argues that the experiences of Guatemalans and Salvadorans—who comprise the largest groups of Central Americans in the United States—were distinct, due to the civil wars in their countries. Arias, "Central American–Americans," 172.

76. While NAFTA contributed to the free movement of corporations, militarized policing in the U.S.–Mexico borderlands starting in the 1990s influenced what De Genova refers to as migrant "illegality." See De Genova, "Legal Production," 160–85.

77. David Bacon, *The Right to Stay Home: How US Policy Drives Mexican Migration* (Boston: Beacon Press, 2013). In a report by Public Citizen, the authors suggested that NAFTA displaced 15 million farmers who were forced to migrate to seek employment. Public Citizen, "Down on the Farm: NAFTA's Seven-Years War on Farmers and Ranchers in the U.S., Canada, and Mexico," http://www.citizen.org, iv.

78. See Denise A. Segura and Patricia Zavella, "Introduction," in *Women and Migration in the U.S.–Mexico Borderlands*, ed. Denise A. Segura and Patricia Zavella (Durham, N.C.: Duke University Press, 2007).

79. This book does not include documentary photography projects involving farm laborers in the 2000s because so few of them have been exhibited. Saundra Sturdevant's Migrant Photography Project, based in Tulare Country,

Central Valley, California, and HRHCare's project with farmworkers from Puebla, Mexico, are exceptions.

80. Monica W. Varsanyi, "Immigration Policy Activism in U.S. Cities and States: Interdisciplinary Perspectives," in *Taking Local Control: Immigration Policy Activism in U.S. Cities and States*, ed. Monica W. Varsanyi (Stanford, Calif.: Stanford University Press, 2010), 10.

81. Schmidt Camacho, *Migrant Imaginaries*, 291. Emphasis in original.

82. She suggests that the day laborers provide "evidence of how the current regime of border surveillance serves as a form of labor discipline." Ibid.

83. Schmidt Camacho contends that the IIRIRA "racialized migrants as a threat to national security and economic health." Schmidt Camacho, *Migrant Imaginaries*, 200. See also Massey and Durand, *Crossing the Border*. According to the chief counsel of the House Subcommittee on Immigration, one of IIRIRA's aims was to "mak[e] it more difficult for illegal aliens to have jobs in this country." George Fishmond, as quoted in Mary Reinholz, "Immigrants Find the Island a Mixed Blessing; A Life Looking over Shoulders in a Land of Freedom," *New York Times*, December 27, 1998.

84. See http://www.ice.gov/287g/.

85. Varsanyi, "Immigration Policy Activism," 11.

86. De Genova, "Conflicts of Mobility," 446.

87. Ibid., 447–48.

88. Monica W. Varsanyi, "Rescaling the 'Alien,' Rescaling Personhood: Neoliberalism, Immigration, and the State," *Annals of the Association of American Geographers* 98, no. 4 (2008): 877–96.

89. Varsanyi, "Immigration Policy Activism," 11.

90. See Varsanyi, *Taking Local Control*.

91. Roxanne Lynn Doty, *The Law into Their Own Hands* (Tucson: University of Arizona Press, 2009), 86.

92. See the preface for more information on the USA PATRIOT Act.

93. The Department of Homeland Security absorbed the Immigration and Nationalization Service and U.S. Customs Service and created three agencies in 2003: the Bureau of Citizenship and Immigration Services, the Bureau of Customs and Border Protection, and the Bureau of Immigration and Customs Enforcement.

94. See ICE's website, http://www.ice.gov/history. Michael Wishnie, Margo Mendelson, and Shayna Strom, "Collateral Damage: An Examination of ICE's Fugitive Operations Program," Migration Policy Institute (MPI) report, February 2009, www.migrationpolicy.org.

95. Wishnie, Mendelson, and Strom, "Collateral Damage," 2. See also Nicholas De Genova and Nathalie Peutz, "Introduction," in *The Deportation Regime: Sovereignty, Space, and the Freedom of Movement*, ed. Nicholas De Genova and Nathalie Peutz (Durham, N.C.: Duke University Press, 2010), 4.

96. In the case of workplace raids, De Genova argues, "Migrants came to be easy stand-ins for the figure of terrorism." Nicholas De Genova, "Spectacle of Terror, Spectacle of Security," in *Accumulating Insecurity: Violence and Dispossession in the Making of Everyday Life*, ed. Shelley Feldman, Charles Geisler, and Gayatri A. Menon (Athens: University of Georgia Press, 2011), 151.

97. See https://www.govtrack.us/congress/bills/109/hr4437.

98. See https://www.congress.gov/bill/109th-congress/senate-bill/2611.

99. For the text of the REAL ID Act, see http://www.dhs.gov/xlibrary/assets/real-id-act-text.pdf. The Secure Fence Act also led to the Bush administration's doubling the size of the Border Patrol, making it the largest law enforcement agency in the United States.

100. Wendy Brown, *Walled States, Waning Sovereignty* (New York: Zone Books, 2010), 36.

101. S-COMM started in fourteen U.S. communities, and it was extended to many more. Provine, Lewis, and Decker, *Policing Immigrants*, 31.

102. Ibid., 5.

103. See Julia Preston, "Illegal Workers Swept from Jobs in 'Silent Raids,'" *New York Times*, July 9, 2010, www.nytimes.com; see also Anna Sampaio, *Terrorizing Latina/o Immigrants: Race, Gender, and Immigration Politics in the Age of Security* (Philadelphia: Temple University Press, 2015), 141.

104. ICE developed NFOP in 2003 to "improve national security by dispatching Fugitive Operations Teams to locate and apprehend dangerous individuals with existing removal orders." Wishnie, Mendelson, and Strom, "Collateral Damage." According to ICE, Operation Community Shield is "a nationwide initiative that targets violent transnational street gangs, by partnering with U.S. and foreign law enforcement agencies at all levels, and making use of its authority to deport criminal aliens." See https://www.ice.gov/national-gang-unit.

105. Sampaio, *Terrorizing Latina/o Immigrants*, 136–37.

106. Ibid., 137.

107. "Editorial: Confusion over Secure Communities," *New York Times*, October 5, 2010, A26.

108. See http://www.ice.gov/doclib/secure-communities/pdf/prosecutorial-discretion-memo.pdf.

109. Ibid.

110. See Cecilia Muñoz, "Immigration Update: Maximizing Public Safety and Better Focusing Resources," August 18, 2011, https://obamawhitehouse.archives.gov/blog/2011/08/18/immigration-update-maximizing-public-safety-and-better-focusing-resources.

111. For details on DACA, see the DHS website: http://www.dhs.gov.

112. Some scholars have noted that the 2006 Immigrant Rights March inspired political activism of undocumented youth in the years that followed. See Roberto G. Gonzales, "Left Out but Not Shut Down: Political Activism and

the Undocumented Student Movement," in *Governing Immigration through Crime: A Reader*, ed. Jonathan X. Inda and Julie A. Dowling (Stanford, Calif.: Stanford University Press, 2013), 269–84.

113. De Genova, "Conflicts of Mobility," 453. Emphasis in original.

114. See Pallares, *Family Activism*, 17; and Gabriela Marquez-Benitez and Amalia Pallares, "Not One More: Linking Civil Disobediences and Public Anti-Deportation Campaigns," *North American Dialogue* 19, no. 1 (2016): 14–15.

115. The DREAM Act proposed that migrant youth of "good moral character" who had lived in the United States for at least five years and graduated from a U.S. high school or the equivalent could apply for a six-year conditional resident status. "Bill Text—112th Congress (2011–2012)—THOMAS (Library of Congress)—S.952.IS," Library of Congress, https://www.congress.gov. DREAM activists not only include undocumented youth from Mexico and Central America, but also those from Asia, the Caribbean, the Middle East, and Africa.

116. Marquez-Benitez and Pallares, "Not One More," 22.

117. For more information on IYJL and DreamActivist.org, see chapter 6.

118. Pallares, *Family Activism*, 100.

119. Ibid., 123.

120. Unzueta Carrasco and Seif, "Disrupting the Dream," 287.

121. Karma R. Chávez, *Queer Migration Politics: Activist Rhetoric and Coalitional Possibilities* (Urbana: University of Illinois Press, 2013), 81.

122. As cofounder Marisa Franco has stated, "We need Latinx leaders who are not simply pro-Latino, but also pro-woman, pro-queer, pro-poor, pro-Black, pro-indigenous, pro-climate because OUR community is all of those things and WE care about all of them. We need to learn how to lead better with each other across these lines." Franco, "An Introduction to Mijente," December 10, 2015, http://mijente.net/2015/12/10/an-introduction-to-mijente/.

123. Discourses around "deserving" versus "undeserving" migrants have circulated in the United States for over one hundred years and have disproportionally affected people of color, including Mexican and Central American migrants. As De Genova contends, "U.S. immigration law has generated the juridical categories of differentiation among various migrations, defined the parameters of 'legality,' and continually revised the possibilities for 'legal' migration in ways that have been disproportionately restrictive for Mexicans in particular." De Genova, *Working the Boundaries*, 8.

124. Unzueta Carrasco and Seif, "Disrupting the Dream," 289.

125. This campaign built on NDLON's previous work with migrant rights activists in states with anti-immigrant laws, such as Arizona, Georgia, and Alabama. Walter Nicholls, *The DREAMers: How the Undocumented Youth Movement Transformed the Immigrant Rights Debate* (Stanford, Calif.: Stanford University Press, 2003), 161.

126. As mentioned earlier, the #Not1More campaign is an initiative to stop the deportation of undocumented migrants.

127. Pallares, *Family Activism*, 1–2.

128. Amalia Pallares and Ruth Gomberg-Muñoz, "Politics of Motion: Ethnography with Undocumented Activists and of Undocumented Activism," *North American Dialogue* 19, no. 1 (2016): 7.

129. Carlos, "5 Years since SB1070: Aquí Estamos, y No Nos Vamos," #Not1More's Virtual Conference, National Day Labor Organizing Network, April 23, 2015, http://www.ndlon.org/en/.

130. Marjorie Garber, "Compassion," in *Compassion: The Culture and Politics of an Emotion*, ed. Lauren Berlant (London: Routledge, 2004), 24; Juliet Koss contends that empathy draws on the German concept of *Einfühlung* (feeling into) "to describe an embodied response to an image, object or spatial environment." Koss, "On the Limits of Empathy," *Art Bulletin* 88, no. 1 (March 2006): 139.

131. Marquez-Benitez and Pallares, "Not One More," 17.

132. Beattie, *Documentary Screens*, 107. Some of this work developed out of social activism, when photography, film, and video were also used to "document social problems." Ibid., 118.

133. Ibid., 112.

134. Patricia Aufderheide, *The Daily Planet: A Critic on the Capitalist Culture Beat* (Minneapolis: University of Minnesota Press, 2000), 219.

135. See Roger Larson and Ellen Meade, *Young Filmmakers* (New York: E. P. Dutton, 1969). In the 1970s and 1980s public access cable television developed in the United States, allowing more people access to video equipment. See Dee Dee Halleck, *Hand-Held Visions: The Impossible Possibilities of Community Media* (New York: Fordham University Press, 2002).

136. In 1979 Ann Marie Rousseau taught homeless women living in New York City shelters how to use cameras. She curated an exhibition, *Because of an Emergency: Work from the New York City Women's Shelter*, that was shown at the Metropolitan Museum of Art. Jim Hubbard, *Shooting Back: A Photographic View of Life by Homeless Children* (San Francisco: Chronicle Books, 1992); Jim Hubbard, *Shooting Back from the Reservation: A Photographic View of Life by Native American Youth* (New York: New Press, 1994); Wendy Ewald, *Portraits and Dreams: Photographs and Stories by Children of the Appalachians* (New York: Writers & Readers, 1985); and Wendy Ewald, *Portraits and Dreams: Photographs by Mexican Children* (Rochester, N.Y.: George Eastman House, 1993).

137. Julia Ballerini, "Photography as a Charitable Weapon: Poor Kids and Self-Representation," *Radical History Review* 69 (1997): 175.

138. Don Slater, "Marketing Mass Photography," in *Language, Image, Media*, ed. H. Davis and P. Walton (Oxford: Blackwell, 1983), 246. Emphasis in original.

139. Ballerini, "Photography as a Charitable Weapon," 175.

140. See Susan Sontag, *On Photography* (New York: Farrar, Straus and Giroux, 1977); and Martha Rosler, "In, Around, and Afterthoughts (on Documentary Photography)," in *The Contest of Meaning: Critical Histories of Photography*, ed. Robert Bolton (Cambridge, Mass.: MIT Press, 1992).

141. See Sekula, "The Body and the Archive." Tagg examined the use of this form in surveillance by state agents. Tagg, *The Burden of Representation*.

142. John Tagg, "A Means of Surveillance: The Photograph as Evidence in Law," in *The Burden of Representation: Essays on Photographies and Histories* (London: Macmillan, 1988), 102. Certain documentary forms fall within Mirzoeff's definition of visuality, including photography that "develop[s] new means of disciplining, normalizing, and ordering vision." Mirzoeff, *The Right to Look*, 23.

143. Solomon-Godeau, *Photography at the Dock*, 179; see also John Tagg, "The Currency of the Photograph: New Deal Reformism and Documentary Rhetoric," in *The Burden of Representation: Essays on Photographies and Histories* (London: Macmillan, 1988), 153–83; and William Stott, *Documentary Realism and Thirties America*, 2nd ed. (Chicago: University of Chicago Press, 1989).

144. Solomon-Godeau, *Photography at the Dock*, 171.

145. See for example Stuart Hall's essays in *Representation: Cultural Representation and Signifying Practices*, ed. Stuart Hall (London: Sage, 1997), as well as the essays in the edited collection *Only Skin Deep*, including Nicholas Mirzoeff, "The Shadow and the Substance: Race, Photography and the Index," in *Only Skin Deep: Changing Visions of the American Self*, ed. Coco Fusco and Brian Wallis (New York: International Center of Photography and Harry N. Abrams, 2003), 111–27.

146. Fusco, "Racial Time," 16. Emphasis in original.

147. Leigh Raiford, *Imprisoned in a Luminous Glare: Photography and the African-American Freedom Struggle* (Chapel Hill: University of North Carolina Press, 2013), 13; see also Erica Duganne, *The Self in Black and White: Race and Subjectivity in Postwar America Photography* (Hanover, N.H.: University Press of New England, 2010).

148. Raiford, *Imprisoned in a Luminous Glare*, 15.

149. Stuart Hall, "Introduction to Media Studies at the Centre," in *Culture, Media, Language*, ed. Stuart Hall, Dorothy Hobson, Andrew Lowe, and Paul Wills (London: Hutchinson, 1987), 117–18. See also Hall, *Representation*.

150. Jay Ruby, "Speaking For, Speaking About, Speaking With, or Speaking Alongside: An Anthropological and Documentary Dilemma," *Journal of Film and Video* 1/2 (1992): 47.

151. Patricia Aufderheide, "Public Intimacy: The Development of First-Person Documentary," *Afterimage* 25, no. 1 (July–August 1997). Aufderheide argues that, while this genre is frequently socially engaged, "it typically does not make a direct argument, but an implicit request for the viewer to recognize the reality of the speaker, and to incorporate that reality into his or her view of the world."

152. See also Paul Ward, *Documentary: The Margins of Reality* (New York: Columbia University Press, 2005), 27. At the time of the film's production, Ziv stated, "The idea is to give the camera to people who are creating reality and then see how this reality takes shape through their eyes." Quoted in Aufderheide, "Public Intimacy."

153. John T. Caldwell, "Representation and Complicity in Suburban Mining Camps: Reflections of a Documentary Filmmaker," *Aztlán* 28, no. 2 (Fall 2003): 216.

154. Yet similar to all visual artifacts, photographs, films, and videos can be read in different ways, depending not just on the context of exhibition and distribution but also on the viewer. See Allan Sekula, "On the Invention of Photographic Meaning," in *Thinking Photography*, ed. Victor Burgin (London: Macmillan Education, 1982), 84–109; Mary Price, *The Photograph: A Strange, Confined Space* (Minneapolis: University of Minnesota Press, 1994); and Stuart Hall, "Encoding/Decoding," in *Culture, Media, Language: Working Papers in Cultural Studies, 1972–79*, ed. Stuart Hall, Dorothy Hobson, Andrew Lowe, and Paul Willis (London: Hutchinson, 1980), 128–38.

155. As Thomas Austin and Wilma de Jong note, "The early years of the 21st century have witnessed significant and ongoing changes in the technological, commercial, aesthetic, political and social dimensions of documentaries produced for, and viewed on, a range of differently configured screens." Austin and de Jong, "Introduction," in *Rethinking Documentary: New Perspectives, New Practices*, ed. Thomas Austin and Wilma de Jong (Maidenhead: Open University Press and McGraw Hill Education, 2008), 1.

156. Yates McKee and Meg McLagan, "Introduction," in *Sensible Politics: The Visual Culture of Nongovernmental Activism*, ed. Meg McLagan and Yates McKee (New York: Zone Books, 2013), 17–18. They also suggest that "Each [platform] demands its own mode of address and techniques of soliciting attention, its own supporting discourses whereby it claims truth, authority and legitimacy." Ibid.

157. One book that focuses on undocumented youth activists' use of digital media in the post-9/11 era is Sasha Costanza-Chock's *Out of the Shadows, Into the Streets! Transmedia Organizing and the Immigrant Rights Movement* (Cambridge, Mass.: MIT Press, 2014).

1. "We See What We Know"

1. In her book *At the Edge of Sight*, Shawn Michelle Smith writes about the significance of the literal and metaphorical edges of photographs, as well as what is just outside the frame. Smith, *At the Edge of Sight: Photography and the Unseen* (Durham, N.C.: Duke University Press, 2013).

2. Carlos Canales, telephone conversation with author, June 23, 2004.

3. Anonymous Workplace Project participant. The materials from the Unseen America exhibition at SUNY–Stony Brook were available at the office of the now-defunct Bread and Roses Cultural Project in New York City.

4. However, Nathalis Guy Wamba and Carolyn Curran remark in their 2003 report on Unseen America, *Shadow Catchers: A Look at Unseen America,* that "it is not accurate to say that they are unseen within their own groups." Wamba and Curran, *Shadow Catchers: A Look at Unseen America* (New York: Bread and Roses Cultural Project Inc., New York Health and Human Service Employees International Union 1199SEIU, 2003), 21.

5. Quoted in ibid., 52.

6. De Genova et al., "Migrant Struggles," 26.

7. Kathleen Woodward, "Calculating Compassion," in *Compassion: The Culture and Politics of an Emotion,* ed. Lauren Berlant (London: Routledge, 2004), 80.

8. As journalist Michael A. Fletcher notes, the Bush administration's DOL was "philosophically hostile to the mission of the agency." Fletcher, "Labor Department Accused of Straying from Enforcement," *Washington Post,* December 1, 2008.

9. Esther Cohen, telephone interview with author, December 23, 2003.

10. Esther Cohen, "Why Roses with Our Bread?" *New Labor Forum* (Fall/Winter 2001): 140.

11. Leon Fink and Brian Greenberg, *Upheaval in the Quiet Zone: A History of Hospital Workers' Union Local 1199* (Chicago: University of Illinois Press, 1989), 191.

12. See http://www.bread-and-roses.com/aboutindex.html. Accessed July 1, 2004.

13. Ibid.

14. Ibid.

15. Karin Becker Ohrn, *Dorothea Lange and the Documentary Tradition* (Baton Rouge: Louisiana State University Press, 1980), 36.

16. Rosler has argued, "Documentary, as we know it, carries (old) information about a group of powerless people to another group addressed as socially powerful." Rosler, "In, Around, and Afterthoughts," 306.

17. See Sekula, "On the Invention of Photographic Meaning," 84–109.

18. Tagg, "The Currency of the Photograph," 110–41; Maren Stange, Sally Stein, et al., *Official Images: New Deal Photography* (Washington, D.C.: Smithsonian Institution Press, 1987); and Maren Stange, *Symbols of Idea Life: Social Documentary Photography in America, 1890–1950* (New York: Cambridge University Press, 1989).

19. William Stott, *Documentary Expression and Thirties America* (London: Oxford University Press, 1973), 14.

20. Duganne, *The Self in Black and White,* 79.

21. Sekula, "On the Invention of Photographic Meaning," 452–73; and Price, *The Photograph.*

22. Sekula, "On the Invention of Photographic Meaning"; and Price, *The Photograph.*

23. Materials from the Unseen America exhibition at SUNY–Stony Brook were available at Bread and Roses Cultural Project, New York.

24. Sara J. Mahler, *American Dreaming: Immigrant Life on the Margins* (Princeton, N.J.: Princeton University Press, 1995), 17.

25. According to Jennifer Gordon, the Workplace Project originally served as a "bare-bones legal clinic," which also offered a "Worker's Course," instructing members in U.S. labor and immigration history, labor law, and organizing techniques. See the documentary film *So Goes a Nation: Lawyers and Communities*, produced by New York Lawyers for the Public Interest, the Louis Stein Center for Ethics, and Public Interest Law at Fordham University School of Law, with the *Fordham Urban Law Journal*, 1997.

26. Members—especially those working as day laborers—were also plagued by harassment as they waited for work on street corners.

27. The Unpaid Wages Prohibition Act increased the minimum penalty for underpayment or nonpayment of wages to $500 and the maximum fine to $20,000. "Pataki Signs Unpaid Wages Bill," *Buffalo News*, September 19, 1997.

28. Jennifer Gordon, *Suburban Sweatshops: The Fight for Immigrant Rights* (Cambridge, Mass.: Belknap Press of the Harvard University Press, 2005), 143.

29. Ibid., 132.

30. Ibid., 180.

31. See Fine, *Worker Centers*, 79–85.

32. Ibid., 85.

33. U.S. federal law on wages and hours was established by the Fair Labor Standards Act (1938), which applies to businesses engaged in interstate commerce or with annual sales over $500,000. Smaller businesses—such as those in landscaping or contracting or restaurants—are not subject to this law. The Migrant and Seasonal Agricultural Worker Protection Act covers only farmworkers.

34. George Fishmond, as quoted in Reinholz, "Immigrants Find the Island." Further, as Alicia Schmidt Camacho argues, the IIRIRA "racialized migrants as a threat to national security and economic health." Schmidt Camacho, *Migrant Imaginaries*, 200. See also Massey and Durand, *Crossing the Border*.

35. Inda, *Targeting Immigrants*, 176–77.

36. Their approach was analogous to the ways that Duggan describes civil rights lobbies during the 1980s, which "engaged the politics of the possible, often with the hope of using liberalism's own languages and rules to force change beyond the boundaries of liberal equality." Duggan, *The Twilight of Equality?* xviii.

37. Gordon, *Suburban Sweatshops*, 251.

38. Ibid., 252. In a *New York Times* article, Steven Greenhouse notes that the Long Island chapter of the New York State Restaurant Association supported the bill, "even though immigrant advocates say restaurants are among the employers who most often failed to pay wages properly." Greenhouse also

notes that the New York Farm Bureau's members most fervently objected to the bill. Greenhouse, "Bill Seeks to Make Sure Immigrants Get Paid," *New York Times*, June 30, 1997, 4.

39. Gordon, *Suburban Sweatshops*, 105.

40. Ibid., 257.

41. Gordon has described this as "very different than traditional advocacy efforts on behalf of poor people." Ibid., 271.

42. Ibid., 272.

43. Ibid.

44. Schmidt Camacho, *Migrant Imaginaries*, 301.

45. In a March 1997 meeting between the Workplace Project and a Republican senator, the senator asked Luz—who had given the opening presentation on the Unpaid Wages Prohibition Act—why "this bill isn't going to flood the state with illegals?" His question was translated to Luz, who responded in Spanish "Esta ley no da a inmigrantes indocumentados ningún derecho que no tenían antes" (This law doesn't give undocumented immigrants any rights they didn't already have). The translator continued, "New York already requires that undocumented workers be paid minimum wage, so that employers don't take jobs away from citizens. This bill only raises the penalties to deter repeat violators." Gordon, *Suburban Sweatshops*, 256.

46. Ibid., 276.

47. Robert D. McFadden, "At Rally, Suffolk Residents Protest Illegal Immigration," *New York Times*, October 15, 2000. The name change borrows from former New York City mayor Rudolph Guiliani's concept of "quality of life."

48. Jackson B. Miller, "'Legal or Illegal? Documented or Undocumented?' The Struggle over Brookhaven's Neighborhood Preservation Act," *Communication Quarterly* 51, no. 1 (2003): 80.

49. In 1999 SQL began to work with anti-immigrant organizations, including the Federation for American Immigration Reform (FAIR) and Glenn Spencer's American Patrol. Southern Poverty Law Center, *Climate of Fear: Latino Immigrants in Suffolk County, New York* (Montgomery, Ala.: SPLC, 2009), 13, http://www.splcenter.org/sites/default/files/downloads/splc_suffolk_report _0.pdf.

50. According to Elizabeth Druback-Celaya, who interviewed members of the Farmingville community in 2001 and 2002, many longtime residents viewed Mexican and Central American migrants as not living according to the "basic 'rules' that defined being a member of the Farmingville community," because they believed that these individuals were neither paying taxes nor buying homes in the area. Furthermore, many longtime residents felt that the migrant population was putting a "strain on physical and financial community resources" and that "valuable space in the community [was] being overtaken by migrants" (e.g., "'open air' hiring halls"). Elizabeth Druback-Celaya, "Making Space: The Integration of Mexican Immigrants into New York State

Communities; Farmingville and Poughkeepsie" (Bachelor's thesis, Vassar College, 2002), 25, 28.

51. Ibid., 28.

52. Miller notes, "Competition over space . . . is a theme which, in many respects, dominates Long Island culture." Miller, "Legal or Illegal?" 74.

53. Ken Greenberg, "The Would-Be Science and Art of Making Public Spaces," *Architecture et Comportment/Architecture and Behavior* 6, no. 4 (1990): 324.

54. Don Mitchell, "The End of Public Space? People's Park, Definitions of the Public, and Democracy," *Annals of the Association of American Geographers* 85, no. 1 (1995): 115.

55. Duggan, *The Twilight of Equality?* 17–18.

56. See Neil Smith, "Giuliani Time: The Revanchist 1990s," *Social Text 57* 16, no. 4 (Winter 1998): 1–20.

57. Druback-Celaya, "Making Space," 28.

58. Migrants' renting—rather than owning—their homes contributed to the Farmingville residents' belief that migrants were "lacking the investment in place that is needed to ensure the care and maintenance of its [their neighborhood's] quality." Ibid., 31. Druback-Celaya obtained this information from her interviews with Farmingville residents.

59. Farmingville is a very small town (population sixteen thousand), which at the time of the workshop was 93.5 percent white, according to the 2000 census. See 2000 Census for Farmingville, New York, http://factfinder.census.gov.

60. In the late 1990s, reporters covering Suffolk County related migrants' housing issues to a lack of affordable housing on Long Island. See, for example, Cooper, "Laborers Wanted"; and Michelle Salcedo, "Left Homeless: Mexican Workers Evicted in Raids at Crowded Rentals," *Newsday*, Suffolk County ed., July 24, 1998.

61. Cooper, "Laborers Wanted."

62. Southern Poverty Law Center, *Climate of Fear.*

63. Cooper, "Laborers Wanted."

64. McFadden, "At Rally, Suffolk Residents Protest."

65. Southern Poverty Law Center, *Climate of Fear,* 13.

66. Charlie LeDuff, "Immigrant Workers Tell of Being Lured and Beaten," *New York Times,* September 20, 2000. For more on the experiences of Long Island day laborers, see the documentary film *Farmingville,* DVD/VHS, dir. Carlos Sandoval and Catherine Tambini (New York: Camino Bluff, 2004).

67. This was clearly hypocritical, since one of SQL's main complaints was that day laborers on street corners created traffic hazards. See Fine, *Worker Centers,* 18. In 2001 the county legislature approved the bill to give $80,000 to create a hiring hall in Farmingville. The center was later vetoed by Republican county executive Robert Gaffney. Al Baker, "In Suffolk, Bill for Day Laborer

Center Is Vetoed," *New York Times*, April 6, 2001, B-5; Elissa Gootman, "Temperature Rise over Immigrants," *New York Times*, April 22, 2001; Cooper, "Laborers Wanted"; LeDuff, "Immigrant Workers Tell."

68. Canales, telephone conversation.

69. Ibid.

70. Cohen, "Why Roses with Our Bread?" 142.

71. Wamba and Curran, *Shadow Catchers*, 13.

72. Ibid., 50.

73. Arias has argued that migrants from Central America—including those from El Salvador, from which many of the Unseen America workshop participants migrated—"keep themselves on the margins of social visibility." Arias, "Central American–Americans," 168. See also Mahler, *American Dreaming*.

74. Cohen, telephone conversation.

75. By 2003, Linda Markstein and Naomi Woronov had developed the *Unseen America Teacher's Guide*. Markstein and Woronov, *Unseen America Teacher's Guide* (New York: Bread and Roses Cultural Project, New York Health and Human Service Employees International Union 1199/SEIU, 2003).

76. Matthew Septimus, interview with author, December 26, 2003.

77. Ibid.

78. Wamba and Curran, *Shadow Catchers*, 15.

79. It should be noted that the photographer who took this picture was unidentified in both local and national exhibitions of this work. In the context of the local exhibition, the day laborers were identified collectively, whereas at the DOL, a few were identified by name, which is how I know who took some of the pictures.

80. Shandray Gabbay, "Latino Laborers Turned a Camera on Themselves," *New York Times*, October 28, 2001. Although these images did not have titles when displayed at SUNY–Stony Brook, they were given titles by the Bread and Roses staff for the DOL exhibition.

81. Liz Wells, *Photography: A Critical Introduction*, 2nd ed. (London: Routledge, 2001), 121.

82. Catherine Zuromskis, *Snapshot Photography: The Lives of Images* (Cambridge, Mass.: MIT Press, 2013), 33.

83. See Wendy Hesford and Wendy Kozol, "Introduction," in *Just Advocacy? Women's Human Rights, Transnational Feminisms, and the Politics of Representation*, ed. Wendy Hesford and Wendy Kozol (New Brunswick, N.J.: Rutgers University Press, 2005).

84. Zuromskis, *Snapshot Photography*, 33.

85. Of all the photographs that they took during the workshop, Workplace Project staff member Carlos Canales indicated that the day laborers viewed the pictures of waiting for work as the most political. Canales, telephone conversation.

86. Materials from the Unseen America exhibition at SUNY–Stony Brook were available at Bread and Roses Cultural Project in New York City.

87. Matthew Septimus, telephone conversation with author, December 26, 2003.

88. Ibid.

89. English translations of the captions were also available at the exhibition. Materials from the Unseen America exhibition at SUNY–Stony Brook were available at Bread and Roses Cultural Project in New York City.

90. Septimus, telephone conversation.

91. There was at least one exception: a photograph of day laborers standing by an inflatable giant rat during a demonstration against a contractor who owed them back wages. For information on these protests against Kevin Dutton, the owner of the Wildflower Landscaping Design and Construction Firm, which started in June 2000, see Valerie Burgher, "Laborers Protest Disputed Back Wages," *Newsday*, November 12, 2000, A-29.

92. See Esther Cohen, ed., *Unseen America: Photos and Stories by Workers* (New York: Reagan Books, 2006), 158.

93. For the DOL exhibition, this image was titled *A Dream Come True* by the staff of Bread and Roses (photograph by Nelson).

94. The other show took place at the Union Gallery, and it also featured the work of Local 32B-J of SEIU and Local 23–25 of the Union of Needletrades, Industrial and Textile Employees. See also Gabbay, "Latino Laborers."

95. The exhibits took place during a campus celebration of Hispanic Heritage Month in October 2001.

96. The exhibition was organized by Betty Angolia after she read an article about the show at SUNY–Stony Brook in *Newsday*. Wamba and Curran, *Shadow Catchers*, 86.

97. All of these captions were from the Unseen America exhibition at SUNY–Stony Brook, and were available at Bread and Roses Cultural Project, New York. I made a few grammatical changes to the text, based on suggestions from Diego Bustos, who helped copyedit the Spanish text.

98. Luis was one of the few Mexicans in the group. Some—but not all—day laborers preferred to remain anonymous, and they did not include their names with the captions. In one caption, an anonymous day laborer wrote: "Los inmigrantes no pretenden hacer ningún daño. Quizás los cuadros ayudarán a otros a entendernos major—basados en algo que es verdadero—no lo que ellos piensan que somos" (Immigrants intend no harm. The pictures will help others to understand us better—based on something that is real—not what they think we are).

99. As mentioned earlier, members of the Workplace Project had not even considered bringing their Unpaid Wages Prohibition Act to President Bill Clinton's DOL in the mid- to late 1990s, due to their concerns that the DOL would pass on information about the complainants' residency to the INS.

100. A July 2008 report by the U.S. Government Accountability Office found that the Wage and Hour Division's (WHD) response to complaints was inadequate, citing numerous "instances where WHD inappropriately rejected complaints, failed to adequately investigate complaints or neglected to investigate until it was too late." U.S. Government Accountability Office, "Department of Labor: Case Studies from Ongoing Work Show Examples in Which Wage and Hour Division Did Not Adequately Pursued Labor Violations" (testimony before the Committee on Education and Labor, House of Representatives, July 15, 2008).

101. "Vision," http://www.dol.gov/_sec/media/reports/annual2003/mess age-mission.htm. According to labor journalist David Moberg, the Bush administration "eliminated many of former President Clinton's initiatives, including rules to prevent cumulative trauma disorders, and the federal government labor-management cooperation programs." Furthermore, the Bush administration also "slashed enforcement of workplace safety and work standards and withdrew two-dozen planned safety regulations." David Moberg, "Forge a Coalition with Labor," *In These Times*, July 15, 2004, 22.

102. Esther Cohen, e-mail to author, June 23, 2004.

103. Rosler, "Post-Documentary," 228.

104. After appearing at the DOL, the exhibition was brought to the Take Back America Conference, the Jobs with Justice Conference, and SEIU Local 150 in Milwaukee in 2003. In 2004 the exhibit traveled to the AFL-CIO Conference, the Social Responsibility Network Conference, the Labor Religion Coalition's annual meeting, and the Society for Photographic Education's annual conference.

105. Esther Cohen, as quoted in Wamba and Curran, *Shadow Catchers*, 14.

106. This show at the DOL was based on an exhibition at Gallery 1199, Bread and Roses' exhibition space in New York City. The show included photographs by workers associated with unions 1199SEIU, DC 37 Social Service Employees Union Local 371, the Union of Needletrades, Industrial and Textile Employees Local 23–25, and SEIU Local 32B-J, as well as non-unionized migrants affiliated with workers' centers, such as the Damayan Filipino workers' center in New York City.

107. Esther Cohen, conversation with author, New York, July 9, 2004.

108. The SEIU added 150,000 new members between 2000 and 2002. Catherine Haughney, "Through Workers' Eyes, a Different City," *Washington Post*, November 25, 2002.

109. Esther Cohen, as quoted in Sarah Marcisz, "A Picture's Worth," *Washington Times*, May 21, 2003.

110. Ibid.

111. Elaine Chao, as quoted in Marcisz, "A Picture's Worth."

112. Lauren Berlant, "Introduction: Compassion (and Withholding)," in *Compassion: The Culture and Politics of an Emotion*, ed. Lauren Berlant (London: Routledge, 2004), 3.

113. Woodward, "Calculating Compassion," 60–61.
114. Berlant, "Introduction," 9.
115. Fletcher, "Labor Department Accused."
116. Berlant, "Introduction," 2.
117. Although many newspapers across the country reviewed local exhibitions of Unseen America, the exhibition at the DOL was reviewed in national magazines, notably *Newsweek*, which displayed a slideshow of Unseen America images on its website, and network television news programs, such as *ABC World News Tonight* (May 10, 2003).
118. See the DOL's "vision" in their annual report of 2006: http://www.dol.gov/_sec/media/reports/annual2006/MDA.htm.
119. Ann Cvetkovich, *An Archive of Feelings: Trauma, Sexuality, and Lesbian Public Cultures* (Durham, N.C.: Duke University Press, 2003), 16.
120. Wamba and Curran, *Shadow Catchers*, 27.

2. The Border's Frame

1. Vilma Velez, Wilfredo Morel, and Nick Cannell, conversation with the author, HRHCare, Peekskill, New York, January 5, 2010.
2. Anne Nolon, telephone conversation with the author, February 8, 2010.
3. David Fitzgerald asserts that what are frequently referred to as transnational relationships are actually translocal ones, and he notes that "migrants' strongest cross-border links are often highly *localistic* ties between particular sending areas and their satellites in the receiving country." Fitzgerald, "Beyond 'Transnationalism': Mexican Hometown Politics at an American Labor Union," *Ethnic and Racial Studies* 27, no. 2 (2004): 231.
4. According to Silvia Esqueda, promotores and promotoras are "community members who serve as liaisons between their community and health, human and social service organizations." In the 1950s, promotores and promotoras were developed in parts of Latin America to bring health care to people who had no previous access to it. By the late 1980s, promotores and promotoras were working in migrant and farmworker communities in the United States. Esqueda, "Implementing a Promotoras Comunitarias Model," http://www.cabhp.asu.edu/about/News/images/BUSTING_Myths/pdfs/9janextended/Session16%20Esqueda%20Slides.pdf.
5. In the introduction to the book *Unseen America: Photos and Stories by Workers*, Esther Cohen describes Unseen America as a form of national culture similar to the Federal Writers' Project, noting that "a strong national culture holds countless different visions—voices of all pitches from the myriads of jobs, experiences, and perspectives that make up our society." Cohen, "Introduction," in *Unseen America: Photos and Stories by Workers* (New York: HarperCollins, 2005), xix.
6. Barbara Hill, telephone conversation with the author, January 16, 2009.

7. Stephen, *Transborder Lives*, 26, 317; Segura and Zavella, "Introduction," 3.

8. Stephen, *Transborder Lives*, 65.

9. Elizabeth Druback-Celaya, telephone conversation with the author, March 8, 2010.

10. Ibid.

11. Participants in La Ciénega spoke about the Communities without Borders project in *Unseen America: Seeking Health through Art*, a short video about the project directed by HRHCare staff member Nick Cannell.

12. Jo Margaret Mano and Linda Greenow, "Mexico Comes to Main Street: Mexican Immigration and Urban Revitalization in Poughkeepsie, New York," *Middle States Geographer* 39 (2006): 76–83.

13. HRHCare's precursor, the Peekskill Area Ambulatory Health Center, was founded in the early 1970s by four African American women from Peekskill, New York: Mary Woods, Pearl Woods, Willie Mae Jackson, and the Reverend Jeanette Phillips. *The Peekskill Founding Mothers*, dir. Nick Cannell, Hudson River HealthCare Inc. Available on Hudson River HealthCare's Facebook page.

14. Mano and Greenow, "Mexico Comes to Main Street." According to Jeffrey H. Cohen and Leila Rodríguez, since the mid-twentieth century, migration from Oaxaca has followed that of Mexico more generally. Cohen and Rodríguez, "Remittance Outcomes in Rural Oaxaca, Mexico: Challenges, Options, and Opportunities for Migrant Households" (Working Papers, Center for Comparative Immigration Studies, University of California, San Diego, August 1, 2004), 5.

15. Allison Mountz and Richard Wright, "Daily Life in the Transnational Migrant Community of San Agustín, Oaxaca, and Poughkeepsie, New York," *Diaspora* 5, no. 3 (1996): 404; and Cohen and Rodríguez, "Remittance Outcomes," 6.

16. Oaxaca is part of the Mixteca-Sur (south-central Mexico), which includes the states of Puebla and Guerrero. Between November 1991 and January 1992, President Salinas revised aspects of Article 27, which as Jones and Ward argue, allowed "*ejidos* (communal lands) to convert 'use' rights into individual rights to sell, rent, or mortgage land to non-*ejido* members, and to set up joint venture contracts with domestic or foreign private companies." Gareth A. Jones and Peter M. Ward, "Privatizing the Commons: Reforming the *Ejido* and Urban Development in Mexico," *International Journal of Urban and Regional Research* 22, no. 1 (March 1998): 77–78.

17. Wayne Cornelius and David Myhre, "Introduction," in *The Transformation of Rural Mexico: Reforming the Ejido Sector*, ed. Wayne Cornelius and David Myhre (La Jolla, Calif.: Center for U.S.–Mexican Studies, University of California, San Diego, 1998), 5.

18. Liliana Rivera-Sánchez, "Expressions of Identity and Belonging: Mexican Immigrants in New York," in *Indigenous Mexican Immigrants in the United*

States, ed. Jonathan Fox and Gaspar Rivera-Salgado (La Jolla, Calif.: Center for U.S.–Mexican Studies, University of California, San Diego, 2004), 419.

19. Stephen, *Transborder Lives,* 125.

20. Mountz and Wright, "Daily Life," 404.

21. As Lawrence A. Brown, Tamara E. Mott, and Edward J. Malecki have argued, Mexican migration since 1990 has significantly increased in small cities and towns across the United States. Brown, Mott, and Malecki, "Immigrant Profiles of U.S. Urban Areas and Agents of Resettlement," *Professional Geographer* 59, no. 1 (2007): 56–73.

22. Mountz and Wright, "Daily Life," 407.

23. Cohen and Rodríguez, "Remittance Outcomes." These statistics were drawn from Anuario Estadístico Oaxaca, vol. 2, Instituto Nacional de Estadística y Geografía (INEGI), Aguascalientes, México, 2001.

24. Cohen and Rodríguez, "Remittance Outcomes." See also Brian J. Godfrey, "New Urban Ethnic Landscapes," in *Contemporary Ethnic Geographies in America,* ed. Inés M. Miyares and Christopher A. Airriess (Lanham, Md.: Rowman and Littlefield, 2007).

25. Brown, Mott, and Malecki, "Immigrant Profiles," 57.

26. Godfrey, "New Urban Ethnic Landscapes," 334; and Mano and Greenow, "Mexico Comes to Main Street," 78, 81.

27. Cohen and Rodríguez, "Remittance Outcomes," 23.

28. Mountz and Wright, "Daily Life," 409.

29. Cohen and Rodríguez, "Remittance Outcomes," 23.

30. In this chapter, I use the term *translocal community* to describe La Ciénega and Poughkeepsie, but Jonathan Fox and Gaspar Rivera-Salgado refer to a "transnational community" in this specific context. Fox and Rivera-Salgado, "Introduction," in *Indigenous Mexican Immigrants in the United States,* ed. Jonathan Fox and Gaspar Rivera-Salgado (La Jolla, Calif.: Center for U.S.–Mexican Studies and Center for Comparative Immigration Studies, University of California, San Diego, 2004), 26.

31. Godfrey, "New Urban Ethnic Landscapes," 334. Between 1990 and 2000, the Latina/o population of Poughkeepsie tripled. This is probably an underestimate, since the census tends not to include undocumented residents in its statistics, and 91 percent of Mexicans in Poughkeepsie who were born in Mexico were undocumented in 2000. Mano and Greenow, "Mexico Comes to Main Street," 77–78.

32. Mano and Greenow, "Mexico Comes to Main Street," 77. See also E. Lynch, "Hispanic Numbers Rise: Mexicans Are Flocking to the City," *Poughkeepsie Journal,* June 27, 2001.

33. Cohen and Rodríguez, "Remittance Outcomes," 6.

34. Schmidt Camacho, *Migrant Imaginaries,* 290. See also Massey and Durand, *Crossing the Border.*

35. The rise in enforcement has meant additional risks for border crossers, as routes have become more difficult and more dangerous, and the fees paid to "coyotes" (smugglers) have also risen. Cohen and Rodríguez, "Remittance Outcomes," 26.

36. Pilar Parra and Max Pfeffer, "New Immigrants and Rural Communities: The Challenges of Integration," in "The Border Next Door: New York Migraciónes," ed. Margaret Gray and Carlos Decena, special issue, *Social Text* (Fall 2006): 85. See also Douglas Massey and Jorge Durand, "What We Learned from the Mexican Migration Project," in *Crossing the Border: Research from the Mexican Migration Project*, ed. Douglas Massey and Jorge Durand (New York: Russell Sage Foundation, 2004); Fernando Riosmena, "Return versus Settlement among Undocumented Mexican Immigrants," in *Crossing the Border: Research from the Mexican Migration Project*, ed. Douglas Massey and Jorge Durand (New York: Russell Sage Foundation, 2004); and Cohen and Rodríguez, "Remittance Outcomes."

37. Parra and Pfeffer, "New Immigrants," 95.

38. Comité Latino was based on a model of grassroots organizing that HRHCare had developed by identifying leaders in the African American community. *The Peekskill Founding Mothers.*

39. Velez, Morel, and Cannell, conversation.

40. Ibid.

41. As Schmidt Camacho notes, this was also the case for Mexican migrants in the United States. Schmidt Camacho, *Migrant Imaginaries*, 304. See also Jeffrey Passell, "Unauthorized Immigrants: Numbers and Characteristics," in *Pew Hispanic Center Project Report* (Washington, D.C.: Pew Research Center, 2005).

42. Druback-Celaya, telephone conversation.

43. Mano and Greenow, "Mexico Comes to Main Street," 76–83.

44. Harvey Flad, "Digital Tour of Poughkeepsie," https://www.youtube.com/watch?v=n2ndeiaI2WM.

45. Godfrey, "New Urban Ethnic Landscapes," 336.

46. Ibid., 336, 348; Mano and Greenow, "Mexico Comes to Main Street," 80.

47. Articles published in the *Poughkeepsie Journal* helped foster an understanding of the Oaxacan migrants living in Poughkeepsie.

48. Mano and Greenow, "Mexico Comes to Main Street," 81. As Parra and Pfeffer have described, the events in Poughkeepsie have also taken place in other small cities and towns in New York State. They argue that the "rejuvenation of some downtown business districts with stores that cater to immigrants provides an indication that the integration of farm workers into community life can prove to be an important resource in revitalizing local economies." Parra and Pfeffer, "New Immigrants," 95.

49. Druback-Celaya, "Making Space." The attitude of long-term Poughkeepsie residents toward Mexican migrants has developed over decades.

50. Ibid., 40. The Family Partnership Center houses twenty different health and human service agencies. The center includes food and emergency services, health care, job training, adult and youth education opportunities, youth development and recreation programs, mediation and legal services, mental health services and emotional support, crime victims and battered women's services, and theater and arts programs. See http://www.familypartnership center.org.

51. As Druback-Celaya contends, the presence of the Mexican population in Poughkeepsie is "not in contradiction to the overall community." Druback-Celaya, "Making Space," 16.

52. Ibid., 40. See also Elizabeth Lynch, "Programs Break Down Barriers for Newcomers," *Poughkeepsie Journal*, July 16, 1998; and Shawn Cohen, "Agencies, Schools Reach Out to Spanish-Speaking People," *Poughkeepsie Journal*, December 27, 1998.

53. Druback-Celaya, "Making Space," 42.

54. Ibid., 41. See also Lynch, "Programs Break Down Barriers"; and Cohen, "Agencies."

55. Godfrey, "New Urban Ethnic Landscapes," 334.

56. Helen J. Johnston, "An Overview of the Growth and Development of the U.S. Migrant Health Program," *Migration Today* 12, nos. 4–5 (1984): 13. Much of the funding for these services came from the Migrant Health Act, which was signed by John F. Kennedy in 1962 and enabled the Public Health Service to disburse grants to organizations to provide health clinics for seasonal migrants and farm workers. In 1964, when the Bracero Program ended, the Department of Health, Education, and Welfare's (HEW) general counsel ruled that Migrant Health Program Services should include "foreign" as well as "domestic" workers. In 1975 Congress permitted neighborhood health centers to serve as "community and migrant health centers." Ibid.

57. More recent federal policies include the Deficit Reduction Act of 2005, which requires that Medicaid applicants provide documentation of citizenship, and the 2010 Affordable Care Act, which excludes undocumented migrants. Gilbert Gee and Chandra Ford, "Structural Racism and Health Inequities: Old Issues, New Directions," *W.E.B. Du Bois Review* 8, no. 1 (2011).

58. Ibid., 123.

59. For a more critical perspective on health promotion, see Hester, "Bodies in Translation," 168–88. Hester notes that while there were good intentions behind the Ottawa Charter of Health Promotion (1986), scholars have critiqued the ways in which it was taken up in the United States and elsewhere, due in large part to neoliberal policies.

60. Bonnie Lefkowitz, *Community Health Centers: A Movement and the People Who Made It Happen* (New Brunswick, N.J.: Rutgers University Press, 2007), 8–9.

61. This vision of the role of community health workers was also part of the Alma Ata Declaration of the World Health Organization (WHO) in 1978. In 1989 the WHO defined community health workers as "members of the communities where they work," who "should be selected by the communities, should be answerable to the communities for their activities, should be supported by the healthcare system but not necessarily a part of its organization." World Health Organization, "Strengthening the Performance of Community Health Workers in Primary Health Care," *World Health Organization Technical Report*, Series 780 (Geneva: World Health Organization, 1989), 6.

62. Morel also helped organize the "Open Doors" art project for children. Wilfredo Morel, conversation with the author, January 5, 2010.

63. Bread and Roses originally contacted Barbara Hill, a social worker at HRHCare, who suggested that the workshop be held in Poughkeepsie so the organization could reach out to the "new immigrant and Mexican day laborer population" in that town. Barbara Hill, e-mail to Hudson River HealthCare staff, Peekskill, New York, February 6, 2003.

64. Jenna Loyd, "Where Is Community Health? Racism, the Clinic, and the Biopolitical State," in *Rebirth of the Clinic: Place and Agents in Contemporary Healthcare*, ed. Cindy Patton (Minneapolis: University of Minnesota Press, 2010), 40–41.

65. According to Seth Holmes, most undocumented migrants do not qualify for Medicare or Medicaid. Holmes, *Fresh Fruit, Broken Bodies: Migrant Farmworkers in the United States* (Berkeley: University of California Press, 2013), 129; Holmes, "An Ethnographic Study of the Social Context of Migrant Health in the United States," *PLOS Medicine* (2006).

66. Loyd, "Where Is Community Health?" 39.

67. Michel Foucault, *History of Sexuality*, vol. 1 (New York: Vintage Books, 1978), 144–45, as quoted in Loyd, "Where Is Community Health?" 42–43.

68. Loyd, "Where Is Community Health?" 40.

69. Ibid., 43.

70. Ibid.

71. Vilma Velez, telephone conversation with the author, January 16, 2009. See also the HRHCare press release about the show in Poughkeepsie, October 9, 2003, Hudson River HealthCare, Peekskill, New York.

72. Velez, Morel, and Cannell, conversation.

73. Ibid.

74. Ibid.

75. Druback-Celaya, telephone conversation. For the workshop at the Family Partnership Center in the summer of 2003, the organization was ultimately successful in recruiting individuals from La Ciénega; close to 95 percent of the participants were from that town. Velez, Morel, and Cannell, conversation.

76. Velez, Morel, and Cannell, conversation

77. Wamba and Curran, *Shadow Catchers*, 63–64.

78. It should also be noted that Unseen America project participants could not share images digitally, since their family members in Oaxaca did have access to the Internet. Elizabeth Druback-Celaya, e-mail communication with the author, April 2, 2010.

79. As part of Unseen America, many of the participants filled out forms that included questions about their background. Hudson River HealthCare, Peekskill, New York.

80. Velez, Morel, and Cannell, conversation.

81. As mentioned previously, this emphasis developed from HRHCare staff's early discussions with the director of the Workplace Project and the Bread and Roses staff. Wamba and Curran, *Shadow Catchers*, 63–64.

82. Hudson River HealthCare, PowerPoint presentation for Communities without Borders workshop.

83. Druback-Celaya, telephone conversation. Also in 2003, there was no Internet access in La Ciénega, so family members could not use technologies such as Skype that would let them see each other. Vilma Velez, conversation with the author, January 5, 2010.

84. Communities without Borders participants, conversation with the author, Hudson River HealthCare, Poughkeepsie, New York, January 5, 2010. Druback-Celaya explained that over the course of the workshop, many participants began to believe that the staff was doing what they could to help their community. Druback-Celaya, telephone conversation

85. Hudson River HealthCare, PowerPoint presentation.

86. Juan Garcia-Nuñez, telephone conversation with the author, February 17, 2010.

87. Patricia Holland, "Introduction," in *Family Snaps: The Meanings of Domestic Photography*, ed. Patricia Holland and Jo Spence (London: Virago, 1991), 4. Photographs like these are records of family life. Esther noted in the caption to *My Son, Grandson, and Angela* that this image was "a recollection for the little girl . . . on her baptism."

88. Tina Campt, "Family Matters: Diaspora, Difference, and the Visual Archive," *Social Text 98* 27, no. 1 (Spring 2009): 92.

89. One of the main rules of photographic composition is the rule of thirds. "In the rule of thirds, photos are divided into thirds with two imaginary lines vertically and two lines horizontally making three columns, three rows, and nine sections in the images. Important compositional elements and leading lines are placed on or near the imaginary lines and where the lines intersect." See http://learnprophotography.com/rule-of-thirds/.

90. Zuromskis, *Snapshot Photography*, 10.

91. Sonja Vivienne and Jean Burgess, "The Remediation of the Personal Photograph and the Politics of Self-Representation in Digital Storytelling," *Journal of Material Culture* 18, no. 3 (September 2013): 280.

92. Zuromskis, *Snapshot Photography*, 34, 35.

93. This comment was on the form Francisca filled out as part of the Unseen America project. Hudson River HealthCare, Peekskill, New York.

94. Velez, Morel, and Cannell, conversation.

95. Ibid.; Druback-Celaya, telephone conversation

96. Velez, Morel, and Cannell, conversation.

97. HRHCare's PowerPoint.

98. Velez, Morel, and Cannell, conversation.

99. There were very few images of men produced during the workshop, although there was one photograph of an elderly man on a donkey in front of a field by Edith Morales Gutiérrez, and another of a man sitting near a field by Elena Celaya Cruz.

100. Nick Cannell, dir., *Unseen America: Seeking Health through Art* (Community Health Productions, 2003), http://vimeo.com/9718725; Velez, Morel, and Cannell, conversation.

101. Wilfredo Morel, conversation with the author, January 5, 2010.

102. Cannell, *Unseen America*.

103. Ibid.

104. Lynn Stephen, "Los Nuevos Desaparecidos y Muertos: Immigration, Militarization, Death, and Disappearance on Mexico's Borders," in *Security Disarmed: Critical Perspectives on Gender, Race, and Militarization*, ed. Barbara Sutton, Sandra Morgen, and Julie Novkov (New Brunswick, N.J.: Rutgers University Press, 2008), 95.

105. Schmidt Camacho, *Migrant Imaginaries*, 287. Schmidt Camacho draws on the concept of migrant sorrows from Matthew Jacobson, *Special Sorrows: The Diasporic Imagination of Irish, Polish, and Jewish Immigrants in the United States* (Berkeley: University of California Press, 2002).

106. These images also relate to organizing that has taken place in recent years in Oaxaca that has focused on the right *not* to migrate. See Bacon, *The Right to Stay Home*; and Cacho, *Social Death*, 123–24.

107. Another exhibition of this work, *Picturing New Destinies: Nuevos Destinos*, took place at the Dutchess County Community College from February 19 to March 19, 2004.

108. Velez, Morel, and Cannell, conversation.

109. Communities without Borders participants, conversation.

110. The exhibition at Oaxaca City's Los Danzantes restaurant took place from October 31 to November 16, 2003.

111. Francisco Ramírez, "La Ciénega, lazo migrante con Estados Unidos," *Noticias: Voz e Imagen de Oaxaca*, October 29, 2003, 20A.

112. She also writes, "The intensity of one's own family photographs and memories can never be matched by someone else's. . . . We bring an emotional involvement as well as a practical knowledge to the people and events we find between its [family album's] covers. Family photography does not seek

to be understood by all. It is a private medium, its simple imagery enriched by the meanings we bring to it." Holland, "Introduction," 2–3.

113. Druback-Celaya, telephone conversation.

114. Communities without Borders participants, conversation.

115. Ibid.

116. Druback-Celaya, conversation.

117. See https://www.govtrack.us/congress/bills/109/hr4437.

118. The Asociación Hispana de Benito Juárez, a hometown association that was established in 2004, was the most powerful Latina/o group in Poughkeepsie at the time. The Asociación Hispana de Benito Juárez sponsors soccer leagues and raises money for projects to help the Poughkeepsie migrant community. The group also contributes to public events organized by Saint Mary's Church, the only Catholic church in Poughkeepsie that offered Mass in Spanish, celebrated religious holidays like Guadalupe Day and the feast day of the Virgen de Juquila (the patron saint of Oaxaca), and organized smaller events, like a Cinco de Mayo festival. Druback-Celaya, telephone conversation. Most members of the organization were permanent residents or immigrants and helped plan some of the events related to "A Day without an Immigrant."

119. While members of HRHCare's Comité Latino helped organize "A Day without an Immigrant" boycott, march, and rally held in Poughkeepsie in 2006 they could not do so through their affiliation with HRHCare. The organization's status as a Federally Qualified Health Center (FQHC) affected the ability of promotores and promotoras to carry their association with HRHCare into another political context. This was related to the HRHCare's conflict of interest policy, which was required for FQHCs by federal law. See "Health Center Program Requirements," U.S. Department of Health and Human Services, updated in October 2012.

120. Inda and Dowling, "Introduction," 3.

121. Cara Anna, "Immigrants across the State Prepare to Demonstrate," *Buffalo News*, April 30, 2006.

122. According to reports in local newspapers, two thousand people participated in the march. See Michael Valkys, "Latinos March in City," *Poughkeepsie Journal*, May 2, 2006, A1; and Patricia Doxsey, "Dutchess Rally Draws Thousands," *Daily Freemen*, May 2, 2006.

123. Chavez notes that these individuals involved themselves in the 2006 immigration rights marches as a "spectacular display of belonging." Chavez, *The Latino Threat*, 155.

124. Schmidt Camacho, *Migrant Imaginaries*, 232.

125. Stephen, *Transborder Lives*, 41.

126. As Anne Nolon, the CEO of HRHCare, stated in *Unseen America: Seeking Health through Art* about the photography project: "It is our hope that through the Unseen America project family members in Mexico and Poughkeepsie, New York, will understand the importance of primary and preventative health

care and will encourage those who can to access healthcare through community health-care centers." Cannell, *Unseen America.*

127. Stephen, *Transborder Lives,* 65.

3. Visible Frictions

1. Chavez, *The Latino Threat,* 144. The title of this chapter references the title of chapter 6 from Chavez's book: "The Minuteman Project's Spectacle of Surveillance on the Arizona–Mexico Border."

2. Wayne Cornelius, "Controlling 'Unwanted Immigration': Lessons from the United States, 1993–2004," *Journal of Ethnic and Migration Studies* 31, no. 4 (July 2005): 784. See also Inter-American Commission on Human Rights of the Organization of American States, "Report N° 78/08, Petition 478–05, Admissibility Undocumented Migrant, Legal Resident, and US Citizen Victims of Anti-Immigrant Vigilantes, United States," August 5, 2009, 4.

3. Chavez, *The Latino Threat,* 151.

4. See Border Film Project's website: http://www.borderfilmproject.com/.

5. For more information on the Minuteman Project, see Chavez, *The Latino Threat*; and Doty, *The Law.*

6. Rudy Adler and Brett Huneycutt, interview on NPR, *Weekend Edition,* September 2006, http://www.borderfilmproject.com/en/press/.

7. I am referring to the photography of David Bacon, Julián Cardona, and Rick Nahmias, as well as the more recent "I Have a Name" project by Tom Feher and Robert Adler.

8. My analysis of the Minutemen's photographs is a response to Laura Wexler's proposal for "scholars of American nationalism to attempt to identify a photographic history of the national gaze." Wexler, "Techniques of the Imaginary Nation," in *Race and the Production of Modern American Nationalism,* ed. Reynolds J. Scott-Childress (New York: Garland, 1999), 379.

9. Pegler-Gordon, *In Sight of America,* 42.

10. Lisa Cartwright and Marita Sturken, *Practices of Looking: An Introduction to Visual Culture* (Oxford: Oxford University Press, 2009), 24.

11. Lawston and Murillo, "Policing Our Border," 186.

12. De Genova, *Working the Boundaries,* 62.

13. Ibid., 60. John Higham, *Strangers in the Land: Patterns of American Nativism, 1860–1925* (New York: Atheneum, 1970), 4.

14. Lawston and Murillo, "Policing Our Border," 186.

15. Roxanne Lynn Doty, "The Double Writing of Statecraft: Exploring State Responses to Illegal Immigration," *Alternatives* 21 (1996): 185.

16. Drawing from John Berger, Nevins describes "ways of seeing" as "metaphors for and manifestations of how we perceive the world and act within it." Joseph Nevins, *Operation Gatekeeper: The Rise of the "Illegal Alien" and the Making of the U.S.–Mexico Boundary* (New York: Routledge, 2002), 8. See also Berger, *Ways of Seeing* (New York: Penguin Books, 1990).

17. Nevins, *Operation Gatekeeper*, 10.

18. Gilberto Rosas, "The Thickening Borderlands: Diffused Exceptionality and 'Immigrant' Social Struggles during the 'War on Terror,'" *Cultural Dynamics* 18, no. 3 (2006): 338.

19. Borderlands Autonomist Collective, "Resisting the Security-Industrial Complex: Operation Streamline and the Militarization of the Arizona-Mexico Borderlands," in *Beyond Walls and Cages: Prisons, Borders, and Global Crisis*, ed. Jenna M. Loyd, Matt Mitchelson, and Andrew Burridge (Athens: University of Georgia Press, 2012), 191.

20. Alicia Schmidt Camacho, "Migrant Melancholia," in "The Last Frontier? The Contemporary Configuration of the U.S.–Mexico Border," ed. Jane Juffer, special issue, *South Atlantic Quarterly* 105, no. 4 (Fall 2006): 835. A 2009 report from the ACLU and Mexico's National Commission on Human Rights (CNDH) stated that since 1994, more than five thousand migrants had died attempting to reach the United States: "U.S.-Mexico Border Crossing Deaths Are Humanitarian Crisis, According to a Report from the ACLU and the CNDH." See American Civil Liberties Union website, https://www.aclu.org. See also Aviva Chomsky, *Undocumented: How Immigration Became Illegal* (Boston: Beacon Books, 2014), 83.

21. De Genova has written about the construction of "migrant illegality," arguing that the "effective equation of 'illegal immigration' with unauthorized border-crossing has served to continuously restage the U.S.–Mexico border in particular as the theater of the enforcement 'crisis' and thus constantly re-renders 'Mexican' as the distinctive national name for migrant 'illegality.'" De Genova, "The Legal Production," 171.

22. Ibid., 179–80.

23. Schmidt Camacho, *Migrant Imaginaries*, 295.

24. See text of the law: https://www.govtrack.us/congress/bills/109/hr6061.

25. Jane Juffer, "Introduction," in "The Last Frontier? The Contemporary Configuration of the U.S.–Mexico Border," ed. Jane Juffer, special issue, *South Atlantic Quarterly* 105, no. 4 (Fall 2006): 671; see also Justin Akers Chacón, *No One Is Illegal: Fighting Racism and State Violence on the US–Mexico Border* (Chicago: Haymarket Books, 2006), 241.

26. Juffer, "Introduction," 666.

27. Doty, *The Law*, 41. Robin Dale Jacobson argues that "the Minuteman Project in the 1990s would have been a fringe group from which the mainstream restrictionist forces would have attempted to distance themselves. In 2006 the line between mainstream and extreme restrictionist forces is not so clear." Jacobson, *The New Nativism: Proposition 187 and the Debate over Immigration* (Minneapolis: University of Minnesota Press, 2008), 143.

28. During these hearings, Chris Simcox was also asked to testify. Doty, *The Law*, 41.

29. Ibid., 97.

30. In September 2005, Governor Napolitano gave $1.5 million in emergency aid for law enforcement, repairing fences, and handling "costs related to illegal immigrants deaths" along the U.S.–Mexico boundary. Jimmy Magahern, "Postcards from the Edge," *Phoenix New Times*, October 20, 2005, 1.

31. Doty, *The Law*, 101.

32. Ibid., 10. Emphasis in original.

33. Ibid., 11.

34. Here Gilberto Rosas cites Gary Spencer, the leader of the American Border Patrol, who stated, "Mexican 'immigrants' dilute American culture." Rosas, "The Thickening Borderlands," 342.

35. In May 2012, the Justice Department sued Sheriff Joseph Arpaio of Maricopa County, Arizona. See *United States of America v. Maricopa County Sheriff's Office and Joseph M. Arpaio, Sheriff of Maricopa County, Arizona*. And in July 2012, the federal civil rights lawsuit *Melendres v. Arpaio* was brought to trial in a class-action suit, representing Latinos/as who had been stopped by Sheriff Arpaio's deputies since 2007.

36. Cornelius, "Controlling 'Unwanted Immigration,'" 784. See Inter-American Commission, "Report N° 78/08," 4.

37. Juffer, "Introduction," 674.

38. Akers Chacón, *No One Is Illegal*, 247. Numerous immigrant rights organizations have documented instances in which vigilantes assaulted undocumented migrants while they rounded them up, detained them at gunpoint, and waited for the Border Patrol to arrive. The federal government ignored the members of vigilante groups who assaulted undocumented migrants. In 2005, Tucson's Border Action Network submitted a petition to the Inter-American Commission on Human Rights (IACHR) of the Organization of American States (OAS), citing the U.S. government for failing to prosecute vigilante violence. See Border Action Network's website section on "No Vigilante Violence": http://www.border action.org. In 2009 the commission ruled that the complaint was admissible and published a report. See Inter-American Commission, "Report N° 78/08."

39. Rudy Adler, Victoria Criado, and Brett Huneycutt, "Project Background," in *Border Film Project: Photos by Migrants and Minutemen on the U.S.–Mexico Border* (New York: Abrams, 2007). According to an article in the *Phoenix New Times*—published when they were developing the project and Rudy Adler was interested in making a documentary film—Huneycutt stated that he wanted to investigate Arizona's border situation with Mexico. As Huneycutt noted, "The natural intersection for us was a film about immigration." See Magahern, "Postcards from the Edge."

40. The organizers' biographies are available on the Border Film Project's website.

41. Daniel González, "Border Exposures," *Arizona Republic*, March 18, 2008, A1, A17.

42. Magahern, "Postcards from the Edge."

43. Ibid.; and Adler, Criado, and Huneycutt, "Project Background."

44. "La frontera, de ambos lados," November 10, 2006, BBC Mundo, http://news.bbc.co.uk.

45. González, "Border Exposures"; see also Border Film Project website, http://www.borderfilmproject.com/.

46. Sara Inés Calderón, "Filmmakers Look at Immigration from Different Angle," *Brownsville Herald*, September 4, 2005.

47. González, "Border Exposures."

48. According to the book's map, the organizers gave cameras to migrants primarily in the northern border states of Sonora and Chihuahua. Adler, Criado, and Huneycutt, *Border Film Project*.

49. Magahern, "Postcards from the Edge."

50. Wendy Grossman, "Exhibit Offers Snapshots from the Border Crisis," *Houston Chronicle*, November 19, 2006.

51. Calderón, "Filmmakers Look at Immigration."

52. Ibid.; Andrew Junker, "Photographs Capture Life on the Border," *Catholic Sun* online, November 2, 2006, http://www.borderfilmproject.com/press/061102_catholicsun.pdf.

53. "La frontera, de ambos lados."

54. Quoted in Junker, "Photographs Capture Life."

55. Adler and Huneycutt, interview.

56. Adler, Criado, and Huneycutt, "Project Background."

57. Zuromskis, *Snapshot Photography*, 63–64.

58. Although some of the Minutemen who surveilled migrants resided in border states, most came from other parts of the country. In many ways, the images produced by Minutemen are informed by what John Urry refers to as the "tourist gaze," which is counter to their "everyday" lives that include work and home. The tourist gaze "is directed to features of the landscape and townscape that separate them off from everyday experience," as well as "certain aspects of the place to be visited which distinguish it from what is conventionally encountered in everyday life." Urry, *The Tourist Gaze: Leisure and Travel in Contemporary Societies* (London: Sage, 1990), 3, 10.

59. Wexler, "Techniques of the Imaginary Nation," 379.

60. See Stephen, "Los Nuevos Desaparecidos," 91.

61. bell hooks contends: "Travel is not a word that can be easily evoked to talk about the Middle Passage, the Trail of Tears, the landings of Chinese immigrants at Ellis [or Angel] Island, the forced relocation of Japanese-Americans, the plight of the homeless." hooks, *Representing Whiteness in the Black Imagination* (London: Routledge, 1992), 176.

62. Schmidt Camacho, "Migrant Melancholia," 846. Emphasis in original.

63. Camera numbers from *Border Film Project* (2007).

64. Rosas, "The Thickening Borderlands," 32.

65. Juffer, "Introduction," 675.
66. Chavez, *The Latino Threat*, 137.
67. Juffer, "Introduction," 665.
68. Ibid., 672.
69. Ibid., 674.
70. Akers Chacón, *No One Is Illegal*, 251.
71. De Genova, "The Legal Production," 176–77.
72. Ibid., 178.
73. Chavez, *The Latino Threat*, 132.
74. Lawston and Murillo, "Policing Our Border," 182.
75. De Genova, "The Legal Production," 161. Frank Luntz, the head of a public opinion company, sent a document to Republican politicians entitled "Respect for the Law and Economic Fairness: Illegal Immigration Prevention" emphasizing a law-and-order frame, in which a undocumented migrant crossing the border is deemed to have committed an "illegal" act.
76. Chavez, *The Latino Threat*, 137.
77. Some of the images include elements of landscape photography and keep within its aesthetic conventions. The width of the photograph is greater than the height, and the composition is of one-third/two-third horizontal proportions. Wells, *Photography*, 296.
78. De Genova, "The Legal Production," 178.
79. Nevins, *Operation Gatekeeper*, 8.
80. Chavez, *The Latino Threat*, 150.
81. Sarah Hill has noted that in the years leading up to NAFTA, the mainstream media linked "'dirty' immigrant Mexicans to a 'dirty' border environment," which "not only reinforced existing stereotypes but also provided nativists with another seemingly natural reason to disparage and denigrate Mexicans." Sarah Hill, "Purity and Danger on the U.S.–Mexico Border," in "The Last Frontier? The Contemporary Configuration of the U.S.–Mexico Border," ed. Jane Juffer, special issue, *South Atlantic Quarterly* 105, no. 4 (Fall 2006): 779.
82. Ibid. See also Mary Douglas, *Purity and Danger* (New York: Praeger, 1966). Hill also argues, "We can know that an environment is degraded by iconic images of human things inappropriately mingled with nature: tires clogging a waterway, plastic flotsam and jetsam strewn across a patch of desert, or factory smokestacks staining the sky black with billowing emissions. The images indexes deteriorated nature, implicitly narrating human imprints on nature: *People* litter, *industries* pollute." Hill, "Purity and Danger," 781.
83. Hill, "Purity and Danger," 793. Here she mentions the websites of the Minuteman Project and other organizations.
84. Ibid., 781.
85. De Genova, "The Legal Production," 176–77.

86. Almost all of the migrants' images document what De Genova describes as the "perilous and sometimes deadly circumstances required to evade detection" while attempting to cross the border. Ibid., 177.

87. Zuromskis, *Snapshot Photography*, 61.

88. James Walsh, "From Border Control to Border Care: The Political and Ethical Potential of Surveillance," in *Governing Immigration through Crime: A Reader*, ed. Jonathan X. Inda and Julie A. Dowling (Stanford, Calif.: Stanford University Press, 2013), 285.

89. Schmidt Camacho, "Migrant Melancholia," 832.

90. Peter Osborne, *Traveling Light: Photography, Travel, and Visual Culture* (Manchester: Manchester University Press, 2000), 147.

91. Stephen, "Los Nuevos Desaparecidos," 94.

92. Magahern, "Postcards from the Edge."

93. Stephen, "Los Nuevos Desaparecidos," 92.

94. I am drawing on Schmidt Camacho's argument that "the narration of migrant sorrows constitutes a political act." Schmidt Camacho, "Migrant Melancholia," 833.

95. Magahern, "Postcards from the Edge."

96. Ibid.

97. Quoted in Junker, "Photographs Capture Life."

98. See http://www.borderfilmproject.com.

99. Photographs from the Border Film Project were exhibited at Creighton University, Omaha, Nebraska; the Scottsdale Museum of Contemporary Art, Scottsdale, Arizona; New York University, New York City; DiverseWorks, Houston, Texas; Harvard University Law School, Cambridge, Massachusetts; Seattle University, Seattle, Washington; Gage Gallery, Chicago, Illinois; University of Texas, El Paso; and Buffalo Arts Studio, New York. The organizers also showed the images at the Comisión Nacional de Derechos Humanos in Mexico City during the International Migration Conference in October 2006. For exhibition dates, see the Border Film Project's website: http://www.borderfilmproject.com.

100. Cassandra Coblentz, telephone conversation with author, October 20, 2015.

101. Quoted in Rena Rapuano, "Bridging the Divide," *Museum News* 5, no. 6 (November/December 2006): 12. Further, senior curator Marilu Knode noted that the show presented immigration in a different way by "giving the cameras to the actual people involved," which "gives us a personal face to a very, very complicated situation." Quoted in Brady McCombs, "Minutemen, Crossers Picture the Border," *Arizona Daily Star*, October 19, 2006.

102. Ljiljana Ciric, "Bridging the Border: Film Project Illustrates Both Sides of Border Debate," October 5, 2006, Arizona State University, WebDevil.com.

103. Wall labels copyright SMoCA.

104. One museum attendee (Lila, from Tucson) commented on the space at the exhibit, noting that it "mimics the feel of a border—inclusion and exclusion." Copyright SMoCA.

105. Coblentz, telephone conversation.

106. Junker, "Photographs Capture Life."

107. Quoted in Ciric, "Bridging the Border."

108. Allan Sekula, "Photography between Labor and Capital," in *Mining Photographs and Other Pictures, 1948–1968: A Selection from the Negative Archives of Shedden Studio, Glatt Buy, Cape Breton*, ed. Benjamin H. D. Buchloh and Robert Wilkie (Halifax: Press of the Nova Scotia College of Art and Design, 1983), 194.

109. Ibid.

110. Chris Kraus also noted that "nowhere in the exhibition does the project suggest a causal relation between first-world wealth and Third-World poverty." Kraus, "The Border Film Project: Scottsdale Museum of Contemporary Art," *Art Forum* (January 2007): 257–58. Art historian Claudia Mesch argued that the exhibition of Border Film Project at SMoCA "echoes the state of current discourse in US border policy, since it too presents localized migration problems as a stalemate that pits one population against the other rather than revealing it as a stage where global markets intertwine and mutate." Mesch, *Art and Politics: A Small History of Art for Social Change since 1945* (London: I. B. Tauris, 2013), 185.

111. Schmidt Camacho, "Migrant Melancholia," 832.

112. Magahern, "Postcards from the Edge."

113. In both Unseen America projects that I describe, the photographers addressed their images primarily to members of their local and translocal communities. It was only the exhibitions at the Department of Labor and at the Danzantes restaurant that were addressed to "outside" audiences.

114. Holland, "Introduction," 2–3.

115. Zuromskis, *Snapshot Photography*, 6.

116. Junker, "Photographs Capture Life"; and Adler and Huneycutt, interview.

117. Junker, "Photographs Capture Life."

118. Sekula, "Photography between Labor and Capital," 195.

119. Some of the critical reviews mentioned the organizers' lack of awareness of the Minutemen's performance for the camera. In a local newspaper article following an exhibition at DiverseWorks in Houston, reviewer Kelly Klaasmeyer noted that when watching the video that was shown as part of the exhibition, "you get the sense that the Minutemen . . . aren't exactly putting all their cards on the table for the filmmakers." Klaasmeyer, "Migrants and Minutemen," *Houston Press*, November 30, 2006, http://www.houstonpress.com.

120. McCombs, "Minutemen, Crossers."

121. Junker, "Photographs Capture Life," 12–13.

122. In a review entitled "Bridging the Divide," Rapuano commented: "Both the project collaborators and the museum curators were struck by how similar themes emerged from the photos of the migrants and the Minutemen." Rapuano, "Bridging the Divide," 12.

123. The organizers interviewed Mexicans and Central Americans who planned to cross the U.S.–Mexico border, those already living in the United States, and their relatives in El Salvador and Mexico. They also interviewed members of the Minuteman Project at "observation sites" along the border and leaders of the Minuteman Project in Washington, D.C. Adler, Criado, and Huneycutt, "Project Background."

124. Ibid.

125. Sekula, "Photography between Labor and Capital," 195–96.

126. The ordering of the images can be determined by consulting with the section on "Camera Photographer's Information" at the center of the book. Some of the notes include information about where the migrants came from—including Mexico and countries in Central America, such as Honduras and Guatemala—as well as where the cameras were mailed from in the United States.

127. Sekula, "Photography between Labor and Capital," 197.

128. Ibid. Emphasis in original.

129. Duggan, *Twilight of Equality?*, xxi.

130. De Genova, *Working the Boundaries*, 72.

131. For example, Jacobson notes, "In August 2006, their Web site featured articles on the Reconquista movement, 'Hezbollah Invading U.S. from Mexico,' undocumented immigrants' claims about political takeover, and a recent MMP demonstration at Ground Zero." Jacobson, *The New Nativism*, 143. Arturo J. Aldama argues that in groups like the Minutemen, "vigilantism is tied to [the] ideas of racial xenophobia and to fears of how they perceive the reconquest of the Southwest by Mexico and Mexican immigrants." Aldama, "Fears of Aztlán/Fears of the Reconquista: White Men as New (Old) Nativ(ist)e Americans," in *Comparative Indigeneities of the Americas: Towards a Hemispheric Approach*, ed. M. Bianet Castellanos, Lourdes Gutiérrez Nájera, and Arturo J. Aldama (Tucson: University of Arizona Press, 2012), 156.

132. Lawston and Murillo, "Policing Our Border," 182.

133. Zuromskis, *Snapshot Photography*, 10.

134. See http://www.borderfilmproject.com/en/photo-gallery/.

135. Cartwright and Sturken, *Practices of Looking*, 29.

136. Chavez, *The Latino Threat*, 135.

137. Sekula, "Photography between Labor and Capital," 195.

138. Ibid., 194.

139. Lawston and Murillo, "Policing Our Border," 186.

140. In the organizers' statement, they note, "When they [Minutemen] spot migrants and smugglers, they avoid direct confrontation and instead call the

Border Patrol. Our time with the Minutemen gave us a view of the so-called 'vigilantes' that was much more nuanced than the caricatures painted by the media. We realized that these *volunteers* are by and large concerned Americans, trying to do their part to make the United States a safer place and to protect American jobs" (my emphasis). Adler, Criado, and Huneycutt, "Project Background."

141. They also emphasize that many of the Minutemen are retired veterans or law enforcement officers, and thus, their work allows them to "continue their lives of public service by volunteering to do what they believe the U.S. government should be doing—regaining control of the U.S. border with Mexico." Ibid.

142. De Genova, *Working the Boundaries*, 91.

143. Bonnie Honig, *Democracy and the Foreigner* (Princeton, N.J.: Princeton University Press, 2001), 96.

144. Akers Chacón describes the Minutemen's media strategy during their monthlong action and publicity event in April 2005, as well as the media's uncritical reception of the group. He contends that the Minutemen "were able to present themselves as a unified, national movement, acting on behalf of U.S. public opinion." In response, he notes that the media "devour[ed] it [their message] whole" by representing the Minutemen as "concerned citizens." Akers Chacón, *No One Is Illegal*, 261.

145. Ibid.

146. For example, Simcox was arrested on a weapons charge. See Doty, *The Law*, 33; and Chavez, *The Latino Threat*, 136.

147. The organizers include a quote from a Minuteman leader in Washington, in which he said that he "works tirelessly to help people focus their anger and frustration on Washington, not on the people who come across the border." However, previous to the mainstreaming of the Minutemen in 2005, one of the group's founders, Chris Simcox, spoke differently about the possible ways that members could interact with unauthorized migrants, noting that "so far we have been restrained, but I'm afraid that our restraint is wearing thin. Take heed of our weapons because we're going to defend our borders by any means necessary." Juffer, "Introduction," 666. This quotation from Simcox was originally published in Amanda Susskind and Joanna Mendelson's "Extremists at the Border: Minuteman Project about More Than Enforcing Policy," *L.A. Daily News*, May 15, 2005.

148. De Genova, *Working the Boundaries*, 62. Emphasis in original.

149. Adler, Criado, and Huneycutt, "Project Background." These statements relate to Lisa Marie Cacho's argument that "the human value of undocumented laborers is measured only in terms of their economic value for the American middle-class." Cacho, *Social Death*, 19.

150. See Linda Bosniak, "'Nativism' the Concept: Some Reflections," in *Immigrants Out: The New Nativism and Anti-immigrant Impulse in the United States*, ed. Juan Perea (New York: New York University Press, 1990), 288.

151. Ibid., 289.

152. David Michael Smith, "Photo Book Looks at Illegal Immigration from Both Sides of the Fence," *Daily News* (Galveston, Texas), May 27, 2007, D6.

153. De Genova, *Working the Boundaries*, 74. Specifically, he argues, "The refusal to recognize the history of colonization in U.S. nation-state formation has a rather direct relevance for any consideration of Mexican migration." Ibid., 75.

154. Ibid., 74–75.

155. Ibid., and Janice Radway, "What's in a Name: Presidential Address to the American Studies Association, 20 November 1998," *American Quarterly* 51, no. 1 (1999): 12.

4. Refusing Disposability

1. According to the Merriam-Webster online dictionary, a maquiladora is "a foreign-owned factory in Mexico at which imported parts are assembled by lower-paid workers into products for export," http://www.merriam-webster .com/dictionary/maquiladora.

2. In Mexico, an *asociación civil* is a nonprofit organization.

3. Rosa-Linda Fregoso, "*Maquilápolis*: An Interview with Vicky Funari and Sergio De La Torre," *Camera Obscura* 25, no. 274 (2010): 177.

4. Ibid. The first quote in the sentence was from De La Torre and the second from Funari.

5. Beattie, *Documentary Screens*, 118.

6. Aufderheide, *The Daily Planet*, 215.

7. Ibid., 216. Beattie notes that "first-person video developed in the United States from a basis in social activism and investigation in which video was used as a tool to document social problems." Beattie, *Documentary Screens*, 118.

8. Although not all women maquila workers are migrants, most of those who participated in the making of the film migrated to Tijuana from elsewhere in Mexico. In an e-mail, Vicki Funari wrote, "The majority of the women in our group (12 in the first video workshop, and then a fluctuating group of about 10 over the next four years, as some women left and new women came into the project during subsequent workshops) were migrants, though they had been in Tijuana for much of their lives." Vicky Funari, e-mail to author, February 12, 2015.

9. I would like to thank Rosa-Linda Fregoso for her comments on a paper that I gave about *Maquilápolis* at the American Studies Association's Annual Meeting, Philadelphia, October 10–14, 2007.

10. Sergio De La Torre, conversation with the author, San Francisco, California, July 31, 2012.

11. Jefferson Cowie, *Capital Moves: RCA's Seventy-four-Year Quest for Cheap Labor* (Ithaca, N.Y.: Cornell University Press, 1999), 106. During the Bracero Program (1942–1964), the populations of Mexican border cities, such as Tijuana

and Ciudad Juárez, grew, since these were the locations where U.S. companies hired Mexican workers. Kathryn Kopinak, "Globalization in Tijuana Maquiladoras: Using Historical Antecedents and Migration to Test Globalization Models," in *Tijuana Dreaming: Life and Art at the Global Border*, ed. Josh Kun and Fiamma Montezemolo (Durham, N.C.: Duke University Press, 2012), 79. Even after the Bracero Program ended, Mexicans migrated to northern border cities, as they believed there might be work there. The end of the Bracero Program led to the repatriation of 178,000 workers from the United States to Mexico, which contributed to the 250,000 unemployed workers living in Mexican border cities in the mid-1960s. Cowie, *Capital Moves*, 110.

12. Devon G. Peña, *The Terror of the Machine: Technology, Work, Gender, and Ecology on the U.S.–Mexico Border* (Austin: Center for Mexican American Studies, University of Texas, 1997), 50; and Milagros Peña, *Latina Activists across Borders: Women's Grassroots Organizing in Mexico and Texas* (Durham, N.C.: Duke University Press, 2007), 78. For information on maquiladoras in Juárez, see Alejandro Lugo, *Fragmented Lives, Assembled Parts: Culture, Capitalism, and Conquest at the U.S.–Mexico Border* (Austin: University of Texas Press, 2008), 72. Donald Baerresen wrote a guide to the BIP in 1971, which also describes the multinational corporate interest in hiring women to work in the maquilas. See Baerresen, *Border Industrialization Program of Mexico* (Lexington, Mass.: Heath—Lexington Books, 1971), 34–35.

13. Cowie, *Capital Moves*, 119.

14. Kopinak, "Globalization in Tijuana Maquiladoras," 80. Here, Kopinak draws on research conducted for her book *Desert Capitalism: Maquiladoras in North America's Western Industrial Corridor* (Tucson: University of Arizona Press, 1996), 105.

15. Peña, *The Terror of the Machine*, 50, 259; and Susan Tiano, *Patriarchy on the Line: Labor, Gender, and Ideology in the Mexican Maquila Industry* (Philadelphia: Temple University Press, 1994), 164.

16. Kopinak, "Globalization in Tijuana Maquiladoras," 76.

17. Peña, *Latina Activists across Borders*, 76.

18. Joshua Kagan, "Workers' Rights in the Mexican Maquiladora Sector: Collective Bargaining, Women's Rights, and General Human Rights; Laws, Norms, and Practices," *Journal of Transnational Literature and Policy* (2005–2006): 174.

19. Ibid., 153.

20. Such as George Kourous, "Workers' Health Is on the Line: Occupational Health and Safety in the Maquiladoras," in *The Maquiladora Reader: Cross-Border Organizing since NAFTA*, ed. Rachel Kamel and Anya Hoffman (Philadelphia: American Friends Service Committee, 1999), 36.

21. Kagan, "Workers' Rights in the Mexican Maquiladora Sector," 159–60.

22. Ibid., 163–64.

23. This is from the Ley Federal del Trabajo (Mexican Federal Labor Law).

24. Tiano, *Patriarchy on the Line*, 221.

25. Peña, *The Terror of the Machine*, 106. Labor historians have written about the collusion between the PRI and U.S.-based multinational corporations to prevent workers from forming unions outside of the Confederation of Mexican Workers (CTM). See, for example, Dan La Botz, *Mask of Democracy: Labor Suppression in Mexico Today* (Boston: South End Press, 1999).

26. COMO was founded by María Elena Villegas, a nurse employed at the RCA plant in Juárez, and Dr. María Guillermina Valdés-Villalva. See Peña, *The Terror of the Machine*.

27. Joe Bandy and Jennifer Bickham Mendez, "A Place of Their Own? Women Organizers in the Maquilas of Nicaragua and Mexico," in *Latin American Social Movements: Globalization, Democratization, and Transnational Networks*, ed. Hank Johnston and Paul Almeida (Lanham, Md.: Rowman and Littlefield, 2006), 133.

28. The concept of promotores (community activists) developed in the health-care field, in which both founders of COMO had previously worked. For more information on health promotion, see Hester, "Bodies in Translation," 168–88.

29. Peña, *The Terror of the Machine*, 145.

30. Ibid., 144.

31. Ibid., 171.

32. Ibid., 171–72.

33. Luz Aida Ruiz Martinez, "The Primer Taller Fotodocumental—Tijuana," http://www.f8.com/FP/TIJUANA/English/PROJECTS/Luz12.htm.

34. Sylvia López Estrada, "Border Women's NGOs and Political Participation in Baja California," in *Women and Change at the U.S.–Mexico Border: Mobility, Labor, and Activism*, ed. Doreen J. Mattingly and Ellen R. Hansen (Tucson: University of Arizona Press, 2006).

35. Doreen J. Mattingly and Ellen R. Hansen, "Women at the Border: Foundations and Frameworks," in *Women and Change at the U.S.–Mexico Border: Mobility, Labor, and Activism*, ed. Doreen J. Mattingly and Ellen R. Hansen (Tucson: University of Arizona Press, 2006), 13.

36. Bandy and Mendez, "A Place of Their Own?" 133.

37. For more information on these organizations see Michelle Téllez and Cristina Sanidad, "'Giving Wings to Our Dreams': Binational Activism and Workers' Rights Struggles in the San Diego–Tijuana Border Region," in *Border Politics: Social Movements, Collective Identities, and Globalization*, ed. Nancy A. Naples and Jennifer Bickham Mendez (New York: New York University Press, 2015), 323–56.

38. Numerous organizations aid maquiladora workers in the U.S.–Mexico borderlands. By the time that this book is published, some of these organizations may no longer exist, and some new organizations may also have been formed.

39. Claire F. Fox notes that inSite played up the "'sister cities' trope prevalent during the NAFTA negotiations." Fox, *The Fence and the River: Culture and Politics at the U.S.–Mexico Border* (Minneapolis: University of Minnesota Press, 1999), 45.

40. Grant H. Kester, *The One and the Many: Contemporary Collaborative Art in a Global Context* (Durham, N.C.: Duke University Press, 2011), 7, 5.

41. George Yúdice, *The Expediency of Culture: Uses of Culture in the Global Era* (Durham, N.C.: Duke University Press, 2004), 288.

42. Ibid., 289.

43. "Historical Background," Register of inSite Archives, 1992–2006, MSS 707, Mandeville Special Collections Library, University of California, San Diego (UCSD).

44. Fiamma Montezemolo, "Tijuana: Hybridity and Beyond; A Conversation with Néstor García Canclini," *Third Text* 23, no. 6 (November 2009): 738. Yúdice relates inSite to other public art programs established in the 1990s, in which artists developed installations using performance, film, and video in local sites and with "local publics, communities, institutions, and corporations." Yúdice, *The Expediency of Culture*, 296.

45. Yúdice, *The Expediency of Culture*, 289, 296; Grant Kester, *Conversation Pieces: Community and Communication in Modern Art* (Berkeley: University of California Press, 2004), 128–29.

46. Yúdice, *The Expediency of Culture*, 300.

47. Kester does not criticize all community-based art projects. For example, see his analysis of Fred Lonidier's work, including *N.A.F.T.A.* (Not a Fair Trade for All, 1997). Kester, *Conversation Pieces*, 176–80.

48. Ibid., 173.

49. Ibid., 173–74.

50. Ibid., 174.

51. Michael Krichman and Carmen Cuenca to Krzysztof Wodiczko, May 13, 1999, inSite Archives, MSS 707, Box 173, Mandeville Special Collections Library, UCSD.

52. Patricia Phillips, "Creating Democracy: A Dialogue with Krzysztof Wodiczko," *Art Journal* (Winter 2003): 34.

53. Cecilia Garza Bolio, e-mail to Krzysztof Wodiczko, February 1, 2000, inSite Archives, MSS 707, Box 173, Mandeville Special Collections Library, UCSD.

54. Krzysztof Wodiczko, Proposal for inSite 2000, inSite Archives, MSS 707, Box 173, Mandeville Special Collections Library, UCSD.

55. *Yeuani* is a Nahuatl word meaning "furious." (I'd like to thank Rafael Martinez for his translation of this word.) Elsa Jiménez founded the organization to provide women working at the maquiladoras with information about their rights. See http://clon.uam.mx.cyberzine/6/yeuani/htm.

56. inSite poster for "Tijuana Projection," inSite Archives, MSS 707, Box 173, Mandeville Special Collections Library, UCSD.

57. This issue was raised by Yúdice in *The Expediency of Culture*.

58. George Yúdice, "Public and Violence," in *Artistic Citizenship: A Public Voice for the Arts*, ed. Mary Schmidt Campbell and Randy Martin (London: Routledge, 2006), 158.

59. See handwritten transcripts of recordings of promotoras from Factor X, including Esperanza, Norma [Moreno], Adela [Rivera], Delfina, Paola, Leticia [Meza], and Diana, n.d., inSite Archives, "Tijuana Projection," MSS 707, Box 223, Folder 11, Mandeville Special Collections Library, UCSD.

60. See, for example, Adela's testimony included with the transcripts from the recordings of promotoras from Factor X, n.d., ibid. Kopinak notes, "The Tijuana area is known to attract migrants from farther away than other maquiladora cities." Kopinak, "Globalization in Tijuana Maquiladoras," 80.

61. See Diana's and Delfina's testimony, inSite Archives, "Tijuana Projection," MSS 707, Box 223, Folder 11, Mandeville Special Collections Library, UCSD.

62. See Delfina's testimony, ibid.

63. See Delfina's and Esperanza's testimony, ibid.

64. According to a report on *Tijuana Projection* in the inSite archives, the testimonies focused on issues like "work-related abuse, sexual abuse, family disintegration, alcoholism, and domestic violence." "Tijuana Projection."

65. Its militarized aesthetics are similar to those of the Homeless Vehicle Project. For a drawing of one of the images, see http://www.pbs.org/art21/ files/images/wodiczko-draw-002.jpg.

66. Wendy Kozol and Wendy Hesford, "Introduction," in *Just Advocacy? Women's Human Rights, Transnational Feminisms, and the Politics of Representation*, ed. Wendy Hesford and Wendy Kozol (New Brunswick, N.J.: Rutgers University Press, 2005), 13.

67. Yúdice, *The Expediency of Culture*, 324. Further, he stated that "the claim to be doing art, however, does not do away with the interrogations about what, exactly, the artist is doing by engaging communities." Ibid., 320.

68. Ibid., 288. During a summer residency in July 1999 to prepare for inSite 2000–2001, Yúdice noted that some artists scrutinized inSite's mission of supporting "interaction" between artists and "communities" to consider the benefits for community members. For example, according to Yúdice, artist Armando Rascón "suggested that an art project should have lasting effects in the community in which it is sited, that is, should leave something that goes beyond instigating awareness of the contradictions attaching to a particular place or situation." Ibid., 318.

69. Montezemolo notes, "I have doubts about relational art in situ. I feel the ethical remains outside of it." Montezemolo, "Tijuana," 749.

70. This quote was from a transcript of a panel, "Image Power: Cultural Interventions as Public Memory in Postmodern Spaces," held on February 25, 2001, at the Centro Cultural Tijuana. The participants included Néstor García Canclini, George Yúdice, and Krzysztof Wodiczko; the moderator was Susan Buck-Morss. Transcript, "Image Power," 18, insite Archives, MSS 707, Box 142, Mandeville Special Collections Library, UCSD.

71. Ibid.

72. Krzysztof Wodiczko, interview with Maria Hinojosa, *One-on-One*, WGBH, February 2, 2010.

73. See transcript for the panel "Image Power: Cultural Interventions as Public Memory in Postmodern Spaces."

74. This point was articulated in an e-mail written by Diana Arias, a promotora who was involved in the *Tijuana Projection*. Diana Arias, e-mail to author, May 21, 2013. Also, see the transcripts of the recordings of promotoras from Factor X, n.d., "Tijuana Projection."

75. Yúdice, *The Expediency of Culture*, 149.

76. Leah Ollman, "Losing Ground: Public Art at the Border," *Art in America* 89, no. 5 (May 2001). The reviews include Karla Gerado, "Vivencias Monumentales," *Frontera*, February 27, 2001; Robert L. Pincus, "Sphere Hosts Big Images at insite 2000," *San Diego Union Tribune*, February 23, 2001; Katrina Paredes, "Bolas de Imagines," *Frontera*, February 22, 2001; Berlin Golonu, "Viewpoint," *Artweek*, February 2001; Karla Gerado, "Mayor de Edad," *Frontera*, October 20, 2000; and Jeannette Sanchez, "Convivencia Artistica el la Frontera," *La Crónica*, October 12, 2000.

77. Arias, e-mail.

78. Kester, *Conversation Pieces*, 171.

79. Ibid., 172.

80. Ibid.

81. Ibid., 174.

82. Krzysztof Wodiczko, "Tijuana Projection," in *inSITE 2000–2001: Parajes Fugitivos/Fugitive Sites*, ed. Osvaldo Sánchez and Cecilia Garza (San Diego, Calif.: Installation Gallery, 2002), 77.

83. Krzysztof Wodiczko, interview with Maria Hinojosa.

84. Kester, *The One and the Many*, 1–2. Kester drew these definitions from the *Complete Edition of the Oxford English Dictionary* (1987).

85. This film is similar to Funari's film *Paulina*, which Rosa-Linda Fregoso argues "call[s] into question the claim of nonfiction film to represent reality." Fregoso, *meXicana Encounters: The Making of Social Identities in the Borderlands* (Berkeley: University of California Press, 2003), 42.

86. *Maquilápolis: City of Factories Discussion Guide*, 11, http://www.newsreel .org/guides/Maquilapolis/MAQ_DiscussionGuide_English.pdf. In *The Fence and the River*, Fox writes about how conventional documentary films produced about the U.S.–Mexico border have a tendency to "replicat[e] the observer/

observed dynamics of much traditional documentary cinema in which testimony of local witnesses is mediated through 'expert' talking heads, and both of these in turn are subsumed by a voiceover narrator's authoritative commentary." Fox, *The Fence and the River*, 60.

87. See the interview with Vicky Funari and Sergio De La Torre, the production journal, and the filmmakers' statement, all on the *POV* website: http://www.pbs.org/pov/maquilapolis.

88. Vicky Funari is a documentary filmmaker who also directed *Live Nude Girls Unite!* (2000). For more information on Funari, see https://www.haverford.edu/users/vfunari.

89. Sergio De La Torre's biography can be found on his website: http://delatorreguerrero.com/bio.html.

90. Members of Grupo Factor X founded Colectivo Chilpancingo. When Grupo Factor X stopped operating in 2004, some members formed Promotoras por los Derechos de las Mujeres (Women's Rights Advocates). The film's credits state that the collaboration included promotoras from Factor X, Colectivo Chilpancingo Pro Justicia Ambiental (Chilpancingo Collective), and Promotoras por los Derechos de las Mujeres.

91. Funari and De La Torre, production journal.

92. *Maquilápolis: City of Factories Discussion Guide*, 2. The coordinating promotoras included Lupita Castañeda, Diana Arias, and Teresa Loyola. The others were collaborating promotoras: Lourdes Luján, Carmen Durán, Eva Balión, Lucia Blanco, Natividad Guizar, Vianey Mijangos, Yesenia Palomares, Delfina Rodríguez, Francis Rodríguez, Adela Rivera, Rocio Salas, Blancha Sánchez, and Cody Valadéz. *Maquilápolis: City of Factories Discussion Guide*, 11.

93. Funari and De La Torre, interview. Funari also commented on making the film: "We talked a lot to the women over the years of making it, we did a lot of discussions and exercises and we consulted with them the whole way along. . . . Through long-term engagement with the workers we came up with a way for them to have a voice and have control."

94. Funari and De La Torre, production journal.

95. Fregoso, "*Maquilápolis*," 175.

96. Kathryn Kopinak and Ma. Del Rocío Barajas contend that by 2002, the fourteen-week course grew to include women from other parts of Mexico who wanted training to become promotoras as well. Kopinak and Del Rocío Barajas, "Too Close for Comfort? The Proximity of Industrial Hazardous Waste to Local Populations in Tijuana, Baja California," *Journal of Environment and Development* 11, no. 3 (September 2002): 238. Edmé Domínguez notes that Factor X was "an initiator and inspirer of regional networks of maquiladora women workers organizing schools of methodology." Domínguez, "Resistance to Global Capital at the Local Level: Search for Solidarity and Transnational Organizing among Women Workers in Mexico: Final Report of Results" (Preliminary Version), 13.

97. De La Torre also describes Factor X's process of training women maquila workers, noting that "Factor X brought 14 factory workers a year to their office, which had a cafeteria, a childcare center, a classroom [and] provided therapy for some of the workers. Every weekend for a whole year, the organization would train these workers on issues like human rights, labor rights, and domestic violence." Funari and De La Torre, interview.

98. "Taller de Video/Video workshop," *Maquilápolis* website, http://www.maquilapolis.com/taller_MAQ_english.pdf.

99. Funari and De La Torre, interview.

100. Ginger Thompson, "Fallout of US Recession Drifts South into Mexico: Jobs Are Scarce and the Outlook Becomes Dismal," *New York Times,* December 26, 2001. According to the "scoreboard," a monthly report in *Twin Plant News,* which bills itself as "The Magazine of the Maquiladora Industry," the number of maquiladoras in Tijuana decreased by 60 from 2001 to 2002 and by 150 from 2002 to 2003. See *Twin Plant News,* January 2000–December 2005. I would like to thank Rafael Martínez for compiling this data.

101. Funari and De La Torre, production journal.

102. See *Maquilápolis.*

103. The original BIP agreement involved importing materials to factories, where they would be assembled by Mexican workers and exported internationally.

104. In *Maquilápolis,* the promotoras note which states they are originally from—Jalisco, Oaxaca, Mazatlán, and Sinaloa, among others.

105. See *Maquilápolis.*

106. Lisa Lowe, "The Gender of Sovereignty," *The Scholar and Feminist Online* 6, no. 3 (Summer 2008): 10.

107. I am referring to the "myth of the disposable Third World woman," as described by Melissa Wright, *Disposable Women and Other Myths of Global Capitalism* (London: Routledge, 2006).

108. In *Capital Moves,* Cowie describes how the BIP "created an enclave in which U.S. industry could use low-wage Mexican labor to produce goods for the U.S. market free of Mexican tariff restrictions." Cowie, *Capital Moves,* 113.

109. Cota speaks about the concessions that the Mexican government made with the IMF in the 1970s, so salaries in Mexico would not increase. He argues that the IMF forced the Mexican government to break its own laws. See *Maquilápolis.*

110. Kopinak, "Globalization in Tijuana Maquiladoras," 82.

111. See Kopinak and Barajas, "Too Close for Comfort?"

112. As Kopinak describes, more migrants to Tijuana took up residency in areas around Chilpancingo—which is downstream from Metales y Derivados—because they could not afford to purchase their own land. Although the

groundwater was contaminated, they nevertheless built wells, which enabled them to live on the land. Kopinak, "Globalization in Tijuana Maquiladoras," 85.

113. Ibid.

114. *Maquilápolis: City of Factories Discussion Guide*, 9.

115. Beattie, *Documentary Screens*, 121.

116. Ibid., 123.

117. Wright, *Disposable Women*, 2.

118. *Maquilápolis: City of Factories Discussion Guide*, 3.

119. Funari and De La Torre, filmmakers' statement.

120. Since *Maquilápolis* was a coproduction of the ITVS, it was broadcast on October 10, 2006, as part of *POV*, which shows independent nonfiction films on public television. In addition to funding from ITVS, the filmmakers also received support from Creative Capital, the Sundance Institute Documentary Fund, and other foundations.

121. *Maquilápolis* was well received, and it won awards at film festivals in Denmark, Spain, South Korea, Mexico, and the United States. These included an Outstanding Achievement Award at the Tribeca Film Festival in New York and the CINE Golden Eagle.

122. See "Outreach," *Maquilápolis* website.

123. *Maquilápolis: City of Factories Discussion Guide*, 3.

124. See "Outreach," *Maquilápolis* website.

125. Lowe, "The Gender of Sovereignty," 10.

126. *Maquilápolis: City of Factories Discussion Guide*, 3.

127. Carmen Durán and Lourdes Luján traveled with the film to New York, parts of Europe, and Asia. See *Maquilápolis: City of Factories Discussion Guide*.

128. "Taller de Video/Video Workshop," *Maquilápolis* website. Edmé Dominguez, who conducted research on Factor X and other nonprofit organizations in Mexico, notes that the success of *Maquilápolis* "inspired these women workers to activate their own agency and continue with other projects of their own." Dominguez, "Resistance to Global Capital," 13.

129. "Taller de Video/Video Workshop," *Maquilápolis* website.

130. Schmidt Camacho, *Migrant Imaginaries*, 256. Schmidt Camacho characterizes the book as a "collaborative exposition of the labor struggle within the plants." Ibid., 255. See also Sandra Arenal, *Sangre joven: Las maquiladoras por dentro* (Mexico City: Editorial Nuestra Tiempo, 1986).

131. I would like to thank Claire Fox for suggesting that I highlight this point in the Conclusion.

132. Schmidt Camacho, *Migrant Imaginaries*, 253. Schmidt Camacho further argues that *Sangre joven* "presented an alternative view of Mexico's political economy, theorized through the laboring bodies of the *obreras* [women workers]." Ibid., 254.

133. Ibid., 256.

134. Tarek Elhaik, "Borderland Ghosts: From *Touch of Evil* to *Maquilápolis: City of Factories*," in *Tijuana Dreaming: Life and Art at the Global Border*, ed. Josh Kun and Fiamma Montezemolo (Durham, N.C.: Duke University Press, 2012), 345.

5. Disappearance and Counter-Spectacle in *Sanctuary City/Ciudad Santuario*, 1989–2009

1. HR 4437—which was sponsored by Jim Sensenbrenner—passed the House of Representatives in December 2005 but not the Senate. For more information about HR 4437, see http://www.ncsl.org/research/immigration/summary-of-the-sensenbrenner-immigration-bill.aspx.

2. Tomás Summers Sandoval Jr., *Latinos at the Golden Gate: Creating Community and Identity in San Francisco* (Chapel Hill: University of North Carolina Press, 2013), 1. Summers Sandoval quoted this individual from Pia Starker's "Humanizing the Debate, Day Laborers More Concerned with Work Than Politics," *San Francisco Chronicle*, May 19, 2006.

3. The 1989 ordinance bans employees from "requesting information about or disseminating information regarding" an individual's immigration status, unless they are required to do so by state or federal law. San Francisco, California, Administrative Code § 12H.2 (c).

4. Chavez, *The Latino Threat*, 155.

5. See for example, Nicholas De Genova, "Production of Culprits: From Deportability to Detainability in the Aftermath of 'Homeland Security,'" *Citizenship Studies* 11, no. 5 (2007): 427; and De Genova and Peutz, "Introduction," 4, 35.

6. As mentioned in chapter 4, Sergio De La Torre is from the Tijuana/San Diego border region, and he now teaches at the University of San Francisco. His biography can be found at http://delatorreguerrero.com/.

7. Chapter 12 of the city's municipal code states, "No department, agency, commission, officer or employee of the City and County of San Francisco shall use any city funds or resources to assist in the enforcement of Federal immigration law." San Francisco, California, Administrative Code §12H.2 (1989).

8. Sergio De La Torre, telephone conversation with author, June 14, 2011.

9. De Genova, "Spectacle of Terror," 153. Emphasis in original.

10. Chavez, *The Latino Threat*, 155.

11. Claude Lomnitz, "2006 Immigration Mobilizations," in *Nongovernmental Politics*, ed. Michel Feher, Gaëlle Kirkorian, and Yates McKee (New York: Zone Books, 2007), 437.

12. McKee, "'Eyes and Ears,'" 339.

13. Further, Judith Butler relates her call for a critical image to post-9/11 "cultural criticism" that would "interrogate the emergence and vanishing of the human at the limits of what we can know, what we can hear, what we can see and what we can sense." Butler, *Precarious Life: The Powers of Mourning and*

Violence (London: Verso, 2004), 146, as quoted in McKee "'Eyes and Ears,'" 339. Emphasis in original.

14. Meg McLagan, "Human Rights, Testimony, and Transnational Publicity," in *Nongovernmental Politics*, ed. Michel Feher, Gaëlle Kirkorian, and Yates McKee (New York: Zone Books, 2007), 310.

15. Ibid., 306.

16. In using this term I relate *Sanctuary City/Ciudad Santuario* to the work of ALARMA (Artists in Los Angeles Reconceptualizing Media Arts), who stated in their "Manifest(o)" that they "appropriate the phantom spectacles of the city and provide counter-spectacles," as well as Krzysztof Wodiczko's projections, which Peter Boswell describes as "counter-spectacles." See Rita González, Ramón Garcia, and C. Ondine Chavoya, "A.L.A.R.M.A.'s Manifest(o) Destiny," *Wide Angle* 20, no. 3 (1998); and Peter Boswell, "Krzysztof Wodiczko: Art and the Public Domain," in *Public Address: Krzysztof Wodiczko* (Minneapolis, Minn.: Walker Art Center, 1992), 21.

17. In 1992 city politicians amended the ordinance, so any noncitizen convicted of crimes was exempt from protection. Thus, police officers could report the immigration status of noncitizens arrested for or convicted of felony crimes to the INS. San Francisco, California, Administrative Code §12H.2 (1992).

18. As Ridgely notes, "From 1984–1987, more than 20 cities and two states (New York and New Mexico), adopted resolutions declaring themselves as sanctuaries for Central American refugees, many issuing statements about cooperation with the INS." Ridgley, "Cities of Refuge," 66–67. Also on the sanctuary movement is Susan Bibler Coutin's *The Culture of Protest: Religious Activism and the U.S. Sanctuary Movement* (Boulder, Colo.: Westview Press, 1993).

19. García, *Seeking Refuge*, 88.

20. Ibid., 86–108. However, the federal government attempted to use section 274(a) of the Immigration and Nationality Act of 1952 to prosecute those "harboring migrants." Ibid., 104. Garcia notes that members of the sanctuary moment were surveilled, and some were prosecuted as part of Operation Sojourner. Ibid., 105.

21. Ridgley, "Cities of Refuge," 55.

22. Varsanyi, "Immigration Policy Activism," 11. Philip Kretsedemas also argues that the federal executive branch "opened the door" for different immigration regimes by affirming "local governments have the authority to enact their own immigration laws." Kretsedemas, "Immigration Enforcement and the Complication of National Sovereignty: Understanding Local Enforcement as an Exercise in Neoliberal Governance," *American Quarterly* 60, no. 3 (September 2008): 554.

23. Provine et al., *Policing Immigrants*, 9.

24. Wishnie, Mendelson, and Strom, "Collateral Damage."

25. Ibid., 2; De Genova and Peutz, "Introduction," 4.

26. Julie Myers, assistant secretary of ICE and DHS, at a hearing on "Immigration Enforcement of the Workplace" before the U.S. Senate Committee on the Judiciary, Subcommittee on Immigration, Border Security and Citizenship, June 19, 2006. See www.ice.gov/doclib/news/library/speeches/060619 MyersSenateJudiciary.pdf.

27. Myers, "Immigration Enforcement of the Workplace."

28. De Genova, "Spectacle of Terror," 151.

29. Michael Dwyer, "U.S. Officials Nab 2,100 Illegal Immigrants in 3 Weeks," *USA Today*, June 14, 2006, http://usatoday30.usatoday.com. By March 2007, thirteen hundred undocumented immigrants had been arrested. Laura Carlsen, "Return to Sender," *Counterpunch*, March 1, 2007.

30. ICE's website describes the NFOP as one that "identifies, locates, and arrests fugitive aliens, aliens that have been previously removed from the United States, removable aliens who have been convicted of crimes." For more on fugitive operations, see http://www.ice.gov/fugitive-operations/.

31. Carlsen, "Return to Sender." The Migration Policy Institute published a 2009 report that noted the drop in criminal aliens arrested by ICE between 2003 and 2007. See Wishnie, Mendelson, and Strom, "Collateral Damage"; see also Malia Politzer, "Most Immigrants Arrested in 'Operation Return to Sender' Had No Criminal Record," *Phoenix New Times*, November 5, 2009, http://blogs.phoenixnewtimes.com.

32. Jennifer Bennett, "Operation Return to Sender," *Slate*, May 30, 2008, http://www.slate.com.

33. Michael Manekin and Kelly Pakula, "Return to Sender Sweeps Begin," www.InsideBayArea.com.

34. Wishnie, Mendelson, and Strom, "Collateral Damage."

35. De Genova, "Spectacle of Terror," 155.

36. David Bacon, interview with Amy Goodman, *Democracy Now*, April 27, 2007, http://www.democracynow.org/.

37. ACLU of Northern California, "Lawsuit Seeks Documents Regarding ICE Raids. Federal Immigration Agency Has Failed to Comply with FOIA Requests from March 2007," June 2, 2008, www.aclunc.org.

38. Margot Pepper, "Deconstructing 'Return to Sender,'" *Counterpunch*, June 2007.

39. Jesse McKinley, "San Francisco Bay Area Reacts Angrily to Series of Immigration Raids," *New York Times*, April 27, 2007.

40. Quoted in Leslie Fulbright, Patrick Hoge, and Vanessa Hua, "Hundreds Rally in Oakland, San Francisco for Immigrant Rights," *San Francisco Chronicle*, May 1, 2007.

41. Quoted in Manekin and Pakula, "Return to Sender Sweeps Begin."

42. Rose Arrieta, "ICE Raids Bay Area Taquería Chain," *El Tecolote*, May 2, 2008, http://eltecolote.org.

43. Michelle Schudel, "ICE Stages Illegal Raids on Bay Area Restaurant Chain," *Liberation News*, May 21, 2008.

44. Matt O'Brien and Jeanine Benca, "Protest in SF Follows ICE Raids," *San Jose Mercury News*, May 5, 2008, http://www.mercurynews.com.

45. City and County of San Francisco, Resolution 003–2008, "Denouncing the Raids Conducted by the Immigration and Customs Enforcement in San Francisco," May 12, 2008, http://sfgov.org.

46. Lori Haley is quoted in Elena Shore, "Immigration Raid Undermines San Francisco's Sanctuary Status," *New American Media*, September 17, 2008, www.alternet.org.

47. Susan Bibler Coutin, "Exiled by Law," in *The Deportation Regime: Sovereignty, Space, and the Freedom of Movement*, ed. Nicholas De Genova and Nathalie Peutz (Durham, N.C.: Duke University Press, 2010), 353.

48. The amendment was approved in October 2009 by the Board of Supervisors.

49. Rose Cuison Villazor, "'Sanctuary Cities' and Local Citizenship," *Fordham Urban Law Review* 37 (2010): 585–87. See also Jesse McKinley, "San Francisco at Crossroads over Immigration," *New York Times*, June 12, 2009, http://www.nytimes.com.

50. Villazor, "'Sanctuary Cities,'" 589. In fact, Ridgley notes that the IIRIRA was a direct attack on local sanctuary policies. Ridgley, "Cities of Refuge," 62.

51. Villazor, "'Sanctuary Cities,'" 589.

52. Ibid., 590.

53. Ibid., 574. Villazor is drawing on Yishai Blank, "Spheres of Citizenship," *Theoretical Inquiries in Law* 8 (2007): 412–21; Saskia Sassen, *Territory, Authority, Rights* (Princeton, N.J.: Princeton University Press, 2006), 315; and Cristina Rodriguez, "The Significance of the Local in Immigration Regulation," *Michigan Law Review* 106 (2008): 577–78.

54. Monica W. Varsanyi, "Interrogating 'Urban Citizenship' vis-à-vis Undocumented Migration," *Citizenship Studies* 10, no. 2 (2006): 239.

55. Miriam Wells, "The Grass-Roots Reconfiguration of US Immigration Policy," *International Migration Review* 38, no. 4 (2004): 1314.

56. De La Torre's grant application to the Creative Work Fund is available on its website: www.creativeworkfund.org.

57. Ibid. The idea for the "Agit-Van" appears to have been drawn from Dziga Vertov's "Agit-train," as well as cinema trucks that travel in rural Mexico.

58. Sergio De La Torre, telephone conversation with author, June 14, 2011.

59. De La Torre also noted, "We have created a positive dialogue with the nonprofits we have partnered with, but have found it hard to translate with undocumented immigrants." Sergio De La Torre, e-mail correspondence with author, June 13, 2011.

60. De La Torre, telephone conversation.

61. De La Torre, e-mail correspondence.

62. During the HRC/IRC Joint Hearing on "The Impacts of Federal Immigration Enforcement Policy on San Francisco Communities," held on April 13, 2009, Mission District residents spoke about the effects of ICE raids on their communities, as well as the "reported alleged vehicle checkpoints targeting undocumented residents."

63. As a result of their house arrest, individuals were required to wear electronic monitoring devices on their ankles. From reports on the ICE raids by the Fugitive Operations unit, migrants under house arrest were required to stay at home between 11:30 P.M. and 6:30 A.M. They also could not leave San Francisco. Although they lacked criminal records, people under house arrest would eventually appear before an immigration judge, who would decide whether to deport them or let them stay. Shore, "Immigration Raid Undermines."

64. Brian J. Godfrey, "Barrio under Siege: Latino Sense of Place in San Francisco, California," in *Hispanic Spaces, Latino Places: Community and Cultural Diversity in Contemporary America*, ed. Daniel Arreola (Austin: University of Texas Press, 2004).

65. This information was provided on the Queen's Nails Project website on July 11, 2011. However, the website is no longer accessible since the Queen's Nails Project closed in 2013.

66. De La Torre, telephone conversation.

67. Jennifer González, *Subject to Display: Reframing Race in Contemporary Installation Art* (Cambridge, Mass.: MIT Press, 2008), 5–6.

68. Catherine M. Cole, "Mediating Testimony: Broadcasting South Africa's Truth and Reconciliation Commission," in *Documentary Testimonies: Global Archives of Suffering*, ed. Janet Walker and Bhaskar Sarkar (London: Routledge, 2010), 202.

69. Roland Barthes, "The Grain of the Voice," in *Image—Music—Text* (New York: Noonday Press, 1977), 188.

70. In reviewing the minutes from the joint hearings, many people spoke, including politicians, academics, LGBT and other activists, lawyers, doctors, and non-Latina/o undocumented migrants. See http://www.sfgov2.org/Modules/ShowDocument.aspx?documentid=562.

71. This audio excerpt was included in the exhibition's sound room. Thanks to Naomi Ambriz for providing the translation.

72. See the minutes from San Francisco's HRC/IRC "Joint Hearing" on April 13, 2009, http://www.sfgov2.org/Modules/ShowDocument.aspx?documentid=562.

73. According to Philip Kretsedemas, the USA PATRIOT Act "gave federal enforcement agencies an ability to search the premises of all U.S. residents without a warrant." Kretsedemas, "Immigration Enforcement," 563.

74. This audio excerpt was included in the exhibition's sound room. Thanks to Naomi Ambriz for providing the translation.

75. Janet Walker and Bhaskar Sarkar, "Introduction," *Documentary Testimonies: Global Archives of Suffering*, ed. Janet Walker and Bhaskar Sarkar (London: Routledge, 2010), 10, 17.

76. Hesford, *Spectacular Rhetorics*, 103.

77. McLagan notes that although it has been challenged, "the underlying assumption [with human rights work] is that the circulation of [specific forms of realism] generates political action." McLagan, "Human Rights," 306, 307.

78. Ibid., 304. Cvetkovich, *An Archive of Feelings*, 38.

79. Walker and Sarkar nevertheless contend that "audiovisual testimonial utterances are always already mediated at the level of the speaking subject whose personal narrative is a product of selection, ordering, interpretation, partisanship, prohibition, character, reflection, and the vicissitudes of memory; and at the level of the media text." Walker and Sarkar, "Introduction," 7.

80. John Beverley, *Testimonio: On the Politics of Truth* (Minneapolis: University of Minnesota Press, 2004), 24.

81. McKee, "'Eyes and Ears,'" 334.

82. Some undocumented Latina/o migrants caught up in ICE raids in the Bay Area were sent to detention centers in Arizona and elsewhere, and were eventually deported. Shore, "Immigration Raid Undermines."

83. McKee, "'Eyes and Ears,'" 334.

84. This piece is similar to the installation work described by Jennifer González, as the electronic ankle bracelet attests to the presence of a body, functioning "as [an] indexical link[s] to a larger social history of people and things" that is shown to "'situate' human subjects, to contribute to the processes of their subject formation and/or subjection." González, *Subject to Display*, 10.

85. De La Torre, telephone conversation.

86. Geographers like Godfrey have explained how the Mission had largely remained a Latina/o neighborhood into the early 2000s, largely due to rent control laws. Godfrey, "Barrio under Siege."

87. Karl Beitel, *Local Protests, Global Movements: Capital, Community, and State in San Francisco* (Philadelphia: Temple University Press, 2013), 68–69. Nancy Raquel Mirabal argues that more than one thousand Latina/o families were displaced from the neighborhood in the late 1990s and early 2000s. Mirabal, "Geographies of Displacement: Latina/os, Oral History, and the Politics of Gentrification in San Francisco's Mission District," *Public Historian* 31, no. 2 (Spring 2009): 13.

88. Describing the MAC protests in 2000, Mirabal contends, "Long-term residents, including a number of Latina/os, held signs describing the number of years they had lived in the Mission." Mirabal, "Geographies of Displacement," 28.

89. Beitel, *Local Protests*, 68.

90. Summers Sandoval, *Latinos at the Golden Gate*, 9.

91. Municipal identification cards were approved in 2007, and the program was launched in January 2009. See www.sfgov2.org/index.aspx?page =110. The first city to have municipal ID cards was New Haven, Connecticut.

92. See San Francisco's General Services Agency website: www.sfgsa.org/index.aspx?page=1072.

93. See the minutes from San Francisco's HRC/IRC's "Joint Hearings," held on April 13, 2009, http://www.sfgov2.org/Modules/ShowDocument.asp x?documentid=562.

94. Sergio De La Torre, telephone conversation with author, September 10, 2010.

95. See video on Sergio De La Torre's Vimeo site: http://vimeo.com/user 7146025.

96. Kretsedemas notes, "The current discourse on the 'immigration problem' also blurs the lines between legal status, 'race,' and culture, where concerns about illegal immigration are conflated with the cultural and demographic changes resulting from immigration in general." Kretsedemas, "Immigration Enforcement," 554.

97. De La Torre, telephone conversation with author, June 14, 2011.

98. Maldonado, Licona, and Hendricks, "Latin@ Immobilities," 323; see also Rosas, "The Managed Violences," 401–18.

99. Maldonado, Licona, and Hendricks, "Latin@ Immobilities," 327.

100. Avery Gordon, *Ghostly Matters: Haunting and the Sociological Imagination*, 2nd ed. (Minneapolis: University of Minnesota Press, 2008), 104.

101. Cari Tuna and Stu Woo, "Tech Influx Transforms Mission Neighborhood," *Wall Street Journal*, May 27, 2010; see also James Christopher, "Locals Protest Tech Bus Invasion of Public Bus Stops," *El Tecolote*, January 16–29, 2014, http://eltecolote.org.

102. Summers Sandoval, *Latinos at the Golden Gate*, 183.

103. De La Torre, e-mail correspondence.

104. De La Torre, telephone conversation with author, June 14, 2011.

105. De La Torre's approach is also similar to that of the Pocho Research Society of Erased and Invisible History (PRS), a collective of anonymous activists, artists, and historians in Los Angeles, who are "dedicated to the systematic investigation of space, memory, and displacement." *Journal of Aesthetics and Protest* 3 (June 2004), http://www.joaap.org/.

106. González, *Subject to Display*, 9. González draws on Butler's summary of Michel Foucault's concept of subjection, "literally, the making of the subject, the principles of regulation according to which a subject is formulated or produced. This notion of subjection is a kind of power that not only unilaterally *acts on* a given individual as a form of domination, but also *activates* or forms the subject." Judith Butler, "Subjection, Resistance, Resignification: Between Freud and Foucault," in *The Identity in Question*, ed. John Rajchman (New York: Routledge, 1995), 230. Emphasis in original.

107. Krzysztof Wodiczko, "Projections," *Perspecta* 26: Theater, Theatricality, and Architecture (1990): 273.

108. Guy Debord, "Towards a Situationist International" (June 1957), in *Situationist International Anthology*, trans. and ed. Ken Knabb (Berkeley, Calif.: Bureau of Public Secrets, 1989), 22.

109. Ibid., 25; Debord, *The Society of the Spectacle*. As Jonathan Crary argues about *Comments on the Society of the Spectacle*, Debord understood the spectacle as "the annihilation of historical knowledge—in particular the destruction of the recent past." Crary, "Spectacle, Attention, Counter-Memory," *October* 50 (Fall 1989): 106.

110. De La Torre, e-mail correspondence.

111. Walker and Sarkar, "Introduction," 11.

112. McKee, "'Eyes and Ears,'" 330.

113. González, *Subject to Display*, 9.

114. De La Torre, e-mail correspondence.

115. Tuna and Woo, "Tech Influx."

116. Mirabal, "Geographies of Displacement," 17.

117. Quoted in Steve Rogers, "Territories 2: Superimposing the City," *Performance Magazine*, August 9, 1985, 38.

118. Howard N. Fox, "Theater of the Inauthentic," in *Phantom Sightings: Art after the Chicano Movement*, ed. Rita González, Howard N. Fox, and Chon A. Noriega (Berkeley: University of California Press, 2008), 81.

119. De Genova, "Spectacle of Terror," 151.

120. Ibid., 159–60.

121. Mirabal, "Geographies of Displacement," 19.

122. Summers Sandoval, *Latinos at the Golden Gate*, 184.

123. As Mirabal describes, there has been "a correlation between urban renewal and race, specifically the exclusion of populations of color for whites." Mirabal, "Geographies of Displacement," 16.

124. *No Vacancies* was displayed between April 2010 and December 2011 at West Wall Gallery.

125. See De La Torre's artist statement about *No Vacancies* on the website for the Walter and Elise Haas Fund: http://www.haassr.org/blog/display/no-vacancies/.

126. Varsanyi, "Immigration Policy Activism," 19. Provine et al. also refer to this as a "multi-jurisdictional patchwork." See Provine et al., *Policing Immigrants*, 3.

127. In reference to the effects of federal immigration policies on undocumented migrants, De Genova and Peutz argue that the "grim spectacle of the deportation of even just a few . . . produces and maintains migrant 'illegality' as not merely an anomalous juridical status but also a practical, materially consequential, and deeply interiorized mode of being—and of being put in place." De Genova and Peutz, "Introduction," 14.

128. McNevin, "Undocumented Citizens?" 177.

129. Ibid., 178.

130. Marquez-Benitez and Pallares, "Not One More," 22.

6. Reconfiguring Documentation

1. See http://www.ice.gov/287g/.

2. See http://www.azleg.gov/legtext/49leg/2r/summary/s.1070pshs.doc .htm.

3. I describe these individuals as "undocumented youth activists," to distinguish them from DREAM and migrant activists who are not eligible for the DREAM Act or Deferred Action for Childhood Arrivals (DACA) due to their age. However, I am aware that it is problematic to use the term *youth* to describe activists whose ages span from teenagers to young adults. Activist and scholar Unzueta Carrasco describes this group as "undocumented 1.5 generation activists," who are "immigrants, born abroad yet raised and educated in the United States." Unzueta Carrasco and Seif, "Disrupting the Dream," 287.

4. Nicholas De Genova, "The Queer Politics of Migration: Reflections on 'Illegality' and Incorrigibility," *Studies in Social Justice* 4, no. 2 (2010): 115.

5. Jonathan X. Inda and Julie Dowling describe policies that advocate "attrition through enforcement"—such as SB 1070 and the SB 1070 copycat laws—as "tactic[s] that seeks to incapacitate immigrants, Latinos in particular, in order to wear down their will to work and live in the United States." Further they note that "attrition through enforcement is not an official government policy, but it does appear to be the de facto way that undocumented immigration is being governed." Inda and Dowling, "Introduction," 23.

6. Gerardo, "Fearless and Speaking for Ourselves," *No Papers No Fears* (blog), August 18, 2012, http://nopapersnofear.org.

7. Papadopoulos and Tsianos, "The Autonomy of Migration," 224.

8. NIYA was "an undocumented youth-LED network of grassroots organizations, campus-based student groups and individuals committed to achieving equality for all immigrant youth, regardless of their legal status." See NIYA's Facebook page. For more information on NDLON and the Puente Movement, see the Introduction.

9. Marquez-Benitez and Pallares, "Not One More," 22.

10. One example is the E-Verify Program, https://www.uscis.gov.

11. Kevin Haggerty, "Tear Down the Walls: On Demolishing the Panopticon," in *Theorizing Surveillance*, ed. David Lyon (London: Willan, 2006), 29.

12. The activists that I write about have something in common with the queer immigrants of color that Monisha Das Gupta describes in her book *Unruly Immigrants*, who do not "uncritically embrac[e] visibility as a mode of political empowerment." Das Gupta, *Unruly Immigrants: Rights, Activism, and*

Transnational South Asian Politics in the United States (Durham, N.C.: Duke University Press, 2006), 165.

13. Diana Taylor, *Performance* (Durham, N.C.: Duke University Press, 2016), 147.

14. Rather, drawing on Richard Schechner's concept of performance, Taylor understands it as "'restored' or 'twice-behaved behavior.'" Taylor, *Disappearing Acts*, 184–85.

15. Pallares, *Family Activism*, 98.

16. Ana Elena Puga explains that the migrant melodramas, "while sympathetic to migrants, stage suffering so as to create the illusion that the undocumented must naturally, inevitably, necessarily endure physical and psychological pain." Puga, "Poor Enrique and Poor María, or, The Political Economy of Suffering in Two Migrant Melodramas," in *Performance in the Borderlands*, ed. Ramón Rivera-Servera and Harvey Young (London: Palgrave Macmillan, 2011), 228.

17. The press release is available on YouTube, under the activists' videos, including one by Martin: http://www.youtube.com/watch?v=TCRiyhUitok.

18. Puga, "Poor Enrique and Poor María," 228.

19. Taylor, *Performance*, 36.

20. McKee and McLagan, "Introduction," 17–18.

21. Peter Nyers, "Abject Cosmopolitanism: The Politics of Protection in the Anti-Deportation Movement," in *The Deportation Regime: Sovereignty, Space, and the Freedom of Movement*, ed. Nicholas De Genova and Nathalie Peutz (Durham, NC: Duke University Press, 2010), 429, 431.

22. See ICE's website for "Secure Communities": www.ice.gov/pi/news/factsheets/ secure_communities.htm.

23. *Si No Nos Invitan, Nos Invitamos Solos: No Papers, No Fear Protest in Alabama* was filmed by Barni Axmed Qaasim (Puente Movement) and can be viewed on YouTube: https://www.youtube.com/watch?v=Iaj95A8ac8U.

24. Nicholls, *The DREAMers*, 13.

25. Undocumented youth participated in these marches in 2006 with other youth as well as family members to protest the passing of HR 4437, the Border Protection, Antiterrorism, and Illegal Immigration Control Act. These marches had a lasting effect on undocumented youth activists for a variety of reasons, including the fact that they saw so many other undocumented youth willing to publically participate in an event to support migrant rights. See Gonzales, "Left Out but Not Shut Down," 269–84.

26. They added "Unapologetic" in 2011.

27. Karma Chávez argues that within the context of the LGBT movement, radical activists come out "to declare their presence, demand systemic changes, and resist and disrupt the assumptions of normative culture." Chávez, *Queer Migration Politics*, 84. For more on this strategy, see "Coming Out as Coalitional Gesture?" in *Queer Migration Politics*.

28. According to Aswini Anbuaja, both public rallies and social media have allowed undocumented migrant activists "to take away the stigma associated with being paperless." Anbuaja, "Immigrant Youth 'Come Out' as Undocumented, Push for DREAM Act," http://news.feetintwoworlds.org/2011/03/21/immigrant-youth-come-out-as-undocumented.

29. Nadia Sol Ireri Unzueta Carrasco made this point during her presentation at the "Everyday Forms of Popular Power: Art, Media, and Immigration" symposium at the University of New Mexico on November 9, 2012, https://www.youtube.com/watch?v=Zm_OJ9PZLEk.

30. Marquez-Benitez and Pallares, "Not One More," 15.

31. Nicholls, *The DREAMers*, 81.

32. Maggie Jones, "Coming Out Illegal," *New York Times Magazine*, October 21, 2010, http://www.nytimes.com.

33. Quoted in Alan Gomez, "DREAMers Personalize Cases to Stall Deportation," *USA Today*, http://usatoday30.usatoday.com.

34. Nicholls, *The DREAMers*, 15, 98.

35. Ibid., 200.

36. See http://puenteaz.org/programs/community-defense-course/.

37. Unzueta Carrasco and Seif, "Disrupting the Dream," 288.

38. In 2010, almost four hundred thousand undocumented migrants were deported, the highest recorded number in U.S. history. Peter Slevin, "Deportation of Illegal Immigrants Increases under Obama Administration," *Washington Post*, July 26, 2010, http://www.washingtonpost.com.

39. Varsanyi, "Immigration Policy Activism."

40. Nicholls, *The DREAMers*, 116–17.

41. Hinda Seif, "Unapologetic and Unafraid: Immigrant Youth Come Out from the Shadows," *New Directions for Child and Adolescent Development* 134 (Winter 2011): 72.

42. For example, see Nataly's statements in Kiri Walton, "Undocumented Pebblebrook Student Speaks Out after Arrest," *South Cobb Patch*, June 29, 2011, http://patch.com/georgia/southcobb/undocumented-pebblebrook-student-speaks-out-after-arrest.

43. This change also affected the migrant rights movement. See Roque Planas, "The Law Kicked Off Immigration Crackdowns across the Country: Five Years Later, Lots of People Still Hate It," *Huffington Post*, April 24, 2015, http://www.huffingtonpost.com.

44. Seif, "Unapologetic and Unafraid," 71.

45. Sasha Costanza-Chock, "Se Ve, Se Siente: Transmedia Mobilization in the Los Angeles Immigrant Rights Movement" (PhD diss., University of Southern California, 2010), 190. Costanza-Chock defines "transmedia mobilization" as media production that is "dispersed systematically across multiple media platforms, creating a distributed and participatory social movement 'world.'" Ibid., 115. See also Costanza-Chock, *Out of the Shadows*.

46. In addition, undocumented Latina/o migrants in Los Angeles have used their cell phones to record aspects of their lives at home and work, which they then upload onto the *VozMob* blog as part of *Mobile Voices* (*VozMob*). *VozMob* was developed by the Annenberg School for Communication and Journalism at the University of Southern California and the Institute of Popular Education of Southern California in 2010. This blog has also been a means for migrants to share their views on political issues, as well as their involvement in immigrant rights marches. They have also used their cell phones to take photographs and videos of their employers' homes and licenses of their cars in case they were not paid. See https://vozmob.net/en/main.

47. See http://www.ice.gov/doclib/secure-communities/pdf/prosecutorial -discretion-memo.pdf.

48. Most of these videos can be viewed on YouTube, under the activists' first name and last initial, the location (North Carolina), and "We Will No Longer Remain in the Shadows." The heading for the press release is "Seven Undocumented Youth Speak Out against Federal Inaction and the Lack of Educational Access."

49. Michael May, "Los Infiltradores," *American Prospect*, June 21, 2013, http: //prospect.org/authors/michael-may.

50. Ibid.

51. As noted in the Introduction, this announcement publicized a June 17, 2011, memo by John Morton, the director of the DHS, who gave the directive for ICE agents to exercise "prosecutorial discretion." The memo stated that ICE should focus its work on undocumented migrants convicted of crimes, but this was largely ignored by federal immigration officials, who continued to arrest, detain, and deport those who had committed only civil violations. See http://www.ice.gov/doclib/secure-communities/pdf/prosecutorial-discretion -memo.pdf.

52. Prosecutorial discretion is issued by a joint task force—composed of staff members from the DHS and the Department of Justice (DOJ)—which reviews pending removals and can grant deferred action on an individual's deportation. Alexa Alonzo and Mary Kenney, "Practice Advisory," September 1, 2011, www.legalactioncenter.org.

53. After 1924, Mexicans who crossed the U.S.–Mexico boundary without documentation were considered to have entered "illegally," perceived as criminals, and treated as being "undeserving" of relief. Ngai, *Impossible Subjects*, 89.

54. Ibid., 57.

55. The press release is available on YouTube, underneath the activists' videos, including one by Martin: http://www.youtube.com/watch?v=TCRiyh Uitok.

56. Unzueta Carrasco and Seif, "Disrupting the Dream," 285.

57. The END campaign was initiated in 2010 "to prevent the deportations of young people, thereby allowing immigrant youths to continue their lives in

the United States, pursue higher education, and achieve their dreams." See http://unitedwedream.org/about/projects/end/.

58. The main targets of these public campaigns included John Morton, director of DHS/ICE, as well as politicians from the individual's state or district. *Education Not Deportation: A Guide for Undocumented Youth in Removal Proceedings*, 34, http://www.e4fc.org/images/E4FC_DeportationGuide.pdf. UnitedWe Dream also made a video, https://www.youtube.com/watch?v=_rDmBQf3qAo.

59. *Education Not Deportation*, 35.

60. Ibid.

61. Unzueta Carrasco and Seif, "Disrupting the Dream," 288.

62. I compare the videos produced in North Carolina to the example included in the *END Guide*. See Herta's video, https://www.youtube.com/watch?v=kMU_DZofuWQ.

63. Cristina Beltrán refers to these videos as "cyber-testimonies." Beltrán, "Undocumented, Unafraid, and Unapologetic: DREAM Activists, Cyber-Testimonio, and the Queering of Democracy," in *Transforming Citizens: Youth, New Media, and Political Participation*, ed. Danielle Allen and Jennifer Light (Chicago: University of Chicago Press, 2015), 20.

64. Nicholls, *The DREAMers*, 13.

65. See Angelica's video, http://www.youtube.com/watch?v=HuqoGX8h P2o.

66. See Santiago's video, http://www.youtube.com/watch?v=XEvokpyUysY.

67. Martin explains that he participated in the action because politicians representing his state—such as Senator Kay Hagan (D-NC)—were doing nothing to help undocumented youth. See Martin's video, http://www.youtube.com/watch?v=TCRiyhUitok.

68. Santiago also noted that undocumented youth should "'embrace' the struggles of LGBTQ communities, African American communities, communities of color, and immigrant communities of all backgrounds" in order to "create a real movement." See Santiago's video, http://www.youtube.com/watch?v=XEvokpyUysY.

69. See Martin's video, http://www.youtube.com/watch?v=TCRiyhUitok.

70. These approaches to publicity have been addressed in essays, including Jennie Choi's "A Web of Power: How Online Tools Are Transforming the Way Social Change Happens," *Sojourner Magazine*, July 2011, http://sojo.net/magazine/2011/07/web-power.

71. McLagan, "Human Rights," 311.

72. Ibid., 312. At this time DreamActivist.org's Facebook page describes the organization as "the largest social media hub for undocumented immigrants to aid organizations, communities, and individuals to come together and find new ways to provide help for immigrant communities."

73. The petition blamed President Obama and the Democratic Party, explaining, "Your recent announcement only acts as a mask to the devastation and injustice that programs like 287(g) and Secure Communities will continue

to have in our communities. Your announcements are a symptom of the problem that is the vicious cycle of immigrant criminalization, not a potential cure to the realities of a broken immigration system. We will not tolerate lies designed to court the votes of our community. We will hold you and other Democratic leaders accountable as we demand to be treated with nothing less than dignity and justice." "Support Undocumented Youth Arrested in North Carolina," September 8, 2011, www.dreamactivist.org.

74. May, "Los Infiltradores." Marco wrote that undocumented migrants began "applying counter-intuitive measures to counter-hegemonic ends." Steve Pavey and Marco Saavedra, *Shadows Then Light* (Lexington, Ky.: One Horizon Institute, 2012).

75. Pavey and Saavedra, *Shadows Then Light*.

76. Mohammad, as quoted in ibid.

77. Inda and Dowling note that "ICE's law enforcement partners are supposed to target dangerous 'criminal aliens,' but most immigrants who get caught are actually low-level offenders or people who simply crossed paths with local police." Inda and Dowling, "Introduction," 22; and Michelle Waslin, *The Secure Communities Program: Unanswered Questions and Continuing Concerns* (Washington, D.C.: Immigration Policy Center, 2010).

78. Pallares, *Family Activism*, 124–25. See also "People of Alabama vs. HB 56," November 16, 2011, http://www.youtube.com/watch?v=wfHQA-zr9-I.

79. Inda and Dowling note, "In some locations . . . police officers are engaging in heavy racial profiling of Latinos, making pretextual stops and arrests of people believed to be immigrants so that their information (such as fingerprints) can be checked against the DHS databases." Inda and Dowling, "Introduction," 22; see also Mary Romero, "Keeping Citizenship Rights White: Arizona's Racial Profiling Practices in Immigration Law Enforcement," *Law Journal for Social Justice* 1, no. 1 (2011): 97–113.

80. See presentation by Jonathan and Isaac at the "Everyday Forms of Popular Power: Art, Media and Immigration" symposium, University of New Mexico, November 9, 2012, https://www.youtube.com/watch?v=4ct6lMyFWfM.

81. See, for example, http://www.youtube.com/watch?v=PkxnPixjTts.

82. These actions involved tactics that, as Peter Nyers notes, "have been proven to be important for how they disrupt the administration, the routines, and, above all, the 'normality' of deportations." Nyers, "Abject Cosmopolitanism," 431.

83. See presentation by Jonathan and Isaac at "Everyday Forms of Popular Power."

84. Jonathan and Isaac, "Interview with Irene Vásquez" (University of New Mexico, December 3, 2011); "Going Undercover at the Border Patrol," *Arts of Aztlán*, https://vimeo.com/33189634.

85. See presentation by Jonathan and Isaac at "Everyday Forms of Popular Power."

86. *Undocumented Youth vs. Border Patrol Round 1—Mobile, Alabama*, http://www.youtube.com/watch?v=iA54ErBfZ8E.

87. Scholars like Mark Andrejevic refer to counter-surveillance as "inverse surveillance," which "relies on the ability to offer a convincing counternarrative to that promulgated by authorities, who may have better access to mainstream media or public relations strategies." Further, he comments that "the success of inverse surveillance depends on the efficacy of such counternarratives—or, similarly, on the availability to subvert a particular dominant narrative." Andrejevic, "Watching Back, Surveillance as Activism," in *Media and Social Justice*, ed. Sue Curry Jansen, Jefferson Pooley, and Lora Taub-Pervizpour (New York: Palgrave Macmillan, 2011), 180.

88. For example, they spoke with one undocumented migrant who was put into deportation proceedings after he walked into a women's bathroom by mistake. Jonathan and Isaac, "Everyday Forms of Popular Power."

89. Ibid.

90. Brenda Medina and Lacey Johnson, "Coming Out as Undocumented, and Gay," *Say Something*, episode 34, *Chronicle of Higher Education*, May 25, 2012, http://chronicle.com. This episode features Jonathan talking about his involvement in undocumented youth activism.

91. Mohammad, "Press Release, November 24, 2011," as quoted in Pavey and Saavedra, *Shadows Then Light*.

92. In Arizona, NDLON worked with organizations like the Puente Movement to strengthen the local migrant rights movement. Similarly, in Georgia, NDLON worked to "reinforce the local social movement infrastructure," to "enhance its mobilization capacities," and to help local activists lead their own campaigns. Nicholls, *The DREAMers*, 161, 163.

93. Mike Ludwig, "Don't Call Me Illegal: An Interview with Youth Immigrant Activist Tania Unzueta," June 17, 2013, http://www.truth-out.org/news/item/16986-dont-call-me-illegal-an-interview-with-youth-immigrant-activist-tania-unzueta.

94. The "undocubus" left Phoenix on July 29, 2012, the first anniversary of Arizona's implementation of SB 1070.

95. Sarah Lai Stirland, "Website Yes, Legal Status, No: 'No Papers, No Fear' Hopes to Build a Movement for Undocumented Immigrations," August 31, 2012, www.TechPresident.com.

96. B. Loewe, telephone interview with author, September 26, 2012. According to its website, "The Turning the Tide Campaign is a collective effort of communities and organizations across the country unified to confront the growing wave of criminalization and separation of immigrant families. The campaign is rooted in local organizing that seeks to resist and move away from bigotry, hatred, and attrition in order to advance human rights, tolerance, and inclusion." See http://altopolimigra.com/. As opposed to how I

defined *translocal* in chapter 2, here I use *trans-local* to refer to organizing across localities that are facing similar restrictive immigration laws within the United States.

97. For more about the Barrio Defense Committees in Arizona, see Nicholls, *The DREAMers*, 162.

98. Interview with Carlos, executive director, Puente Movement, by members of Generation Justice, KUNM, Albuquerque, New Mexico, broadcast September 16, 2012.

99. These individuals included Barni Axmed Qaasim, Jorge, and Perla, all of whom worked on videos, and Fernando, who documented the actions through photography. For biographies, see http://nopapersnofear.org/; and Barni Axmed Qaasim, telephone conversation with author, September 8, 2015.

100. See the press release, http://www.usccr.gov/press/2012/PR_07-26-12_Immigration.pdf.

101. *Ganando el derecho de hablar por nosotros mismos: Winning the Right to Speak for Ourselves* and *Si No Nos Invitan, Nos Invitamos Solos: No Papers, No Fear Protest in Alabama* were filmed on August 20, 2012.

102. Diane McWhorter, "The Strange Career of Juan Crow," *New York Times*, June 16, 2012, http://www.nytimes.com. In Alabama, this law includes "requiring schools to verify the immigration status of newly enrolled K–12 students; criminalizing the solicitation of work by unauthorized immigrants; a provision that made it a crime to provide a ride to undocumented immigrants or to rent to them; a provision that infringed on the ability of individuals to contract with someone who was undocumented and a provision that criminalized failing to register one's immigration status." Southern Poverty Law Center, http://www.splcenter.org/get-informed/news/civil-rights-coalition-victorious-in-suit-against-alabama-s-anti-immigrant-law. See also Julia Preston, "Alabama: Deal Reached over Immigration Crackdown," *New York Times*, October 30, 2013, A17.

103. See their mission statement: http://www.usccr.gov/about/index.php.

104. The press release indicates, "Members of the public and interested organizations are invited to submit written statements for the record on the specific topic of the briefing by sending them to immigration 2012@USCCR.gov." See http://www.usccr.gov/press/2012/PR_07-26-12_Immigration.pdf.

105. Cacho, *Social Death*, 6.

106. Borcilǎ with Marciniak and Tyler, "The Political Aesthetics," 48.

107. Nyers, "Abject Cosmopolitanism," 425.

108. Kobach helped author SB 1070 with Arizona state senator Russell Pearce, so it is not surprising that activists planned an action to coincide with Kobach's testimony.

109. Since those who presented at the briefing spoke in English, the activists brought a translator so they could hear a Spanish translation of the testimony.

110. Miller, "'Legal or Illegal?'" 83.

111. This transcript is from the video of an action, *Si No Nos Invitan, Nos Invitamos Solos*, by NDLON. See http://www.youtube.com/watch?v=Iaj95A8a c8U.

112. De Genova, "The Queer Politics of Migration," 101, 103. De Genova also contends that the chant reflected "the migrants' exuberant and outspoken proclamations of their existence—their presence, their 'here'-ness . . . and the incorrigibility they celebrated in their defiant refusal to be silenced, suppressed, or expelled." Ibid., 110.

113. McNevin, "Undocumented Citizens?" 177.

114. Engin F. Isin, *Being Political: Genealogies of Citizenship* (Minneapolis: University of Minnesota Press, 2002), 275–76, as quoted in Nyers, "Abject Cosmopolitanism," 424.

115. Pallares, *Family Activism*, 2. As Pallares notes, however, "the immigrant rights movement does not share one collective identity stemming from a singular process of identification among movement participants." Ibid.

116. Cacho, *Social Death*, 131.

117. This is what Ana Elena Puga calls a "casting competition." Puga, "Migrant Melodrama and Elvira Arellano," *Latino Studies* 10, no. 3 (2012): 356.

118. Ibid.

119. Nyers, "Abject Cosmopolitanism," 427, 432.

120. Qaasim, telephone conversation.

121. McKee and McLagan, "Introduction," 15.

122. Schmidt Camacho, *Migrant Imaginaries*, 215.

123. See http://nopapersnofear.org/blog/post.php?s=2012–08–29-all-four -immigrant-rights-advocates-arrested-on-gay-street-released-no-papers-no -fear-bus-tour-heads-towards-democratic-national-convention-local-groups -continue-fight.

124. Stirland, "Website Yes, Legal Status, No."

125. This website was based on one that NDLON created for the ¡Alto Arizona! Campaign—www.AltoArizona.com—which included an action center, press releases, photographs, videos of protests, and forms of "creative resistance," including posters, videos, music, and poetry that activists uploaded onto the website.

126. See http://nopapersnofear.org/.

127. For details on DACA, see the DHS website: http://www.dhs.gov/de ferred-action-childhood-arrivals.

128. Unzueta Carrasco and Seif, "Disrupting the Dream," 286.

129. For more information about the #Not1More campaign, see http://www .notonemoredeportation.com/.

130. Adrian Carrasquillo, "How the Immigrant Rights Movement Got Obama to Save Millions from Deportations," November 22, 2014, Buzz Feed, http://www.buzzfeed.com.

131. More for information on DAPA, see https://www.ice.gov/daca#wcm -survey-target-id. It is noted on the website that "on February, 2015, a federal district court temporarily enjoined the government from proceeding forward on the Secretary's policy of DAPA and expanded DACA."

132. See, for example, Marisa Franco, "A Movement That's Committed, Experienced, and Ready," November 22, 2014, http://www.notonemoredepor tation.com/2014/11/22/marisa-franco-committed-experienced-and-ready/; and Alicia Schmidt Camacho, "Obama's Executive Order on Immigration: Two Faculty Experts Weigh In on the Subject," *Yale News*, November 24, 2014, http://news.yale.edu/2014/11/24/president-obama-s-executive-order-immi gration-two-faculty-experts-weigh-subject.

133. During the speech, an activist in the audience called him out, stating: "Mr. President, that has been a lie. You have been deporting every . . ." when he was cut off. Lawrence Downes, "Smooth Pivot on Immigration by the Deporter-in-Chief," *New York Times*, December 1, 2014.

134. B. Loewe, "Before You Pull Down That Protest Sign, Think Again" (or "For Those Who Celebrate the Victory but Condemn the Tactics"), http:// www.notonemoredeportation.com.

135. Unzueta Carrasco and Seif, "Disrupting the Dream," 279.

136. Pallares, *Family Activism*, 1–2; see also Nyers, "Abject Cosmopolitanism," 427.

137. This relates to Schmidt Camacho's notion of "nomadic counterpublics—for locating political and cultural agency beyond the sanctioned boundaries of liberal nationalism." Schmidt Camacho, *Migrant Imaginaries*, 232.

138. Ibid., 12.

139. De Genova et al., "Migrant Struggles," 26.

140. Vicki Squire, *The Contested Politics of Mobility, Borderzones, and Irregularity* (London: Routledge, 2011), 5.

141. Peter Nyers and Kim Rygiel, "Introduction," in *Citizenship, Migrant Activism, and the Politics of Movement*, ed. Peter Nyers and Kim Rygiel (London: Routledge, 2012), 6.

142. McLagan, "Human Rights," 315.

143. McKee and McLagan, "Introduction," 9.

Conclusion

1. Marquez-Benitez and Pallares, "Not One More," 17.

2. See, for example, http://www.notonemoredeportation.com/2013/10/14/ protest-closes-phoenix-ice-office-prevents-deportations/.

3. See http://www.notonemoredeportation.com/tag/2million2many/. In addition to these actions, migrant detainees have also organized hunger strikes in detention centers.

4. It should be noted that the MODC action resembles Francis Alÿs's performance walking with a block of ice through Mexico City, entitled "Paradise

of Praxis 1: Sometimes Making Something Leads to Nothing," http://francis alys.com/sometimes-making-something-leads-to-nothing/.

5. Borcilă with Marciniak and Tyler, "The Political Aesthetics," 54.

6. Ibid., 52.

7. Artivists also uploaded photographs, videos, performance art, poetry, 3-D art, music, and posters onto #Not1More's website, creating an online gallery of artwork. The website also has information about open deportation cases, photographs of individuals in deportation proceedings, and how supporters can help stop these individuals' deportations using online petitions. See http://www.notonemoredeportation.com/portfolio-type/open-cases/. The #Not1More campaign has also influenced youth media collectives, such as Puente Vision in Arizona, which was created by young people whose family members were released from detention centers, due to the success of media campaigns. See http://puenteaz.org/programs/art-and-culture/puente-vision/.

8. Borcilă with Marciniak and Tyler, "The Political Aesthetics," 56. Emphasis in original.

9. Unzueta Carrasco and Seif, "Disrupting the Dream," 296. Similarly, as Cacho describes, these activists "search beyond U.S. law and U.S. borders for alternatives to racialized rights-based and U.S. centric struggles." Cacho, *Social Death*, 142–43.

10. As Cacho notes, presenting some undocumented migrants as "deserving" and others as "undeserving" involves "rendering the violences of the law invisible," while also "concealing the forces of transnational capital." Cacho, *Social Death*, 130–31.

11. As mentioned earlier, this includes "border control, detention, and deportation." De Genova et al., "Migrant Struggles," 26.

12. Borcilă with Marciniak and Tyler, "The Political Aesthetics," 55–56. Emphasis in original.

13. Marciniak and Tyler, "Introduction," 18; and Imogen Tyler, *Revolting Subjects: Social Abjection and Resistance in Neoliberal Britain* (London: Zed Books, 2013).

14. McKee and McLagan, "Introduction," 22.

15. Borcilă with Marciniak and Tyler, "The Political Aesthetics," 53.

Index

REBECCA M. SCHREIBER is associate professor of American studies at the University of New Mexico. She is author of *Cold War Exiles in Mexico: U.S. Dissidents and the Culture of Critical Resistance* (Minnesota, 2008).